DEVELOPMENTAL PSYCHOLOGY:
Historical and Philosophical Perspectives

CHILD PSYCHOLOGY

A series of books edited by **David S. Palermo**

DEVELOPMENTAL PSYCHOLOGY:
Historical and Philosophical Perspectives

Edited by

RICHARD M. LERNER
Pennsylvania State University

LEA LAWRENCE ERLBAUM ASSOCIATES, PUBLISHERS
1983   HILLSDALE, NEW JERSEY   LONDON

Lawrence Erlbaum Associates, Inc., Publishers
365 Broadway
Hillsdale, New Jersey 07642

Library of Congress Cataloging in Publication Data
Main entry under title:

Developmental psychology.

  (Child psychology)
  Includes bibliographical references and index.
  1. Developmental psychology—History. 2. Developmental
psychology—Philosophy. I. Lerner, Richard M. II. Series.
[DNLM: 1. Human development—History—Congresses.
BF 713 D4893 1980]
BF713.D479 1983   155   83-1513
ISBN 0-89859-247-X

Printed in the United States of America
10 9 8 7 6 5 4 3 2 1

Contents

Foreword

It is a pleasure indeed to write the Foreword for *Developmental Psychology: Historical and Philosophical Perspectives*. The editor has compiled a volume which, I believe, will become a milestone in the history of developmental psychology. It is especially noteworthy that this book is being published in 1983—a time when we have just commemorated the 100th anniversary of one of the first significant volumes in developmental psychology. Wilhelm T. Preyer (1841–1897), an ardent advocate of Darwinism and the German pioneer of child psychology, published his classic, *Die Seele des Kindes* (The Mind of the Child) in 1882. During the ensuing century developmental psychology has steadily matured. As a specialty it has now come of age. From the beginning, principally under the influence of evolutionary theory, developmental psychology focused on the child and adolescent. Today it has expanded to become the study of the life span and it has accumulated a vast amount of empirical data on the various stages of human development. Now developmental psychology can reflect on its history and the achievements and findings of its numerous investigators.

Lerner and his associates in developmental psychology have produced in this volume a group of excellent essays describing and analyzing its philosophical and historical roots. The authors are eminent scholars who, as Lerner says, have notably influenced the history of their specialty and who will continue to do so. All are principal contributors to the current historical-philosophical-theoretical-methodological debates in developmental psychology. Each has his own philosophical, methodological, and theoretical stance which he enunciates in his paper. Moreover, they are all keenly aware that the nature of their research, the facts that they discover, and the significance assigned to these facts depend on the particular philosophical assumptions from which they originate. Perhaps most significantly, the authors included in this volume recognize that the indiscriminate accumulation of empirical data is of little consequence unless results are meaningfully based in some theoretical frame of reference. In their expositions of diverse philosophical and theoretical underpinnings in developmental psychology the authors make a major contribution to the understanding of the past and present of this vital specialty as well as to its future growth.

It is perhaps appropriate to conclude this foreword with a note about personal developmental history. The editor of this volume, Dr. Richard M. Lerner, as an eager and enthusiastic adolescent, attended my introductory psychology, experimental psychology, and history of psychology courses at Hunter College of the City University of New York. Subsequently, for almost two decades, I have had the pleasure of following his career in developmental psychology. I have observed his professional growth and development from early college days to his current status as a mature psychological scientist and scholar. I have read with interest and pride his numerous articles and several textbooks in developmental psychology, and now am quite pleased to take part in one of his scholarly efforts.

Virginia Staudt Sexton
St. John's University
Jamaica, N.Y.

Preface

Over the last 50 years developmental psychologists have paid increasing attention to issues of process, theory, and explanation, as compared to those of description. During the last 10 to 15 years this growing concern with theory and explanation has been associated with an interest in: (1) the philosophical and scientific antecedents of current methodological and substantive foci in developmental psychology; and in turn (2) the contemporary role of philosophy (e.g., paradigms or world views) in lower-order theoretical, methodological, and empirical endeavors. Today, then, developmental psychologists are more appreciative of the philosophical foundations of their past and present scientific endeavors, and many are actively exploring the potential empirical use of theoretical ideas derived from several philosophical paradigms, for example, the organismic, mechanistic, dialectical, and contextual world views.

This book derives both from this historical tradition and from this contemporary situation. The purpose of this book is to discuss the relations between philosophy and developmental psychology, as those relations have existed over the course of the history of the discipline and as they may currently exist. Although all portions of developmental psychology are not surveyed, major proponents of several currently key areas are represented (e.g., organismic developmental theory, stage theory, life-span developmental psychology, and the ecological approach to development). In addition, discussion of many currently prominent issues are included (e.g., constancy and change in human development, the use of multivariate models and methods, the role of the context in individual development, and the use of developmental theory in public policy and political arenas. The diversity of approaches and of interests present in the book are representative of the breadth of theoretical and empirical interests found in contemporary developmental psychology. As the authors of the chapters review the historical and present role of philosophical issues in their particular areas of interest (Part Two of the book), and as they critically exchange ideas (Part Three of the book, and portions of Parts Two and Four of the book as well), we see, first, the ubiquitous role of philosophy in developmental psychology. In addition then, we see the need to be constantly aware of the ways in which our pre-empirical beliefs influence our empirical ones, and, in turn, of how it is sometimes difficult for empirical findings to influence our assumptions. In addition, we see that there exists a range of interpretation about the nature of the historical bases of our contemporary work and about the appropriate role of particular philosophical positions in usefully facilitating these current scientific endeavors.

Edwin G. Boring, in the Preface of the first edition of his *A History of Experimental Psychology* (New York: Appleton–Century–Crofts, 1929), wrote that: "the gift of professional maturity comes only to the psychologist who knows the history of his science [p. xii]." However, in the Preface to the second edition (1950), he added that: "As time goes on, there come to be second thoughts about the interpretation of it [history]." Developmental psychologists are more mature, then, than they were 50 years ago, in that they are more cognizant of, and concerned with, the history of their discipline and with the significant but often veiled role that philosophical issues have played in the discipline's development. However, our discipline's development has not ended; we have not reached any final level of maturity. As evidenced by the range of interpretation present in this volume, the development of developmental psychology is an open-ended process; it is a discipline whose past history may be told in many ways and whose future history is always just beginning.

There are several people who have enabled me to move this volume from idea to reality. First and foremost, I thank the authors of the book's chapters. Their scholarship, diligence, patience, and commitment to the project are the key reasons for this book's existence. I am also grateful to Virginia Staudt Sexton, to whom this book is dedicated, for giving me the opportunity to organize a symposium at the 1980 American Psychological Association meetings, on which this book is based, and for agreeing to write the Foreword for this book. The feedback of several scholars was invaluable through the several phases of this project. I thank Roger A. Dixon, David F. Hultsch, Karen Hooker, David S. Palermo, and, especially, William A. Clebsch—whose articulateness and knowledge were great sources of stimulation and encouragement for me. I would also like to thank Rebecca Gorsuch, Kathie Hooven, and Joy Barger for their excellent secretarial support.

Most of my work on this book took place while I was a Fellow at the Center for Advanced Study in the Behavioral Sciences during the 1980–81 academic year. I am grateful for financial support provided by National Institute of Mental Health grant #5-T32-MH14581-05 and by the John D. and Catherine T. MacArthur Foundation, and for the assistance of the Center's staff. An additional grant from the John D. and Catherine T. MacArthur Foundation in part supported my remaining work on the book upon my return to Penn State. I am also grateful for this additional support.

Finally, and not at all least, I express my appreciation to and love for my wife, Jacqueline, and my son, Justin, for tolerating an all-too-often absent husband and father and for giving him the support he needed to complete this work.

Richard M. Lerner
University Park, PA.

To
Virginia Staudt Sexton:
A dedicated and superb teacher
and scholar, a devoted and
constant friend

INTRODUCTION

1

The History of Philosophy and the Philosophy of History in Developmental Psychology: A View of the Issues

Richard M. Lerner
The Pennsylvania State University

Much of psychology's early history is, of course, a part of philosophy . . . I do not hesitate to use philosophical terminology because psychology cannot be completely divorced from philosophy either in its history or in its present functioning. This state of affairs is cause for neither congratulation nor commiseration. Psychology is not the more scientific by trying to brush this sometimes embarrassing fact under the rug, as do some of our colleagues, by teaching and preaching psychology as if it had no philosophically based commitments . . . Denying there is need to consider philosophical questions does not solve the problem. The very denial is one form of philosophical solution [R. I. Watson, 1977].

INTRODUCTION

Today, most scientists would agree that there is a relation between philosophy and their empirical endeavors. However, disagreement would likely rapidly emerge if scientists were asked to indicate the precise features of the relation between philosophy and science. At one extreme the view might be that modern science emerged historically from philosophy, and that the chief remnant of this disciplinary heritage is the logic of scientific verification/falsification and proof. At the other extreme might lie the view that science is a social institution shaped by the cultural and historial variables influencing all human constructions; as such, scientific methodology and "truths" are always relativistic phenomena, embedded in particular constellations of social, cultural, and historial variables (Gould, 1981; Kagan, 1980; Kuhn, 1970). Views between these extremes would also certainly exist.

The diversity that exists today in science regarding views about the relation(s) between philosophy and science is no less than the variation that has been present historically. Over the course of its history, the explicitness with which developmental psychology has engaged philosophical issues has changed. The purpose of this chapter is to describe some of the major instances of this historically changing relation. Several approaches to fulfilling this purpose are reasonable. The range of choices is not unlike that available to a person who has a one month vacation period available for an ''around-the-world'' tour (cf. Whitehurst, 1982): If one dwells too long on any one point, the intensity and depth that may be achieved may be lessened because one will cover fewer points; if one opts to cover more points, then each must be viewed in a more general way. I have chosen to cast this chapter closer to the latter alternative.

In deciding on this approach I recognize that neither I nor most of my audience are professional historians or professional philosophers; rather, we are developmental psychologists, whose primary interest with the history of the relation between philosophy and developmental psychology is its use for facilitating understanding of current scientific activity (see Blight, 1981, and Weimer, 1979, for corresponding rationales for interest in such history). Moreover, the chapters that follow this one in this book, and several other relatively recent (e.g., Dixon, in press; Robinson, 1976; Smith, 1981) and classic references (Boring, 1950; Misiak & Sexton, 1966; Roback, 1952), provide—in their combination—the in-depth treatments of many, if not all, of the points that I can only treat in overview in the space available to me.

The history of developmental psychology is, of course, not completely separate from the history of psychology in general. As such, to fulfill the purpose of this chapter it is useful to describe first some features of the history of the relation between philosophy and psychology in general. The relation between philosophy and psychology has changed repeatedly both in regard to any acknowledged role of philosophical issues in psychological theory and research and in respect to formal, academic-institutional relations between the two disciplines.

Trends in the Relations Between Philosophy and Psychology During the 18th, 19th, and 20th Centuries in America

To illustrate the historically changing relations between philosophy and psychology, we may briefly consider major features of the links between the two disciplines, as they existed across the last 200 or so years in America (as noted, more detailed discussions of these relations are found in Boring, 1950; Misiak & Sexton, 1966; Roback, 1952; Robinson, 1976; and Smith, 1981).

The bases of psychological thought in America can be traced first to theology, then to moral philosophy, and, until the work of William James, to mental philosophy. The ideas of Jonathan Edwards and of Samual Johnson are representative of these first two influences. For example, in 1752 Johnson published *Elementa Philosophica,* the first textbook of philosophy published in America; it contained discussion of topics such as sensation, cognition, and affect (Misiak & Sexton, 1966).

However, in the 100 years prior to the work of William James it was the mental philosophy of the Scottish school of realism that dominated American psychological thought. This philosophical school was founded by Thomas Reid (1710–1796), who advocated the notion of mental facilities, thus providing the basis for what has been termed *faculty psychology* (Misiak & Sexton, 1966). Other leading contributors to the Scottish school were Dugald Stewart (1753–1828) and Thomas Brown (1778–1820). In America an initial major promoter of the Scottish tradition was John W. Witterspoon (1722–1794) at Princeton University (then the College of New Jersey).

From the revolutionary period until the late 19th century (and the advent of James), the books of philosophers such as Reid and Stewart were the principal textbooks of moral philosophy in the United States. However, during the 19th-century textbooks written in America began to appear and find some use (e.g., Thomas Upham published *Elements of Intellectual Philosophy* in 1827 and *Elements of Mental Philosophy* in 1831, and Noah Porter published *The Human Intellect* in 1868 [Misiak & Sexton, 1966]). Misiak and Sexton (1966) believe that the content of these books suggested some movement in American psychology from philosophy to a scientific orientation. Nevertheless, they (Misiak & Sexton, 1966) believe these texts, and psychological academic activity in general, were merely: "dilutions of the Scottish philosophers . . . and were . . . in the interests of religious orthodoxy. Mid-nineteenth century philosophy was a kind of Protestant scholasticism which derived its psychology from theological dogma [p. 128]."

Despite its pervasive presence the influence of the Scottish school decreased precipitously with the promotion of the views of William James. The last major representatives of the Scottish school were both professors of mental philosophy, as psychology was called in 19th-century academe (Misiak & Sexton, 1966), and presidents of their respective universities: Noah Porter (1811–1882) of Yale University, and James McCosh (1818–1894) of Princeton University.

The beginning of the influence of William James (1842–1910) can be traced at least to a letter he wrote in 1875 to President Eliot of Harvard University. James said (in Misiak & Sexton, 1966) that: "A real science of man is now being built out of the theory of evolution and the facts of archeology, the nervous system, and the senses [p. 130]." James' declaration of psychology as a science and his active publicizing of this "new" discipline began to forge for the first time in the United States a separation between philosophy and psychology; his work helped create both the academic and popular perception of psychology as an independent and scientific discipline.

James' career at Harvard mirrors the evolving separation between philosophy and psychology in the United States. In 1875 James taught a graduate course at Harvard entitled "The relation between Physiology and Psychology" (Boring, 1950). Whereas in 1880 he had been appointed an assistant professor of philosophy at Harvard and by 1885 had risen to the rank of Professor of Philosophy, he had his title changed in 1890 to Professor of Psychology. In that same year James published *The Priniciples of Psychology* in two volumes. James described the book as being written from a positivistic viewpoint, and certainly its influence was to markedly promote psychology as a scientific discipline in the United States (Misiak & Sexton, 1966). Indeed, 2 years later James founded, with Hugo Müunsterberg, Harvard's psychological laboratory, and by 1900 there were about 40 psychological laboratories in the United States.

Interestingly, and perhaps foreshadowing the waxing and waning closeness of philosophy and psychology that would characterize scientific psychology's history, James, after doing so much to launch psychology as a science and as a discipline distinct from philosophy, changed his title once again, in 1897, to Professor of Philosophy. However, the science he had vigorously promoted continued on the trajectory he had set for it, despite the fact that James himself had withdrawn from the fray. Indeed, as presaged by James in his 1875 letter to President Eliot, by 1900 not only had the number of scientific laboratories grown enormously but the characteristics of American psychology had become well-defined. As Boring (1950) has stated: "It had inherited its physical body from German experimentalism, but had got its mind from Darwin [p. 506]."

The positivistic, experimental, and functional features of psychology continued to be characteristic of the "new" science in the 20th century (White, 1968), the number of laboritories continued to increase rapidly (e.g., the number almost doubled from 1900 to 1915; Misiak & Sexton, 1966), and the distinction between philosophy and scientific psychology was increasingly drawn more rigidly and was enforced by both intellectual argument and academic-institutional separations (Smith, 1981). As Smith (1981, p. 29) points out:

> The plain fact was that experimentalists typically had no desire for philosophical intercourse, and one need look no further than Watson and Edward L. Thorndike for instances. Although both had considerable contact with important philosophers as students, both doubted the value of philosophy. Watson claimed that his extensive philosophical training "wouldn't take hold" and that he understood neither his illustrious teachers, John Dewey and George Herbert Mead. Thorndike reacted even more negatively to philosophy, calling his teacher, Josiah Royce, "too much a performer," and remarking that the best thing that could be said for a philosophy course was that it does not meet often.
>
> The path of independence that most psychologists had blazed for themselves by 1910 was by and large adhered to for the next twenty-five years.

Nevertheless, however necessary or immutable the division between philosophy and psychology may have seemed, we see that by the middle portion of the

20th century events conspired to once again change the intellectual relation between philosophy and psychology (e.g., see Smith, 1981). In fact, by 1962 the first official function of a then newly organized division of the American Psychological Association—the Division of Philosophical Psychology—was held. At that function Joseph R. Royce, one of the Division's organizers, said (in Misiak & Sexton, 1966) that the beginning of the Division was a celebration of the: "official remarriage of psychology and philosophy after almost 100 years of legal separation [p. 29]."

Events pertaining to numerous areas in psychology interacted in the first two-thirds or so of this century to recreate an acknowledged relation between philosophy and psychology. Smith (1981), for example, described those events pertinent to experimental psychology and learning theory. As noted, however, the purpose of this chapter is to highlight those events involved in the area of developmental psychology. An overview of this history thus allows us to appreciate the bases of current relations between philosophy and developmental psychology; in addition, it allows us to appreciate key issues pertinent to the major focus of this volume: the ways in which the history and nature of the relation between philosophy and developmental psychology are involved in past and current theoretical, methodological, and substantive concerns in the study of human development.

The Role of Philosophy in Developmental Psychology: An Historical Overview

Discussions of the history of developmental psychology have appeared repeatedly (Baltes, 1979a; Bronfenbrenner, 1963; Dixon, in press; Havighurst, 1973; Looft, 1972; Sears, 1975; White, 1968). We need not reiterate these presentations in the present chapter. Instead, our goal is to indicate those features of the history of developmental psychology that mark the changing relations between philosophical and scientific endeavors.

One may speculate that a factor motivating the drawing and sharpening of the distinctions between philosophy and psychology, by the early contributors to scientific psychology, was a perceived need to create disciplinary boundaries in order to establish and protect intellectual and academic-institutional domains of proprietorship (cf. Smith, 1981). Such boundaries may have thus been initially quite functional. However, we have noted earlier that in the years between the turn of the century and the early 1960s the perception of the potential role of philosophy in psychology had changed to an extent sufficient for the establishment of a division of the American Psychological Association explicitly designed to explore philosophy–psychology interrelations.

Developmental psychology changed in this period from a descriptive, normative discipline to one concerned centrally with theory and metatheory (Bronfenbrenner, 1963; Looft, 1972; Mussen, 1970). Interestingly, these metatheoretical or paradigmatic (Kuhn, 1970) concerns in part pertain to the role of historical change in an organism's development across life. Moreover, the change in disciplinary focus from description to theory and metatheory was fostered by historical events affecting science and scientists in the 1900 to 1960 period. It is useful to divide our consideration of this history into events preceding and following World War II.

Events Prior to World War II

G. Stanley Hall's (1904) recapitulationist theory was the first scientific theory of human ontogenetic development to reach prominence in the psychological literature. However, due to criticism that became quite prominent almost immediately upon the publication of Hall's (1904) ideas (Thorndike, 1904), recapitulationism per se found few adherents in developmental psychology; that is, Hall's impact was not to create an active area of research devoted to documenting that ontogeny recapitulates phylogeny. However, Hall's was a "nature"-based conception of development (Lerner & Hultsch, in press; Lerner & Spanier, 1980), and Hall had both personal and academic influence in American psychology. Thus, Hall's students—the two most prominent of whom were Lewis Terman and Arnold Gesell—were influenced by Hall to an extent sufficient to adopt his general "nature" orientation of ontogeny (if not his specific, nature-based theory).

Terman's work on mental measurement and Gesell's research on infant and child growth and maturation were associated with explicit theoretical interests. Terman's (1925; Terman & Oden, 1959) research was aimed at supporting the view that intellectual ability was hereditarily based (Gould, 1981) and Gesell's (1929, 1931, 1934, 1946, 1954) empirical work built on his concern with depicting the inherent timetable of human growth and with providing support for his notion of "maturational readiness." Nevertheless, despite these theoretical agendas a major impact of Terman's and Gesell's work was to foster developmental psychology's becoming a descriptive, normative discipline.

The empirical work associated with mental measurement was test construction, norm establishment, and description of various groups' performances. The empirical work associated with Gesell's laboratory involved the systematic cataloging of growth norms. In a discipline so recently emerged from philosophy, it is perhaps understandable that empirical work would be stressed, and the stress in this empirical work was clearly description and norm-generation. However, a contrast to these emphases, a "nurture"-bases theory of behavior, arose in psychology. Although the proponents of this view were not primarily developmentalists, their work came to influence developmental research and, as such, provided a counterpoint to the descriptive, nature focus provided by Hall, Terman, and Gesell.

In the second decade of this century and continuing through the 1950s, American psychology, as well as other areas of social science (e.g., sociology; Homans, 1961) were quite influenced by a behavioristic, learning-theory view of behavior. Although, no learning theory has ever been devised on the basis of information derived *primarily* from children (White, 1970), extensive application to human development was made. John B. Watson, who developed this view under the label *Behaviorism* (Watson, 1913, 1918), stressed that stimuli and responses combine under lawful, empirical conditions—the laws of conditioning; by focusing on how stimuli in the environment gained control over the behavior of organisms, one could know how behavior was acquired and, by implication, developed. Indeed, Watson applied these ideas to children, both in his research (Watson & Raynor, 1920) and in his prescriptions for child care (Watson, 1928).

Behaviorism gave psychologists an intellectual orientation that allowed them to be viewed as objective and natural scientists (cf. Smith, 1981). As such, Behaviorism and variants and extensions of it (Hull, 1929; Skinner, 1938) became the predominant conceptual focus in American psychology. As was the case with Watson's work, ideas and principles derived primarily from nonhuman organisms, primarily rats (Beach, 1950; Herrnstein, 1977), were applied to humans. Again, ideas pertinent to human development and socialization arose (Dollard, Doob, Miller, Mowrer, & Sears, 1939; Miller & Dollard, 1941).

The behavioristic-oriented research tradition was associated with manipulative research; such investigations tended to concentrate on readily observable aspects of behavior (e.g., aggressive behaviors) and constituted a compendium, and an elaborate and fairly precise one, of how variations in particular stimulus characteristics were related to variations in responses of certain groups of children (basically white, middle-class children of highly educated parents). Moreover, some of the work done within this tradition, for example, that of Dollard et al. (1939) and Miller and Dollard (1941), can be viewed as an attempt to translate organismic, psychoanalytic concepts into terms compatible with mechanistic, social learning theory. Of course, metatheoretical differences between the two theories make such translation difficult (cf. Reese & Overton, 1970), and the contrasting methodological strategies associated with the two types of theories complicate this issue (cf. Overton & Reese, 1973). Thus, whether for reasons associated with these and/or with other problems, there were not in the 1940s—as there are still not today—many attempts to translate theories derived from one metatheory into the terms of a theory derived from another metatheory in order to conduct empirical tests. However, one major point of difference between the 1940s—wherein the predominant emphasis in developmental work was description—and today, wherein a major concern is with process and explanation (Mussen, 1970)—is the frequency with which theorists associated with different metatheories engage each other in debate about their philosophical orientations. Events surrounding World War II helped serve to bring this alteration about.

World War II

The events surrounding World War II irrevocably altered the nature of American social science. First, even before the United States entered the war in December, 1941, effects of events in Europe were felt. Nazi persecution led many Jewish intellectuals to flee Europe during the 1930s, and many sought refuge and a new start for their careers in the United States. Great pains were often taken to find these refugees positions in American universities and associated institutions (Gengerelli, 1976); not infrequently, these people brought with them ideas counter to those predominating the American academic scene. For instance, many psychoanalytically oriented people came to this country (e.g., Peter Blos and Erik Erikson).

In addition, once America entered the war, and numerous soldiers needed to be tested for psychological as well as physical trauma, the federal government gave universities large amounts of money to train clinical psychologists. This program allowed many professionals with psychoanalytic orientations to become faculty members in universities, previously dominated by behaviorists (Misiak & Sexton, 1966), because they were the people with backgrounds appropriate for teaching clinical skills to the new and larger groups of future clinicians that were needed.

Thus, one impact of World War II was to encourage psychoanalytic thinking in many psychology departments. This orientation presented not only the introduction of nature-based thinking into departments where behaviorists previously resided in total control of the intellectual domain (Gengerelli, 1976). Additionally, it represented just *one* of many different theoretical accounts of human functioning derived from the contributions of European scholars—accounts that stressed either nature or both nature and nurture as sources of behavior and development—that were now making inroads into American thinking. For instance, nativistic, gestalt ideas about perception and learning, were introduced by people like Wertheimer, Koffka, Kohler, Goldstein, and Lewin and were shown to be pertinent also to areas of concern such as brain functioning, group dynamics and social problems (Sears, 1975). Similarly, at about this time the developmental concepts of Heinz Werner (1948) became known and began to be used in relation to both basic and applied problems.

One outcome of the changes fostered by events relating to World War II was thus to provide a pluralism of ideas about development. Now there were numerous interpretations of behavior and development, interpretations that were based on substantially different conceptions of the source of human functioning, and these different alternatives were advanced by respected advocates often working in the same academic contexts (Gengerelli, 1976).

The 1950s and 1960s

Because of the pluralism of perspectives now increasingly present in academe, developmentalists became less concerned with issues primarily pertinent to the description of development and became more focused on issues of interpretation. As such, they primarily became concerned with the *comparative use* and evaluation of various theories in integrating the facts of development into an understandable whole. For instance, one instance of this change of focus is the rediscovery of the theory of Jean Piaget; this theory was known in America in the 1920s (Piaget, 1923); but Piaget's ideas were not given much attention at that time because of the "clinical" nature of Piaget's research methods, his nonstatistical style of data analysis, and the abstract constructs with which he was concerned, all of which ran counter to then predominant trends in the United States. As a consequence, Piaget's theory did not become popular until the European influences on America began to alter the character of developmental psychology. Indeed, it can be fairly said that concern with the components of Piaget's theory was one of the predominant features of American developmental psychology throughout the 1960s.

In essence then, the years preceding 1970 were characterized by an increasing movement away from the descriptive and normative study of human development (Sears, 1975) to a primary focus on process and explanation (Bronfenbrenner, 1963; Looft, 1972). Philosophical and theoretical essays (McCandless & Spiker, 1956; Spiker & McCandless, 1954) illustrated this trend by involving calls for studies of developmental processes and mechanisms, especially ones involving learning (Lipsitt, personal communication, 1979). In addition, the theoretical and editorial work of Harris (1956, 1957) furthered the concern with process and explanation, instead of with descriptive, normative work. Characterizing the emphases by 1970, Mussen (1970) noted: "The major contemporary empirical and theoretical emphases in the field of developmental psychology, however, seem to be on explanations of the psychological changes that occur, the mechanisms and processes accounting for growth and development [p. vii]."

The 1970s Through Today

The 1970s saw an increasingly more abstract concern with the study of development. Two interrelated themes emerged. First, there was a trend toward the multidisciplinary, life-span study of human development. Second, there occurred a renewed appreciation of the metatheoretical, or paradigmatic, bases of developmental theories (Overton & Reese, 1973; Reese & Overton, 1970).

The Life-Span Perspective.   As discussed by Havighurst (1973) and by Baltes (1979a), the historical bases of the life-span perspective can be traced to 18th- and 19th-century publications by Tetens (1777), Carus (1808), and Quetelet (1835), and in the 20th century to contributions in both Europe and in the United States, such as those by Sanford (1902), Hall (1922), Hollingworth (1927), Bühler (1933), Pressey, Janney, and Kuhlen (1939), Erikson (1950), and by the faculty of the Committee on Human Development at the University of Chicago (Havighurst, 1948, 1953, 1956; Neugarten, 1964, 1966, 1969; Neugarten &

Guttman, 1958). For example, in the work of Havighurst (1948, 1953) we find a stress on an active organism changing across life (as a consequence of having to confront new "developmental tasks") and an emphasis on the need to use a multidisciplinary perspective to understand organism-context relations across life.

By the late 1960s and throughout the 1970s these historical antecedents began to be synthesized, and interest in adult development and aging began to grow rapidly. This interest in adult development and aging provided the recent, major impetus to the current empirical concern with life-span development because, most obviously, it moved scientific investigation beyond the child and adolescent years. However, this life-span research interest was also critically concerned with issues of explanation and theory.

Attempts to use a unidimensional biological model of growth, based on an idealistic, genetic-maturational (organismic) paradigm, to account for data sets pertinent to the adult and aged years were not completely successful (Baltes, Reese, & Lipsitt, 1980; Baltes & Schaie, 1973). Viewed from the perspective of this organismic conception, the adult and aged years were seen as periods of decline. However, all data sets pertinent to age changes (e.g., in regard to intellectual performance) during these periods were not consistent with such a unidirectional format for change. Instead, increasingly greater interindividual differences in intraindividual change were evident in many data sets (Baltes, 1979a; Baltes & Schaie, 1974; Schaie, Labouvie, & Buech, 1973). On the basis of such data, Brim and Kagan (1980) observed that: "growth is more individualistic than was thought, and it is difficult to find general patterns [p. 13]."

Variables associated with membership in particular birth cohorts and/or with normative and non-normative events occurring at particular historical times of measurement appeared to account for more of the variance in behavior change processes with respect to adult intellectual development than did age-associated influences (Baltes et al., 1980). Data sets pertinent to the child (Baltes, Baltes, & Reinert, 1970) and the adolescent (Nesselroade & Baltes, 1974) that considered these cohort and time effects also confirmed their saliency in developmental change. Ultimately, conceptualizations useful for understanding the role of these non-age-related variables in development were induced (Baltes, Cornelius, & Nesselroade, 1977).

In summarizing the implications of this work for the understanding of the human life course, Brim and Kagan (1980) note that: "humans have a capacity for change across the entire life span . . . there are important growth changes across the life span from birth to death, many individuals retain a great capacity for change, and the consequences of the events of early childhood are continually transformed by later experiences, making the course of human development more open than many have believed [p. 1]."

As a consequence of this empirical and conceptual activity, the point of view labeled *life-span developmental psychology* or the *life-span view of human devel-*

opment (Baltes, 1979a,b; Baltes et al., 1980) became crystallized. The emerging nature of this orientation has become clear over the course of several conferences (Baltes & Schaie, 1973; Datan & Ginsberg, 1975; Datan & Reese, 1977; Goulet & Baltes, 1970; Nesselroade & Reese, 1973), the initiation of publication of an annual volume devoted to life-span development (Baltes, 1978; Baltes & Brim, 1979, 1980), and the publication of numerous empirical and theoretical papers (Baltes et al., 1980). From this perspective, the potential for developmental change is seen to be present across all of life; the human life course is held to be potentially multidirectional and necessarily multidimensional (Baltes, 1979b; Baltes et al., 1980). In addition, the sources of the potentially continual changes across life are seen to involve both the inner-biological and outer-ecological levels of the context within which the organism is embedded. Indeed, although an orientation *to* the study of development and not a specific theory *of* development (Baltes, 1979b), it is clear that life-span developmentalists are disposed to a reciprocal model of organism-context relations. As Baltes (1979b) has indicated:

> Life-span developmental psychologists emphasize *contextualistic-dialectic* paradigms of development (Datan & Reese, 1977; Lerner, Skinner, & Sorell, 1980; Riegel, 1976a) rather than the use of "mechanistic" or "organismic" ones more typical of child development work. There are two primary rationales for this preference. One is, of course, evident also in current child development work. As development unfolds, it becomes more and more apparent that individuals act on the environment and produce novel behavior outcomes, thereby making the active and selective nature of human beings of paramount importance. Furthermore, the recognition of the interplay between age-graded, history-graded, and non-normative life events suggests a contextualistic and dialectical conception of development. This dialectic is further accentuated by the fact that individual development is the reflection of multiple forces which are not always in synergism, or convergence, nor do they always permit the delineation of a specific set of endstates [p. 2].

In essence, the currently popular formulation of the life-span view of human development arose as a consequence of the failure of ideas associated with theories derived from the extant, major paradigms of development (the organismic and the mechanistic; Overton & Reese, 1973; Reese & Overton, 1970) to be completely useful in accounting for changes across the life-span. In turn, developmental psychologists associated with life-span and adult development and aging research found it of use to derive ideas from another philosophical orientation—the contextual (Pepper, 1942). This paradigm leads to the view that the features of human development—its content and the constancy or change of its structures and functions—are reciprocally linked to the historically changing contexts of human life. Thus, the history of developmental psychology has involved not only a return to considering the role of philosophy in formulating useful theory and method but, at the same time, to an appreciation of a philosophical position stressing the role of historical change in human development. In short, the history of philosophy in developmental psychology has led to a concern with the philosophy of history.

Paradigms of Development.   This historical change can be documented by reference to the second theme that has been identified previously as emerging in the 1970s—the concern with the paradigmatic bases of developmental theory. Indeed, it seems evident that this second theme was simultaneously a product and a producer of the first theme. For example, many of the papers associated with this second theme were initially presented at conferences and were then published in volumes, wherein life-span developmental psychology was promoted. Thus, the opportunity for, and presence of, cross-fertilization seems clear.

In the 1970s, discussions occurred concerning how the "family of theories" (Reese & Overton, 1970) derived from the organismic and the mechanistic world view, respectively, were associated with different ideas about the nature and nurture bases of development (Overton, 1973), with different stances in regard to an array of key conceptual issues of development (e.g., the quality, openness, and continuity of change (Looft, 1973), with contrasting methodologies for studying development (Overton & Reese, 1973), and, ultimately, with alternative truth criteria for establishing the "facts" of development (Overton & Reese, 1973; Reese & Overton, 1970).

This focus on the philosophical bases of developmental theory, method, and data led to considering the use of still other paradigms in the study of development (Riegel, 1973). In part, this concern occurred as a consequence of interest in integrating assumptions associated with prototypic organismic- and mechanistic-derived theories (Looft, 1973). For instance, Riegel (1973, 1975, 1976a,b) attempted to formulate a paradigm of development including both the active organism focus in organicism and the active environment focus in mechanism. In addition, however, interest in continual, reciprocal *relations* between active organism and active context (and not in either element per se) and concern with these relations as they existed on all phenomenal levels of analysis was a basis of proposing a dialectical (Riegel, 1975, 1976a), transactional (Sameroff, 1975), or relational (Looft, 1973) model of human development.

Contrary to assumptions associated with the other paradigms of human development, Riegel's (1975, 1976a,b) view emphasized the continual conflict among inner-biological, individual-psychological, outer-physical, and sociocultural levels of analysis; he assumed that constant changes among the multiple, reciprocally related levels of analysis were involved in development (Overton, 1978). Thus, his dialectical model can be seen as consistent with the paradigm that Pepper (1942) labeled as contextualism (Hultsch & Hickey, 1978; Lerner et al., 1980).

The dialectical model, as summarized by Riegel (1976a), involves a commitment to the study of "ceaseless flux," of actions and changes, and to a concern with short-term (e.g., situational) changes, long-term (e.g., individual and cultural) changes, and, *especially,* to the interrelation between the two. Thus, ceaseless, interrelated changes are the core ideas in the paradigm promoted by Riegel. These ideas are also basic to the contextual paradigm of Pepper (1942). According to Hultsch and Hickey (1978), from this view: "every behavior and incident in the world is a historic event" and "change and novelty are accepted as fundamental [p. 79]." Pepper (1942) states that the basic facts of existence are: "complexes or contexts [p. 142]," where "the real historic event, the event in its actuality, is when it is going on *now,* the dynamic dramatic active event [p. 232]," and where "the relations involved in a historic event are inexhaustable, and a set of contextualistic categories does not so much determine the nature of our world as lead one to appreciate fair samples of the world's events [p. 237]." Thus, constant change of the "now" (the event) and the total interrelation of this event are the basic ideas of Pepper's contextual paradigm. Riegel's (1975, 1976a,b) ideas then, along with those of Pepper (1942), promoted interest in the developmental implications of active organisms being engaged in relations with their active context.

In sum, from this perspective, developmental changes occur as a consequence of reciprocal (bidirectional) relations between the active organism and the active context. Just as the context changes the individual, the individual changes the context. As such, by acting to change sources of their own development, by being both a product and a producer of their contexts, individuals effect their own development (Riegel, 1976a; also see Schneirla, 1957). Moreover, because the context is seen as a multilevel one—having interrelated biological, sociocultural, physical-environmental, and historical components—Riegel's ideas were consonant with the multidisciplinary, life-span view of human development we have discussed earlier.

In summary, when scientific psychology emerged from philosophy in the years preceding and following the turn of the century, the leading proponents of the "new" science were at pains to demonstrate that their discipline was a quantitative, natural science area of inquiry (Boring, 1950; Misiak & Sexton, 1966). In developmental psychology these orientations to scholarship were associated with the emergence of a descriptive, normative, and largely nature-based approach to child psychology, and then with the development of an experimental, manipulative approach to studying behavior, one based largely on the application of nurture-based conditioning principles to children (White, 1970).

The events in the late 1930s to early 1960s historical era fostered a change in the concern with philosophy in developmental psychology (e.g., in regard to the relativism of explanation). This alteration, brought to the fore by the increasing presence in American academe of scholars with diverse, nature, interactionist, and nurture conceptions, helped prompt the increasing concern with explanation and theory that characterized developmental psychology throughout this period. By the late 1960s and through the 1970s this concern was made increasingly more abstract, as developmentalists came to focus with increasing frequency on the philosophical bases of their theories (Bronfenbrenner, 1977, 1979; Overton, 1973; Overton & Reese, 1973; Reese & Overton, 1970; Riegel, 1975). Paradigms or models other than the organismic and mechanistic were considered— both for reasons of promoting theoretical integration (Looft, 1973; Mischel, 1977; Riegel, 1975; Sarbin, 1977) and for resolving anomolies in data sets extending beyond childhood and adolescence (Baltes, 1979b; Lerner & Ryff, 1978). These alternative contextual, ecological, or dialectical paradigms or models stressed the role of ecological structures and historical events as being causally involved in intraindividual development. Thus, prompted by historical changes in the world within which the discipline of developmental psychology was developing, a renewed concern with philosophy–psychology relations occurred; and one key component of this historical change in the role of philosophy is that philosophical positions incorporating the role of history in the person's individual development emerged as prominent.

Conclusions: Philosophical and Theoretical Pluralism in Contemporary Developmental Psychology

At this writing the field of developmental psychology is characterized by the presence of multiple paradigmatic, theoretical, and methodological orientations. Such pluralism has perhaps always been present (Reese & Overton, 1970; von Bertalanffy, 1933). However, what may be unique about the current historical era is:

1. The explicit attention being paid to this pluralism.
2. The amount of journal and book space and conference time being devoted to issues pertinent to this pluralism. One example of such an issue is the nature of the links among: (a) a paradigm; (b) either one, or the family, of theories associated with it; and (c) the methods derived from the theory; a second example of such an issue is whether different paradigms lead to irreconcilable theoretical and methodological differences (Reese & Overton, 1970), or whether there may be particular substantive areas wherein integration may be achieved (Kuhn, 1978; Overton & Newman, 1981).
3. The willingness current developmental psychologists have to devote their scholarly time to, and engage each other in scholarly debates about, issues pertinent to philosophical concerns. For example, for more than a decade the journal *Human Development* has been devoted almost exclusively to publishing papers pertinent to such issues. The *International Journal of Behavioral Development* has been strongly committed to publishing philosophical and theoretical papers, and a relatively new journal, *Developmental Review,* also has such an emphasis.

Moreover, given the emphasis on the role of historical change in individual development, found in one of the currently prominent metatheoretical perspectives—the contextual—these philosophical and theoretical papers and debates have often included discussions of potential historical influences on development and of historical analyses of the development of particular theoretical positions (Meacham, 1977, 1978, 1981; Riegel & Rosenwald, 1975). Issues here have included whether the "history" that is studied when one assesses individual development (ontogeny) is formally related to the history of that individual's species (Gould, 1977) and/or context (e.g., society or culture, Brent, 1978; Lerner & Busch–Rossnagel, 1981). In other words, is there homology, analogy, or no useful relation between levels or, perhaps more accurately, types of "history" (e.g., of the organism's life course; of the organism's evolution and of its physical and cultural context; and of the discipline [developmental psychology] that studies the organism's life course)? Said yet another way, how do the activities of the historian—who, for example, may be recounting the changes involved in the social context of the 19th or 20th century and/or who may be detailing the changes in the discipline of developmental psychology during this period—correspond to the activities of the developmental psychologist who may be attempting to account for the changes in one or several human lives? Are developmental psychologists merely historians of the life course, and, if not, what are the key distinctions between history *qua history* and human ontogeny and/or the disciplines that study it?

Other, related issues exist. Independent of whether the activities of the developmental psychologist and of the historian are distinct, a key issue that remains is how are we to include or exclude the role of historical events and change (in respect to the species and/or in regard to the person's context) in our theories of human development? Do we remain impressed that features of human behavior change across life? For instance, there is relatively little general predictability from infancy to adulthood (Lipsitt, 1982) and for selected behaviors from one historical era to another (Baltes et al., 1977; Elder, 1974) (i.e., there are cohort effects). Or, do we focus on either idealized (Piaget, 1970) or, to some extent, empirical constancies (Costa, McCrae, & Arenberg, 1980) and see them as sufficient to exclude the role of history in human developmental theory? What implicit and explicit philosophical stances lead us to be inclusionary or exclusionary? Of what *use* is either route for description, for explanation, and perhaps also for enhancing human development? Indeed, does the topic of developmental enhancement even make sense if one excludes contextual change as an influence on human *ontogeny* (Brim & Kagan, 1980; Lerner, in preparation)? In sum, what is the role of historical analysis and of historical change in understanding human development?

In conclusion, developmental psychology is today characterized by an acknowledged and attended to diversity of philosophical, theoretical, and methodological orientations, and of views about the nature and role of history in one's philosophical, theoretical, and methodological endeavors. More importantly, this diversity of perspective generates considerable debate and cross-fertilization among proponents of contrasting positions. It is the purpose of this book to present essays by key contributors to the current historical–philosophical–theoretical–methodological debates, essays that represent their own work on, and views of issues involved in, these debates. It is also the purpose of this book to represent the potential cross-fertilization of ideas that exists as a consequence of debate among these scholars. The format of this book facilitates the accomplishment of these two goals.

The Plan of the Book

As may be evident from the preceding discussion, the discipline of developmental psychology has itself developed. The scholars contributing to this volume have both worked with and are among the people who have notably influenced this history. Their work is likely to continue to influence the field. One reason for this likely continued influence is that the work of these scholars itself changes, and one major way that this change is brought about is by confronting, in the arena of ideas, those with different views. Syntheses that emerge from such interchanges have in the past helped change the field (e.g., Harris, 1957). Such interactions are likely to have similar benefits in the future.

Divergence, interchange, and perhaps some integration are reflected in this book. The book is divided into four parts, the first and last of which are relatively brief. The present chapter constitutes the introductory section of the volume. The second section of the book presents the historical and philosophical essays of Kagan, White, Baltes, Dixon and Nesselroade, Bronfenbrenner, and Kaplan. Kaplan's chapter includes his analysis of differences between his perspective and those of the other contributors. It sets the stage for the third section of the book; that is, using Kaplan's chapter as a springboard many of the other authors comment on the positions taken by Kaplan as well as on other issues. Finally, a brief concluding chapter by me constitutes the last section of this book. In order to illustrate the range of perspectives and topics covered by the authors in this book, it is useful to briefly indicate key themes in their essays.

Kagan's essay on developmental categories and the premise of connectivity in many ways serves as the keynote chapter for this volume; that is, a key implication of his presentation is that over the course of the history of the discipline developmental psychologists have not paid sufficient attention to their philosophical "presuppositions" (pre-empirical, often culturally deep-rooted, beliefs), and that because such presuppositions bias or constrain theory or research, more explicit attention needs to be paid to such philosophical issues. Kagan notes that key features of the role of developmental psychology are to adopt theoretically useful categories and to select the best constructs to describe change. However, such selection is limited not only by one's "tacit hypotheses," or presuppositions, but as well by one's consciously articulated hypotheses and by categorical bias. In addition, although there are at least three potential referents in developmental classification (others of the same age, others of different ages, and animals other than homo sapiens), it is rare in the history of developmental classification that the referent being used is clearly specified.

All these potential problems in developmental classification, illustrated by Kagan through a discussion of the classification of motives, may be complicated by one's unarticulated presuppositions. To demonstrate this role of presuppositions, Kagan shows how the presupposition of *connectivity*—a belief, common to Western societies, that there exists an unbroken, virtually immutable and continuous path from earlier to later life—has influenced classification. He traces the history of this presupposition from early Eastern and Western cultures through the history of developmental psychology in this century, and he indicates both the relevance of the connectivity presupposition to current theory and research and to the continuing resistance that exists among many developmentalists to the idea of discontinuity.

White's essay discusses the historical development of the idea that there is development, specifically development of the child's cognitive abilities through stages. White contrasts the use of induction versus the use of abduction among early, 19th-century "stage" theorists. These theorists—George J. Romanes, Ivan M. Sechenov, and James Mark Baldwin—did rely to some extent on data; but White points out that their theories were not grounded on data in the way in which 20th-century idealizations of the philosophy of science have held that contemporary theories ought to relate to data. Instead, these theorists' use of abduction involved a movement from experience to conjecture, from consequences to antecedents.

White indicates that this historical analysis has several uses for current developmental psychologists. First, an analysis of these early theories suggests that one does not need much formal data about children to generate ideas basic to current stage theories. Second, White's historical analysis is useful in helping current developmental psychologist's deal with a concept of development that has features congruent and incongruent with their contemporary ones. White argues that, whereas the ideas of development we today deal with were elaborated in the social histories and evolutionary theory of the last two centuries, few current developmental psychologists recognize and use the generic nature of developmental theory, a nature that may be derived from the historical bases of current ideas of development. Finally, White notes that the developmental ideas he reviews were built with activist and political intentions, and that one can understand the history of these ideas as an attempt to use developmental science to identify the good.

Baltes' essay describes how, beginning in the 18th century, the history of developmental psychology has involved the repeated espousal (albeit in insular ways) of a life-span approach to the study of behavioral development. He reviews the early contributions to a life-span perspective of Tetens, Carus, and Quetelet in the 18th and 19th centuries and then traces the development of this approach through the 20th century.

The antecedents of the currently popular life-span perspective coalesced to provide the current view with several key features: Because of a primary concern with long-term processes, the life-span approach tends to stretch the boundaries of any developmental orientation. This long-term process emphasis has relevance to theoretical and methodological issues (e.g., reformulating the concept of development to encompass models other than only biological ones, thus expanding the substantive scope of developmental constructs in order to link ontogenetic and biocultural change in an interactive, contextual framework; and devising research methods and designs suitable for validly measuring across life the developing person in a changing world).

The essay by Dixon and Nesselroade notes certain commonalities between pluralism and correlational analysis in the history of developmental psychology. Dixon and Nesselroade observe that a pluralistic approach to theory and method in developmental psychology is often associated with a contextual or pragmatic metatheory. In turn, those who promote this linkage between pluralism and pragmatic metatheory also often forward a multivariate approach to empirical endeavors. Dixon and Nesselroade set as their primary aim the specification of the conceptual and historical links among these three ideas. They view these three ideas as the key features of current life-span developmental psychology and, as such, observe historical instances of pluralism in philosophy, and most notably in the pragmatics of William James; in turn, they discuss the origin of the method of correlation in philosophy and psychology.

Dixon and Nessleroade integrate these historical analyses by indicating how pluralism leads to a concept of development that is promoted by current life-span developmental psychologists, and, in turn, how the philosophical, theoretical, and methodological development of contemporary multivariate models similarly combine to provide life-span developmentalists with empirical means to conduct research consonant with this concept of development. Finally, Dixon and Nesselroade indicate how both pragmatics/pluralism and multivariate correlational analysis coalesce to create several specific propositions and themes basic to the current life-span perspective.

Bronfenbrenner's essay traces the evolution of the concept of environment in systematic research on human development. His emphasis is on how constructs pertinent to the environment were being explicitly or implicitly used in empirical investigation. Bronfenbrenner identifies the earliest empirical studies as appearing in the 1870s, first in Germany, and then in England, with the work of Sir

Francis Galton, and finally in the United States in the 1880s with G. Stanley Hall. Bronfenbrenner traces the change from structural to dynamic models of the environment as it occurred in this century, largely in the United States, noting the innovation and enrichment that emerged in the 1930s in the theoretical conceptions underlying research models for the study of human development in context.

Bronfenbrenner notes several sources of scientific progress in research on environmental influences. In particular, he identifies how the course of social change has itself provoked investigators to adopt a broader and more complex conception of the environment as it affects human development. In addition, he indicates how the most significant scientific advances that have occurred over the last three decades have involved the gradual elaboration of latent structures underlying the research designs employed by investigators in the field.

In the first major portion of his chapter, Kaplan notes that scholars reconstruct the domains of "philosophy of history" and "history of philosophy" in quite different ways, depending on their values and interests. Given this constraint on all developmental psychologists, Kaplan then presents his definition of developmental psychology as a practico-theoretical discipline, a policy discipline, concerned with the perfection (including liberation or freedom) of the individual. He then discusses those philosophers of history and philosophers in history whose ideas have foreshadowed his views. In the second major portion of his essay, Kaplan discusses some problems and issues for a theoretically oriented life-span developmental psychology. Here he emphasizes the need to distinguish between development and change and notes that development does not exist directly in the populations studied but resides fundamentally in the perspective used. However, he also notes that, because different "theories" will yield different "facts" about development, a key issue for a theoretically oriented life-span developmental psychologist to face is the choice of a theory or a perspective for use in examining the phenomena of human life.

The final major portion of Kaplan's chapter clarifies his positions regarding development vis-à-vis the views found in the essays of Kagan, White, Baltes, Dixon and Nesselroade, and Bronfenbrenner. This last section therefore constitutes a discussion of the preceding chapters and serves as the initiation of a dialogue among authors in the book. This last section of Kaplan's chapter serves then as a transition between the second and third portions of this book.

In sum, the chapters that follow this one focus on a rather diverse array of philosophical and substantive issues of concern to contemporary developmental psychologists. This diversity of interests and the divergence of perspectives found across chapters illustrate that developmental psychologists are aware of their history and of the past importance of philosphy in that history, and that today they are still actively involved in historical and philosophical debate. Such awareness and interchange augers well for the future development of the discipline.

ACKNOWLEDGMENTS

The writing of this chapter was supported in part by a grant from the John D. and Catherine T. MacArthur Foundation. I am grateful to Roger A. Dixon, David F. Hultsch, and Karen Hooker for their comments on an earlier draft of this chapter.

REFERENCES

Baltes, P. B. (Ed.). *Life-span development and behavior* (Vol. 1). New York: Academic Press, 1978.

Baltes, P. B. Life-span developmental psychology: Some converging observations on history and theory. In P. B. Baltes & O. G. Brim, Jr. (Eds.), *Life-span development and behavior* (Vol. 2). New York: Academic Press, 1979. (a)

Baltes, P. B. On the potential and limits of child development: Life-span developmental perspectives. *Newletter of the Society for Research in Child Development*, 1979 (Summer), 1–4. (b)

Baltes, P. B., Baltes, M. M., & Reinert, G. The relationship between time of measurement and age in cognitive development of children: An application of cross-sectional sequences. *Human Development*, 1970, *13*, 258–268.

Baltes, P. B., & Brim, O. G., Jr. (Eds.). *Life-span development and behavior* (Vol. 2). New York: Academic Press, 1979.

Baltes, P. B., & Brim, O. G., Jr. (Eds.). *Life-span development and behavior* (Vol. 3). New York: Academic Press, 1980.

Baltes, P. B., Cornelius, S. W., & Nesselroade, J. R. Cohort effects in behavioral development: Theoretical and methodological perspectives. In W. A. Collins (Ed.), *Minnesota symposia on child psychology* (Vol. II). New York: Thomas Crowell, 1977.

Baltes, P. B., Reese, H. W., & Lipsitt, L. P. Life-span developmental psychology. *Annual Review of Psychology*, 1980, *31*, 65–110.

Baltes, P. B., & Schaie, K. W. (Eds.). *Life-span developmental psychology: Personality and socialization*. New York: Academic Press, 1973.

Baltes, P. B., & Schaie, K. W. The myth of the twilight years. *Psychology Today*, 1974, *7*, 35–40.

Beach, F. A. The Snark was a Boojum. *American Psychologist*, 1950, *5*, 15–124.

Blight, J. G. Toward the reconstruction of psychology and its historiography. *Journal of the History of the Behavioral Sciences*, 1981, *17*, 136–143.

Boring, E. G. *A history of experimental psychology* (2nd ed.). New York: Appleton–Century–Crofts, 1950.

Brent, S. B. Individual specialization, collective adaptation and rate of environment change. *Human Development*, 1978, *21*, 21–33.

Brim, O. G., Jr., & Kagan, J. Constancy and change: A view of the issues. In O. G. Brim, Jr. & J. Kagan (Eds.), *Constancy and change in human development*. Cambridge, Mass.: Harvard University Press, 1980.

Bronfenbrenner, U. Developmental theory in transition. In H. W. Stevenson (Ed.), *Child Psychology. Sixty-second Yearbook of the National Society for the Study of Education. Part I*. Chicago: University of Chicago Press, 1963.

Bronfenbrenner, U. Toward an experimental ecology of human development. *American Psychologist*, 1977, *32*, 513–531.

Bronfenbrenner, U. *The ecology of human development*. Cambridge, Mass.: Harvard University Press, 1979.

Bühler, C. *Der menschliche Lebenslauf als psychologisches Problem*. Leipzig: Hirzel, 1933.

Carus, F. A. *Psychologie Zweiter Theil: Specialpsychologie*. Leipzig: Barth & Kummer, 1808.

Costa, P. T., McCrae, R. R., & Arenberg, D. Enduring dispositions in adult males. *Journal of Personality and Social Psychology*, 1980, *38*, 793–800.

Datan, N., & Ginsberg, L. H. (Eds.). *Life-span developmental psychology: Normative life crises*. New York: Academic Press, 1975.

Datan, N., & Reese, H. W. (Eds.). *Life-span developmental psychology: Dialectical perspectives on experimental psychology*. New York: Academic Press, 1977.

Dixon, R. A. Human development: History of research. In T. Husen & T. N. Postlethwaite (Eds.), *International encyclopedia of education: Research and studies*. Oxford: Pergamon Press, in press.

Dollard, J., Doob, L. W., Miller, N. E., Mowrer, O. H., & Sears, R. R. *Frustration and aggression*. New Haven, Conn.: Yale University Press, 1939.

Elder, G. H. *Children of the great depression*. Chicago: University of Chicago Press, 1974.

Erikson, E. H. *Childhood and society*. New York: Norton, 1950.

Gengerelli, J. A. Graduate school reminiscence: Hull and Koffka. *American Psychologist*, 1976, *31*, 685–688.

Gesell, A. L. Maturation and infant behavior pattern. Psychological Review, 1929, *36*, 307–319.

Gesell, A. L. The individual in infancy. In C. Murchison (Ed.), *Handbook of child psychology*. Worcester, Mass.: Clark University Press, 1931.

Gesell, A. L. *An atlas of infant behavior*. New Haven, Conn.: Yale University Press, 1934.

Gesell, A. L. The ontogenesis of infant behavior. In L. Carmichael (Ed.), *Manual of child psychology*. New York: Wiley, 1946.

Gesell, A. L. The ontogenesis of infant behavior. In L. Carmichael (Ed.), *Manual of child psychology* (2nd ed.). New York: Wiley, 1954.

Gould, S. J. *Ontogeny and phylogeny*. Cambridge, Mass.: The Belknap Press of Harvard University Press, 1977.

Gould, S. J. *The mismeasure of man*. New York: Norton, 1981.

Goulet, L. R., & Baltes, P. B. (Eds.). *Life-span developmental psychology: Research and theory*. New York: Academic Press, 1970.

Hall, G. S. *Adolescence*. New York: Appleton, 1904.

Hall, G. S. *Senescence: The last half of life*. New York: Appleton, 1922.

Harris, D. B. Child psychology and the concept of development. Presidential address to the Division of Developmental Psychology, American Psychological Association, September 3, 1956. Reprinted in D. S. Palermo & L. P. Lipsitt (Eds.), *Research readings in child psychology*. New York: Holt, Rinehart, & Winston, 1963.

Harris, D. B. (Ed.). *The concept of development*. Minneapolis: University of Minnesota Press, 1957.

Havighurst, R. J. *Developmental tasks and education*. New York: David McKay, 1948.

Havighurst, R. J. *Human development and education*. New York: David McKay, 1953.

Havighurst, R. J. Research on developmental task concept. *School Review*, 1956, *64*, 215–223.

Havighurst, R. J. History of developmental psychology: Socialization and personality development through the life-span. In P. B. Baltes & K. W. Schaie (Eds.), *Life-span developmental psychology: Personality and socialization*. New York: Academic Press, 1973.

Herrnstein, R. J. The evolution of behaviorism. *American Psychologist*, 1977, *32*, 593–603.

Hollingworth, H. L. *Mental growth and decline: A survey of developmental psychology*. New York: Appleton, 1927.

Homans, G. C. *Social behavior: Its elementary forms*. New York: Harcourt, Brace, & World, 1961.

Hull, C. L. A functional interpretation of the conditioned reflex. *Psychological Review*, 1929, *36*, 498–511.

Hultsch, D. F., & Hickey, T. External validity in the study of human development: Theoretical and methodological issues. *Human Development*, 1978, *21*, 76–91.

Kagan, J. Perspectives on continuity. In O. G. Brim, Jr. & J. Kagan (Eds.), *Constancy and change in human development*. Cambridge, Mass.: Harvard University Press, 1980.

Kuhn, D. Mechanisms of cognitive and social development: One psychology or two? *Human Development*, 1978, *21*, 92–118.

Kuhn, T. S. *The structure of scientific revolutions*. (2nd ed.). Chicago: University of Chicago Press, 1970.

Lerner, R. M. *On the nature of human plasticity*. Manuscript in preparation.

Lerner, R. M., & Busch–Rossnagel, N. A. Individuals as producers of their development: Conceptual and empirical bases. In R. M. Lerner & N. A. Busch–Rossnagel (Eds.), *Individuals as producers of their development: A life-span perspective*. New York: Academic Press, 1981.

Lerner, R. M., & Hultsch, D. F. *Human development: A life-span perspective*. New York: McGraw–Hill, in press.

Lerner, R. M., & Ryff, C. D. Implementation of the life-span view of human development: The sample case of attachment. In P. B. Baltes (Ed.), *Life-span development and behavior* (Vol. 1). New York: Academic Press, 1978.

Lerner, R. M., Skinner, E. A., & Sorell, G. T. Methodological implications of contextual/dialectic theories of development. *Human Development*, 1980, *23*, 225–235.

Lerner, R. M., & Spanier, G. B. *Adolescent development: A life-span perspective*. New York: McGraw–Hill, 1980.

Lipsitt, L. P. Personal communication, December, 1979.

Lipsitt, L. P. (Chair). *Symposium on Enduring and reversible effects of early experience*. Annual Meeting of the American Association for the Advancement of Science, Washington, D.C., January 4, 1982.

Looft, W. R. The evolution of developmental psychology: A comparison of handbooks. *Human Development*, 1972, *15*, 187–201.

Looft, W. R. Socialization and personality throughout the life-span: An examination of contemporary psychological approaches. In P. B. Baltes & K. W. Schaie (Eds.), *Life-span developmental psychology: Personality and socialization*. New York: Academic Press, 1973.

McCandless, B. R., & Spiker, C. C. Experimental research in child psychology. *Child Development*, 1956, *27*, 78–80.

Meacham, J. A. A transactional model of remembering. In N. Datan & H. W. Reese (Eds.), *Life-span developmental psychology: Dialectical perspectives on experimental research*. New York: Academic Press, 1977.

Meacham, J. A. Research on remembering: Interrogation or conversation, monologue or dialogue. In D. F. Hultsch (Chair), *Implications of a dialectical perspective for research methodology*. Symposium presented at the meeting of the American Psychological Association, Toronto, August, 1978.

Meacham, J. A. Political values, conceptual models, and research. In R. M. Lerner & N. A. Busch–Rossnagel (Eds.), *Individuals as producers of their development: A life-span perspective*. New York: Academic Press, 1981.

Miller, N. E., & Dollard, J. *Social learning and imitation*. New Haven, Conn.: Yale University Press, 1941.

Mischel, W. On the future of personality measurement. *American Psychologist*, 1977, *32*, 246–254.

Misiak, H., & Sexton, V. S. *History of psychology: An overview*. New York: Grune & Stratton, 1966.

Mussen, P. H. (Ed.). *Carmichael's manual of child psychology* (3rd ed.). New York: Wiley, 1970.

Nesselroade, J. R., & Baltes, P. B. Adolescent personality development and historical change: 1970–1972. *Monographs of the Society for Research in Child Development*, 1974, *39* (1, Serial No. 154).

Nesselroade, J. R., & Reese, H. W. (Eds.). *Life-span developmental psychology: Methodological issues*. New York: Academic Press, 1973.

Neugarten, B. L. *Personality in middle and late life.* New York: Atherton Press, 1964.

Neugarten, B. L. Adult personality: A developmental view. Human Development, 1966, *9*, 61–73.

Neugarten, B. L. Continuities and discontinuities of psychological issues into adult life. *Human Development,* 1969, *12*, 121–130.

Neugarten, B. L., & Guttman, D. L. Age–sex roles and personality in middle age: A thematic apperception study. *Psychological Monographs,* 1958, *72* (No. 470).

Overton, W. F. On the assumptive base of the nature–nurture controversy: Additive versus interactive conceptions. *Human Development,* 1973, *16,* 74–89.

Overton, W. F. Klaus Riegel: Theoretical contribution to concepts of stability and change. *Human Development,* 1978, *21,* 360–363.

Overton, W. F., & Newman, J. *Life-span cognitive intervention research: A competence-performance model.* Paper presented at the sixth biennial meeting of the International Society for the Study of Behavioral Development, Toronto, August, 1981.

Overton, W. F., & Reese, H. W. Models of development: Methodological implications. In J. R. Nesselroade & H. W. Reese (Eds.), *Life-span developmental psychology: Methodological issues.* New York: Academic Press, 1973.

Pepper, S. C. *World hypotheses: A study in evidence.* Berkeley: University of California Press, 1942.

Piaget, J. La pensée symbolique et la pensée l'enfant. *Archives of Psychology,* Genève, 1923, *18,* 273–304.

Piaget, J. Piaget's theory. In P. H. Mussen (Ed.), *Carmichael's manual of child psychology* (3rd ed.). New York: Wiley, 1970.

Pressey, S. L., Janney, J. E., & Kuhlen, R. G. *Life: A psychological survey.* New York: Harper, 1939.

Quetelet, A. *Sur l'homme et le developpement de ses facultes.* Paris: Bachelier, 1835.

Reese, H. W., & Overton, W. F. Models of development and theories of development. In L. R. Goulet & P. B. Baltes (Eds.), *Life-span developmental psychology: Research and theory.* New York: Academic Press, 1970.

Riegel, K. R. Developmental psychology and society: Some historical and ethical considerations. In J. R. Nesselroade & H. W. Reese (Eds.), *Life-span developmental psychology: Methodological issues.* New York: Academic Press, 1973.

Riegel, K. F. Toward a dialectical theory of development. *Human Development,* 1975, *18,* 50–64.

Riegel, K. F. The dialectics of human development. *American Psychologist,* 1976, *31,* 689–700. (a)

Riegel, K. F. From traits and equilibrium toward developmental dialectics. In W. Arnold (Ed.), *Nebraska symposium on motivation.* Lincoln: University of Nebraska Press, 1976. (b)

Riegel, K. F., & Rosenwald, G. C. (Eds.). *Structure and transformation: Developmental and historical aspects.* New York: Wiley, 1975.

Roback, A. A. *History of American psychology.* New York: Library Publishers, 1952.

Robinson, D. N. *An intellectual history of psychology.* New York: Macmillan, 1976.

Sameroff, A. Transactional models in early social relations. *Human Development,* 1975, *18,* 65–79.

Sanford, E. C. Mental growth and decay. *American Journal of Psychology,* 1902, *13,* 426–449.

Sarbin, T. B. Contextualism: A world view of modern psychology. In J. K. Cole (Ed.), *Nebraska symposium on motivation, 1976.* Lincoln: University of Nebraska Press, 1977.

Schaie, K. W., Labouvie, G. V., & Buech, B. V. Generational and cohort-specific differences in adult cognitive functioning: A fourteen-year study of independent samples. *Developmental Psychology,* 1973, *9,* 151–166.

Schneirla, T. C. The concept of development in comparative psychology. In D. B. Harris (Ed.), *The concept of development.* Minneapolis: University of Minnesota Press, 1957.

Sears, R. R. Your ancients revisited: A history of child development. In E. M. Hetherington (Ed.), *Review of child development research* (Vol. 5). Chicago: The University of Chicago Press, 1975.

Skinner, B. F. *The behavior of organisms.* New York: Appleton, 1938.

Smith, L. D. Psychology and philosophy: Toward a realignment, 1905–1935. *Journal of the History of the Behavioral Sciences,* 1981, *17,* 28–37.

Spiker, C. C., & McCandless, B. R. The concept of intelligence and the philosophy of science. *Psychological Review,* 1954, *61,* 255–266.

Terman, L. M. (Ed.). *Genetic studies of genius, I: Mental and physical traits of a thousand gifted children.* Stanford, Calif.: Stanford University Press, 1925.

Terman, L. M., & Oden, M. H. *Genetic studies of genius, V: The gifted group at mid-life.* Stanford, Calif.: Stanford University Press, 1959.

Tetens, J. N. *Philosophische Versuche über die menschliche Natur und ihre Entwichlung.* Leipzig: Weidmanns Erben & Reich, 1777.

Thorndike, E. L. The newest psychology. *Educational Review,* 1904, *28,* 217–227.

von Bertalanffy, L. *Modern theories of development.* London: Oxford University Press, 1933.

Watson, J. B. Psychology as the behaviorist views it. *Psychological Review,* 1913, *20,* 158–177.

Watson, J. B. *Psychology from the standpoint of a behaviorist.* Philadelphia: Lippincott, 1918.

Watson, J. B. *Psychological care of infant and child.* New York: Norton, 1928.

Watson, J. B., & Raynor, R. Conditional emotional reactions. *Journal of Experimental Psychology,* 1920, *3,* 1–14.

Watson, R. I. Psychology: A prescriptive science. In J. Brozek & R. B. Evans (Eds.), *R. I. Watson's selected papers on the history of psychology.* Hanover, N. H.: University of New Hampshire Press, 1977.

Weimer, W. *Notes on the methodology of scientific research.* Hillsdale, N.J.: Lawrence Erlbaum Assoc., 1979.

Werner, H. *Comparative psychology of mental development.* New York: International Universities Press, 1948.

White, S. H. The learning-maturation controversy: Hall to Hull. *Merrill–Palmer Quarterly,* 1968, *14,* 187–196.

White, S. H. The learning theory tradition and child psychology. In P. H. Mussen (Ed.), *Carmichael's manual of child psychology* (3rd ed.). New York: Wiley, 1970.

Whitehurst, G. J. Language development. In B. Wolman (Ed.), *Handbook of developmental psychology.* Englewood Cliffs, N.J.: Prentice-Hall, 1982.

PERSPECTIVES ON HISTORY AND PHILOSOPHY

2

Developmental Categories and the Premise of Connectivity

Jerome Kagan
Harvard University

INTRODUCTION

Descriptions of phenomena, the bedrock of empirical science, function either as incentives for inferential propositions or affirmations of deductive ones. Although scholars have always acknowledged the potential distortion that human perception and presupposition can impose on real events, during the 19th century both historians and scientists became more seriously skeptical over their ability to know the world in its natural state (Hughes, 1958). The initial reaction to this crisis of certainty was an argument for a qualitative difference between the natural sciences and disciplines that studied history and human nature. This initial, but less than adequate, defense was followed several decades later by three quite different intellectual reactions—a harder line toward meaningful propositions, a flight from objectivity to the celebration of intuition, and pragmatism.

Even though contemporary physicists and chemists recognize the arbitrariness of the division between the observing agent and the observed (D'Espagnat, 1979), they manage to contain the distortion through the use of machines and elegant deductive sequences that stipulate the relation between the signs generated by apparatus and the phenomena of interest. But the sciences that study human nature are generally without such advantage. Observer error looms large for anthropology, sociology, and psychology and affects both the language of description as well as the constructs of explanation. Developmental psychology is especially vulnerable because such a large proportion of empirical work involves observations of children in natural contexts. But even in laboratories, descriptions of play with objects, interactions with peers and adults, the solving of problems and changes in posture and facial expression—all of which are central to modern theory—permit the observer's suppositions to exaggerate some of what happened, ignore most of what happened, and occasionally invent phenomena that never happened.

A central problem for disciplines like developmental psychology that seek to describe and explain change is parsing the flux of objective events into theoretically useful categories and selecting the best constructs to describe and interpret change during particular temporal epochs. The history of biology provides many examples of the importance of the initial descriptive phase in an investigation. When 17th-century scholars assumed that the world of living things formed a closely connected linear chain of organisms from algae to chimpanzees, which had not been altered since the creation, animals were classified by their physical resemblance to man. Modern biologists characterize evolution as branching, dynamic, and occasionally discontinuous and are as likely to use similarities in biochemistry as morphology in grouping organic varieties. The change in presupposition from static to evolving had a profound effect on classification.

The influence of traditional assumptions on codification of the events of psychological development is more obvious and, occasionally, more resistant to change because almost every citizen has some a priori conception of human nature. If, as many hold, children are born with little or no predispositions but learn ideas and skills as a result of interactions with objects and people, it is reasonable to invent names for classes of interaction and their occasions and consequences. And for half a century, child psychologists have been preoccupied with the form of feeding, soothing, and play between adults and infants during the first years of life, but relatively indifferent to sleep patterns, laughter, and the balance between quiescence and action. I do not criticize those decisions, for some selection is necessary before data are gathered. It is neither possible nor wise to begin observation with no prior ideas. But how do we know what dimension to select? If our subject is a 4-month-old infant, do we describe the individual movements of fingers, or of arms? Do we quantify direction and velocity of movement or its outcome and incentive? The bases for these decisions usually originate in theory, even if it is folk theory. Investigators committed to Piagetian ideas create constructs for goal-directed actions with objects. Those who are loyal to psychoanalytic theory name drive states like hunger and pain and the behaviors that involve the satisfaction of those drives, usually at the hands of caretaking adults. The behaviorist notes responses with immediate consequences in the environment. The investigator who is convinced that the infant's temperament is a dimension of significance, quantifies crying, alertness, and inhibition to the unfamiliar.

The Selection of Events

There are at least three different factors that influence the phenomena classifiers choose to describe (I am not concerned here with the specific words chosen, but with the aspect of the complex selected for naming).

The first influence is a tacit hypothesis as to the immediate antecedents or consequences of an observed event, suppositions that are easily projected on to an event. Rarely do observers perceive and name the event as it happens in the present moment. A child who has spilled some glue on a table "runs to his mother and kisses her." The act of kissing the parent is an event that, only with difficulty, can be viewed as an isolated touching of lip to cheek. It takes effort for the observer to resist assigning to the child internal states that followed the spilling of the glue or the change in state after the act of kissing. Both intrusions color the perception of the event. Film can capture a splash of water frozen in space and time; such perceptions are difficult for human beings. Most classifications imply an inference as to origin or future state. If the classifier believes in the primacy of a certain cause for a behavior, he or she tends to focus on those phenomena that affirm that belief. For example, Tiedemann (1897) believed that maximizing pleasure was the primary incentive for action in the infant. Thus, when he looked at his newborn son he noted first that the boy turned to the light and added that the sensations that resulted from this action were pleasurable (actually he used the word agreeable). Millicent Shinn (1907) also shared that perspective; her first description of the infant she summarized in her full diary was: "The child that I observed seemed for the first hour to feel a mild light agreeably [p. 21]." By contrast, Darwin's first diary descriptions dealt with his child's reflexes (yawning, stretching, and sucking), because Darwin believed the major causes of behavior resided in phylogenetic adaptation.

Contemporary observers of infants are becoming persuaded that structural aspects of the central nervous system set necessary conditions for behavior; hence, they describe responses they assume reflect developmental states of the brain. Some quantify the infant's attention to stimuli varying in contour, curvilinearity, hue, and symmetry and conclude that the central nervous system is prepared to organize the environment in a structured way (Bornstein, 1979). Those who believe in a relation between present and future behavior describe preferentially those responses they believe have consequences in the future—dispositions or competences that are preserved, albeit through transformation.

Suppositions about historical antecedents also affect descriptions of the present. Most scholars since the Enlightenment have wanted to believe in a connection between infancy and later developmental periods. Nineteenth-century observers sought to detect a relation between signs of will in the infant and older child. The modern preoccupation with perception, memory, and reasoning in adults makes it natural for child psychologists to search for early signs of these functions in infants and to apply to their data the same labels that are applied to different phenomena in the adult. Bornstein (1979), for example, offers as evidence for prototypicality in infants the fact that they look longer at vertical symmetrical than at asymmetrical patterns. However, the typical basis for the classification of prototypicality in the adult comes from data on linguistic classification of objects (Rosch, 1977).

Many 19th-century scholars regarded the helplessness of the child as beneficial because it made the young child receptive to training and made adults cooperative in their nurture of the child; "the helplessness of the child was necessary to bring about the helpfulness of mankind" (Chamberlain, 1907), [p. 441]." But 20th-century observers who were influenced by Freudian theory regarded the helplessness of infants as detrimental, because it made them too dependent upon the parents. A physician at London's Tavistock Clinic (Miller, 1922) warned that: "The greatest of all the sins of parenthood is to stand between the child and self-realization—to obstruct his psychological freedom [p. 19]."

The consciously articulated hypothesis of the observer forms a second influence on classification. Bernfeld (1929) wanted to prove sensory processes were pleasant and described the smiling and cooing of the baby while it looked at an interesting sight. Sroufe (1979) wants to show that securely attached infants become more exploratory than the less-securely attached and so codes the older child's constructive play with toys. Izard (1977), who believes that the muscles of the face reveal the primary affect states, classifies the changing form of the infants' eyes, brows, and mouth to the brief pain of an injection, whereas other investigators focus on limb movement and vocalization (Haith, 1980; Kagan, 1971). It is unlikely that any articulated hypothesis will violate a presupposition as to the cause of an event. Most observers believe that 1-year olds do not have any representation of right or wrong; hence they would not present an infant with visual stimuli representative of social and asocial actions in order to see if the infant's reactions were different to the two classes of events. But this experiment could have been performed by a 19th-century psychologist.

The third influence on classification, often unconscious, is a categorical bias. It is the disposition to classify an event as similar to or different from some other referent. Tiedemann (1897) wanted to maximize the differences between humans and animals and described actions that would exaggerate the differences between those two species. Darwin, on the other hand, wanted to minimize those differences and described the infant reflexes that were most similar to those displayed by animals. This categorical bias reveals itself in three different perspectives in classification.

Three Perspectives in Classification.   One basis for the disparity in classifications of the human infant is the fact that classifiers assume different referents when using descriptors that are comparative, and often evaluative, in meaning. Rarely does the classifier specify the referent and, as a result, the descriptors can be ambiguous. One of three possible referents is available and each provides a different perspective.

From the perspective of individual differences the referent is children of the same age. Descriptions like irritable, easy to placate, and attached are usually intended to differentiate among infants, not between infants and older children or between infants and animals. The second perspective is developmental; the implied referent is children of a different age or adults. Descriptive terms like undifferentiated, helpless, dependent, and asymbolic are usually intended to compare infants with older members of the species. The third perspective is comparative. Its implied referent is animals other than Homo sapiens—terms like linguistic, social, symbolic, and moral are intended to differentiate children from animals—or in the 19th and early 20th centuries—a referent that is absent today; a comparison of infant with savage.

"That the child in many respects resembles the savage is an idea familiar even to some of the writers of antiquity, who saw that the childhood of the race and the childhood of the individual had not a few things in common." (Chamberlain, 1907, [p. 291])."

Nineteenth-century writers, many of whom were under the influence of Darwinian theory, typically used terms that assumed animals to be the counterclass (Fiske, 1909); hence, two very popular descriptions were *volitional* and *possessing consciousness*. Twentieth-century writers were more likely to assume an individual-difference perspective. But note how ambiguous the statement, "Infants have no sense of self" can be if the referent is not given. That sentence has one meaning if other mammals are the referent, but quite another if 3-year olds are.

The Classification of Motives

The classification of human motives provides a particularly nice example of how the referent chosen and the scholar's purpose influence the motivational term selected. Because there are literally thousands of specific goals a person can generate, it is necessary to decide how the representations of goals states should be classified. (We take an axiomatic that a large number of similar events are capable of satisfying a particular motive—the hungry child will accept many different edible foods.) The answer to this question depends on the purpose of the classifier. The correlates of a motive include the cognitive representation of a goal, prior incentive, accompanying feeling state, and relevant instrumental behavior. Motives can be classified on the basis of similarities in one or more of these properties.

A pragmatic strategy that categorizes motives by similarity in behavioral consequence is popular in American psychology. All acts that hurt another are said to be produced by a motive of hostility; responses that result in closer social relationships are said to be caused by a motive for affiliation, even though these behavioral events often have different incentives, ideas, and affective profiles. A second basis for classification of motives uses the content of the cognitively represented goal state rather than behavioral consequences. This strategy is preferred by theorists who wish to classify people of similar age cohorts into different abstract types and use fantasy or verbal report as the index of a motivational hierarchy. Thus, ideational concern with assuming power over a peer, affiliation with the opposite sex, or acceptance by authority are named in accord with those mental representations, even though each of the preceding motives might result in the same behavior (working conscientiously at one's job), or different behaviors (those who wish to dominate others may seek nurturant roles with younger people or politics). There is no necessary relation between classifications based on the cognitive representations of goals and those based on behaviors.

A third basis for classifying motives focuses on similarity in the intensity or quality of feeling that accompanies the ideation. Cognitive representations of hostile intentions are grouped with cognitive representations of sexuality when both are associated with intense excitement, even though the ideas and actions differ. An observer who names a person as involved or apathetic implies concern with a great number of varied goals. There must be some inherent attractiveness to this strategy for Freud's concept of libido, Pavlov's notion of an excitatory nervous system, Hull's concept of drive, Spence's concept of general anxiety, and the neuroscientists' postulation of arousal all make the presence of some primary feeling state the basis for behavioral attempts to gain goals.

The least popular strategy classifies motives in accord with similarities in incentive events. Some theorists, Bowlby is an example, suggest that children who have been rejected by their parents should be classified as similar in a motivational disposition because they are insecurely attached, even though this motive can lead to hostility toward adults, excessive desire for reassurance, or mastery of a skill that gains acceptance or power.

The differential utility of these four ways to classify motives depends on the scholar's purpose. If the purpose is to predict the likelihood of a motivational idea capturing consciousness, selection of intensity and quality of feeling is probably the most relevant criterion, for motives associated with salient feeling states are likely to dominate awareness. But if the purpose is to explain the cause of a change in goal-related behavior, a theorist would be likely to classify by similarities in incentive events. If the purpose is to classify motives in accord with their likelihood of facilitating adjustment to society, similarity in behavioral outcome is the preferred criterion. Motives for autonomy, harmonious social relations, and mastery might be grouped together because all are apt to produce behaviors that maximize adjustment. Finally, if the purpose is to explain diverse and alternative ways to gratify a wish, especially when the investigator assumes stability of a motive hierarchy over time, classification by the content of the mental representation of the goal sought is likely to be the strategy of choice. Hostility often leads to disobedience to parents in 6-year olds; to school failure in adolescents.

The Nesting of Motives.   A motive term is a category and, therefore, like most categories is part of a nested set of concepts. Each classification intended to name a unitary event exists in a hierarchy based on the number of events permitted into the classification. This continuum can be viewed as an uncertainty dimension; the more events in the class, the more uncertain one is about the specific object that provoked the classification. To name a particular dog *Jojo* permits no other objects in that category. To name the same event *dog, pet, mammal,* or *living thing* permits an increasing number of objects into the classification. Thus, one primary dimension inherent in any classification is its specificity, by which we mean how many objects are permitted into the category. This dimension of specificity is very similar to Rosch's vertical dimension of inclusiveness (Rosch, 1977).

Thus a motive for a concrete goal—a friendship with a particular person, for example—is part of a more inclusive category, say, reassurance of one's acceptability. But that motive may belong to an even more inclusive class we might call the desire to regard self as good. A 10-year-old girl who leaves her friends in order to go home might do so because of a motive: (1) to complete her algebra assignment; (2) to be ranked high in her class; (3) to please her parents; or (4) to meet a private standard of virtue or self-worth.

If observers wish to explain a particular action at a particular time, they usually select the least inclusive criterion. If, however, the purpose is to explain a diverse group of actions over a longer period, a more inclusive motive, like hostility, recognition, or status, is chosen. Traditionally, American psychologists have chosen intermediate levels of classification because they wanted to discriminate among persons of the same age cohort with respect to persistent behaviors over a prolonged period of time. They were not interested in differentiating among categories of behavioral change within one person or among classes of living things (i.e., the motives of infrahuman animals and people). Hence motive names like affiliation, achievement, and power have been popular.

Although the psychologist's typical purpose is to differentiate one class of persons from another, when adults talk in a nonscientific frame about a person they know very well, they usually use motive terms at a less-inclusive level because they implicitly compare the person with him or herself. They wish to differentiate the person's behavior today from behavior on a previous occasion. A parent says of her whining child, "He is upset because he wants to go to the movies," or "She wants a new bicycle." But the same parent is likely to describe the same behavior in an unfamiliar child with a more inclusive motive term (e.g., "She is a controlling or demanding child"), for the purpose is to differentiate the less-familiar child from other children.

The Relation Between Procedure and Classification

The meaning of a scientific classification depends not only on its theoretical presuppositions but also on its procedural origin. When an observer says, "This flower is red," we assume she/he is looking at the flower, not touching or smelling it; when an observer says a person's heart rate is 135 beats per minute, we assume she/he is looking at the record of a cardiotachometer, not the color of the person's face. The relation between the procedures used to generate observations and the descriptors or constructs applied to the observations is better appreciated by investigators in the natural sciences than by those in the social sciences. When chemists report the acidity or temperature of a solution their colleagues know, and usually approve of, the methods used and have articulated the relation between the method and the descriptive statement. For controversial classifications like *particle,* the physicist is careful to tell his/her colleagues whether his/her observations came from a Wilson cloud chamber or a linear accelerator, for the meaning of particle is not identical in those two procedures.

Social scientists are more indifferent to method and too often treat statements about a person's self-concept, motivation to achieve, or anxiety over agression as equivalent, even though some descriptions are based on answers to interviews, some on stories to pictures, and some on autonomic reactions to electric shock. The investigator who uses a group administered, paper–pencil questionnaire to evaluate a child's self-concept may conclude that poor black children have a positive self-concept. The second scientist interviews the same children in their homes over a period of 8 weeks and concludes that these children have fragile self-concepts. When observers say that a 1-year old is attached to the mother it is not always clear what method was used—reunion behavior in the Ainsworth Strange Situation, crying upon separation from the mother in the home, clinging to the mother in a waiting room, or smiling and vocalizing when the caretaker picks the child up. Because each source of information lends a different meaning to the statement "This child is attached," each is, in fact, a classification-cum-method unit. This is why many have made a plea for multiple assessments of the same quality (Brunswik, 1956; Campbell & Fiske, 1959).

There is much empirical support for the notion that the meaning of constructs used to summarize data is tied to procedure. Weiskrantz (1977) has shown that the truth value of statements describing the cross-modality matching ability of monkeys (haptic to visual) depends on the procedures used. The monkeys fail on some procedures but succeed on others. Similarly, infants' disposition to look longer at a novel than a familiar stimulus depends on the specific method of presentation (Ruff, 1981), as does the 4-year old's tendency to sort objects by their taxonomic status (Markman, Cox, & Machida, 1981). Propositions about the perceptual salience of particular stimulus dimensions, like the size or distance of an object, must add a statement describing the subject's prior familiarity with the object, a point I made over 15 years ago (Kagan, 1967). Groups of 6-month-old children were habituated on one of two three-dimensional representations of the human head (large or small) at one of two distances. All groups were dishabituated to the same head, which differed in size, distance, or both dimensions from the habituated standard. The greatest increase in attention occurred among the children who were exposed to a head that changed in size, not distance from the child. But when the same procedure was implemented with cubes rather than heads, the increase in attention to the transformed stimulus was much smaller in magnitude, and the largest gain in attention was displayed by those children exposed to the stimuli presented at an altered distance, not one of different size. It is not possible to make universal statements about the salience of size, distance, color, or shape; the salience of any dimension is specific to a procedure (McKenzie, Tootell, & Day, 1980).

This problem is of particular relevance to developmental psychology because it is in transition from a tradition characterized by almost total dependence on observations of molar behavior in natural contexts to the use of experimental and interview procedures that generate data not readily observable without some intervention. Although 19th-century classifications of intelligent or moral were based on evidence that differed from those employed today, psychologists continue to use the same terms. When Preyer said his son was emotionally labile, his readers knew that the classification was based on watching his son's behavior at home. When a modern observer makes the same statement, we must be told if the source is the mother's report, heart rate variability, changes in GSR, EMG, EEG, or a microanalysis of film recordings of the child's facial expressions. The meaning of the statement, "The child is emotionally labile," varies with the method used.

Recognition of the many potential influences on observation predicates has led psychologists to be skeptical of the program of the logical positivists. Shea (1974) has stated: "The meaning of all scientific terms, whether factual or theoretical, is governed by the paradigm or general intellectual stance which underlies them and in which they are imbedded [p. 178]."

Because the meaning of an observation statement is dependent on presuppositions, it is best to make those presuppositions explicit. When an observer studying the facial expressions of a child says, "She is experiencing fear," we must appreciate that the statement, parading as an observational predicate, assumes a relation between the arrangement of facial muscles and a feeling experience. A visitor from outer space, unfamiliar with the idea of gravity, watching a tree in late October, is as likely to think, "The tree dropped a leaf," as "The leaf fell." Developmental psychologists bring a variety of suppositions to their observations, including the assumption of a general intellectual ability, stages of cognitive and moral development, a purpose for each action, the law of effect, self-consciousness, and a connectivity between past and present structures and dispositions.

Connectivity

The remainder of this chapter explores one of the presuppositions that monitors classification—the assumption of connectivity. I select this idea in preference to the others because it has been fundamental to Western science and continues to be one of the most important rationales for the study of children (Brim & Kagan, 1980). The presence of an origin myth and its connection to the present is one of the major dimensions of difference between the philosophies of the ancient near

Eastern cultures of Egypt, Mesopotamia, and Greece, on the one hand, and ancient China, on the other. The former societies were concerned with the beginnings of the world and humanity; whereas, the Chinese regarded the world as uncreated. According to Mote (1971), the world of life constituted the: "central functions of a spontaneously self-generating cosmos having no creator, god, ultimate cause or will external to itself [p. 18]."

The Greeks, who made reason and inquiry the greatest good, assumed that the observable world was derived from and connected to a small number of basic material elements. For Thales it was water. For Anaximenes air was the fundamental entity from which substances were derived by a transformation. Fire resulted from the dilation of air into a rarer form. Wind represented condensation. If that condensation proceeded further, stone was created. Parmenides insisted that reality was the unchanging and visible unity beneath sensory experience. If an entity exists, then it must be indestructible, eternal, and unchangeable. Democritus put Parmenides' ideas into a more material form with two related assumptions that can be detected in the thought of future centuries. "Nothing can come into being from that which is not nor pass away from that which is not . . . atoms are impassive and unalterable." The mind was a material entity constituted of atoms. The difference between the perception of an event (the *nomos*) and the essence of the event (the *physis*) is due to differences in the two motions of the atoms that constitute the mind. But both Thales' water and Democritus' atoms, though dynamic entities, were indestructible. Both Thales' proclamation that water is the first cause and the modern developmental assumption that the first interactions between mother and infant lay a foundation for the child's future essence assume a material link between the deep past and this moment. How different this Western view is from the Buddhist insistence on the "impermanence of things in the world" and the illusion of any material connection between then and now.

The supposition of connectivity imposes a nontrivial bias on what is observed and described. If an observer believes that a hidden structure is preserved over two points in time, he or she is biased to look for actions on the later occasion that might be classified (usually on the basis of physical resemblance) with those manifested earlier. Piaget, for example, groups the newborn's grasping of a finger placed in its palm with the 18-month old's imitative opening and closing of the hand, implying that some residue of the former displayed on the first day is participating in the later act. Piaget's insistence on the indefinite preservation of remnants of old structures, which appears in his mature writings on the child, can be traced to his first scientific papers on the classification of mollusks written before he was 20 years old (Vidal, 1981). The young Piaget defended the Lamarckian hypothesis that morphological changes could be induced by the organism's continued commerce with the environment and disagreed sharply with the naturalists who defended sudden mutation as the primary basis for evolutionary change (the genus in question was *Limnaea*). These morphological changes, according to Piaget, occurred slowly over time and eventually became hereditary; therefore, preserved indefinitely. For example, Piaget suggested that brackish ponds are gradually converted into fresh-water lakes (in Vidal, 1981) so that: "its fauna evolves slowly . . . . and gives rise to species absolutely authentic and hereditary [p. 32]." "Duration alone will have a real effect. Moreover, it is not the factors which must be new but the ensemble of those factors and their relationship, their synthesis [p. 54]."

These statements, written in 1914 about *Limnaea,* are key premises in his later writings on the origins of intelligence in children.

Piaget (1951) wrote: "Thus, when we studied the beginnings of intelligence we were forced to go as far back as the reflex in order to trace the cause of the assimilating activity which finally leads to the construction of adaptive schemas, for it is only by a principle of functional continuity that the indefinite variety of structures can be explained [p. 6]."

Following the spirit of Piagetian theory, Langer (1980) suggests that the origins of adult logic can be detected in the object manipulations of infants 6- to 12-months old. When a 6-month old raises an object to his or her face with the left hand while his or her right hand slides a second object to the right, Langer (1980) writes: "The most advanced binary mappings produced at this stage consist of two-step sequences of simultaneous but different transformations [p. 29]." A child who bangs a block three times on a table is displaying a: "three unit equivalence which is an instance of two distinct proto-responding reproductions [p. 136]."

These assumptions of preservation of structure are intuitively appealing to those who believe in the connectivity premise. Recall that when Freud's writings were more popular many scholars accepted as reasonable the suggestion that the verbal aggression of a 22-year-old woman toward her professor rested on structures that began to be established following premature weaning from the breast at 9 months of age.

The presumption of connectivity is also evident in the predilection of Western physiologists and psychologists to try to alter the biologically based properties of systems through the creation of unnatural conditions during early infancy (Hubel & Wiesel, 1970). The discovery of cells in the visual cortex that respond to lines of different orientation suggests many different experiments that might be performed. The attempt to evaluate the effect of early occlusion of one or two eyes on the cells' future function is not the most obvious. It is only reasonable to a community of scholars who believe in connectivity and the power of original experience to constrain the future in a serious way.

Most 19th-century philosophers, historians, and natural scientists supported the connectivity premise, maintaining that in order to understand any phenomenon one had to have access to its entire history from origin to present—a position Mandlebaum (1971) has called the bias of historicism. The 19th-century historians who had rejected the mechanical view of man held by Enlightenment philosophers took biology as the most informative model and likened the history of society to the growth of plants and animals. This frame assumed that any phenomenon that was part of a fixed sequence was a complex function of all that happened earlier. Each new stage grew out of a prior one, contained some of the past, and moved inexorably toward a stage that was better than the one before. Reflect on E. B. Tylor's (1878) view of the history of civilizations: "It is indeed hardly too much to say that civilization being a process of long and complex growth can only be thoroughly understood with studied through its entire range; that the past is continually needed to explain the present and the whole to explain the part [p. 2]."

Although this view of the history of civilizations became far less popular among 20th-century historians, it remains regnant in developmental psychology. The faith in a connectivity between the deep past and the present has been an essential premise in theories of development since the beginning of formal study of the child in the decades following Darwin's great work. All theorists assumed a structural link between all phases of development and wrote in affirmation of Russell's bold assertion (in Hanson, 1961): "The chain of causation can be traced by the inquiring mind from any given point backward to the creation of the world [p. 50]." Many implied that no part of the child's past could ever be lost; every psychological property in the adult could, in theory, be traced to a distant origin,

If, then, from this law of habit there is no escape as long as we have bodies, if, by the time we are six years old, three-fourths of our actions are the result of habits formed; if, by the time we are grown up, 99 hundredths of our actions are so determined; if, in this way, our very life and destiny are dependent on the habits we form as we grow; then it follows that we cannot exaggerate the importance of the formation of right habits in childhood, neither can be exaggerate our own responsibility, as parents, in their formation (Mumford, 1925, [pp. 69–70]).

Richardson (1926) wrote:

But there seems to be no manner of doubt, among those whose studies have best qualified them to speak with authority, that the mind of any person, child or adult, is made up of the sum total of all of the experiences through which he has passed since birth, plus every impression that has ever touched him in passing, no matter how fleeting and transitory some of these may have seemed. That is to say, that every thought, feeling, experience, or image that has ever impinged upon one's consciousness becomes, once and for all, a component of a great, constantly growing, indestructable body, his mind—which is to say, his real self [pp. 33–34].

Bernfeld (1929) believed all of adult cognition had its origin in early infancy. "The powerful significance of the intellectual processes—perception, phantasy, thinking and their social results in science, art, and philosophy in the human being—have their first roots in this specifically human mental structure of the 3 months old child [p. 138]." "Historically all phenomena of adult mental life must be traceable to birth [p. 213]."

One author, faithful to the psychoanalytic assumption that overstimulation was dangerous, regarded the cinema as a particularly dangerous source of excessive stimulation. Parents who took their infants to the movies were exposing the child to a toxic experience analogous to the viruses that lie dormant for years and then, suddenly, strike.

> Nor should the young child be taken to public entertainments of any sort. It is not only the ignorant who take their babies to moving picture shows or other entertainments, they may be found at concerts and lectures which draw their audiences from the most cultured. The baby may show no signs of restlessness and be as good as you please, or may make up for lost sleep by an extra nap the next day, and yet be harmed thereby. No serious immediate symptoms of nervous overstimulation may appear, but some day the accounting must come—it may be 20 or even 40 years later before it is paid in full, but paid it will be, (Fenton, 1925, [pp. 293–294]).

Even authors uncommitted to a single theoretical view disseminated this catechism. Tracy and Stimpfl (1909) stated casually that the proprietary instinct grows out of the grasp reflex of the infant, and Rand, Sweeny, and Vincent, (1930) believed that the adult's sense of the aesthetic grew out of infant experiences: "General opinion agrees that aesthetic taste can be influenced even at such an early age. It is probably not desirable, then, to give him ugly toys which he may come to love because of the associations with them [p 260]." John Watson (1928) was unambiguous: "At three years of age the child's whole emotional life plan has been laid down, his emotional disposition set [p. 45]."

In one of the most popular psychology texts of the first decade of this century, Edward L. Thorndike (1905) ended his final chapter with a ringing affirmation of the permanence of early acquisitions:

> Though we seem to forget what we learn, each mental acquisition really leaves its mark and makes future judgments more sagacious . . . . nothing of good or evil is ever lost; we may forget and forgive, but the neurones never forget or forgive . . . It is certain that every worthy deed represents a modification of the neurones of which nothing can ever rob us. Every event of a man's mental life is written indelibly in the brain's archives, to be counted for or against him [pp. 330–331].

And modern authors, like Hetherington and Parke (1979), write: "Variations in the early environment may exert profound effects on the individual's emotional and social development and possibly on intellectual development. The child's capacity for responding flexibly and adaptively to changing stimulus conditions, a necessity for proper development, may be impaired if his early experience is impoverished [p. 153]." Mussen, Conger, and Kagan (1969) sug-

gest a connection between toilet training during the second year and later confor-
mity: "excessive timidity and over-conformity may also stem from unduly severe toilet training [p. 264]. Toilet training is a learned situation . . . in which
the mother–child relationship may deteriorate, handicapping subsequent, healthy
emotional and social adjustment [p. 265]."

All the preceding statements contain the same premise evident in John
Locke's writing (in Mandelbaum, 1971) 200 years earlier:

> The little, or almost insensible, impressions on our tender infancies, have very
> important and lasting consequences: and there it is, as in the fountains of some
> rivers, where a gentle application of the hand turns the flexible waters into chan-
> nels, that make them quite contrary courses; and by this little direction, given them
> at first, in the source, they receive different tendencies, and arrive at last at very
> remote and distant places. I imagine the minds of children as easily turned, this or
> that way, as water itself [p. 151].

Connectivity is implied not only by statements asserting directly that the
dispositions shaped during the early years will be preserved but also, in indirect
form, by labeling a behavior in an infant with a name that was appropriate for the
adult. Kline and France (1907) projected the adult concern with property on to
the infant and saw this motive in the simplest behavior. A 4-month-old baby
cries: "Whenever a bottle is taken from her. Even if the bottle was empty she
would not let it leave her sight unless given another [p. 256]. We have found that
the desire to own is one of the strongest passions in child life; that selfishness is
the rule: that children steal, cheat or lie without scruple to acquire property; that
they have no idea of a proprietary right [p. 266]. These things are natural in the
child [p. 266]."

Arlitt (1928) calls the infant's tendency to stop crying when he or she is with a
familiar person a sign of *gregariousness*. The infant's tendency to cry when
another baby does so is indicative of the instinct to "do as others do" which
"makes for good adjustment in society." Bullying and tormenting are "traceable to the instinctive tendency to self-assertion [p. 110]." Arlitt posits six instincts in the infant, five of which are more applicable to older children and
adults than to infants. They are: self-assertion, to do as others do, to be uncomfortable at the sight of suffering, play, sex, and gregariousness. The reason why
this declaration does not strike Arlitt or her audience as odd is that both she and
her readers assume a strong connectivity in development. Adult behavior has its
origins in infancy. Therefore, if one sees a response that could be an origin of a
later disposition, both author and audience are receptive to assume that it is.

A third sign of the belief in connectivity is the awarding of primacy to the
affects that appear early in development. Because crying (indicative of fear),
motor discharge (indicative of rage), and babbling while being touched (indica-

tive of love) are seen during the first year, whereas signs of shame, guilt, and pride are not, Arlitt writes that the latter three cannot be basic emotions. For some writers, the doctrine of connectivity implied that the earlier a disposition appeared the more significant it was for development. Phenomena that occurred later in development were likely to be structural derivatives of the earlier processes.

What Entity is Preserved?

The statement that a psychological disposition is preserved can have at least two meanings. The most obvious, but least likely, is that the same reaction occurs to a specific incentive, context, or theoretically reasonable surrogate. The Moro reflex to vestibular stimulation is preserved from birth to about 4 months of age in the human infant but not after that time; clinging to the mother when a strange adult enters the room is preserved in some children from about the first to the fourth birthday. It is difficult, perhaps impossible, to find preservation of a particular response over very long periods of time because the response profile of the young child is so different from that of the adolescent. It is for this reason that preservation has a second, more popular meaning.

It is assumed that underlying structures and predispositions are preserved, even though the surface display changes. The preservation takes one of two quite different forms. The most popular refers to the preservation of individual differences in behavior; the second to the participation in later competences of structures that were part of an earlier stage for those characteristics that develop inevitably in all human beings. McCall (1981) suggests that "stability" be used to refer to the former phenomenon. But, in both phenomena, investigators search for a connection between theoretically related behaviors at two points in time and infer the stability of some inner predisposition that mediates the link of past to present.

Investigators search for a connection between theoretically related behaviors at two points in time and infer the stability of some inner predisposition or structure. Although the specific reactions required on "intelligence" scales at 3 and 10 years of age are dramatically different, some believe that the underlying quality of *intelligence* is stable over the 7-year interval, permitting correct answers on both occasions.

The problem with this strategy is that because developmental theory is weak it is easy to invent hypothetical structures that might be preserved to account for a correlation between two different behaviors at two different times in ontogeny. Sroufe (1979) suggests that the positive relation between a particular profile of behavior in the Ainsworth Strange Situation (child cries to maternal departure but greets the mother upon her return) and the 3-year old's tendency to show exploration and curiosity with toys reflects stability of a "secure attachment." Kagan

(1971) has suggested that the positive relation between a slow tempo of play with toys at 1 year and long response times and low errors on the Matching Familiar Figures Test at 10 years of age reflects a hidden disposition toward inhibition.

Although these hypotheses as to what is preserved might be correct, neither is intuitively obvious. Indeed, the positive relation between two behaviors at two points in time is likely to be the result of many intermediate changes between the original and final response. Evolutionary biologists tell us that the origin of the flamingo lies with the primitive aquatic vertebrate *Amphioxus*. Although both share some structural similarities, a great deal of change has occurred in the thousands of years that separated the appearance of these two forms. It seems more accurate to say that the original structure made the final structure a little more likely.

I acknowledge that some structures might be preserved. Fear of an abusive father created in a 10-year-old girl could be preserved and display itself in fear of men at 20 years of age. However, every correlation between two different behaviors at two different points in time is not obvious evidence for the preservation of a structure.

There is an important distinction between an outcome that is constrained by an initial structure and one that contains part of the original structure. The cells of the spinal cord of the newborn, in contrast to those of the surrounding, supporting muscles, were determined by the spatial position of its parent cells in the stage prior to gastrulation. But no unique structures in the blastula were preserved to participate in either spinal cord or muscle. We might regard this example from embryology as analogous to the fact that a middle-class 3-year old with an unusually large vocabulary is more likely to become a successful lawyer than a working-class 3-year-old child who is not yet speaking. But it is as reasonable to suggest that these different outcomes were due to the maintenance of certain conditions for three decades, as to argue for the preservation of different cognitive structures or processes from age 3 to adulthood.

The popular approach to inferring preservation of structures requires detecting within a sequence of many events those few that cohere as a causal chain. The stage theories of Freud and Piaget imply that selected competences or dispositions in the adolescent depend on and are consequences of earlier structures. But these two theories, like all essays on development, whether theoretical or empirical, are essentially histories. They are sets of sentences that attempt to tell a coherent story. In this sense theories of psychological development resemble both *The Origin of Species* and *The Rise and Fall of the Roman Empire*.

Developmental psychology, like history, consists of descriptions of events over a time period and, depending on the author's premises, propositions that attempt to relate the events—the presumed explanation. But the biases of the narrator pose a major problem in both disciplines. Between any two points in time lie many more events than can be seen or recorded. The scholar must select a very small number and ignore many others. Between 1900 and 1978 the automobile, the television, the nuclear weapon, the laser, and the contraceptive pill were invented; the Germans lost World War I, there was an economic depression, Germany was divided following the end of World War II, the Peoples' Republic of China was created, there was a long, bitter struggle in Vietnam, an American president resigned, and the price of oil and postage increased dramatically. Which of these events are part of a coherent sequence and which are not? Only theory can produce an answer to that question. The same problem confronts child psychologists. Between 1 and 15 months of age most infants will smile to a face, show anxiety toward a stranger, sit, stand, walk, and run, solve the object permanence problem, show symbolic play, and begin to speak single words. Which of these phenomena are connected and which not?

The developmental psychologist tries to detect which of these phenomena are structurally related and to invent reasons. The validity of the explanation rests, in part, on the accuracy with which the theorist selects from the stream of development the events considered to be connected. And that selection is guided by suppositions that are not always articulated, suppositions that also influence the historian's account of a sequence of events.

The most important factual bases for the popularity of the connectivity premise come from the preservation of some individual-difference dimensions from school entrance forward. Few studies fail to find stability of individual differences in IQ, academic grade, and related cognitive performances from age 6 through early adulthood, even though the magnitudes of the correlations decrease linearly with age (Kagan & Moss, 1962). Olweus (1981) also finds stability of individual differences in aggression across periods of 10 to 20 years but notes that there is decreasing interage correlations as the duration of the interval increases.

There is good reason for the robust nature of this generalization. The child's entrance into the concrete operational stage is accompanied by an ability to seriate self with others with respect to culturally valued qualities, like academic ability and sociability, and, as a consequence, children establish an expectation of success or failure that influences their motivation for change. Thus, few dispute the selective stability of qualities from school entrance forward, at least among American and European children. There is considerably more controversy over comparable stability of the variation noted as the phase of infancy ends, at about age 2. The cognitive profile of the infant seems to be more vulnerable to change, for investigators do not find persuasive preservation of individual differences in intellectual competences from age 2 forward when social class is controlled. When it is not controlled the apparent preservation, as we suggested earlier, is likely to be due to the continuous action of the environments associated with the earlier variation.

Most recently a group of investigators have found a relation between security of attachment (usually measured by behavior in the Ainsworth Strange Situation) at 12 and 18 months of age and theoretically reasonable outcomes 1 to 3 years later (Arend, Gove, & Sroufe, 1979; Egeland & Sroufe, 1981; Sroufe & Waters, 1977; Vaughn, Egeland, Sroufe, & Waters, 1979). These data suggest that perhaps the combination of temperamental qualities and experiential events that produce secure and less-secure attachments in 1-year olds might have a life that extends a few years, or perhaps longer. But even if these relations are replicated—and we hope they will be—few would insist that the dispositions that accompany a secure or less-secure attachment are impenetrable and resistant to alteration, should particular environmental events occur. The truth value of statements about preservation and change assumes comparable stability or lack of stability in environments. A dense set of threats or loss of attachment objects can make the most secure child anxious, and we know that a benevolent environment can repair, to some degree, the fear and apathy created by a traumatic infancy (see Rathbun, DiVirgilio, & Waldfogel, 1958; Winick, Meyer, & Harris, 1975). Some degree of malleability is always possible.

Many believe that behavioral dispositions influenced by the child's biological properties and earliest experiences are likely to be preserved for a long time. The biological dispositions with the most substantial futures included the temperamental qualities of activity, irritability, and timidity. The tendency to show behavioral inhibition to unfamiliar events is one of the most stable characteristics of young children, at least across the first 3 to 4 years of life. Some 2-year olds cling to their mother and stop playing or talking when in an unfamiliar place or with an unfamiliar adult or child. They stare at the unfamiliar person, are likely to withdraw when approached or attacked, and wait for the other to initiate play with a novel toy before they will do so. This behavioral propensity comes very close to the temperamental dimension of approach–withdrawal studied by Thomas and Chess (1977). About one-third of extremely inhibited 2- to 3-year-old children show higher and more stable heart rates than most children while processing discrepant visual and auditory information that requires accomodation. This autonomic reaction is presumably due to sympathetic blockade of vagal influence on the heart and disruption of sinus arrhythmia. This autonomic pattern could reflect a lower threshold for sympathetic arousal due to genetic factors and/ or events occurring during the embryogenesis of the autonomic nervous system.

But even though the biological propensity to become sympathetically aroused by the unfamiliar might not change, the behavioral reactions might be more malleable. A child could, through effort and the proper arrangement of environmental contingencies, overcome his or her disposition to behavioral inhibition in the face of uncertainty. Behaviors that are under the child's potential control should be poor candidates for preservation. Many behaviors fit this criterion—unprovoked aggression, seeking of help when uncertain, and withdrawal to the unfamiliar are potentially capable of change. Behaviors are most likely to be preserved when the local conditions render the response adaptive because it reduces uncertainty, is in accord with the norms of the child's context, or there is serious external constraint on change.

All culturally valued behaviors fit this criterion; hence, behaviors that meet cultural expectations are more likely to be stable than those that do not (Kagan & Moss, 1962). Most research supports this hypothesis. Successful school performance is more stable than failure; the probability of children who have no psychological symptoms developing them is considerably smaller than the probability of children with symptoms losing them. There is a general growth toward health, at least through early adolescence. But this assumption implies the obviously invalid prediction of a straight line diminution of psychological problems with age. Most acknowledge that during late adolescence and adulthood new incentives for uncertainty arise.

A profitable strategy is to ask during what phases of development particular sources of uncertainty and associated symptoms are likely to occur. The era from 6 to 20 months is potentially stressful because children are vulnerable to anxiety following separation from caretakers and environmental unpredictability. The period from 6 to 8 years is stressful because of the demands of school. The interval from 14 to 18 years contains conflicts over heterosexuality and vocational choice for all in our society; for those who are failing in school there is a need to deal with that fact. The fourth and fifth decades can contain tension due to work. There is no reason to expect that those who are vulnerable to the early stresses of childhood should be the same ones who are vulnerable to the work stresses of middle age. The American child who has established a strong attachment to its parents and has successful school experiences is more likely, as an adult, to be in a vocation with heavy responsibility and, therefore, more vulnerable to potential failure and the anxiety it generates. Children who experience failure during the early school years are likely to set lower expectations in their vocational choice. Hence, when they choose a job, mediocre performance will have less-serious consequences, and they will be working under less-threatening conditions. This may be one reason why it has been difficult to predict later vulnerability to symptoms and degree of adjustment from childhood symptomatology (Cass & Thomas, 1979).

Gradualness in Growth

Few would quarrel with the statement that significant dispositions—some undesirable—can emerge late in life. Individuals are not dynamic entities progressing gradually, in connected stages, to higher states of organization in accord with fixed nautral law. But many more would resist the suggestion that some emergent phenomena may not have a long connected history. A nice example of the hypothesis that some competences may appear with a short history is found in a recent discovery of the behaviors emerging during the second year of life. During the last half of the second year the child displays for the first time a preoccupation with adult standards on dirtiness, aggression, and destruction, affect appropriate to successful and unsuccessful mastery, directions, requests, and orders to adults to change their behavior, and language that is descriptive of the child's own actions (Kagan, 1981). The temporal contiguity in age of onset and period of growth for the previous responses, across both Western and non-Western samples of children, implies that these diverse phenomena are likely to be consequences, in part, of maturational changes in the central nervous system in children growing up in any environment with people and objects. It is not obvious that this set of behaviors, which might be regarded as reflecting the emergence of self-awareness, is a result of a long, connected history of material experiences with objects and people.

Most Western scholars are reluctant to posit the relatively sudden emergence of endogenous mechanisms that might be responsible for new behaviors, because there is a prejudice against postulating significant entities that can arise with a short history. Western philosophers and scientists prefer to impose a gradual, continuous, and connected transition on all instances of change. This preference was captured in its quintessence by Leibniz's insistence on a seamless continuum in nature in which no event could "take place by a leap."

Leibniz conceived of nature as consisting of distinct monads ranging in hierarchical sequence from God to the lowest grade of life. Although no two monads were alike, each differed from the one just below it and the one above it by the least possible difference. A sentence from a letter captures Leibniz's deep conviction that without such a continuum there would be only disorder (quoted in Lovejoy, 1936): "It is necessary that all the orders of natural beings form but a single chain in which the various classes, like so many rings, are so closely linked one to another that it is impossible for the senses or the imagination to determine precisely the point at which one ends and the next begins [p. 145]." The implication was that there must be a cause or principle of sufficient reason for each ring; whatever exists must have an origin, and understanding is attained when each of the consequences derived from the origin can be shown to be necessary.

Kant recognized that the assumption of continuity in nature did not rest on empirical grounds but believed it to be one of the mind's necessary constructions. As cited by Lovejoy (1936): "Neither observation nor insight into the constitution of nature could ever establish it as an objective affirmation [Nevertheless] the method of looking for order in nature according to such a principle and the maxim of admitting such order (though it may be uncertain just where and how far) as existing in nature, certainly constitute a legitimate and excellent regulative principle of reason [p. 241]."

Despite this caveat Kant's (1966) prose reads as though he were describing nature, not the mind's invention: "All phenomena are therefore continuous quantities . . . as every number must be founded on some unity, every phenomenon, as a unity, is a quantum and, as such, a continuum . . . Of quantities in general we can know one quality only *a priori*, namely, their continuity [pp. 141, 144]." Kant restated the Greek notion of stable essences by asserting the principle of the permanence of a substance: "In all changes of phenomena the substance is permanent and its quantum is neither increased nor diminished in nature [p. 149]." But the section that reflects his views on connectedness most clearly deals with causality (Kant, 1966):

> All change therefore is possible only through a continuous action of causality . . . This is the law of continuity in all change, . . . neither time nor a phenomenon in time consists of parts which are the smallest possible and . . . the state of a thing which is being changed passes through all these parts, as elements, to its new state [pp. 164–165].

Thomas Henry Huxley warned Darwin that his insistence on gradual continuous evolution represented "an unnecessary difficulty" in the theory, and Gould (1980) has argued that speciation can, on occasion, be rapid—a phenomenon Gould calls "punctuated equilibria." Increasingly sophisticated studies of morphological embryogenesis indicate that differentiation produces distinct, discontinuous cell types not connected by intergradations. Biologists now describe aspects of organ development with sentences that assume abruptness of change. Newman and Frisch (1979) suggested that in the early formation of the chick limb there appeared to be sudden structural changes. As a specific illustration, an enzyme that inhibits precartilege cells from responding to a certain protein: "makes its abrupt appearance in the developing chick limb immediately before the onset of chondrogenesis [p. 664]." The authors (Newman & Frisch, 1979) suggest that: "it is not the amount of time spent by a population of cells in the subridge region that determines the proximodistal character of the elements they will become part of [p. 667]." If morphological growth of the embryo provides a useful model for early psychological growth, it would follow that a sudden change in central nervous system function would be more important than the amount of time spent in a particular class of interactional experience, at least for selected competences. It is reasonable, therefore, to suggest, with D'Arcy Wentworth Thompson, that new developmental functions can occur without long connected periods of transition. "We cannot transform an invertebrate into a vertebrate, nor a coelenterate into a worm by any single and legitimate deformation . . . Nature proceeds from one type to another . . . to seek for stepping stones across the gaps between is to seek in vain forever (cited in Gould, 1980, [p. 193])."

Resistance to the Idea of Discontinuity

There are good reasons for the widespread resistance to positing discontinuities in the growth and emergence of novel structures. First, the doctrine of connectedness makes original forms useful. If the origin of important adult properties occurs during later childhood or adolescence, the first years of life would appear to have a less-significant function, much like the embryonic notochord that vanishes after its mission is completed. The possibility that the products of an era of development might be temporary or transitional is bothersome to many who want to believe that all psychological products are permanent and that "everything we learn is permanently stored in the mind (Loftus and Loftus, 1980, p. 410)."

Further, arguments for connectivity have the illusion of being mechanistic. When each new function is preceded by another that makes a substantial contribution to it, one is better able to state the cause–effect sequence than if a function emerges relatively rapidly as a result of a new endogenous change. In the second instance, the mind is left with an explanatory gap, as it was for 18th- and early 19th-century biologists who had to deal with the proposal of spontaneous generation of new life forms. This assumption was troubling to minds who insisted on knowing the mechanisms for a new form. Fortunately, the hypothesis of the ovum reduced the dissonance and affirmed Harvey's suggestion, made 2 centuries earlier, that the uterus did not contain a mass of tissue that gradually grew into a fetus. But the possibility of the egg created its own theoretical problems, for no one could see the visceral organs and limbs in the tiny cell, and the organ, not the cell, was the primary theoretical entity. Thus, the idea of preformation was invented in order to save gradualism and continuity. It was not until the cell as a unit and mitosis as a process were accepted that the continuist view became ascendant once more and the 19th-century English microbiologist and minister, William Dallinger, could write (Farley, 1974) that there is a: "continuity—an unbroken chain of unity—running from the base to the apex of the entire organic series [p. 149]."

The extraordinary advances in Western biology may be due, in part, to the motivation to defend the continuity axiom, for in order to deal with discoveries that seem to challenge its validity, increasingly extensive and sophisticated analysis is necessary. The law of practice protracted the emergence of will and self-consciousness; the relocations of libido, labeled fixation and regression, smoothed the sudden appearance of adult phobias; the law of effect removed the surprise from the child's first words; and Piaget's stages of intelligence transformed the abrupt display of conservation into an extended but seamless achievement. The gradualness imposed on psychological growth represents a modern solution to the ancient question of whether qualities could be reduced to quantities. The medieval scholars who believed that mathematics was the language God used to construct the world insisted that discrete events could be described in a language of continuous numbers reflecting the smooth surface that lay beneath the boundaried nature of experience. But modern physical science implies that nature is a layered cake of continuous and discontinuous descriptions. The cones of the retina and cells of the thalamus respond categorically to the continuous wavelengths that describe the visible spectrum. Brain—or mind—parse the continuum into categorical packages with rather abrupt boundaries. Many of the surface phenomena in early development seem to be sudden in appearance, implying that they rest on more continuous phenomena that will have to be described in propositions that contain biological terms. That conclusion is not an argument for reductionism, but rather support for the complementarity Bohr insisted was necessary to understand reality. As MacKay (1958) notes, the languages of psychology, biology, and neurophysiology belong to different logical levels and are not simply translations of one another.

There may be a third source of the persuasiveness of connectivity. During each historical period there is a dominant philosophical view that most scholars avoid confronting—an intellectual electric fence. From the Renaissance to the 19th-century philosophers and scientists were reluctant to infer or deduce propositions that would refute or contradict Biblical statements on man and nature. Although few contemporary scientists worry about the implications of their work for Christian teaching, many are concerned, often unconsciously, about the implications of their data and ideas for the ethic of egalitarianism. The attacks on Arthur Jensen, Richard Herrnstein, and E. O. Wilson, among others, have less to do with data than with the implications of their writings for the doctrine of equality.

The assumption of connectedness in the growth of human characteristics is in greater accord with egalitarian principles than discontinuous growth for the latter is likely to be due to maturational changes in the central nervous system. Emphasis on the role of biological changes in the brain implies that an individual's biology has formative force. Because each person is biologically unique (except for one-egg twins), scholars are forced to assume different rates of psychological growth that have their roots in biological processes. That conclusion is regarded by some as inconsistent with egalitarian premises, although it need not be. By contrast, positing continuous development usually implies the formative action of experiences that gradually establish new properties. Because most believe that the experiences of children are potentially controllable, the connected view implies, but does not prove, that one can arrange similar experiences for all infants.

Although developmental psychologists favor a continuist interpretation of change, the most revolutionary scientific ideas during the last 75 years have been discontinuist in their essence. The photon has replaced the wave, the discrete gene replaced the continuous effects of climate, diet, and environmental challenge, and the possible disintegration of protons may replace steady state theories of the universe and imply an end, far, far in the future, of what we would like to regard as a continuous cosmos.

The connectivity that is implied is epigenesis raises different issues. If, as experimental psychologists have shown, the mind creates representations of events that were not experienced—prototypes created from the mental average of encountered events—it is necessary to assume that the structures of mind are continually subject to change. Like the proverbial ship's planks replaced one by one until no piece of wood in the original was present in the restoration, it is possible for a child at age 12 to possess no structure that existed at age 2, even though there is always overlap between the structures created a moment ago and those established a year earlier. This metaphor implies connectivity of structures over short rather than long periods. I rather like this idea because it is in accord with evolutionary theory. Although biologists recognize theoretically a connection between all of today's living forms and ancient forms of life, many of the latter are now extinct.

ACKNOWLEDGMENT

Preparation of this chapter was supported by research grant HD10094 from the National Institute of Child Health and Human Development and a grant from the Foundation for Child Development.

REFERENCES

Arend, R., Gove, F., & Sroufe, L. A. Continuity of individual adaptation from infancy. *Child Development*, 1979, *50*, 950–959.

Arlitt, A. H. *Psychology of infancy and early childhood*. New York: McGraw–Hill, 1928.

Bernfeld, S. *The psychology of the infant*. New York: Brentano's, 1929.

Bornstein, M. *Two kinds of perceptual organization near the beginning of life*. Presented at Minnesota Symposium on Child Psychology. Minneapolis, October, 1979.

Brim, O. G., & Kagan, J. (Eds.). *Constancy and change in human development*. Cambridge, Mass.: Harvard University Press, 1980.

Brunswik, E. *Perception and the representative design of psychological experiments*. Berkeley: University of California Press, 1956.

Campbell, D. T., & Fiske, D. W. Convergent and discriminant validation by the multitrait– multimethod matrix. *Psychological Bulletin*, 1959, *56*, 81–105.

Cass, L. K., & Thomas, C. B. *Childhood pathology and later adjustment*. New York: Wiley, 1979.

Chamberlain, A. F. *The child: A study in the evolution of man*. Cambridge, Mass.: Cambridge University Press, 1907.

D'Espagnat, B. The quantum theory and relativity. *Scientific American*, 1979, 241, *5*, 158–181.

Egeland, B., & Sroufe, L. A. Attachment and early maltreatment. *Child Development*, 1981, *52*, 44–52.

Farley, J. *The spontaneous generation controversy from Descartes to Oparin*. Baltimore: Johns Hopkins University Press, 1974.

Fenton, J. C. *A practical psychology of babyhood*. Boston: Houghton–Mifflin, 1925.

Fiske, J. *The meaning of infancy*. Boston: Houghton–Mifflin, 1909 (first published in 1883).

Gould, S. J. *The panda's thumb*. New York: Norton, 1980.

Haith, M. M. *Rules that babies look by*. Hillsdale, N.J.: Lawrence Erlbaum Associates, 1980.

Hanson, N. R. *Patterns of discovery*. Cambridge, Mass.: Cambridge University Press, 1961.

Hetherington, E. M., & Parke, R. *Child psychology* (2nd ed.). New York: Holt, Rinehart, & Winston, 1979.

Hubel, D. H., & Wiesel, T. N. The period of susceptibility to the physiological effects of unilateral eye closure in kittens. *Journal of Physiology*, 1970, *206*, 419–436.

Hughes, H. S. *Consciousness and society*. New York: Vintage Books, 1958.

Izard, C. *Human emotions*. New York: Plenum, 1977.

Kagan, J. On the need for relativism. *American Psychologist*, 1967, *22*, 131–142.

Kagan, J. *Change and continuity in infancy*. New York: Wiley, 1971.

Kagan, J. *The second year*. Cambridge, Mass.: Harvard University Press, 1981.

Kagan, J., & Moss, H. A. *Birth to maturity*. New York: Wiley, 1962.

Kant, I. *Critique of pure reason*. New York: Anchor Books, 1966.

Kline, L. W., & France, C. J. The psychology of ownership. In T. L. Smith (Ed.), *Aspects of child life and education*. Boston, Ginn, 1907.

Langer, J. *The origins of logic*. New York: Academic Press, 1980.

Loftus, E. F., & Loftus, G. R. On the permanence of stored information in the human brain. *American Psychologist*, 1980, *35*, 409–420.

Lovejoy, A. O. *The great chain of being*. Cambridge, Mass.: Harvard University Press, 1936.

MacKay, D. M. Complementarity. *Symposium of the Aristotelian Society*, 1958, *32*, 105–122. London: Harrison Ltd.

Mandelbaum, M. *History, man and reason*. Baltimore: The Johns Hopkins University Press, 1971.

Markman, E. M., Cox, B., & Machida, S. The standard object sorting task as a measure of conceptual organization. *Developmental Psychology*, 1981, *17*, 115–117.

McCall, R. B. Nature–nurture and the two realms of development. *Child Development*, 1981, *52*, 1–12.

McKenzie, B. E., Tootell, H. E., & Day, R. H. Development of visual size constancy during the first year of human infancy. *Developmental Psychology*, 1980, *16*, 163–174.

Miller, H. C. *The new psychology and the parent*. London: Jarrolds, 1922.

Mote, F. W. *Intellectual foundations of China*. New York: Knopf, 1971.

Mumford, E. E. R. *The dawn of character in the mind of the child*. New York: Longmans Green, 1925.

Mussen, P. H., Conger, J. J., & Kagan, J. *Child development and personality* (3rd ed.). New York: Harper & Row, 1969.

Newman, S. A., & Frisch, H. L. Dynamics of skeletal pattern formation in developing chick limb. *Science*, 1979, *205*, 662–668.

Olweus, D. *The stability of aggression*. Presented at the meeting of The Society for Research in Child Development, Boston, April, 1981.

Piaget, J. *Play, dreams and imitation in childhood* (trans. by C. Gattegno & F. M. Hodgson). London: Routledge & Kegan, Paul, 1951.

Rand, W., Sweeny, M. E., & Vincent, E. L. *Growth and development of the young child*. Philadelphia: Saunders, 1930.

Rathbun, C., DiVirgilio, L., & Waldfogel, S. The restitutive process in children following prolonged separation from family and culture. *American Journal of Orthopsychiatry*, 1958, *28*, 408–415.

Richardson, F. H. *Parenthood and the newer psychology*. New York: Putnam, 1926.

Rosch, E. Principles of Categorization. In E. Rosch & B. Lloyd (Eds.), *Cognition and categorization*. Hillsdale, N.J.: Lawrence Erlbaum Associates, 1977.

Ruff, H. A. Effect of context on infants' responses to novel objects. *Developmental Psychology*, 1981, *17*, 87–89.

Shea, W. R. The classification of scientific terms as theoretical and observational in contemporary philosophy of science. In *Conceptual Basis of the Classification of Knowledge*. Proceedings of the Ottawa Conference, 1971. Edited by J. A. Wojciechowski, Munchen: Verlag Dokumentation, 1974, p. 172–185.

Shinn, M. *Notes on the development of a child*, (Vol. 1). University of California Series, 1893 to 1899. Notes on the Development of a Child (Vol. 2). University of California Publications in Education (Vol. 4), 1907.

Sroufe, L. A. The coherence of individual development. *American Psychologist*, 1979, *34*, 834–840.

Sroufe, L. A., & Waters, E. Attachment as an organizational construct. *Child Development*, 1977, *48*, 1184–1199.

Thomas, A., & Chess, S. *Temperament and development*. New York: Brunner Mazel, 1977.

Thorndike, E. L. *The elements of psychology*. New York: Seiler, 1905.

Tiedemann, D. *Beobachtungen über die Entwickelung der Seelenfanigkeiten bei Kindern*. Altenburg: Oskar Bonde, 1897.

Tracy, F., & Stimpfl, J. *The psychology of childhood* (7th ed.). Boston: Heath, 1909.

Tylor, E. B. *Researches into the early history of mankind*. New York: Holt, 1878.

Vaughn, B. E., Egeland, B., Sroufe, L. A., & Waters, E. Individual differences in infant–mother attachment at 12 and 18 months: Stability and change in families under stress. *Child Development*, 1979, *50*, 971–975.

Vidal, F. *Piaget on evolution and morality*. Unpublished Honors Thesis. Harvard University, 1981.

Watson, J. *Psychological care of infant and child*. New York: Norton, 1928.

Weiskrantz, L. Trying to bridge some neuropsychological gaps between monkey and man. *British Journal of Psychology*, 1977, *68*, 431–445.

Winick, M., Meyer, K. K., & Harris, R. C. Malnutrition and environmental enrichment by early adoption. *Science*, 1975, *190*, 1173–1175.

3 The Idea of Development in Developmental Psychology

Sheldon H. White
Harvard University

In the late 1800s, George Romanes in England, Ivan Sechenov in Russia, and James Mark Baldwin in the United States each argued at some length that the growing child's thought is perfected in stages. These writers were moved by the Evolutionism of their time to spell out some similar arguments: (1) Children show changing organizations of action and thought, or changing "logics", as they grow up; (2) the later actions and logics are built upon the earlier ones, and they are more powerful and perfect than the earlier ones; (3) the emergences of growth move children's thought and action into more and more correspondence with events of the world around them; (4) children begin by dealing with the perceived and the immediate and the concrete; as they grow up, they become able to deal with the distant, the abstract, the conceptualized, and the symbolic.

These four theses amount to an assertion that a child's mind *develops*. Today such an assertion seems truistic in a field that, after all, calls itself developmental psychology. If a child's mind did not "develop," then what would developmental psychology be the psychology of?

Today we can see that the four 19th-century theses are alive in Werner's and Piaget's 20th-century theories of cognitive development. "Fine!," say some of us, "Exactly right! All great ideas have their historical foreshadowings." But some of us are less than enthusiastic about the foreshadowings. Piaget's claim that there are stages of cognitive development is giving us a lot of trouble. Much evidence now runs against it—for example, work reviewed by Gelman (1978) and Brainerd (1978). If research following Piaget's writings does not support his claim that cognition develops in stages, is it helpful or confusing to find that scholars before Piaget have also made the claim that stages exist?

INDUCTION AND ABDUCTION IN THE LATE 19TH CENTURY

The early stage theories of cognitive development were not based on data in the way that contemporary theories are . . . or, rather, they were not grounded on data in the way in which 20th-century idealizations of the philosophy of science have held that contemporary theories *ought* to relate to data.

To begin with, there were not great quantities of data on which to base those early theoretical writings. A sizable and organized empiricism directed toward children would not exist until the child development movement of the 1930s. Toward the end of the 19th century, there were many free-floating pieces of scientific, philosophical, and professionally oriented writing about childhood, these writings often offering or embodying data. G. Stanley Hall was to pull together the diverse people who produced such writings into the loose coalition called the child study movement. This seems to be the historical point of origin for what becomes, in time, an organized research enterprise (Sears, 1975). But Hall never put forward a convincing method of child study. His work with the questionnaire method was not widely cited nor was it much pursued by others after his death.[1]

The early cognitive stage theorists used some of the data of their time. Romanes in his 1889 book, *Mental Evolution in Man,* makes reference to books about children by Sully, Perez, and others.[2] He cites other contemporary data in his book. The stereotype that pictures him as only a gullible anecdotalist is

---

[1]Ross's (1972) biography states that between 1894 and 1915 Hall performed 194 questionnaire studies. In a 1903 review, Hall listed 102 "topical syllabi" completed to date as well as a long bibliography of articles and books based on them. Among the titles of the syllabi are: *Anger; Appetites and Foods; Spontaneously Invented Toys and Amusements; Straightness and Uprightness of Body; Stillness, Solitude, Restlessness.* Writing in 1903, Hall seemed defensive about child study. He said: "Some four or five years ago, when the critics were loudest and most aggressive, many superficial observers thought the movement dead." But Hall argued that child study was alive and well. "It is doing a work for the child at school akin to that of the Reformation for the religious life of the adult."

The questionnaire method yielded some useful data, but it was not equal to the various scientific and practical demands placed upon it. G. Stanley Hall's child study movement was an exercise in the politics of research in which six audiences with differing motives for child study—psychologists, university presidents, educators, social workers, clinicians, and parents—sought methods, findings, and justifications that were far beyond the resources of a discipline of Psychology that was just being born (Siegel & White, 1982). Why did so many turn to this hope of a science for support? Conceivably, they saw "development" as a naturally good thing, so that those who studied children and development might be expected to discover values and goals to guide adults in their work with children.

[2]Romanes (1889) does not give extended citations, but American editions of the work he refers to are: Perez, Bernard, *The first three years of childhood* (Ed. & Transl. by Alice M. Christie). Syracuse, N.Y.: C. W. Bardeen, 1889; Sully, J. *Studies of childhood.* New York: Appleton, 1896.

oversimplified. Sechenov's *The Elements of Thought* does not cite any publications or formal data about childhood. This may be stylistic, however. Sechenov does not directly cite any scientific work on the brain and sensory processes, and yet it is clear he is using such work in his book. Baldwin reports some of his early studies of infants in his 1895 book, *Mental Development in the Child and the Race*. Baldwin presents data or observations on infant distance and color perception, hand preference, imitative copying of drawings, and suggestion. He discusses his methods and data to illustrate the *possibility* of a "dynamogenic method" of child study. (He seems to be groping toward a more motoric and behavioristic Psychology and away from a sensory and ideational Psychology, as a number of his contemporaries were at that time.) All in all, it is clear that any modern research psychologist would regard the data of Romanes, Sechenov, and Baldwin as scanty and quite out of line with their theoretical claims.

But these writers were not proceeding inductively, nor did they make any pretense of doing so. They were trying to show that *ideas* of development and evolution, discovered and elaborated through the study of topics quite distinct from childhood, could be extended to fit the facts of children's cognitive development.

The early theories of cognitive development seem to have been advanced by a process of scientific reasoning in which some facts about children were fitted into a pattern with a variety of other facts according to criteria of coherence, simplicity, fittingness, and harmony. This movement from experience to conjecture, from consequents to antecedents, was set forth not as an end of inquiry but as a beginning of inquiry. A nice work for this process of anticipatory theorizing is Charles Sanders Peirce's word *abduction*.

Peirce argued that, standing beside induction and deduction, abduction is the third great mode of scientific reasoning, absolutely essential to scientific work. Like induction and deduction, abduction takes you from particulars to generals, from what you are seeing in the here and now to the possibility of beliefs about the "all" or "any" of things. The group of three—induction, deduction, abduction—is complete; there is no other way we can move from particulars to generals. Abduction is a negligibly persuasive form of scientific reasoning. It is in large measure what we usually speak of as speculation or conjecture. But it is nonetheless essential because, as Peirce points out, it is the only reasoning process through which new ideas come into science.[3]

----

[3]In the writings brought together as his collected papers, Charles Sanders Peirce repeatedly contends that there are three basic forms of reasoning or argument: Induction, Deduction, and something that he variously calls Abduction, Retroduction, Hypothesis, Probable Inference, or Presumption. In his notes toward a history of science written about 1896, Peirce wrote: "There are in science three fundamentally different kinds of reasoning, Deduction . . . Induction . . . and Retroduction [Vol. *I*, par. 65, p. 28]." In an analysis of signs in 1897, Peirce posited: "a trichotomy of all simple arguments into Deductions, Inductions and Abductions [*II*, 266, p. 152]." In the entry on

The writings of the early cognitive stage theorists were abductive and conjectural. Occasionally, however, such writings were put forward as though they were announcements of a discovery.

GEORGE JOHN ROMANES

George J. Romanes (1848–1894) was a British biologist who began his career with research on jellyfish, starfish, and sea urchins. A friend and disciple of Charles Darwin, he turned his major attention to writings about the development of intelligence. He maintained as a kind of minor counterpoint a series of writings on theology and its relation to science.

Romanes wanted to show that there was an unbroken evolutionary line con-

---

"Reasoning" that Peirce wrote for the *Dictionary of Philosophy and Psychology,* he said "Reasoning is of three elementary kinds . . . *induction, deduction,* and *presumption* [for which the present writer proposes the name *abduction*] [*II,* 774, p. 495]."

Further on in the same dictionary entry, Peirce states: "Presumption is the only kind of reasoning which supplies new ideas, the only kind which is, in this sense, synthetic [*II,* 777, p. 497]." Peirce's formal, functional, and introspective comparisons of deduction, induction, and abduction are quite striking and interesting. He says, for example, that abduction (in this particular paper "hypothesis") produces the *sensuous* element of thought. Using abduction, a harmony among diverse facts and ideas is grasped emotionally as a unity, just as the diverse sounds emitted by the instruments of an orchestra are grasped as: "a peculiar musical emotion, quite distinct from the sounds themselves [*II,* 643, p. 387]."

The sensuous unity that is felt in abduction, and that guides it, reflects the design of the mind. Abduction is, at bottom, a coherence-finding process in which a person finds form in experience as experience is resonant with pre-existing forms in the mind. Keil (1981) has recently discussed children's cognitive development as resting upon an abductive, "constrained" process.

Abduction seems to be the core of a logic of discovery used by developmental psychology but rarely articulated in a principled way. Many developmental analyses consist in the discovery and/or assertion of similarities and correspondences in the formal organizations governing diverse data series. Time series data taken *here* show a systematicity that looks much like the systematicity of the time series data taken *there;* the linking term *looks much like* denotes a rather complex form of Peircian abduction.

In the systematic preface of his *Comparative Psychology of Mental Development,* Heinz Werner acknowledges that "genetic parallelisms" exist. Werner (1948) states: "For all practical purposes one may speak of a principle of parallelism: development in mental life follows certain general and formal rules, whether it concerns the individual or the species [p. 26]." Seeking to disentangle his developmental psychology from the problematic hypotheses of recapitulationism and "the primitive mind," Werner than proceeds to downplay the developmentalist's method of paralleling that tends to generate those problems. Yet those problems are, so to speak, "occupational diseases" of thought engendered as a kind of undesirable byproduct of the developmental psychologist's frequent use of an abductive method of paralleling. The method has scientific benefits that probably substantially outweigh its costs. In a recent paper, Teitelbaum (1977) appears to have recognized the generative potential of the method when he speaks of "synthesis by parallel."

For a broad view of the analogistic tradition in the study of development, see the early chapters in Gould's (1977) *Ontogeny and Phylogeny.*

necting the minds of animals with the mind of man. He wrote *Animal Intelligence* in 1882, and *Mental Evolution in Animals* in 1883, to argue that properties of Mind run continuously through the animal kingdom. His book *Mental Evolution in Man* (Romanes, 1889) was intended to show that science had now encompassed the essence of human psychology:

> After centuries of intellectual conquest in all regions of the phenomenal universe, man has at last begun to find that he may apply in a new and most unexpected manner the adage of antiquity—*Know thyself*. For he has begun to perceive a strong probability, if not an actual certainty, that his own living nature is identical in kind with the nature of all other life, and that even the most amazing side of this his own nature—nay, the most amazing of all things within reach of his knowledge—the human mind itself, is but the topmost inflorescence of one mighty growth, whose roots and stem and many branches are sunk in the abyss of interplanetary time [p. 2].

The prose of the quote says that the human mind is now within the reach of science, whereas the poetics of the quote say that the reader is to feel stupefaction or awe. Words like "new," "amazing," "mighty," "abyss," bid for those feelings from the reader. There are overtones of the evangelical in many late 19th-century writings about evolution and development and psychology and children. I believe those evangelical overtones had an important meaning for the writers and the readers of those books.

The book that follows says that there is a natural ordering of forms of thought. Part of that ordering is seen if we compare the mental activities of creatures whose historical origins fall at different points along evolutionary phylogeny. Part shows up in the intellectual ontogeny of the growing child. Romanes (1889) stated: "Of course my object eventually is to show that in the history of a growing child, just as sensations give rise to percepts and percepts to recepts (as they do among animals) so do recepts give rise to pre-concepts, pre-concepts to concepts, concepts to propositions, and propositions to syllogisms [p. 185]."

Evolutionism and associationism are blended together in the quote. A series of more and more complex knowledge-forms may be formed associationistically out of experience—sensations, percepts, recepts (percepts with sign value, something like conditioned stimuli), preconcepts, concepts, etc. A series of mental activities of more and more complex construction shows up in men and animals if we look at them in just the right way, evolutionistically.

Romanes has explored the thought that is common to man and animals in his previous books. In a chart at the beginning of *Mental Evolution in Man* he summarizes the scheme arrived at in his previous *Mental Evolution in Animals*.

The chart shows 20 "products of intellectual development" arranged in a series of 17 steps. In order, from low to high, the mental activities are: (1) protoplasmic movements; (2) non-nervous adjustments; (3) partly nervous adjustments; (4) nervous adjustments; (5) pleasures and pains; (6) memory; (7) primary instincts; (8) association by contiguity; (9a) recognition of offspring; (9b) secondary instincts; (10) association by similarity; (11) reason; (12) recognition of persons; (13) communication of ideas; (14a) recognition of pictures; (14b) understanding of words; (14c) dreaming; (15) understanding of mechanisms; (16) use of tools; (17) indefinite morality.

These are 20 forms of intellectual activity of increasing sophistication. Now, by parallel alignment, the chart aligns the 20 with a "Phycological Scale"—an evolutionary order—that extends from protoplasmic organisms at the bottom to anthropoid apes and the dog together at the top. Another column of the chart aligns the 20 mental activities as emergences in the "Psychogenesis" of man along a time line of embryogenesis that stretches from ovum and spermatazoa to 15 months of postnatal age.

The design of this opening chart is worth a moment's notice. Romanes is effectively arguing that there is an ordering of mental activities that exists somewhat apart from the manifestations of that ordering in animals and men. One may *discover* the ordering by watching what animals and men do, but the ordering is not a pure and simple induction from observations of either. It is in part a principled ordering.

We would express the principle of Romanes's ordering, in modern terms, as resting upon information-processing complexity. The intellectual products that are lower on Romanes's scale, things like "protoplasmic movements" and "non-nervous adjustments" integrate much less information in their control structures (are associationally much simpler) than are advanced intellectual products such as "use of tools" and "indefinite morality." Romanes is by no means clear about the exact quantitative composition of his ordering. If one wanted to get sticky about things, one might challenge him to count up exactly the informational or associational elements in his 20 intellectual products. But, of course, those counts are not given in Romanes's book nor are they possible at the vague level of prescription he has offered for the mental abilities.[4]

We have discussed, so far, Romanes's description of a developmental series of mind that is common to both animals and young children. Human mental

---

[4]Romanes's (1884) chart is first offered in his preceding book, *Mental Evolution in Animals,* and there he says: "I have thought it a good plan to draw a diagram or map of the probable development of Mind from its first beginnings in protoplasmic life up to its culmination in the brain of civilized man [p. 63]." The intellectual attack on mental development set forth in Romanes's diagram, uses both synthetic and analytic tactics and offers an excellent illustration of the developmentalist's method of paralleling discussed in the preceding footnote. Romanes orders his several series in part using *facts* of historicity. He knows that some things on his lists occur later in time than others. Part of his order depends on his *idea* that greater and greater information-processing complexity will be found in (will be central to the definition of) a developmental series of psychological organizations. Exactly the same idea is central to Pascual–Leone's (1970, 1976) and Fischer's (1980) contemporary theories of cognitive development.

development ascends beyond the highest level attained by any animal. Animal thought at its very highest attains what Romanes terms the *logic of recepts*. Human infants are born using the logic of recepts; they pass beyond animals to a pre-conceptual stage and then finally to a conceptual stage in which their thought is governed by the *logic of concepts*.

Romanes takes the idea of several logics in the human mind from the French philosopher of Positivism, August Comte, acknowledging that that idea has been transmitted to him in writings by John Stuart Mill (pp. 41–42) and George Henry Lewes (p. 47). The doctrine of Comte had been that the human mind can make use of a logic of feelings, a logic of images, and a logic of signs. On various technical grounds, Romanes reformulates Comte's doctrine to envisage a logic of recepts and a logic of concepts in the human mind. He arrives, finally, at the argument that children show four types of ideation as they move from birth to adulthood, the lower receptual, the higher receptual, the pre-conceptual, and the conceptual (pp. 184ff.).

How and when does the child definitively transcend the mental life of the brute? The key event seems to be the child's recognition of its own individuality and the emergence of self-consciousness. From Sully and Wundt, Romanes estimates that self-consciousness arises in children at about 3 years of age because this is when children begin to refer to themselves in speech (p. 201). It is here, then, that the thought of the human takes flight beyond the work of phylogenesis. Uniquely and characteristically human stages of cognitive development are shown during the course of the child's growth. Romanes analyzes reasoning, judgment, imagery, communication, naming, and conceptualization as they are made possible or enhanced by his stages of mental development. Most of his discussion looks congruent with what we are familiar with today in our more detailed and evidential accounts of cognitive development.

IVAN MIKHAILOVITCH SECHENOV

A second theorist of cognitive development was Ivan Sechenov, a Russian physiologist who took his doctorate in 1851 and then spent some time in France and Germany working in the laboratories of DuBois–Reymond, Ludwig, and Helmholtz. During this early phase of his career he achieved some fame for his studies of corticospinal inhibitory effects in the nervous system. Sechenov was led to see the nervous system as, functionally, a hierarchical system of reflexes. Returning to Russia, he published a book, *Reflexes of the Brain,* in 1863, that described the human brain and mind in reflexological terms.

Sechenov's book was one of a number of prospectuses for a physiological or scientific psychology that appeared in Europe in the latter half of the 19th century. But Sechenov published his book in the Russia of the czars. The Petersburg Censorial Committee forbade sale of the book and brought an action against Professor Sechenov in the Petersburg High Court of Justice with a statement of charges that included the following (Shaternikov, in Sechenov, 1935):

> This materialistic theory reduces the best of men to the level of a machine devoid of consciousness and free will, and acting automatically; it sweeps away good and evil, moral duties, the merit of good deeds and the responsibility for bad ones; it undermines the moral foundations of society and thereby destroys the religious doctrine of eternal life; it militates against the views of Christianity and the claims of the Penal Code; consequently, it leads to the corruption of morals. Mr. Sechenov has given his theory the form of a scientific treatise; but its style is far from scientific, it is written so as to be easily understood by the layman. This fact, and the low price of the book [80 kopeks] prove that the author's intention is to make his theory accessible to a wide circle of readers. It follows that Mr. Sechenov's book "The Reflexes of the Brain" is directed to the corruption of morals [p. XXIII].

The charges against Sechenov were dropped and the ban on his book was lifted within a year. With Sechenov, as with Romanes, we find an argument for stages of children's cognitive development embedded in broader claims about the human mind, and we find a whiff of evangelism in the air. Sechenov was not purposefully trying to be evangelical, but some Russian officials took him to be so nevertheless.[5]

The 1863 book, *Reflexes of the Brain,* makes periodic references to children's learning and growth to illustrate Sechenov's reflexological theses. Sechenov

---

[5]The political implications of Sechenov's work and his scientific stance were apparently crystal clear in the Russia of his time. Frolov's (1937) account of Pavlov and his school points out that the 1860s was a time of "exceptional development" of Russian science and philosophy. Sechenov was taken as a model figure, a hero of the liberal intelligentsia of his time. Sechenov was the model for Barazov in Turgenev's *Fathers and Sons,* the scientific "son" who strove against the "father" of the gentry. Frolov (1937) describes the double-edged thrust of *Reflexes of the Brain* in this way:

> By his work on the physiology of the brain, Sechenov not only dealt a blow to the old clerical view of the soul—with a boldness such as Descartes could not boast of—he also created . . . a harmonious theory of the evolution of psychical faculties . . . . It can be easily understood that the enthusiasm of Sechenov and his fellow-thinkers was viewed with extreme disquiet by the tsarist government [p. 4].

Note that Frolov's book was published in 1937 at a time when Stalin had taken the iron fist out of the velvet glove and when attacks that were sometimes lethal were being made on intellectuals. Frolov might be expected to emphasize the prorevolutionary zeal of his scientific ancestors.

But Sechenov's autobiographical notes written in 1905, a year before his death, still reflect the political sensitivity of his 1863 *Reflexes of the Brain.* He notes that an editor had censored out his first title of the work, *An Attempt to Bring Physiological Bases Into Mental Processes.* He is still not sure all of his 1905 notes will get through the censor (Sechenov, 1952, p. 111, footnote 4). He takes some pains to argue that his reputation as a "nihilist philosopher" who absolves people of guilt for immorality is unjustified. He (Sechenov, 1952) quotes his earlier avowal regarding the book: "One must nevertheless have the courage to express his convictions [p. 129]."

extended his reflexological argument in his long paper in 1873, "Who Must Investigate the Problems of Psyhcology and How." Again he used illustrative examples of cognitive development to advocate reflexology. Finally, Sechenov published his *Elements of Thought* in the 1870s.[6] Boring (1950) characterizes this work as explicating Sechenov's "mature mechanistic views" (p. 661). The book offers a number of discussions of mechanisms and time sequences of cognitive development in children.

There are three stages in the growing child's thought: a stage of *automatic sensory thinking*, a kind of thought that the young child shares with animals; a higher stage of *concrete object thinking;* and a still higher stage of *abstract thinking* or thinking in symbols. The dominant theme is the child's passage from the sensory to the symbolic, the abstract, or the "extra-sensory." Sechenov (1935) states:

> This mysterious work of the transformation of sensory products into apparently less and less sensory symbols, together with the innate capacity of speech, enables man to combine the products of the experience of another person with those of his own (i.e., to learn what is taught to him), and is the most characteristic feature of all his mental development . . . The child was thinking in terms of concrete sensations and suddenly the objects of his thoughts, instead of copies of reality, become reflections of this reality; at first these reflections are very close to reality, but gradually they deviate so far from their source that all noticeable connections between the sign or symbol and its sensory origin disappears [p. 455].

Sechenov is a neurophysiologist, intensely aware of the brain and nervous system as a physical system. The brain meets the world through energy exchange processes at the sensory surfaces transduced into the limited language of neural irritability. There are strict rules of coding and all thought, plain or fancy, must begin with the categories of physiology. Sechenov (1935) italicizes the point:

> *All those properties or features of objects which are accessible to the senses, are the products of the physiological process of perception; the number of these properties or features is strictly determined by the number of perceptions [p. 459].*

Before Sechenov, the first steps in the construction of the world out of rudimentary physical energies and physiological responses had been traced out by Hermann von Helmholtz in his classic *Physiological Optics* and *Sensations of Tone* published in the 1850s and 1860s. The announced purpose of Sechenov's *Elements of Thought* was to show the consistency of Helmholtz's molecular

---

[6]Robert Epstein has been of considerable help in my search for an exact date of publication for *The Elements of Thought*, but the closest I have been able to come with his help is to a date for the second edition of this work in 1878. All citations to his work in the text that follows are to a translation of selected works published in 1935.

analyses of the development of sensation with the broad-gauged developmental-ism that was in the process of being set forth by Herbert Spencer in the 10 volumes of his *Synthetic Philosophy* published between 1860 and 1896.

The child stands in the middle of Sechenov's reconciliation of Helmholtz and Spencer, serving as an expository aid. About 100 years before Sechenov, Etienne Condillac wrote a famous exposition of empiricism in which he imagined a statue that was organized inwardly like a man but that had never received a sense impression. Condillac gave the statue one sensory channel after another and argued that with time and amount of sensory experience that statue would build a complete psychology—first attention, then pleasure and pain, then memory, then comparison, etc. Sechenov's child is like Condillac's statue and, in fact, is only a trifle more lively than that statue. Sechenov discusses aspects of young children's behavior—that they have poor memories, that they make mistakes in naming and classifying things, that they ask a lot of "Why?" questions, that they learn to count—but he is not giving his audience information about children. He is drawing upon what he expects they know. Sechenov is outlining a constructivist epistemology and a developmental stage theory appears as a byproduct.

Herbert Spencer's *Principles of Psychology* gives a generalized account of stages of mental development that seems to be the basis for Sechenov's three stages of children's thought. Spencer talks about why there ought to be stages of mental evolution, and he gives an elaborated account of a developmental distancing of thought from sensation that Sechenov will later characterize as a movement from the sensory to the extra-sensory.

There are stages in mental evolution because there is a recursive growth pattern. Function, elaborated, turns into form. Products built at one level of mental growth become building blocks for the next. Spencer (1872) asserted: "It is quite evident that the growth of perception involves representation of sensations; that the growth of simple reasoning involves representation of perceptions; and that the growth of complex reasoning involves representation of the results of simple reasoning. So that the remoteness from sensation necessarily increases with the intellectual elevation [pp. 517–518]."

Spencer's stages of mind—presentation, representation, rerepresentation— are like a set of stairs. The higher you climb, the more remote you are from sensation, the more you increase your intellectual elevation, and the farther you see around. Spencer (1872) spells out what this means:

> Let us look at the matter in the concrete—let us compare the mental activities of the child, the savage, and the civilized man in his various grades of culture. An infant gazing, grasping all it can, and putting to its mouth whatever it lays hold of, shows us a consciousness in which presented feelings greatly predominate. An urchin, pulling to pieces his toys, building card-houses, whipping his top, gathering flowers and pebbles, and shells, passes an intellectual life that is mainly percep-tive—presented feelings are here being associated with represented feelings, form-ing knowledge of the properties and actions of things around; and what goes on of

higher representation, as in that dramatizing to which dolls and sets of miniature tea-things minister, is limited to actions in the household. In the boy and in the savage there is greater excursiveness of representation; but still, representation that passes not much beyond those wider concrete experiences which larger spheres of activity have disclosed. Adventures, triumphs of strength and skill—these furnish subject-matter for the talk of the uncivilized man and the air-castles of the youth: representations are practically limited to the transactions of individuals. Only as maturity is approached do we find in a few of the civilized such higher degree of representation, here passing into re-representation, as that which groups particular modes of human action under general truths. When, rising to intellectual activity of high type, we take for example a statesman, we find that he is habitually absorbed in highly-representative thought [pp. 518–519].

The more your thought stretches across person, time, and space, the larger your *umwelt,* then the higher your level of mental development according to Spencer. The statesman may study statistics representative of the conditions of thousands of men stretched across thousands of miles. The scientist may use scattered data to make an inference about geological processes extending over a billion years in time. These kinds of people are engaging in mental activities at a very high level.[7]

Spencer has an idea of development that is principled and systematic, then, just as Romanes had. He applies this idea to the things of the world to say that some fall into developmental series. The adult is more developed than the infant. The civilized man is more developed than the savage. The higher type of man— the more educated man, the leader, he who sees and knows more broadly—is more developed than the ordinary man.

JAMES MARK BALDWIN

James Mark Baldwin is the third of our 19th-century cognitive stage theorists. We are here trying to explore the ideas of development that lie historically embedded as the intellectual nucleus of developmental psychology; for our pur-

---

[7]Spencer argued that increasing development brought greater *intelligence*—that is, greater and greater correspondences between mind and the material universe, leading to a larger and larger *umwelt.* See, in Volume 1 of his *Principles of Psychology,* the chapters entitled "Life and Mind as Correspondence," "The Correspondence as Extending in Space," "The Correspondence as Extending in Time," "The Nature of Intelligence." Contemporary treatments of mind and intelligence from a paleoneurological perspective (Jerison, 1973, 1976) and from a genetic epistemological perspective (Piaget, 1952, 1954) rest on elaborated forms of the same basic idea. As with Romanes's idea of development discussed in footnote 4 earlier, we find contemporary reassertions of a nuclear 19th-century conception laid down on a broader and richer web of evidence and articulated through more thorough and detailed analytic structures. I have elsewhere argued that this kind of transposition of old ideas on new data bases and conceptual mappings is a fundamental form of scientific progress in Psychology (White, 1977).

poses it is most useful to consider Baldwin's first draft of a theory of cognitive development, his *Mental Development in the Child and the Race* first published in 1895.

Baldwin states his affinity with the authors and issues we have been considering thus far. In his preface, he says that his book is directed toward the problem of Spencer and Romanes (Baldwin, 1906, p. vii). Later (1906) he speaks of the special integrative possibility grasped only by those two men and himself: "with the two great exceptions, Spencer and Romanes, I know of no biologists approaching the first rank, who have attempted to bring the phenomena of mental development—the class of facts most open to scrutiny and most important everywhere in the animal series—and those of organic adaptation, under the terms of a single concept [p. 202]."

Baldwin is united with Spencer and Romanes in the belief that there must be some deep systematic resemblances between the principles of evolution and the principles of mind.

The ideas of development we have discussed so far have all had to do with quality of mental representation or process. A mental activity is more developed as it embraces a larger sensory and ideational field. Baldwin, in contrast, is a theorist of volition and action. He discusses three stages of development but those stages are not so much epistemological stages as forms of internalization of the evolutionary process. Mind is an evolution of evolution. Thinking is an outgrowth of the evolutionary process and an efficient substitute for it.

Baldwin (1906) asks the reader to imagine: "a process by which the theatre of the application of natural selection is transferred from the outside relations of the organism, its relations to its environment, to the inside relations of the organism [p. 197]." Imagine two theaters. The theater of outside relations is the real world around the creature full of rocks, trees, food, predators, opportunities, risks. The theater of inside relations is the shadow world of the mind, full of images of the objects of the real world—these images embedded in internal simulative processes that, for rather ingenious theoretical reasons, Baldwin insists must be based on imitations.

Simple creatures, with little mind and little of the shadow theater, must play out their destinies amongst the external relations of the real world. They live or die according to whether they can modify their bodies and/or their instinctive repertoires to keep adapted to a changing environment. Natural selection corrects and regulates their adaptive process. More complex creatures recreate the objects of the world in the shadow theaters of their mind. In that shadow theater a representation of natural selection—looking more than a little like "reinforcement"—acts to correct and regulate the fit of their motor behaviors to the world by allowing something like vicarious trial and error or planning.

As a child grows up it slowly builds and uses its shadow world. It makes external relations into internal relations. This is the essence of cognitive development. Baldwin's (1906) stages of cognitive development are expressions of this idea of development:

To make these three spheres plain to psychologists we may designate them as, first 'biological adaptations' [modifications of structure, of instinct, the correlation of parts, and organic adaptations in general]; second, the reactions in which so-called 'reflex attention' dominates [simple imitation, suggestive accommodation and control, the learning of infants short of voluntary effort]; third, the conscious selection of ends and their pursuit by volition [voluntary attention, effortful action, 'conduct']. These three forms of adaptation are treated in the course of this work under the headings, respectively, of 'Organic Imitation', 'Conscious Imitation', and 'Volition' [pp. 170–171].

Baldwin's 1895 book seems to be a preliminary work in which he contends rather slowly and carefully with fundamental issues. One problem he addresses is that of a meaningful empiricism for genetic study. He gives several examples of his dynamogenic method of research, but they are not given in a very inspirational tone nor do they seem very inspiring. Nevertheless, he is saying in 1895 in a field full of sensory introspectionists that Psychology ought to be studying the structure of children's actions. By 1980 he will look right. But Baldwin, like his good friend William James, was unenthusiastic about the task of developing a psychological laboratory.

Where Baldwin does seem to be motivated in 1895, and where his writing retains depth and flavor even today, is in his analysis of the subtle systematics of behavioral adaptation. He gives much attention to various forms of suggestion in childhood, to the importance of repetition in adaptation, to habit and accommodation, and to kinds of imitation. What he seems to be groping for are the best elementary terms that might be used in setting forth an idea of development based on the progressive sophistication of control over activities. He only begins here his sketch of a child who not only thinks more and knows more as it grows up but who becomes more autonomous and liberated. The full creation of his stage theory of development will emerge later in the four volumes of his *Thought and Things* (Baldwin, 1906–1915).[8]

---

[8]It is interesting to ask where James Mark Baldwin's ideas are carried forward in today's developmental psychology. Lawrence Kohlberg and his students have done developmental psychology a service by keeping Baldwin's name and work alive in contemporary discussion (Broughton, 1981; Broughton & Freeman–Moir, 1982). It is generally recognized now that Baldwin has had a significant influence on Piaget's work. The critical Piaget books on infancy make much use of terminology developed in Baldwin's infant work, and Baldwin (1906–1915) subtitles Volume III of his *Thought and Things* "Genetic Epistemology"—that is, with the general name that Piaget later came to assign to his overall program of inquiry.

But Baldwin's writings hold that the social and the individual completely interpenetrate one another in development. This is not Piagetian nor Kohlbergian. Baldwin repeatedly appeals to a subtle dialectical interplay through which subject becomes object and object becomes subject. Vygotsky's (1978) recently translated Marxist writings best approximate this feature of Baldwin's writings. It must be remembered, of course, that Hegel was a very influential philosopher of development among turn-of-the-century American psychologists who were philosophically inclined, as Baldwin was.

Finally, Baldwin's mature analysis in *Thought and Things* culminates in what he calls *Pancalism,*

SOME COMMENTS ON DEVELOPMENTAL THEORY

We have looked briefly at the late 19th-century theories of cognitive development of George Romanes, Ivan Sechenov, and James Mark Baldwin. Is there
anything that might be useful today in such an historical examination? There are
several things, I think.

First, the three older theories seem to show that you do not need much formal
data about children to formulate the basic ideas of our current stage theories. You
can use everyday and unsystematic observations of children, mixing those with
knowledge about other things (zoology, botany, archaeology, the brain, anthropology, etc.), if you begin with a reasonably strong systematic idea about
what development is.

The theories of Romanes, Sechenov, and Baldwin—and the theories of
Freud, Werner, and Piaget we use currently—do not sit directly on the data of
child development, and they do not ''jeopardize'' in the easy and complete way
that falsificationist tradition says scientific theories ought to. In the first place,
they are abductive and preliminary in the Peircian sense we discussed earlier—
not inductive and conclusive. Many facts and ideas are blended into a consistent
pattern in order to construct such theories. In the second place, the developmental theories are cross-disciplinary and eclectic, sitting on facts and conclusions
coming out of many fields of inquiry. No one scientist can practically contend
with all the data bases they appeal to. Finally, the older theories of development
were not designed to be regulated solely by facts. They were designed to bring
facts into patterns having simplicity, coherence, orderliness, and harmony. Developmental theories are regulated by beauty as well as truth.

THE IDEA OF DEVELOPMENT IN THE 19TH CENTURY

A second point to a look backward is to help developmental psychologists
contend with an idea of development that is both theirs and not theirs. ''Cognitive development'' is historically linked to the ''evolution'' that is central to
biology, the ''development'' that political scientists tell us rich countries have
and poor countries need, the ''modernization'' and ''cultural complexity'' used
by some nowadays to order cultures, and the organicism that some historians see
as organizing and governing the trend of public affairs. ''Cognitive development'' has a cloud of Marxist and psychoanalytic terminological relatives. It
relates to prominent usages of ''progress,'' ''education,'' and ''therapy.''

---

a ''constructive affectivism.'' Our most adequate and complete knowledge of reality comes in
aesthetic contemplation. The writings of contemporary aesthetic philosophers—Ernst Cassirer
(1955), Susan Langer (1942), Nelson Goodman (1976)—best approximate this view of knowledge.
Amongst the writings of contemporary developmental psychologists, only Werner and Kaplan's
(1963) *Symbol Formation* sets forth a conception of development grounded on this view of knowing.

If ideas of development were brought toward children's cognition in the 19th century, where did they come from? Romanes's stages of cognitive development, it will be remembered, were versions of the three logics of August Comte. Sechenov took his stages from Herber Spencer. Baldwin's formulation, more complex and original, still is linked backward by him to Spencer's and Romanes's work.

Auguste Comte and Herbert Spencer both wrote very elaborate and ambitious philosophical systems in the 19th century, and both were widely read and discussed. Auguste Comte set forth his Positivist philosophy in the first half of the 19th century. He wrote, in 1822, *A Plan for the Scientific Works Necessary to Reorganize Society,* between 1830 and 1842 the six volumes of his *Course of Positive Philosophy,* and between 1851 and 1854 the four volumes of his *System of Positive Polity.* Comte ordered all the sciences that give positive knowledge into a genetic series: mathematics, astronomy, physics, chemistry, biology, and sociology. Each science builds upon those before. With the emergence of sociology, science ripens to become an instrument of rational social planning. The positive society is a culmination. Comte argued for a law of three stages through which societies, and branches of human knowledge, must pass during the course of their development. The three stages are the theological or fictitious, the metaphysical or abstract, and the scientific or positive (DeGrange, 1931; Konig, 1968). One hundred years before Comte, Giambattista Vico had argued in his New Science that humans have three natures. One is poetic—creative, imaginative, religious, forming world views. One is heroic—honoring force and valor, creating status and order. One is human—capable of reason, creating understanding. There is an invariant genetic order in which men can contend with the world around them because they must use one nature and then the next and the next. Human history shows a developmental progression of three ages, passing first through the governance of divine law, then heroic law, then the law dictated by human reason. Vico's New Science is sometimes regarded as the beginning point for the human sciences, just as Comte's Positivist philosophy is sometimes characterized as a beginning point of sociology (Caponigri, 1953; Pompa, 1975; White, 1976). It seems clear that in the 18th and 19th centuries many were excited by the idea that history shows a developmental pattern and that human society may be regulated by laws of social development. Burrow (1968), in his study of Victorian social theory, argues that in the 19th century the social sciences were virtually synonymous with the proposal and study of forms of social development.[9]

---

[9]Burrows (1968) says that the idea of social development came to predominate overwhelmingly as "the central concept of nineteenth-century social theory." He argues: "It is often difficult in the nineteenth century to distinguish between sociology and the philosophy of history and, if the central preoccupation of sociology is with discovering laws of social development, this is not surprising [p. 83]." Burrows is writing about Victorian England. Apparently reacting to a similar trend in

Both Vico and Comte said that the stages of human history resembled the stages of growth of a child's mind. It is conceivable that children contributed some ideas to development to the developmental historians. But these early social theorists were not interested simply in pretty patterns or nice coincidences. Most of them believed in a providential history, a history that forcefully sought out a kind of perfection. Spencer said (in Hofstadter, 1955):

> The ultimate development of the ideal man is logically certain—as certain as any conclusion in which we place the most implicit faith; for instance that all men will die . . . Progress, therefore, is not an accident, but a necessity. Instead of civilization being artificial, it is a part of nature; all of a piece with the development of the embryo or the unfolding of a flower [p. 40].

Notice that the perfection of man, the growth of civilization, the development of the embryo, and the unfolding of a flower are all aligned as natural inevitabilities in the Spencer quote. If you believe in a providential history—if you believe that history is trying to "get somewhere"—then you have to have an idea of development. Something-or-other is the end state toward which all history strives. After you specify the end toward which things go, you need to suggest the nature of the mechanisms that act in the here and now to keep things steering toward providence.

As far as end states go, Condorcet, a French mathematician who wrote a developmental history at the time of the French Revolution, proposed equality, freedom, and knowledge. History moves toward equality of rights among men and classes, the universal liberation that this brings, and the full physical, moral, and intellectual perfection of the individual. (One can hear the strains of the "Marseillaise" faintly behind this argument.) Hegel, lecturing on the philosophy of history in Berlin in the early 1820s, said that human history strives toward God, Freedom, Reason, and the State. The several end states of Condorcet and Hegel seem to be a reasonably complete catalogue of the end states proposed in various accounts of providential history in the past.

What are the local mechanisms that act in the here and now to drive history toward its providential destiny? The great motor of history for Hegel, of course, was the dialectical process. Subject and object tend to become one during the course of the historical process. The master incorporates the slave and the slave incorporates the master. Hegel's proposal of a mechanism of history, amended somewhat by Marx and Engels, was to have a very large political influence. But

---

mid-19th-century Germany, Isaiah Berlin (1980) speaks of: "the farrago of metaphysics, social messianism, and personal ardour that constituted the normal matter of the innumerable historico-theological systems with which German universities were at this time [around 1837] flooding the philosophical public [p. 217]." Berlin gives the name *historiosophy* to "the attempt to make history do the work of theology or speculative metaphysics."

the dialectical idea was an abstract and abstruse idea. In general, the developmental historians were better at proposing final causes—end states, goals, design logics, motives, ideas of history—than they were at proposing efficient causes.

In the 1860s and 1870s, there begins a kind of explosive culmination of the movement toward developmental histories. The idea that human history is principled, orderly, and developmental becomes joined with, and grounded upon, the findings in the natural sciences that establish the theory of evolution.[10] Evolutionary theory was not then, and is not now, a completely clear and evidential theory. But it was immensely more clear and evidential than the developmental histories. One could try to move back and forth between biology and history, using facts and ideas derived from the one to shed enlightenment on the other. This is precisely what Herbert Spencer did in the 10 volumes of his *Synthetic Philosophy*. Spencer reviewed enormous quantities of the science and scholarship of his time, ranging from geology to political science. He proposed efficient, here-and-now causal mechanisms in development. His most famous, pervasive, all-embracing efficient cause was, of course, the Development he described in his Development Hypothesis. In his *First Principles* (Spencer, 1888) he gives the following definition of it: "Evolution is an integration of matter and concomitant dissipation of motion; during which the matter passes from an indefinite, incoherent homogeneity to a definite, coherent heterogeneity; and during which the retained motion undergoes a parallel transformation [p. 396]."

---

[10]It is sometimes argued that "Social Darwinism" was a stimulus to "Darwinism"—that is, that historically theories of social development preceded and encouraged the emergence of a biological theory of evolution. However, there are historical reasons for arguing that evolutionary theory was not completely new with Darwin (Mayr, 1972). Both "Darwinism" and "Social Darwinism" antedated Darwin (Gould, 1977; Greene, 1959; Hofstadter, 1955; Lovejoy, 1936).

The explosive event in the 1860s and the 1870s may have been the joining of social developmentalism and biological evolutionism to form the image of a scientific theology. Thomas Huxley, the knight of Evolution, believed that this joining had taken place. Writing on evolution and ethics he said Science was like Cinderella amongst two ugly sisters, Theology and Philosophy. In the essay (quotes taken from Irvine, 1955), he says:

> She lights the fire, sweeps the house, and provides the dinner; and is rewarded by being told that she is a base creature, devoted to low and material interests. But in her garret she has fairy visions out of the ken of the pair of shrews who are quarrelling down stairs . . . . She knows that the safety of morality lies . . . in a real and living belief in that fixed order of nature which sends social disorganisation upon the track of immorality, as surely as it sends physical disease after physical trespasses [p. 315].

Natural order gives a truer morality than men can create. We must combine the spirit of science with the practices of the church.

> And it is to be recollected in view of the apparent discrepancy between men's acts and their rewards that Nature is juster than we. She takes into account what a man brings with him into the world, which human justice cannot do. . . . The absolute justice of the system of things is as clear to me as any scientific fact. The gravitation of sin to sorrow is as certain as that of the earth to the sun [pp. 129–130].

Spencer's Development is a curiously general efficient force. It drives geology, all forms of plant and animal life, the human mind, the shape and form of any number of human customs and institutions, the general shape and form of human history. Some may prefer the parody of Spencer's definition that William James used to offer his classes (Hofstadter, 1955): "Evolution is a change from a nohowish untalkaboutable all-alikeness to a somehowish and in general talkaboutable not-all-alikeness by continuous sticktogetherations and something-elseifications [p. 129]."

The parody was not meant to be kind. James had mixed feelings about Spencer's theory. It is nonetheless an interesting restatement and something of a simplification of the Spencer definition. Something like a simplification of Spencer's principle was set forth in modern times when Werner and Kaplan (1956) offered their orthogenetic principle: "wherever development occurs, it proceeds from a state of relative lack of differentiation to a state of increasing differentiation, articulation, and hierarchic integration [p. 866]." Like Spencer, Werner felt that development was a general efficient force. The data of child development provided an *occasion* for the study of principles of great relevance to human affairs in many ways. Children offer an externalization, an objectification—in everyday language, a way of getting your hands on the idea of development (Kaplan, 1959, 1967).

The ideas of development we deal with today in developmental psychology are, for the most part, modern forms of the ideas of development that were elaborated in the social histories and evolutionary theory of the last two centuries behind developmental psychology. Werner's theory shows resemblances to Spencer's theory. Baldwin's theory shows resemblances to Hegel's theory. His idea that the external relations surrounding the child become reconstituted as internal relations in the child's mind during cognitive development is classically Hegelian. The subject incorporates the object in cognitive development (and, as the physical world surrounding the child gradually holds more and more of the instruments and artifacts of the child, the object incorporates the subject). Did Werner get his ideas from Spencer, Baldwin from Hegel? There are many bridging possibilities between the pairs of men, and it is hard to know. The more interesting question might be whether this package of historical linkages reveals some interesting possibilities for contemporary linkages.

I have elsewhere argued (White, 1976) that a great deal of what we call "developmental theory" is generic, a form of control systems analysis or organizational theory. This point of view is, I think, well-expressed in Kaplan's (1967) paper, "Meditations on Genesis." To recognize this is to recognize the deep relationships of developmental psychology to analytic philosophy (where a notion like "the idea of development" can be spelled out as something more than a marker for real-world phenomena, where the beauty of an idea can be explored) and to a variety of other theories not in developmental psychology. We can give to, and receive from, data bases other than those that exist in developmental psychology. Only a few people today recognize and use the generic nature of developmental theory—Werner (1948), Piaget (1971, 1972), Campbell (1974), Maturana and Varela (1975), Teitelbaum (1977), Brent (in press)—and yet this is the fundamental strength of the theory.

DEVELOPMENT AS THE IDEA OF THE GOOD

There is, finally, one last reason for a reexamination of the roots of our contemporary ideas of development. I mentioned earlier a smell of evangelism in or near the writings of Romanes and Sechenov. You may have thought I was stretching the argument by focusing my discussion first on a few breathless adjectives of one author, and next on a rather frivolous and hastily dropped charge directed at the second. It seems reasonably clear that the developmental theories of history we have been discussing were built with activist and political intentions. This does not have to mean that every single person who wrote such accounts was striving for power. Yet the story of the developmental histories is largely the story of people trying to divine what the good and the providential is in human affairs through an analysis of the systematics of human history. If providential history will reveal its principles to you, then you have made science and scholarship and evidence tell you what the good is. You do not need religion. You have found a source of values that is stronger than faith.[11]

---

[11]Prior to the consolidation of the academic disciplines near the turn of this century, many of those whom we today call philosophers were social activists and reformers. Their philosophies and their psychologies were subordinated to their political interests. Looking back at Hobbes, Locke, Hume, etc. through modern disciplinary lenses, we have a tendency to screen out all but the technical in their work and then to discuss the men as more or less successful technicians. I believe this seriously distorts the history of Psychology, and have elsewhere argued (White, 1978) that the influential ideologies of Comte, Spencer, and Marx in the 19th century look like fulfillments of Sir Francis Bacon's 17th-century prospectus for a *Great Instauration*—a step-by-step renovation of philosophy and the sciences to ground power and government upon true knowledge of nature. A beautiful description of this larger vision is given by Becker (1932).

Could 20th-century psychological science lead to the understanding of human spiritual perfection? Some thought so. In their *Ethics,* John Dewey and James Tufts (1909) argued that the growth of habits, recycled, becomes the growth of morality. The psychologists, they say, give three stages of human conduct: (1) instinctive activity; (2) attention used to direct and control activity through use of anticipatory imagery; (3) habit, a higher-order automatization of attentionally regulated actions (pp. 8–9). All this produces *unmoral* behavior. "To apply this to the moral development we need only to add that the process repeats itself over and over. The starting-point for each later repetition is not the hereditary instinct, but the habits which have been formed" (p. 9).

We arrive by a recursive process at the growth of the moral. The repetitions lead to: "(a) Instinctive or habitual action; (b) Action under the stress of attention, with conscious intervention and reconstruction; (c) Organization of consciously directed conduct into habits and self of a higher order. Character" (pp. 12–13). The ethics book was published as part of Holt's "American Science Series." The books' two authors, one professor of philosophy at Columbia and the other professor of philosophy at Chicago, treat the topic of ethics largely through expositions of contemporary behavioral and social science.

The religious and political aspirations of the great developmental histories of the 19th century—those of Comte, Spencer, and Marx—are reasonably obvious. Comte crowned his lengthy exposition of Positivism with a four-volume "system of positive polity." He sought a humanitarian religion and Thomas Huxley once characterized his doctrine as "Catholicism minus Christianity" (König, 1968). Spencer makes no bones about the ultimate intent of his developmental history. He opens in volume one with an account of what is valid in the social functions of religion, and he proposes to use scientific knowledge to provide something truer in place of the dogmas of religion. He proposes, in short, to use his developmental history to ground that which he offers in the last volumes of his series, principles of ethics. Comte and Spencer used their scholarship to set forth a scientific account of the Good. The enormous vogue both men had suggests that they were listened to and believed by some. Marx was not delicate about his political aspirations. He said in his *Theses on Feuerbach:* "The philosophers have only interpreted the world in different ways. The point is to change it."[12]

The lever of political change for Comte and Spencer and Marx is their idea of development. More generally, for developmental historians and for developmental psychologists—and for developmental political scientists and economists and for developmental educators and for developmental psychiatrists—the idea of development arrived at in a systematic analysis becomes the idea of the Good in the arena of practical affairs. This must logically be the case if one espouses a providential history. If history points the way to what is good, then it is good to help history. If we state the end state toward which history aspires, then we can state an end-state that is a worthy goal of our own efforts. (If the *summum bonum* of child development is formal operations, then it is good to do anything that helps bring about formal operations.) If we can state the mechanism in the here and now that steers things toward providence, then it is good to enhance the activity of that mechanism. (If it is decentration—or active play, or taking the role of the other, or metacognitive activities—that drives a child toward formal operations, then we know what it is good for educators to do with children.)

The idea of development in developmental psychology is a systematic idea, but it is very likely to be treated as an ethical idea. Piaget so treated the idea of development at the beginning of his investment in it (Vidal, 1980). If we look at the emergence of developmental psychology out of its historical context, we see that one thing that was entailed was the hope of building naturalistic ethics that might serve as foundations for secular professions devoted to human salvation and development.

---

[12]An excellent recent treatment of Marx's developmental view of history is given by Gould (1978), who analyzes an early work that appears to be foundational for Marx's entire scheme (Marx, 1973). Marcuse (1941) links Marx's thinking to that of Hegel and, thus, to the broad tradition of universal history writing. Venable (1945) and Meszaros (1970) pay particular attention to the psychological ideas in Marx's ideology.

ACKNOWLEDGMENTS

Some of the historical analysis in this chapter was begun in collaboration with Harold Fishbein several years ago. It is a pleasure to recall our work together and to acknowledge my debt to his digging and his thinking. Alexander Siegel's comments on an earlier draft were very helpful in the preparation of this chapter.

REFERENCES

Baldwin, J. M. *Mental development in the child and the race: Methods and processes*. New York: Macmillan, 1906 (3rd ed., revised), original 1895.

Baldwin, J. M. *Thought and things: A study of the development and meaning of thought, or genetic logic* (4 vols.). New York: Macmillan, 1906–1911; New York: Putnam, 1915.

Becker, C. L. *The heavenly city of the eighteenth-century philosophers*. New Haven: Yale University Press, 1932.

Berlin, I. The life and opinions of Moses Hess. In H. Hardy (Ed.), *Against the current: Essays in the history of ideas*. New York: Viking, 1980.

Brent, S. *Psychological structures and their functions* (Vol. 1), *Formal and developmental aspects*. New York: Springer, in press.

Boring, E. G. *A history of experimental psychology* (2nd ed.). New York: Appleton–Century-Crofts, 1950.

Brainerd, C. J. The stage question in cognitive-development theory. *Behavioral and Brain Sciences*, 1978, *1*, 173–181.

Broughton, J. M. The genetic psychology of James Mark Baldwin. *American Psychologist*, 1981, *36*, 396–407.

Broughton, J. M., & Freeman–Moir, D. J. (Eds.). *The cognitive-developmental psychology of James Mark Baldwin*. Norwood, N.J.: Ablex, 1982.

Burrow, J. W. *Evolution and society: A study in Victorian social theory*. Cambridge, Mass.: Cambridge University Press, 1968.

Campbell, D. T. Evolutionary epistemology. In P. A. Schilpp (Ed.), *The philosophy of Karl Popper*. LaSalle, Ill.: Open Court Publishing, 1974.

Caponigri, A. *Time and idea: The theory of history in Giambattista Vico*. Notre Dame, Ind.: University of Notre Dame Press, 1968 (original 1953).

Cassirer, E. *The philosophy of symbolic forms* (3 vols.). New Haven, Conn.: Yale University Press, 1955.

DeGrange, M. The method of August Comte: Subordination of imagination to observation in the social sciences. In S. A. Rice (Ed.), *Methods in social science: A case book*. Chicago: University of Chicago, 1931.

Dewey, J. & Tufts, J. H. *Ethics*. New York: Holt, 1909.

Fischer, K. W. A theory of cognitive development: The control and construction of hierarchies of skills. *Psychological Review*, 1980, *87*, 477–531.

Frolov, Y. P. *Pavlov and his school: The theory of conditioned reflexes* (transl. C. P. Dutt). London: Kegan, Paul, Trench, Trubner, 1937.

Gelman, R. Cognitive development. *Annual Review of Psychology*, 1978, *29*, 297–322.

Goodman, N. *Languages of art: An approach to a theory of symbols*. Indianapolis: Hackett, 1976.

Greene, J. C. Biology and social theory in the nineteenth century: Auguste Comte and Herbert Spencer. In M. Clagett (Ed.), *Critical problems in the history of science*. Madison: University of Wisconsin Press, 1959.

Gould, C. C. *Marx's social ontology: Individuality and community in Marx's theory of social reality*. Cambridge, Mass.: MIT Press, 1978.

Gould, S. J. *Ontogeny and phylogeny*. Cambridge, Mass.: Belknap Press, 1977.

Hall, G. S. Child study of Clark University: An impending new step. *American Journal of Psychology*, 1903, *14*, 96–106.

Hofstadter, R. *Social Darwinism in American thought* (rev. ed.). Boston: Beacon Press, 1955.

Irvine, W. *Apes, angels, and Victorians: The story of Darwin, Huxley, and evolution.* New York: McGraw–Hill, 1955.

Jerison, H. J. *Evolution of the brain and intelligence.* New York: Academic Press, 1973.

Jerison, H. J. Paleoneurology and the evolution of mind. *Scientific American*, 1976, *234*, 90–101.

Kaplan, B. The study of language in psychiatry: The comparative developmental approach and its application to symbolization and language in psychopathology. In S. Arieti (Ed.), *American handbook of psychiatry* (Vol. 3). New York: Basic Books, 1959.

Kaplan, B. Meditations on genesis. *Human Development*, 1967, *10*, 65–87.

Keil, F. C. Constraints on knowledge and cognitive development. *Psychological Review*, 1981, *88*, 197–227.

Konig, R. August Comte. In D. I. Sills (Ed.), *International Encyclopedia of the social sciences* (Vol. 3). New York: MacMillan, 1968.

Langer, S. *Philosophy in a new key.* Cambridge, Mass.: Harvard University Press, 1942.

Lovejoy, A. O. *The great chain of being.* Cambridge, Mass.: Harvard University Press, 1936.

Marcuse, H. *Reason and revolution: Hegel and the rise of social theory.* New York: Oxford University Press, 1941.

Marx, K. *Grundrisse: Foundations of the critique of political economy* (transl. M. Nicolaus). New York: Vintage Books, 1973.

Maturana, H., & Varela, F. *Autopoietic systems.* Urbana: University of Illinois Biological Computer Laboratory (Report No. 94), September 1, 1975.

Mayr, E. The nature of the Darwinian revolution. *Science*, 1972, *176*, 981–989.

Mészáros, I. *Marx's theory of alienation.* London: The Merlin Press, 1970.

Pascual–Leone, J. A mathematical model for the transition rule in Piaget's development stages. *Acta Psychologica*, 1970, *32*, 301–345.

Pascual–Leone, J. Metasubjective problems of constructive cognition: Forms of knowing and their psychological mechanism. *Canadian Psychological Review*, 1976, *17*, 110–125.

Peirce, C. S. *Collected papers* (6 vols.), C. Hartshorne & P. Weiss (Eds.). Cambridge, Mass.: Belknap Press, 1978.

Piaget, J. *The origins of intelligence in children* (transl. M. Cook). New York: International Universities Press, 1952.

Piaget, J. *The construction of reality in the child* (transl. M. Cook). New York: Basic Books, 1954.

Piaget, J. *Genetic epistemology* (transl. E. Duckworth). New York: Columbia University Press, 1971.

Piaget, J. *The principles of genetic epistemology* (transl. Wolfe Mays). New York: Basic Books, 1972.

Pompa, L. *Vico: A study of the "New Science."* Cambridge, Mass.: Cambridge University Press, 1975.

Romanes, G. J. *Animal intelligence.* New York: Appleton, 1883.

Romanes, G. J. *Mental evolution in animals.* New York: Appleton, 1884.

Romanes, G. J. *Mental evolution in man: Origins of human faculty.* New York: Appleton, 1889.

Ross, D. *G. Stanley Hall: The psychologist as prophet.* Chicago: University of Chicago Press, 1972.

Sears, R. R. *Your ancients revisited: A history of child development.* Chicago: University of Chicago Press, 1975.

Sechenov, I. In A. A. Subkov, (Ed.), *Selected works.* Moscow–Leningrad: State Publishing House for Biological and Medical Literature, 1935.

Sechenov, I. *Autobiographical notes.* Moscow: Publishing House of the Academy of Medical Sciences, USSR, 1952.

Siegel, A. W., & White, S. H. *The child study movement: Early growth and development of the symbolized child*. In H. Reese & L. P. Lippitt (Eds.), *Advances in child development and behavior* (Vol. 17). New York: Academic Press, 1982.

Spencer, H. *A system of synthetic philosophy* (Vol. I). *First principles*. New York: Appleton, 1888.

Spencer, H. *A system of synthetic philosophy* (Vol. V). *The principles of psychology* (Vol. II). New York: Appleton, 1897 (original 1872).

Teitelbaum, P. Levels of integration of the operant. In W. K. Honig & J. E. R. Staddon (Eds.), *Handbook of operant behavior*. Englewood Cliffs, N.J.: Prentice–Hall, 1977.

Tyack, D. B. *The one best system: A history of American urban education*. Cambridge, Mass.: Harvard University Press, 1974.

Venable, V. *Human nature: The Marxian view*. New York: Knopf, 1945.

Vidal, F. *Jean Piaget's conception of morality*. Paper presented at the Tenth Annual Symposium of the Jean Piaget Society, Philadelphia, 1980.

Vygotsky, L. S., Cole, M., John–Steiner, V. Scribner, S. & Souberman E.(Eds.), *Mind in society: The development of higher psychological processes*. Cambridge, Mass.: Harvard University Press, 1978.

Werner, H. *Comparative psychology of mental development*. New York: Science Editions, 1961 (original 1948).

Werner, H., & Kaplan, B. The developmental approach to cognition: Its relevance to the psychological interpretation of anthropological and ethnolinguistic data. *American Anthropologist*, 1956, *58*, 866–880.

Werner, H., & Kaplan, B. *Symbol formation: An organismic-developmental approach to language and the expression of thought*. New York: Wiley, 1963.

White, S. H. Developmental psychology and Vico's concept of universal history. *Social Research*, 1976, *43*, 659–671.

White, S. H. Social proof structures: The dialectic of method and theory in the work of psychology. In N. Datan & H. Reese (Eds.), *Life-span developmental psychology: Dialectical perspectives on experimental research*. New York: Academic Press, 1977.

White, S. H. Psychology in all sorts of places. In R. A. Kasschau & F. S. Kessel (Eds.), *Psychology and society: In search of symbiosis*. New York: Holt, Rinehart, & Winston, 1978.

4

Life-Span Developmental Psychology: Observations on History and Theory Revisited

Paul B. Baltes
Max Planck Institute for Human Development and Education
Berlin, FRG

It is often observed that the field of life-span developmental psychology has emerged during the 1960s and 1970s (Baltes, Reese, & Lipsitt, 1980; Lerner & Busch–Rossnagel, 1981). However, this recent growth of life-span research has been preceded by a lengthy historical gestation of life-span developmental ideas, as documented in a variety of historical chapters concentrating on both Europe and the United States (Charles, 1970; Groffmann, 1970; Lehr, 1980; Reinert, 1976, 1979). The field of adult development and aging has played a pivotal role in this development, most probably because aging is easily conceptualized as an outcome of life history. Eminent psychological gerontologists, such as Pressey, Kuhlen, Havighurst, Shock, Birren, Neugarten, Riegel, Schaie, and Thomae, all, at one point or another, have argued for and contributed to the advancement of life-span developmental conceptions.

Note also that there is an outpouring of life-span work not only in psychology but also in neighboring disciplines such as sociology (Brim & Wheeler, 1966; Clausen, 1972; Elder, 1975; Featherman, 1981; Hill & Mattessich, 1979; Hill & Rodgers, 1964; Kohli, 1978; Riley, 1976, 1979; Riley, Johnson, & Foner, 1972; Rosenmayr, 1978; Van Dusen & Sheldon, 1976). As is true for psychology, a comprehensive history of the life-span or life-course tradition in sociology or other disciplines has not yet been attempted. Efforts in that direction (Featherman, 1981) are promising. They suggest that much could be learned from such a venture, for example, about possible historical linkages between disciplines and about the essential questions and methods associated with a life-span perspective.

The explosion and scientific institutionalization of life-span work in psychology during the post-WW II decades is evident in numerous types of publications.

79

Following earlier contributions by Bayley (1963), Birren (1964), Bühler and Massarik (1968), Erikson (1959), Havighurst (1948), and Neugarten (1969), the 1970s were particularly fertile. The volumes resulting from the West Virginia Conferences on Life-span Developmental Psychology (Baltes & Schaie, 1973a; Datan & Ginsberg, 1975; Datan & Reese, 1977; Goulet & Baltes, 1970; Nesselroade & Reese, 1973; Turner & Reese, 1980) are illustrative and notable examples of life-span work during the last decade.

There are also several handbooks on human development and aging that exhibit a life-span framework. Prior to the 1970s, a German handbook of developmental psychology edited in 1959 by Thomae and a handbook on socialization edited in 1969 by Goslin represented the prologue. Since then, strong life-span perspectives are evident, for instance, in the recently published handbooks on aging (Binstock & Shanas, 1976; Birren & Schaie, 1977) in which about 10 chapters pay explicit tribute to a life-span conception of sociological and psychological aging. Furthermore, there are at least a dozen textbooks or readers on developmental psychology and human development claiming a life-span orientation, conception, or coverage (Baltes, Reese, & Nesselroade, 1977; Birren, Kinney, Schaie, & Woodruff, 1981; Charles & Looft, 1973; CRM, 1971; Craig, 1976; Goldberg & Deutsch, 1977; Hurlock, 1959; Kaluger & Kaluger, 1974; Kastenbaum, 1979; Kuhlen & Thompson, 1963; Lerner & Hultsch, in press; Lerner & Spanier, 1980; Lugo & Hershey, 1974; Mussen, Conger, Kagan, & Geiwitz, 1979; Newman & Newman, 1975; Oerter, 1978; Pikunas, 1976; Pressey & Kuhlen, 1957; Rebelsky, 1975; Turner & Helms, 1979).

Adding to the scientific and professional institutionalization of the field are also research journals (e.g., *Developmental Psychology, Human Development, International Journal of Behavioral Development, Journal of Applied Developmental Psychology*) and research series (e.g., *Life-span Development and Behavior*) that are conceived of as life-span in approach. The institutionalization of a life-span developmental psychology in graduate training is especially relevant. This trend had begun with the earlier commitment to the approach in at least one major university each in Europe (University of Bonn: Thomae) and the United States (University of Chicago: Havighurst, Neugarten). In the 1970s, a similar posture was then adopted in an increasingly larger number of universities, with West Virginia University perhaps playing a further catalytic role. Finally, and perhaps most importantly, results from long-term longitudinal investigations covering extended periods of the life-span are appearing. Research by Block (1971), Elder (1974, 1979), the Sears' (Sears, 1977; Sears & Barbee, 1977), and Schaie (1979) are good examples of the increasing nourishment of life-span developmental psychology by solid empirical work.

A number of neglected questions need to be addressed however. For example, is this explosion in the quantity of life-span work and its institutionalization paralleled by an increasing insight into its historical, theoretical, and methodological foundations? To what degree is this surge of life-span thinking reflected in a change in actual empirical developmental work, data interpretation, and theoretical conception? Moreover, are there any reasons to believe that this recent outpouring is more than a short-lived fad and that we are not dealing with mere rhetoric rather than with a cogent theoretical argument and framework?

One option for addressing these questions is to present a conceptual rationale for life-span developmental psychology and the predominant theoretical orientation associated with it. This would be repetitious because a number of recently published papers with this aim are available (Baltes & Schaie, 1973b; Baltes, Reese, & Lipsitt, 1980; Featherman, 1981; Lerner & Ryff, 1978; Riley, 1979). However, one comment on the meaning of life-span developmental psychology is relevant here for the sake of clarification: The term *life-span* is not intended to imply that chronological age is the primary organizing variable for life-span developmental work. Rather, the primary focus is on developmental processes that attain their salience in a life-span or life-course context. It is important not to commit the fallacy of equating life-span developmental work with age-developmental work because this would result in an extremely limited model of life-span development. Indeed, recent discussions of life-span developmental models (Baltes et al., 1980; Hultsch & Plemons, 1979; Lerner & Ryff, 1978) have emphasized that a life-span orientation suggests conceptions of development that, especially in the latter part of life, go beyond the use of chronological age as an important theoretical variable. Thus, the term *life-span* is not at all intended to communicate a sole concern with age change. Rather, developmental processes occurring throughout life are of major concern. Age changes and age-related explanations represent only one class of ontogenetic change sequences.

The primary goal of this chapter is to place the recent surge of a life-span orientation into a historical perspective by specifying some of its theoretical and methodological underpinnings and by articulating some recurrent themes that may serve as guides in the current period of quantitative explosion. A life-span orientation is surprisingly old in the history of developmental psychology. In fact, it is argued that there are a number of theoretical and methodological themes that have been identified repeatedly throughout its history. These themes may help to explicate and amplify the special role of a developmental approach to the study of behavior and to place in perspective current endeavors in life-span work.

NOTES ON THE HISTORY OF LIFE-SPAN DEVELOPMENTAL PSYCHOLOGY

A number of reviews on historical facets of developmental psychology are available (Birren, 1961a,b; Cairns & Ornstein, 1979; Charles, 1970; Groffmann, 1970; Hofstätter, 1938; Munnichs, 1966b; Reinert, 1976, 1979; Riegel, 1977). Together, they provide much insight into the origins of life-span developmental psychology. Let me, however, begin my notes on the history of life-span developmental psychology by quoting from the preface to a textbook of developmental psychology:

> The author . . . has for many successive years conducted a course in developmental psychology. . . . With the remarkable progress in psychology during those years, two things have happened. The older volumes on genetic psychology have become inadequate. . . . The more recent volumes have been devoted to rather narrow sections of human growth, such as preschool age, adolescence, and senescence . . . . But the general student is interested in the whole career of human life, not merely in its infancy and school days [p. vi, vii].

These statements reflect the search for life-span coverage and are very representative of what many authors of current developmental psychology textbooks maintain. The fact is, however, that these quotations are 50 years old! They are found in the preface to a forgotten, but excellent, textbook by H. L. Hollingworth published in 1927 entitled *Mental Growth and Decline: A Survey of Developmental Psychology*.

The quotations from Hollingworth (1927) illustrate an important though often neglected historical fact. The emergence of life-span developmental psychology is seen as a recent event; this is not true. On the contrary, a life-span view of behavioral development has origins that antedate the emergence of any age-specific developmental speciality, such as child psychology.

The recognition of a strong life-span emphasis in the formative stages of developmental psychology is due largely to a group of European scholars. Review articles by Hofstätter (1938), Groffmann (1970), and particularly a recent *tour de force* historical review by Reinert (1976, 1979) have provided much evidence. These authors have identified at least three major developmental-psychological works of the 18th and 19th centuries advocating an explicit life-span orientation toward the study of human development. These are publications by Tetens in 1777, F. A. Carus in 1808, and Quetelet in 1835 (1838 in German, 1842 in English). Indeed, a careful examination of these heralds of developmental psychology is most educational and humbling. Their works exemplify remarkable depth and scope in theory and methodology.

Early Precursors: Tetens, Carus, and Quetelet

During the recent decades, Johann Nicolaus *Tetens* (1736–1807) has experienced a period of renewed attention, not only because of his early contributions to developmental psychology, but also because of his work on language and language development. A comprehensive bibliography of Tetens' writings is contained in Pfannkuch (1971). In the present context, Tetens' 1777 two-volume effort on *Philosophische Versuche über die menschliche Natur und ihre Ent-*

Joh: Nicolaus Tetens
Könige: Dänischer Conferenz.
Rath Mitglied der Societät der
Wissenschaften zu Copenhagen

gebohren d. 16 September 1736.

John Nicolaus Tetens (1736–1807)

wicklung is especially pertinent. Table 4.1 presents a summary of the content of the second volume of this work to illustrate the wide-ranging scope of Tetens' endeavor.

In his 1777 book Tetens states with much clarity many of the essentials of developmental-psychological thinking. Attending to the entire life-span from conception to death, he addresses questions such as the relationship between nature and environment, the origin and extent of interindividual differences (variation), the degree to which human development can be "perfected," and

TABLE 4.1
Table of Contents of Tetens (1777), Vol. 2: On the Perfectability and
Development of Man[a]

Chapter	Title
1	On the perfectability of human psyche (Seelennatur) and its development in general
2	On the development of the human body
3	On the analogy between the development of psyche (mind) and the development of the body
4	On the differences between men (humans) in their development
5	On the limits of development and the decline of psychological abilities
6	On the progressive development of the human species
7	On the relationship between optimization (Vervollkommnung) of man and his life contentment (Glückseeligkeit)

[a]Translation by author. The second volume (pp. 369–834) is part of the two–volume work entitled *Philosophische Versuche über die menschliche Natur und ihre Entwicklung.*

the extent to which human nature is undergoing progressive development with historical and evolutionary time.

It is for his vision on human development that Reinert (1979) labels Tetens: "a true giant among the precursors of developmental psychology [p. 211]." Reinert goes on to say that, in his opinion: "neither before nor since Tetens has the true program of human developmental psychology been so impressively formulated." One may wonder about this singular place of eminence assigned to Tetens by Reinert. However, a reading of Tetens' original text and also of the recent commentaries that his work on the development of language has received (Pallus, 1966; Pfannkuch, 1971) support Reinert's conclusion. Although his book is primarily speculative in its data base, Tetens emphasized the need for empirical methodology as the vehicle by which scientific knowledge about human development and psychology can be obtained. In fact, it is occasionally argued (Pallus, 1966) that Tetens' role for German psychology was somewhat equivalent to that of the British empiricists (e.g., Locke) for Anglo-American psychology, and moreover, that he has been a forerunner of a dialectical-materialistic approach in the behavioral and social sciences.

To illustrate Tetens' avant-garde views, one example from his discussion of aging as a component of life-long development should suffice. In his section on the limits and the decline of mental abilities (pp. 729ff), Tetens posits and elaborates on three fundamental issues dealing with the nature and explanation of psychological aging: (1) the question of whether performance decrement as observed in older persons necessarily indexes decline or whether certain aspects of apparent performance decrement can be seen instead as evidence for further development; (2) the question of to what degree performance decrement in older persons is a function of "nonuse" (disuse) of functions; and (3) whether decline in old age should be conceptualized as regression, that is, as a process that occurs in reverse order from that observed in the first half of life. Throughout, and this is much in line with modern discussions (Labouvie–Vief, 1980), Tetens uses concrete examples such as memory functioning to illustrate these issues. In the case of memory, for example, he emphasizes that memory decrement in elderly persons could be seen as adaptive and that a major problem in memory performance of older persons is not one of memory trace but one of retrieval, of reaching the "enveloped" memory material. Furthermore, here and in other areas of human development, Tetens appears committed to a view that is essentially contextual, differential, concerned with plasticity, and with the active role that individuals play as producers of their own development. As a theoretical orientation, Tetens' posture is in convergence with current perspectives on life-span development (see Baltes et al., 1980; Lerner & Busch–Rossnagel, 1981, for reviews).

Friedrich August *Carus* (1770–1808), a relative of the well-known romanticist Carl Gustav Carus (Reinert, 1979), was another German philosopher and developmental psychologist living around the turn of the 19th century who deserves much attention. Because he died young, Carus' work was published posthumously and, for the most part, his contribution was not widely recognized in the history of psychology.

In the second volume of his two-volume work, *Psychology,* published in 1808 and entitled *Special Psychology,* one finds that Carus, like Tetens, treats psychological development as a life-long affair and conceptualizes it very broadly. Of

Friedrich August Carus (1770–1808)

interest here is, for example, his effort to distinguish between a "general age-oriented science" and a "specialized age-oriented science." The former is akin to a nomothetic approach, whereas the latter permits the description and explanation of interindividual differences in development and of the conditions under which such differential development comes about. Among these conditions is living in a particular historical time. A specialized age-oriented science deals with the individual as he (trans. by author): "could be, really is, or usually is under special external conditions and circumstances. The conditions and modifications are either . . . gender-related . . . or related to different conditions of education, work, and social systems [p. 36–37]."

Carus identifies four periods of the life-span: childhood, youth, adult(man)hood, and senescence ("Greisenalter"). To depict Carus' theoretical stance, his views of psychological aging can be used again as an illustration. He is not only concerned with aging as decline but also as a stage of progression. For example, Carus emphasized that if one were to take a "teleological view of the developmental periods," one should expect to find in old age "the most perfect human being [p. 79]." He goes on to state that "age as senescence denotes the last and highest stage of development, maturity." Again, as was true for Tetens, the convergence between Carus' concern for differential development, including the systemic interplay between features of progression and decline during life-span development, and current conceptions of the same issue is astonishing. His position on life-span development, as being relative to contingent and modifying circumstances, is highly similar to current fashionable research approaches that emphasize variability and plasticity. Moreover, Carus' notions on the possibly progressive features of human aging (despite the apparent biological deterioration of elderly persons) bear much resemblance to conceptions such as those of Erikson and Jung, as well as to a view representing aging as a process of specialization and/or "selective optimization and compensation [Baltes & Baltes, 1980; Brent, 1978; Labouvie–Vief, 1980]."

Adolphe *Quetelet* (1796–1874), a Belgian statistician–demographer, is the third precursor who deserves much historical credit. As already suggested in 1938 by Hofstätter, Quetelet's (1842) volume, *A Treatise on Man and the Development of his Faculties,* merits particular attention because of its comprehensiveness and methodological quality.

Quetelet's book is full of empirical data covering the entire life course and considering a host of demographic (birth, fecundity, mortality), physical (stature, weight, height, strength, swiftness, respiration), and psychological variables (crime, morality, intellectual qualities). Quetelet's theoretical conceptions are equally impressive for his joint concern for general developmental laws and the import of sociohistorical change. Last, but not least, Quetelet's nascent insights into methodological issues in the study of development are most astonishing. For example, close to 150 years ago, Quetelet, when evaluating his empirical findings, carefully enumerated a large number of problems in research

Adolphe Quetelet (1796–1874) (From the collection of David Eugene Smith.)

design. Thus, Quetelet (1842) identified the notion of critical periods in the life-span (pp. 31, 57), elaborated the effects of period-specific historical events on age functions (see also Süssmilch, 1741), suggested the need for multiple-period (rather than time-specific) data in the study of age changes (pp. 33, 97–100), touched on salient issues in measurement validity and equivalence (pp. 72–74), and drew attention to selective survival effects (pp. 62–63).

In many respects, Quetelet presented not only the first comprehensive account of life-span developmental findings but also the first glimpse of many issues in developmental research methodology. Unfortunately, as was true by and large for Tetens and Carus, his contributions to developmental psychology lay dormant for more than 100 years.

20th-Century Precursors

It is beyond the scope of this manuscript to elucidate why the late 19th century and early 20th century did not see a continuation of this early ascendance of a life-span conception of developmental psychology as articulated in the works of Tetens, F. A. Carus, and Quetelet. Except for rare cases, the dominant focus in the study of behavioral development, both in Europe and the United States, became clearly that of child development and child psychology. Why? Among the possible reasons is that the intellectual and societal climate of the 19th century (Cairns & Ornstein, 1979; Dixon, 1982) was not supportive. For example, the 19th-century interest in examining the linkage between evolution and ontogeny set the stage for a predominant biological treatment of human development. Furthermore, one could argue that an exposition of the interconnection between biological and psychological development suggested also a focus on the early phases of life. Finally, there were likely during the 19th-century conditions of societal and institutional structure (e.g., relatively short span of education, small proportion of older persons in population) that did not demand a particular emphasis on the second half of life. It will take much careful historical work, however, in order to achieve a better understanding of whether and why the early life-span developmental ideas did not have a more immediate impact on the work of developmental psychologists.

The relative neglect of life-span thinking continued into the 20th century. In the early decades of the 20th century, occasional contributions to an understanding of all stages of the human life-span appeared, including those that resulted in the establishment of the field of gerontology (Hall, 1922; for reviews see Birren, 1961a,b; Freeman, 1979; Lehr, 1980; Munnichs, 1966b; Riegel, 1977). Gerontology is particularly prone to suggest a life-span conception because of its concern with life processes that lead to aging. However, with one notable exception it was not until the late 1920s and 1930s that a concerted effort to develop an integrative view of life-span development was again attempted. The early 20th-century exception is a largely unknown review article by Edmund Clark Sanford published in 1902 in the *American Journal of Psychology* with the title "Mental Growth and Decay." In this article, Sanford (1902) treats development as a continuous process from birth to death, applying this view of development to: "the course of mental development from the first beginnings of mind . . . at birth . . . to old age [p. 426]."[1]

In the third and fourth decades of the 20th century, there is evidence of an increasing concern for issues of life-span development. Three books in particular mark the reappearance of a life-span conception: Hollingworth (1927), Charlotte Bühler (1933), and the coauthored volume by Pressey, Janney, and Kuhlen (1939). The 1927 text by Hollingworth, although the earliest of the three, is perhaps the least known. Each of these books is inherently life-span developmental in that the authors do not simply present an accumulation of age-specific information (infancy, childhood, adolescence, etc.) but instead attempt also to articulate developmental processes that attain their significance in a life-span framework. It is interesting that, although these three books were published within a dozen years of each other, they exhibit more or less complete independence in citation and practically no reference to their 19th-century precursors (Charlotte Bühler makes a reference to F. A. Carus in a footnote). This is particularly surprising in the case of the Pressey et al. book, which did not acknowledge the 1927 American text by Hollingworth but acknowledged Charlotte Bühler's 1933 German work.

In any case, each of these three books is unique and quite remarkable in the conception and in-depth treatment of life-span developmental events and processes. Similar to Quetelet's early 1835 work, and also to the approach of Tetens and Carus, the Hollingworth (1927) and Pressey et al. (1939) books especially present a basic conception of human development that is empirical, process oriented, multidimensional, multidirectional, contextual, and clearly cognizant of the impact of social change and ecological contingencies. For example, Hollingworth (1927, p. 326; see also Figure 1B, this chapter) contains a chart that summarizes the complexity of life-span development in a format that is standing the test of modern times. Furthermore, Pressey and his co-workers' rich exposition of the macro and microlevel "conditions and circumstances of life," of the embeddedness of human development in a changing culture, and their concern with real-life behaviors represent a powerful forerunner of what is now termed an ecological (Bronfenbrenner, 1977), dialectical-contextual (Datan & Reese, 1977; Lerner & Busch–Rossnagel, 1981; Riegel, 1976a,b), or external-validity (Hultsch & Hickey, 1978) orientation. Pressey and his co-workers' empirical data may lack precision; however, their basic theoretical orientation is amazingly

---

[1]A quote from Browning is often used in gerontological writings to communicate an optimistic view of behavior change in aging and the need for a life-span conception of aging. Browning makes Rabbi Ben Ezra say: "Grow old along with me! The best is yet to be. The last of life, for which the first was made." Sanford (1902, p. 448) appears to be the first to have used Browning's quote.

similar to what the current trends in developmental psychology appear to be (i.e., a movement toward models of development that are nonpersonological, contextualistic, and multilinear).

The fact that practically all the historical marker publications dealing with a life-span orientation present a very explicit concern with what are now seen as contemporary trends is a noteworthy situation in my view. This is especially remarkable because the cross-references in these works are so few. It indicates that the involvement of current life-span researchers in such themes as development-specific methodology, issues of developmental paradigms, cohort effects, social change, and other macrolevel features might be intrinsic to a life-span orientation rather than a reflection of the personal interest of the individual researchers. In fact, it is this hitherto unrecognized historical continuity in ideas and issues that is the focus of the remainder of this chapter.

RECURRENT THEMES IN LIFE-SPAN DEVELOPMENTAL THEORY

What are some of the current themes in life-span developmental theory and research that exhibit historical continuity? Moreover, what are some of the reasons why I judge the recurrence of these themes to be significant for an evaluation of their theoretical power? Four themes are discussed as illustrative examples.

It becomes evident that each of the themes covered has achieved a high degree of articulation and resolution primarily because studying human development from a life-span perspective stretches the conceptual boundaries of the developmental approach (Baltes et al., 1980; Brim & Kagan, 1980). Life-span process extend over long time periods; they involve explanatory mechanisms requiring an explicit concern for distal causality and developmental discontinuity. These extreme conditions of life-span research are apt to exemplify and magnify the basic rationale and foundation of developmental psychology. These extreme conditions, however, also exemplify the limits and boundaries that an uncritical use of the developmental orientation might confront.

Reformulating the Concept of Development

Most of the publications aimed at identifying the key features of life-span developmental research (Baltes et al., 1980; Bayley, 1963; Brim & Wheeler, 1966; Elder, 1975; Labouvie–Vief & Chandler, 1978; Lerner & Ryff, 1978; Neugarten, 1969; Schaie & Willis, 1978, Thomae, 1979) emphasize that the traditional concept of development needs expansion or modification when applied to life-span change. Typically, it is argued that the developmental "growth" concept borrowed from biology, whereas useful for some purposes, has some features that are inappropriate or too restrictive for the study of ontogenetic change in a life-span framework. Most historical forerunners, with the possible exception of Charlotte Bühler, also rejected implicitly the application of simple biological growth models as good representations of life-span change. This is particularly true for Quetelet (1835), Hollingworth (1927), and Pressey et al. (1939) but also consistent with the early writings of Tetens and Carus.

The Definition of Development

Let me illustrate this argument in greater detail. Traditionally, conceptions of developmental change (Harris, 1957; Lerner, 1976; Wohlwill, 1973) have focused on defining behavioral change as development if it manifests characteristics of: (1) sequentiality; (2) unidirectionality, (3) an end state; (4) irreversibility; (5) qualitative-structural transformation, and (6) universality. This definitional position has much conceptual strength and good support from biological approaches to child development, especially maturational-personological ones.[2] Research on life-span development in a variety of areas, however, most notably cognitive and social development, has resulted in the conclusion that such a conception of development is unduly restrictive (Baltes & Willis, 1977; Brim & Kagan, 1980).

During the recent decades in the United States, dissatisfaction with the aforementioned definition of development was probably first expressed in Havighurst's (1948) concept of developmental tasks and the contention of several gerontologists (see also Benedict, 1938; Birren, 1964; Neugarten, 1969) that there is much discontinuity between child development and the remainder of the life span. Similarly, in the extensive German literature on life-span development after World War II (for reviews, see Lehr, 1972; Löwe, 1977; Thomae, 1959, 1979), it has been consistently argued that "one-factor" (biological) and unidimensional (growth–decline) conceptions of life-span development are inappropriate. On the contrary, German writers have espoused a position that includes multidimensionality, multidirectionality, and discontinuity as key features of any theory of human development through the life span.

Figures 4.1A and B are taken from Baltes and Willis (1979). They illustrate a

---

[2]Child development as a field represents a rather diversified set of approaches, some of which (e.g., social learning) do not follow the biological growth-oriented perspective to the degree described in this section. Therefore, it needs to be recognized that the present discussion, for heuristic purposes, is an oversimplification. The implication is that the requirements outlined for appropriate life-span models of development are similar more to some than to other models of child development. For instance, a cognitive-structural model of development (Piaget, etc.) represents an extreme point of contrast. A similar note of caution applies to the discussion of biological growth models. The intent here is not to summarily classify all developmental biologists as advocates of a simple maturational-personological growth model. This would be inappropriate (Gollin, 1981; Lerner, 1976). However, it is maintained that this conception historically has been extremely influential.

view of development that is more complex than those represented in simple cumulative and unidirectional conceptions. The upper part of Fig. 4.1A depicts the notion that interindividual variability in behavior increases as life-span change evolves.[3] Furthermore, the lower part of Fig. 4.1A suggests that life-span changes can be rather diverse in nature: Multidimensionality and multidirectionality of behavior-change processes are frequent outcomes.

Fig. 4.1B portrays the further complexity of life-span development. Besides the notions of large interindividual differences, multidimensionality, and multidirectionality (Fig. 4.1A), it shows graphically the possible discontinuity due to life-course grading (Neugarten, 1969) and represents the life course as a series of developmental functions that are only partially connected or continuous. Behavior-change processes in life-span development do not always extend across the entire life-span nor are they always outcomes of continuous influences and processes. Thus, behavior-change processes can differ in terms of onset, duration, and termination when charted in the framework of the life course. Moreover, as illustrated in Havighurst's (1948) formulation of developmental tasks, novel behavior-change processes can emerge at many points in the life span, including old age.

Among current research, the area of intellectual functioning is perhaps the best example to support the views on development expressed in Fig. 4.1. Here, a number of researchers (Baltes & Schaie, 1976; Baltes & Willis, 1979, 1982; Labouvie–Vief, 1980; Labouvie–Vief & Chandler, 1978; Riegel, 1973b) have argued that life-span intellectual development is not so much a unidirectional continuation of childhood intelligence with universal sequences. Rather, it evidences features of multilinearity, multidimensionality, large interindividual differences, and much contextually based plasticity. Evidence on cohort effects, differential change functions for distinct dimensions of intelligence, and sensitivity to intervention programs in the elderly support, in concert, such a conclusion.

As researchers consider development after childhood, then, there is a need for a conception of development that includes the traditional growth-oriented views of development as one important but special class of developmental phenomena. A more comprehensive taxonomy of developmental-change models is needed to permit us to go beyond the constraints specified by our early colleagues in biology and embraced by many developmentalists. For the most part, we do not yet have a good grasp of what the salient behavior dimensions for life-span developmental models are. However, it appears that restricting developmental

---

[3]Although the evidence is less clear, it may be possible to argue that an age-correlated increase in interindividual differences is paralled by an age-correlated decrease in intraindividual variability (plasticity). As to the concepts of multidirectionality, multilinearity, and multidimensionality, reference to Gollin (1981) is helpful. Reviewing evidence from developmental psychobiology, he expresses similar views in articulating what he calls a "multimodal-polyphasic" model of development.

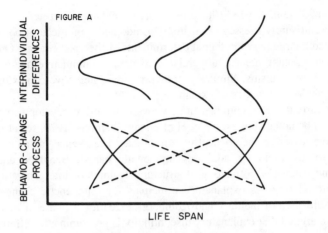

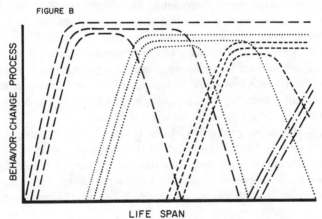

FIG. 4.1.   Selective examples of life-span developmental processes: Fig. 4.1A illustrates multidimensionality, multidirectionality, and age-correlated increases in interindividual variability. Figure 4.1B summarizes notions of life-course grading and discontinuity. Developmental functions (behavior-change processes) differ in terms of onset, duration, and termination when charted in the framework of the life course; moreover, they involve both quantitative and qualitative aspects of change (from Baltes & Willis, 1979).

events to those that have the features of a biological growth concept of development is not desirable (see also Gollin, 1981).

The Explanation of Development

This expansion or modification of a monolithic concept of development is important in answering not only the descriptive question: What does development look like?; it also applies to its explanatory counterpart: Where does development come from? Again, the 18–19th-century precursors such as Tetens, Carus, and Quetelet, and surely Pressey et al. in 1939, adopted a multicausal position and enumerated a large list of potential determinants of life-span change. Only some of the determinants are usefully related to simply cumulative age-associated factors and mechanisms. Similarly, they espoused interactive-contextual rather than personological modes of explanation.

In the current scene, commensurate views in regard to developmental explanations can be noted. For example, Hultsch and Plemons (1979; see also Filipp, 1981) have reviewed the concept of "significant life events" as an organizing explanatory principle for adult-developmental change; Bengtson and Black (1973) and Riley (1976) have used structural features of intergenerational and age-cohort relations as explanatory principles for ontogenetic change; Reese (1976) in the area of memory and Kohlberg (1973) for the case of moral judgment have argued that explanatory discontinuity is predominant. Different models (e.g., mechanistic versus organismic) and combinations of developmental explanation become attractive in that they can account for developmental changes at different segments of the life span. As a final example, Labouvie–Vief's (1977, 1980) review of cognitive development through the life span and suggestions for future theory emphasized the need for alternative conceptions of intelligence that would include multilinear and contextual explanatory features, rather than only the traditional models that have emphasized simple cumulative explanations based on invariant mechanisms.

Figure 4.2 summarizes one model that is aimed at representing the kind of multicausal view necessary to account for the complexity of life-span development. The scheme outlined postulates three major sets of antecedent factors influencing and codetermining individual development: normative age-graded, normative history-graded, and non-normative life events. The three sets of influ-

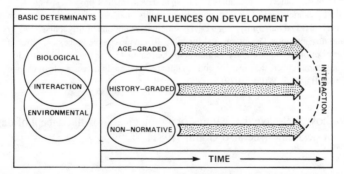

FIG. 4.2.   Three systems of influences regulate the nature of life-span development: ontogenetic (age-graded), evolutionary (history-graded), and non-normative. Further explanation of the figure is contained in Baltes, Cornelius, and Nesselroade (1979).

ences interact in the production of developmental change processes. The scheme outlined does not represent a theory of development. It is a heuristic device aimed at generating a new set of coordinated questions about the causes of life-span development. Note also that the term *normative* is used not in a prescriptive sense but rather as a descriptive term specifying statistical frequency of occurrence and covariation.

Normative age-graded influences refer to biological and environmental determinants exhibiting a high correlation with chronological age. They are the ones usually considered in traditional developmental psychology. Examples of such age-graded influences include processes of biological maturation and socialization when the latter is viewed as consisting of the fairly universal acquisition of a series of age-correlated roles or competencies.

Normative history-graded influences consist of fairly general events or event patterns experienced by a given cultural unit in connection with biosocial change, for example, as evidenced by cohort effects (Baltes, Cornelius, & Nesselroade, 1978). As was true for normative age-graded influences, history-graded influences can involve both environmental and biological characteristics. Such biosocial change effects vary with historical time and can produce unique cohort-related constellations of influences (Elder, 1979; Riley, 1976).

Non-normative influences on life-span development refer to environmental and biological determinants that, although significant in their effect on individual life histories, are not general. They do not occur for everyone nor do they necessarily occur in easily discernible and invariant sequences or patterns. Events and event patterns related to idiosyncratic life experiences (migration, winning in a lottery, etc.) or to certain features of occupational careers (unemployment), family life (divorce, death of a significant other), or health (serious but unexpected sickness) for examples.

Figure 4.2 suggests that these three sets of influences interact with each other and that individual development occurs within their context. The arrows to the right also indicate that these influences accumulate in their effects and may change over time. It is also important to recognize that there is a convergence between the complexity of life-span development on the descriptive level depicted in Fig. 4.1 and the multicausal system of influences postulated in Fig. 4.2. This is plausible because diversity and discontinuity in the patterning of influences (in terms of content, sequencing, duration, patterning, etc.) are prerequisites for diversity in developmental outcomes.

Furthermore, it might be useful to speculate about the relative significance of age-graded, history-graded, and non-normative influences on development at varying points in the life span or on a given behavior-change process. For instance, one could hypothesize that age-graded influences are primarily important in child development and perhaps in advanced aging, whereas history-graded and non-normative influences are relatively more dominant influence systems in early and middle adulthood. Such a *differential life profile* of the relative magnitude of the influence systems would explain why much work in child development has been focused on age-graded influences, whereas the reverse has been true for recent work in adult development (Hultsch & Plemons, 1979). A further discussion of why and how the three systems of influence may exhibit differential life profiles, in terms of their relative impact on development, is contained in Baltes et al. (1980).

In short, when the task is descriptive identification of development, a biological growth concept of development and a simple continuity view of development, perhaps predominant in the early 20th-century work of developmental psychologists, are being recognized increasingly as special cases or subclasses of a larger category of developmental phenomena. Moreover, when the task is developmental explanation, simple personological and cumulative forms are judged to be of restricted value. These perspectives are in accord with the basic view espoused by historical proponents of a life-span approach.

Some Caveats on Pluralism in Definition and Explanation

The interest of life-span developmentalists in formulating a pluralistic conception of development has potential drawbacks. For theoretical reasons, there is not only promise in postulating a conception that is reflective of interindividual variability, intraindividual plasticity, multidimensionality, and multidirectionality, but also caution or even despair. Caution and critical reflection about a pluralistic conception arise because such a conception may endanger the usefulness of a developmental approach (Baltes & Baltes, 1980; Montada, 1979).

Thus, whereas the trend toward complex, multilinear, and multivariate models of development is likely to be necessary, it is imperative to be aware of potential dangers that may result from overgeneralizing this trend. For example, it would be unwise to let this expansion of the concept of development evolve into a total lack of specificity (i.e., of equating any behavioral change with developmental change). Indeed, it will be important to specify some minimum definitional criteria or boundaries so that the uniqueness of a developmental orientation is not lost in toto. This concern applies both to the descriptive characteristics of development as well as to its explanation.

Consider, for instance, the question of defining what constitutes development on the descriptive level discussed previously. Which of the characteristics mentioned before (sequentiality, unidirectionality, end state, irreversibility, qualitative-structural transformation, universality) is one willing to delete or to modify in order to capture pluralism in life-span development? The decision about this is likely to vary depending on content. However, if one were to consider any behavior change as development, the paradigmatic strength of a developmental approach (Baltes, Reese, & Nesselroade, 1977; McCall, 1977; Wohlwill, 1973) would be lost entirely. In other words, some of the characteristics that delineate which change is development will need to be maintained, though in varying combinations, as one attempts to formulate alternative models.

There are similar issues of caution dealing with the explanatory level of developmental analysis. Consider the logical status of each of the three influence systems mentioned (age-grade, history-graded, non-normative) and their role in formulating appropriate research paradigms. Even though each of these systems is likely to operate during development, they do not lend themselves equally well to a developmental process analysis from a psychological point of view, nor is it imperative that all are considered in a concrete research situation.

In the case of non-normative life events, for example, such a conception would only be amenable to a developmental explication if the nature and consequences of non-normative life events either varied to some degree as a function of developmental state, or if a behavior-change theory of chance encounters and life paths can be articulated (Bandura, 1982). Baltes, Cornelius, and Nesselroade (1979) have made similar observations on the logical status that history-graded cohort effects may hold in constructing explanatory developmental theory. They distinguished among four prototypical treatments of cohort effects: error, disturbance, quantitative variation, and theoretical process. Each of these treatments is useful in principle. It is not advisable, however, to elevate one prototypical treatment to a dominant position (e.g., viewing cohort variations as an ubiquitous process associated with qualitative differences in functioning) or to make cohort variation an important and ubiquitous feature of any developmental theory. Riegel (1973a, 1976a,b), for example, tended to do this when deriving from cohort effects the need for a "full-blown" dialectical analysis. Yet, an overeager use and expansive formulation of a dialectical paradigm has its methodological drawbacks (Baltes & Cornelius, 1977). Thus, it is important to recognize under which conditions one or the other type of cohort definition and explication is useful. It may very well be that treating cohort as a theoretical process variable is for developmental psychologist the exception rather than the rule (see also McCall, 1977).

These caveats on the definition and explanation of development are not intended to downgrade the benefits resulting from the quest for a more pluralistic and comprehensive conception of development advanced by life-span developmentalists. The intent is to protect the strength of a developmental approach from excessive and eclectic pluralism and to continue the dialogue about how an appropriate taxonomy of developmental-change processes can be achieved (see also Van den Daele, 1974; Dixon & Nesselroade, this volume; Gollin, 1981; Toulmin, 1981). In the search for a pluralistic conception of development, it is also likely that different disciplines (anthropology, psychology, sociology, etc.) will approach the task of defining and explaining development in different ways. For example, whereas psychologists may opt not to treat cohort variation in many cases as an index for qualitative differences in functioning, sociologists (Elder, 1979) may generally prefer to concentrate on cohort variation as a central process to be explained. On the one hand, then, it does not appear useful for a life-span developmentalist to be monolithic about how development should look and how a developmental analysis should proceed. On the other hand, this openness should not be used as a justification for lack of precision.[4]

Expanding the Scope of Developmental Constructs

The expansion of the concept of development is paralleled by an expansion of the substance of developmental constructs. A life-span approach tends to draw attention to important but neglected classes of developmental behavior. Again, historical forerunners, such as Tetens (1777), Quetelet (1835), and Pressey et al. (1939), had already proposed a much larger array of substantive areas to be the province of developmental psychology than is evidenced in the territory claimed by many standard contemporary textbooks. In Pressey's and his co-workers' 1939 text, for example, such areas as work, occupation, leisure, and family life were given much more prominent consideration than a topical review of developmental psychology (especially of the child-developmental genre) of recent decades would indicate.

The expansion of classes of developmental behavior suggested by life-span research follows in principle two directions. One is to expand a specific construct to include a life-span perspective; the other is to delineate classes of behavior that researchers in age-specific fields, such as child development, could easily overlook.

Let me use attachment as an example of the first strategy, where the expansion in the scope of a construct is likely to occur when conceptualized in a life-span framework. As discussed recently by Lerner and Ryff (1978; see also Hartup & Lempers, 1973), attachment behaviors do not occur only in early life in the context of parent–child relations. Attachments may be developed on many occasions in the life span, such as in the formation and transformation of adolescent and adult friendships; in occupational settings; in family systems such as marriage, divorce, or remarriage; or associated with the death of spouses and friends. As soon as the life-span nature of attachments is recognized, it becomes apparent that the methodology and theory of attachment needs expansion in descriptive and explanatory scope. Moreover, a life-span perspective of attachment makes it apparent that studying the acquisition of attachments is only one significant feature. Attachment behaviors are likely to undergo many subsequent transformations involving not only acquisition but also aspects of maintenance,

---

[4]Some of Kaplan's (this volume) critical observations on life-span developmental psychology can be understood in the context of this section. Kaplan focuses on the problems that are generated if one decides to take a more pluralistic view of development than is true for traditional genetic structuralism or for other conceptions that have much historical linkage to developmental biology and Gestalt psychology, such as is true for Wernerian developmental theory (see also Gollin, 1981; Toulmin, 1981).

dissolution, and transfer. Similar expansive perspectives may be applied to other constructs such as achievement motivation, love, self-concept, or the development of life ideologies. In the case of achievement motivation, for example, it has been suggested that the traditional focus on childhood acquisition needs to be supplemented by mid-life behavior-change studies aimed at clarifying the maintenance (or extinction) of achievement motivation and its transformation into alternative behavior constructs required for successful life adjustment during adulthood.

The second strategy associated with expanding the scope of developmental constructs (i.e., identifying neglected classes of developmental behavior through use of a life-span perspective) is easily evident in classical research on the nature of life biographies or life histories (Bühler, 1933; Dollard, 1949). In life-history research, Elder (1977, 1979) has recently provided a comprehensive and insightful review of the need for temporal constructs aimed at delineating the social course of lives. This strategy of identifying novel classes of behavior is also illustrated by some research in adult development and aging. Work by Clayton (1982, in press; Clayton & Birren, 1980) on wisdom; Munnichs (1966a) and Marshall (1975) on finitude; Bortner and Hultsch (1974) on time perspective; Brim (1974) on the sense of personal control over one's life and on life crises (Brim, 1976a, 1976b); Neugarten, Havighurst, Lowenthal–Fiske, and Chiriboga on life styles (Neugarten, 1964; Lowenthal, Thurnher, Chiriboga, & Associates, 1975); or Bengtson and Black (1973) on generational relations are all examples where somewhat new classes of developmental behavior have been identified. In a simple age-specific approach, particularly when oriented toward childhood, one could easily overlook such constructs. These constructs acquire immediate saliency, however, when a life-span perspective is adopted as a guiding principle.

Linking Ontogenetic and Biocultural Change

Another theme of a life-span orientation emerging from both a historical review and the current research scene is the recognition that individuals develop in a changing biocultural context. Research on cohort effects and on intergenerational relations is an example. This theme implies that the study of development must deal with at least two streams of interactive changing systems: the individual and society broadly defined, or ontogeny and biocultural evolution (Baltes, 1968; Baltes, Cornelius, & Nesselroade, 1978; Elder, 1975, 1979; Neugarten & Datan, 1973; Riegel, 1976a,b; Riley, 1976; Schaie, 1965, 1979; Van Dusen & Sheldon, 1976). The focus on age-graded and history-graded influences in Fig. 4.2 already has indicated a concern with linking individual and biosocial change. Again, it is the extreme demands of a life-span developmental perspective that accentuate this theme. When long-term processes are the focal concern, the assumption of an invariant biocultural or ecological context is generally not a fruitful one.

The role of historical change in the study of individual development can take several forms and may vary according to conceptual beliefs in a given research area. The example given earlier, namely, the different ways of treating the cohort variable, is illustrative. None of the strategies possible for conceptualizing cohort (error, historical disturbance, etc.) is true or false. A life-span approach, however, because of its extension in both individual and historical time (Neugarten & Datan, 1973), makes it less likely that a history-irrelevant or error-type approach would be the predominant option.

It is again impressive to see how our historical forerunners have forcefully tackled this issue. Both Tetens' and Carus' concern for the role of historical conditions has been mentioned already. Similarly, Quetelet in 1835 extensively discussed the roles of evolutionary change and historical periods as modifiers of specific age-developmental functions. Furthermore, he provided a lengthy discussion of conditions under which it would be possible to discern in a changing world what he called "general developmental laws." General developmental laws, as defined by Quetelet (1835), transcend the perturbations created by period-specific effects. Quetelet's view on general developmental laws, incidentally, is similar to Wohlwill's (1973) conceptualization of developmental functions.

The same is true for Quetelet's successors in the history of life-span developmental psychology. Thus, Hollingworth (1927, p. 34) is apparently the first American to have examined intensively the relative advantages of cross-sectional and longitudinal methods. Moreover, he does this in the context of two types of change: individual and societal-institutional. Furthermore, the issue of historical-cultural change is paramount in the 1939 textbook of Pressey, Janney, and Kuhlen. They devote considerable attention to an elaboration of the effects of the changing conditions of the macrocultural context on the nature of human development throughout the life span. Thus, it is not surprising that one of the co-authors, R. B. Kuhlen (1940, 1963), wrote in 1940 the perhaps classical historical paper on cohort effects in psychology and thereby antedated in principle the methodological work of many present investigators.

In short, there is an impressive continuity evident in life-span writings on the relationship between individual and biocultural change. An understanding of current discussions about the meaning and import of cohort effects is greatly aided by a historical perspective. For example, it helps to separate arguments regarding the import of cohort effects for developmental theory from relatively trivial questions concerning the empirical magnitude of cohort effects (Baltes & Schaie, 1976, and Schaie & Baltes, 1977 versus Horn & Donaldson, 1976, 1977). Paraphrasing Anastasi's (1958) classical paper on the nature–nurture issue, the central question is not "How much cohort variance?" but rather "*How* do historical and ontogenetic factors interact in codetermining individual development?" It is in this clarification of the theoretical significance of the dialectic between individual and biocultural development that Riegel's (1976a,b) seminal contributions lie.

Advancing Development-adequate Methodology

The fourth theme in the history, as well as the current scenario, of life-span developmental psychology deals with the need for methodologies that are specifically designed for the analysis of ontogenetic change. Again, it is striking to me that most historical publications, as is true for the life-span work in recent decades, evidence a high level of interest in and treatment of methodological issues.

As an illustration, Hayne Reese, John Nesselroade, and I (Baltes, Reese, & Nesselroade, 1977) have recently attempted to summarize development-specific research methods. The general conclusion (see also Lerner, Skinner, & Sorell, 1980; Nesselroade & Baltes, 1979; Nesselroade, Stigler, & Baltes, 1980; Petermann, 1978; Rudinger, 1982 in press; Wohlwill, 1973) is that many of the methods contained in the methodological arsenal of psychology are ill-suited to the study of developmental change. In fact, existing methods often result in a situation where the phenomenon of development is either ruled out on an a priori methodological basis or captured only in an inadequate manner due to a lack of development-sensitive methodology. This situation has resulted because the traditional focus in psychological research methodology has been oriented toward such features as optimal prediction (rather than representation of change), stability (rather than change), and interindividual differences (rather than patterns of intraindividual change).

Again, because of the radicalism in its developmental formulation, the life-span approach highlights the inappropriateness of existing methodologies. For example, if one acknowledges that change is pervasive, that individuals live in a changing biocultural context, that the explanation of long-term processes is apt to involve complex historical paradigms, and that long-term processes are likely candidates for explanatory discontinuity rather than simple cumulative causal explanations, then the search for new methodologies becomes a critical task. The need for new development-specific methodologies is amplified to such a degree by life-span thinking that it cannot be avoided.

In our historical review, an immediate concern for development-specific methodologies was expressed by practically all precursors. In Tetens' and Carus' work, the methodological concerns dealt, for example, with questions of variability, modifiability, and the competence–performance distinction. From Quetelet in 1835, to Hollingworth in 1927, to Pressey, Janney, and Kuhlen in 1939, the methodological discourse became more and more specific and reflected concrete proposals aimed at formulating appropriate methodologies. Quetelet's (1842) concerns, noted earlier, with critical periods in the life-span (pp. 31, 57), selective survival (pp. 62–63), measurement equivalence (pp. 72–74), and the impact of social change and specific historical moments on age functions (pp. 33, 97–100) exemplify this pressing interest in development-specific methodologies. Likewise, as alluded to earlier, Hollingworth, Pressey, and Kuhlen all devoted considerable attention to development-specific methodology, as did Charlotte Bühler (1933), who proposed the use of life biographies as a major tool of developmental analysis.

Thus, it is not surprising that the search for development-appropriate methodology continues among current researchers with life-span interests. For instance, in addition to methodological discussions of cohort-sequential methodology, there are efforts by life-span oriented researchers to advance models aimed at assessing developmental changes in measurement validity (Schaie, 1978), to consider external validity as a research dimension both equal in significance to internal validity and also as a contextual component intrinsic to any developmental explanation (Hultsch & Hickey, 1978), and to advance the use of structural equation models in identifying long-term causal chains (Jöreskog, 1979; Kohn & Schooler, 1978; Labouvie, 1974; Rogosa, 1979). In my judgment, in each of these cases there is a logic to life-span thinking that pushes the formulation of development-specific methodology beyond the level of articulation likely to be reached within any age-specific developmental speciality, such as child development or gerontology. In other words, the fact that many life-span researchers are interested in theoretical and methodological issues is not accidental. Rather, it reflects the stimulation resulting from the conceptual extremities inherent in life-span conceptions. Moreover, the conceptual extremity required by life-span questions requires the formulation of new methodologies that may advance the state of developmental design in general.

CONCLUSION

The primary purpose of this chapter was to outline some major elements of an often neglected part of the history of developmental psychology, that associated with the life-span perspective. In addition, an effort was made to identify common themes and to examine whether something could be learned from such a historical excursion about current theory and methodology in developmental psychology. In my view, and notwithstanding the difficulties associated with any attempt at historical analysis (Fischer, 1970), these examples from the history and current state of life-span developmental psychology illustrate several perspectives.

First, the life-span approach has a long history and it is useful to be aware of its historical origins and initial rationales. As with most intellectual movements, it takes experience and reflection to sort out the strengths from the weaknesses. For example, whereas the tenor of this chapter has been the theoretical and methodological promise generated from life-span thinking, some observations on caution have been made as well. The examples chosen were the treatment of a pluralistic concept of development and the different interpretations one can place on the existence of cohort effects. In each instance, an uncritical and overeager acceptance could lead to unwanted side effects such as the rejection of the developmental approach in principle, or the embracing of an extreme dialectical posture that would preclude empirical study; that is, not only the strengths but also the potential weaknesses of a developmental approach become easier to grasp when placed in the amplifying context of a life-span framework.

Second, my suggestion is that the strong continuity of certain historical themes expressed in life-span work will be helpful for guiding future research. On the one hand, one can argue, of course, that historical continuity of ideas reflects a sad state of affairs. Usually, ideas that are inherently nonfalsifiable or are not properly articulated are the ones that do not fade away. On the other hand, and here is admittedly my emphasis, historical contiuity in ideas can index significance and fertility. In the present case, the proposition is that historical convergence and continuity help us in articulating what it means conceptually to study development, how a particular developmental event is embedded in a larger context, and why a developmental process or state is better understood (or at least amplified) if placed in a life-span framework. These ideas were part of the original scene in developmental psychology; they have survived and still await the true developmental scholars who mean what they say. In this sense, if we trust my collection of historical observations, a life-span approach, because of the apparent concern with the extreme boundaries of a developmental orientation, helps to keep us on track as developmental psychologists and, thereby, functions as a conceptual guide for the importance of ideas.

The challenges provided by the historical themes identified in life-span work, then, emphasize and highlight what classical developmental psychology is actually about on the conceptual–theoretical level. At the same time, the history of life-span thinking has underscored the need for close interaction between theory and methodology. Throughout, a concern with methodology appropriate to represent and identify development has been of central interest. How to study change adequately, how to assess the relationship between ontogeny and evolution (especially biocultural change), and how to use developmental paradigms without becoming caught in the fallacies of historical analysis are all examples of the questions considered fundamental by early scholars.

It is occasionally argued that 20th-century developmental psychology has been in danger of forgetting its conceptual and methodological uniqueness or "challenges," as McCall (1977) so aptly expressed the situation. In the often more expedient experimental study of individual age differences rather than longitudinal change and developmental processes, much of the unique and historical foundation of developmental research is easily neglected. Therefore, what is also impressive in this historical excursion is the recognition that not much may be gained by taking shortcuts when attempting to describe and explain behavioral development. Insufficient data bases, expediently collected with little use of developmental methodology and little concern for salience in a life-span framework, can quickly lead to an explosion of data. At the same time, however, such research may fade away quickly with little lasting impact.

Let me conclude these observations on the history and theory of life-span developmental psychology by citing a passage from the Preface to Solzhenitsyn's (1973) *Gulag Archipelago*. The passage deals with the costs and benefits associated with a developmental-historical stance. Solzhenitsyn quotes a Russian proverb that nicely illustrates the dilemma developmentalists face when choosing between the "right" but tedious developmental-historical approach and the non-developmental shortcut. He says (Solzhenitsyn, 1973): "Dwell on the past and you will lose one eye. . . . Forget the past and you'll lose both eyes [p. x]." Such appears to be our future in the study of development and aging. On the one hand, if we commit ourselves to a life-span orientation, it will promote the application of more complex research paradigms and models of development. This conceptual virtue, however, will be at the expense of procedural simplicity and perhaps methodological purity. On the other hand, if we choose one of the many shortcuts, we may be productive for the moment and thereby own more of the present but less of the future.

SUMMARY

Observations are offered on the confluence of history, theory, and methodology of life-span developmental psychology. Contrary to most current beliefs, it is shown that throughout the history of developmental psychology, beginning in the late eighteenth century, a life-span approach to the study of behavioral development has been espoused repeatedly, though in an insular fashion.

Life-span developmental psychology stretches the boundaries of any developmental orientation because of its primary concern with long-term processes. Therefore, a life-span approach tends to accentuate, amplify, and articulate important theoretical and methodological issues and principles beyond the level of clarity usually available in age-specific developmental specialties, such as child development or gerontology. Examples are used to illustrate the enduring significance of several theoretical and methodological themes. These themes include (a) the reformulation of the concept of development to encompass models in addition to biological growth models, (b) the expansion of the substantive scope of developmental constructs, (c) the linkage of ontogenetic and biocultural change in an interactive and contextual framework, and (d) the formulation of appropriate development-specific methodologies.

It is argued that life-span researchers should continue to focus on explicating the methodological and theoretical uniqueness and challenge of the developmental orientation expressed in these themes. Continual awareness of and concern for the themes will not only increase the general impact of a life-span orientation but also promote more significant research endeavors. At the same time, some caveats are added. It is suggested that a life-span perspective does not accentuate only the strength and paradigmatic uniqueness of a developmental orientation. Because of its extremity in approach and the associated tendency by life-span scholars to push for alternative, more open-ended, and dynamic conceptions, they are inclined also to go beyond what is useful and to risk, for example, the danger of unsystematic pluralism and lack of precision. The current task is to generate a theoretical orientation on development that is innovative and appropriate in conceptual approach but also contains a sufficient measure of scientific order.

ACKNOWLEDGMENT

This chapter is based largely on an earlier publication (Baltes, 1979) contained in the second volume of *Life-span development and behavior* published by Academic Press. For the present publication, the chapter was modified in three main respects. First, the section on Carus, Tetens, and Quetelet was enlarged, for example, by adding photographs and giving further information on their work. Second, the section on the concept of development was expanded to consider the potential costs associated, for instance, with the use of a pluralistic notion of development and the risks inherent in an overeager acceptance of an extreme dialectical position. Third, the list of references was amplified and updated.

The chapter owes much to the intellectual support provided by the Committee on "Life-course Perspectives on Human Development" of the Social Science Research Council. In addition, specific comments by Albert Bandura, Roger A. Dixon, Kurt Kreppner, John R. Nesselroade, Ellen A. Skinner, and Doris Sowarka were helpful in improving the quality of the manuscript. Note also that the original chapter was derived from a presidential address delivered to Division 20 (Adult Development and Aging) of the American Psychological Association in 1977, and that it was published initially as a tandem piece to Reinert (1979). Reinert's chapter on the history of developmental psychology contains much background information relevant for the present work.

REFERENCES

Anastasi, A. Heredity, environment, and the question "How?" *Psychological Review*, 1958, *65*, 197–208.

Baltes, P. B. Longitudinal and cross-sectional sequences in the study of age and generation effects. *Human Development*, 1968, *11*, 145–171.

Baltes, P. B. Life-span developmental psychology: Some converging observations on history and theory. In P. B. Baltes & O. G. Brim, Jr. (Eds.), *Life-span development and behavior* (Vol. 2). New York: Academic Press, 1979.

Baltes, P. B., & Baltes, M. M. Plasticity and variability in psychological aging: Methodological and theoretical issues. In G. E. Gurski (Eds.), *Determining the effects of aging on the central nervous system*. Berlin: Schering, 1980.

Baltes, P. B., & Cornelius, S. W. The status of dialectics in developmental psychology: Theoretical orientation versus scientific method. In N. Datan & H. W. Reese (Eds.), *Life-span developmental psychology: Dialectical perspectives on experimental research*. New York: Academic Press, 1977.

Baltes, P. B., Cornelius, S. W., & Nesselroade, J. R. Cohort effects in behavioral development: Theoretical and methodological perspectives. In W. A. Collins (Ed.), *Minnesota Symposium on Child Psychology* (Vol. 11). Hillsdale, N.J.: Lawrence Erlbaum Associates, 1978.

Baltes, P. B., Cornelius, S. W., & Nesselroade, J. R. Cohort effects in developmental psychology. In J. R. Nesselroade & P. B. Baltes (Eds.), *Longitudinal research in the study of behavior and development*. New York: Academic Press, 1979.

Baltes, P. B., Reese, H. W., & Lipsitt, L. P. Life-span developmental psychology. *Annual Review of Psychology*, 1980, *31*, 65–100.

Baltes, P. B., Reese, H. W., & Nesselroade, J. R. *Life-span developmental psychology: Introduction to research methods*. Monterey, Calif.: Brooks/Cole, 1977.

Baltes, P. B., & Schaie, K. W. (Eds.). *Life-span developmental psychology: Personality and socialization*. New York: Academic Press, 1973. (a)

Baltes, P. B., & Schaie, K. W. On life-span developmental research paradigms: Retrospects and prospects. In P. B. Baltes & K. W. Schaie (Eds.), *Life-span developmental psychology: Personality and socialization*. New York: Academic Press, 1973. (b)

Baltes, P. B., & Schaie, K. W. On the plasticity of intelligence in adulthood and old age: Where Horn and Donaldson fail. *American Psychologist*, 1976, *31*, 720–725.

Baltes, P. B., & Willis, S. L. Toward psychological theories of aging and development. In J. E. Birren & K. W. Schaie (Eds.), *Handbook of the psychology of aging*. New York: Van Nostrand–Reinhold, 1977.

Baltes, P. B., & Willis, S. L. Life-span developmental psychology, cognitive functioning and social policy. In M. W. Riley (Ed.), *Aging from birth to death: Interdisciplinary perspectives*. Washington, D.C.: American Association for the Advancement of Science, 1979.

Baltes, P. B., & Willis, S. L. Plasticity and enhancement of intellectual functioning in old age: Penn State's Adult Development and Enrichment Program (ADEPT). In F. I. M. Craik & S. E. Trehub (Eds.), *Aging and cognitive processes*. New York: Plenum Press, 1982, in press.

Bandura, A. The psychology of chance encounters and life paths. *American Psychologist*, 1982, *37*, 747–755.

Bayley, N. The life-span as a frame of reference in psychological research. *Vita Humana*, 1963, *6*, 125–139.

Benedict, R. Continuities and discontinuities in cultural conditioning. *Psychiatry*, 1938, *1*, 161–167.

Bengtson, V. L., & Black, K. D. Intergenerational relations in socialization. In P. B. Baltes & K. W. Schaie (Eds.), *Life-span developmental psychology: Personality and socialization*. New York: Academic Press, 1973.

Binstock, R., & Shanas, E. (Eds.). *Handbook on aging and the social sciences*. New York: Van Nostrand–Reinhold, 1976.

Birren, J. E. A brief history of the psychology of aging, Part I. *Gerontologist*, 1961, *1*, 69–77. (a)

Birren, J. E. A brief history of the psychology of aging, Part II. *Gerontologist*, 1961, *1*, 127–134. (b)

Birren, J. E. (Ed.). *Relations of development and aging*. Springfield, Ill.: Thomas, 1964.

Birren, J. E., Kinney, D. K., Schaie, K. W., & Woodruff, D. S. *Developmental psychology: A life-span approach*. Boston: Houghton Mifflin, 1981.

Birren, J. E., & Schaie, K. W. (Eds.). *Handbook of the psychology of aging*. New York: Van Nostrand–Reinhold, 1977.

Block, J. *Lives through time*. Berkeley: Bancroft Books, 1971.

Bortner, R. W., & Hultsch, D. F. Patterns of subjective deprivation in adulthood. *Developmental Psychology*, 1974, *10*, 534–545.

Brent, S. B. Individual specialization, collective adaptation and rate of environmental change. *Human Development*, 1978, *21*, 21–23.

Brim, O. G., Jr. *The sense of personal control over one's life*. Invited address to Divisions 7 and 8 at the 82nd Annual Convention of the American Psychological Association, New Orleans, September, 1974.

Brim, O. G., Jr. Life-span development of the theory of oneself: Implications for child development. In H. W. Reese (Ed.), *Advances in child development and behavior* (Vol. 11). New York: Academic Press, 1976. (a)

Brim, O. G., Jr. Theories of the male mid-life crisis. *Counseling Psychologist*, 1976, *6*, 2–9. (b)

Brim, O. G., Jr., & Kagan, J. Constancy and change: A view of the issues. In O. G. Brim, Jr. & J. R. Kagan (Eds.), *Constancy and change in human development*. Cambridge, Mass.: Harvard University Press, 1980.

Brim, O. G., Jr., & Wheeler, S. *Socialization after childhood: Two essays*. New York: Wiley, 1966.

Bronfenbrenner, U. Toward an experimental ecology of human development. *American Psychologist*, 1977, *32*, 513–531.

Bühler, C. *Der menschliche Lebenslauf als psychologisches Problem*. Leipzig: Hirzel, 1933.

Bühler, C., & Massarik, F. (Eds.). *The course of human life*. New York: Springer, 1968.

Cairns, R. B., & Ornstein, P. A. Developmental psychology. In E. Hearst (Ed.), *The first century of experimental psychology*. Hillsdale, N.J.: Lawrence Erlbaum Associates, 1979.

Carus, F. A. *Psychologie. Zweiter Theil: Specialpsychologie*. Leipzig: Barth & Kummer, 1808.

Charles, D. C. Historical antecedents of life-span developmental psychology. In L. R. Goulet & P. B. Baltes (Eds.), *Life-span developmental psychology: Research and theory*. New York: Academic Press, 1970.

Charles, D. C., & Looft, W. R. (Eds.). *Readings in psychological development through life*. New York: Holt, Reinhart, & Winston, 1973.

Clausen, J. A. The life-course of individuals. In M. W. Riley, M. Johnson, & A. Foner (Eds.), *Aging and society* (Vol. 3), *A sociology of age stratification*. New York: Russell Sage Foundation, 1972.

Clayton, V. Wisdom and intelligence: The nature and function of knowledge in the later years. *International Journal of Aging and Development*, 1982, in press.

Clayton, V. P., & Birren, J. E. The development of wisdom across the life span: A reexamination of an ancient topic. In P. B. Baltes & O. G. Brim, Jr. (Eds.), *Life-span development and behavior* (Vol. 3). New York: Academic Press, 1980.

Communications Research Machines (Ed.). *Developmental psychology today*. Del Mar, Calif.: Communications Research Machines, 1971.

Craig, G. J. *Human development*. New York: Prentice–Hall, 1976.

Datan, N., & Ginsberg, L. H. (Eds.). *Life-span developmental psychology: Normative life crises*. New York: Academic Press, 1975.

Datan, N., & Reese, H. W. (Eds.) *Life-span development psychology: Dialectical perspectives on experimental research*. New York: Academic Press, 1977.

Dixon, R. A. *Darwinism and the emergence of developmental psychology*. Unpublished manuscript, Max Planck Institute for Human Development and Education, Berlin, West Germany, 1982.

Dollard, J. *Criteria for the life history*. New York: Peter Smith, 1949.

Elder, G. H., Jr. *Children of the Great Depression*. University of Chicago Press, 1974.

Elder, G. H., Jr. Age-differentiation in life-course perspective. *Annual Review of Sociology*, 1975, *1*, 165–190.

Elder, G. H., Jr. Family history and the life course. *Journal of Family History*, 1977, *2*, 279–304.

Elder, G. H. Historical change in life patterns and personality. In P. B. Baltes & O. G. Brim, Jr. (Eds.), *Life-span development and behavior* (Vol. 2). New York: Academic Press, 1979.

Erikson, E. H. Identity and the life cycle: Selected papers. *Psychological Issues*, 1959, *1*, 50–100.

Featherman, D. L. The life-span perspective in social science research. New York: Social Science Research Council, September, 1981.

Filipp, S. H. (Ed.). *Kritische Lebensereignisse*. Munich: Urban & Schwarzenberg, 1981.

Fischer, D. H. *Historian's fallacies: Toward a logic of historical thought.* New York: Harper & Row, 1970.

Freeman, J. T. *Aging: Its history and literature.* New York: Human Sciences Press, 1979.

Goldberg, S. R., & Deutsch, F. *Life-span individual and family development.* Monterey, Calif.: Brooks/Cole, 1977.

Gollin, E. S. Development and plasticity. In E. S. Gollin (Ed.), *Developmental plasticity: Behavioral and biological aspects of variations in development.* New York: Academic Press, 1981.

Goslin, D. A. (Ed.). *Handbook of socialization theory and research.* Chicago: Rand McNally, 1969.

Goulet, L. R., & Baltes, P. B. (Eds.). *Life-span developmental psychology: Research and theory.* New York: Academic Press, 1970.

Groffmann, K. J. Life-span developmental psychology in Europe. In L. R. Goulet & P. B. Baltes (Eds.), *Life-span developmental psychology: Research and theory.* New York: Academic Press, 1970.

Hall, G. S. *Senescence: The last half of life.* New York: Appleton, 1922.

Harris, D. B. Problems in formulating a scientific concept of development. In D. B. Harris (Ed.), *The concept of development.* Minneapolis: University of Minnesota Press, 1957.

Hartup, W. W., & Lempers, J. A problem in life-span development: The interactional analysis of family attachments. In P. B. Baltes & K. W. Schaie (Eds.), *Life-span developmental psychology: Personality and socialization.* New York: Academic Press, 1973.

Havighurst, R. J. *Developmental tasks and education.* New York: David McKay, 1948.

Hill, R., & Mattessich, P. Family development theory and life-span development. In P. B. Baltes & O. G. Brim, Jr. (Eds.), *Life-span development and behavior* (Vol. 2). New York: Academic Press, 1979.

Hill, R., & Rodgers, R. H. The developmental approach. In H. T. Christiansen (Ed.), *Handbook of marriage and the family.* Chicago: Rand McNally, 1964.

Hofstätter, P. R. Tatsachen und Probleme einer Psychologie des Lebenslaufs. *Zeitschrift für Angewandte Psychologie,* 1938, *53,* 273–333.

Hollingworth, H. L. *Mental growth and decline: A survey of developmental psychology.* New York: Appleton, 1927.

Horn, J. L., & Donaldson, G. On the myth of intellectual decline in adulthood. *American Psychologist,* 1976, *31,* 701–719.

Horn, J. L., & Donaldson, G. Faith is not enough: A response to the Baltes–Schaie claim that intelligence does not wane. *American Psychologist,* 1977, *32,* 369–373.

Hultsch, D. F., & Hickey, T. External validity in the study of human development: A dialectical perspective. *Human Development,* 1978, *21,* 76–91.

Hultsch, D. F., & Plemons, J. K. Life events and life-span development. In P. B. Baltes & O. G. Brim, Jr. (Eds.), *Life-span development and behavior* (Vol. 2). New York: Academic Press, 1979.

Hurlock, E. B. *Developmental psychology.* New York: McGraw-Hill, 1959.

Jöreskog, K. G. Statistical estimation of structural models in longitudinal-developmental investigations. In J. R. Nesselroade & P. B. Baltes (Eds.), *Longitudinal research in the study of behavior and development.* New York: Academic Press, 1979.

Kaluger, G., & Kaluger, M. F. *Human development: The span of life.* St. Louis: Mosby, 1974.

Kastenbaum, R. *Humans developing: A life-span perspective.* Boston: Allyn & Bacon, 1979.

Kohlberg, L. Continuities in childhood and adult moral development revisited. In P. B. Baltes & K. W. Schaie (Eds.), *Life-span developmental psychology: Personality and socialization.* New York: Academic Press, 1973.

Kohli, M. (Ed.). *Soziologie des Lebenslaufs.* Darmstadt: Luchterhand, 1978.

Kohn, M. L., & Schooler, C. The reciprocal effects of the substantive complexity of work and intellectual flexibility: A longitudinal assessment. *American Journal of Sociology,* 1978, *84,* 24–52.

Kuhlen, R. G. Social change: A neglected factor in psychological studies of the life-span. *School and Society,* 1940, *52,* 14–16.

Kuhlen, R. G. Age and intelligence: The significance of cultural change in longitudinal versus cross-sectional findings. *Vita Humana,* 1963, *6,* 113–124.

Kuhlen, R. G., & Thompson, G. G. (Eds.). *Psychological studies of human development.* New York: Appleton–Century–Crofts, 1963.

Labouvie, E. W. Developmental causal structures of organism-environment interactions. *Human Development,* 1974, *17,* 444–452.

Labouvie–Vief, G. Adult cognitive development: In search of alternative interpretations. *Merrill Palmer Quarterly,* 1977, *23,* 227–263.

Labouvie–Vief, G. Beyond formal operations: Uses and limits of pure logic in life-span development. *Human Development,* 1980, *23,* 141–161.

Labouvie–Vief, G., & Chandler, M. Cognitive development and life-span developmental theories: Idealistic versus contextual perspectives. In P. B. Baltes (Ed.), *Life-span development and behavior* (Vol. 1). New York: Academic Press, 1978.

Lehr, U. *Psychologie des Alterns.* Heidelberg: Quelle & Meyer, 1972.

Lehr, U. Die Bedeutung der Lebenslaufpsychologie für die Gerontologie. *Aktuelle Gerontologie,* 1980, *10,* 257–269.

Lerner, R. M. *Concepts and theories of human development.* Reading, Mass.: Addison–Wesley, 1976.

Lerner, R. M., & Busch–Rossnagel, N. Individuals as producers of their development: Conceptual and empirical bases. In R. M. Lerner & N. A. Busch–Rossnagel (Eds.), *Individuals as producers of their development: A life-span perspective.* New York: Academic Press, 1981.

Lerner, R. M., & Hultsch, D. F. *Human Development: A Life-Span Perspective.* New York: McGraw–Hill, 1983, in press.

Lerner, R. M., & Ryff, C. D. Implementation of the life-span view of human development: The sample case of attachment. In P. B. Baltes (Ed.), *Life-span development and behavior* (Vol. 1). New York: Academic Press, 1978.

Lerner, R. M., Skinner, E. A., & Sorrell, G. T. Methodological implications of contextual dialectic theories of development. *Human Development,* 1980, *23,* 225–235.

Lerner, R. M., & Spanier, G. B. *Adolescent development: A life-span perspective.* New York: McGraw–Hill, 1980.

Löwe, H. *Einführung in die Lernpsychologie des Erwachsenenalters.* Berlin: VFB Deutscher Verlag der Wissenschaften, 1977.

Lowenthal, M. E., Thurnher, M., Chiriboga, D., & Associates. *Four stages of life. A comparative study of women and men facing transitions.* San Francisco: Jossey–Bass, 1975.

Lugo, J. O., & Hershey, G. L. *Human development.* New York: Macmillan, 1974.

Marshall, V. W. Age and awareness of finitude in developmental gerontology. *Omega,* 1975, *6,* 113–129.

McCall, R. B. Challenges to a science of developmental psychology. *Child Development,* 1977, *48,* 333–344.

Montada, L. Entwicklungspsychologie auf der Suche nach einer Identität. In L. Montada (Ed.), *Brennpunkte der Entwicklungspsychologie.* Stuttgart: Kohlhammer, 1979.

Munnichs, J. M. A. *Old age and finitude.* Basel: Karger, 1966. (a)

Munnichs, J. M. A. A short history of psychogerontology. *Human Development*, 1966, *9*, 230–245. (b)

Mussen, P. H., Conger, J. J., Kagan, J., & Geiwitz, J. *Psychological development: A life-span approach.* New York: Harper & Row, 1979.

Nesselroade, J. R., & Baltes, P. B. (Eds.). *Longitudinal research in the study of behavior and development.* New York: Academic Press, 1979.

Nesselroade, J. R., & Reese, H. W. (Eds.). *Life-span developmental psychology: Methodological issues.* New York: Academic Press, 1973.

Nesselroade, J. R., Stigler, S. M., & Baltes, P. B. Regression toward the mean and the study of change. *Psychological Bulletin*, 1980, *88*, 622–637.

Neugarten, B. L. *Personality in middle and late life: Empirical studies.* New York: Atherton, 1964.

Neugarten, B. L. Continuities and discontinuities of psychological issues into adult life. *Human Development*, 1969, *12*, 121–130.

Neugarten, B. L., & Datan, N. Sociological perspectives on the life cycle. In P. B. Baltes & K. W. Schaie (Eds.), *Life-span developmental psychology: Personality and socialization.* New York: Academic Press, 1973.

Newman, B. M., & Newman, P. R. *Development through life.* Homewood, Ill.: Dorsey Press, 1975.

Oerter, R. (Ed.). *Entwicklung als lebenslanger Prozess.* Hamburg: Hoffmann & Campe, 1978.

Pallus, H. Einleitung. In H. Pallus (Ed.), *Johann Nicolaus Tetens: Über den Ursprung der Sprachen und der Schrift.* Berlin: Akademie Verlag, 1966.

Petermann, F. *Veränderungsmessung.* Stuttgart: Kohlhammer, 1978.

Pfannkuch, H. (Ed.). *J. N. Tetens: Sprachphilosophische Versuche.* Hamburg: Meiner Verlag, 1971.

Pikunas, J. *Human development: An emergent science.* New York: McGraw–Hill, 1976.

Pressey, S. L., Janney, J. E., & Kuhlen, R. G. *Life: A psychological survey.* New York: Harper, 1939.

Pressey, S. L., & Kuhlen, R. G. *Psychological development through the life-span.* New York: Harper & Row, 1957.

Quetelet, A. *Sur l'homme et le développement de ses facultés.* Paris: Bachelier, 1835.

Quetelet, A. *Über den Menschen und die Entwicklung seiner Fähigkeiten.* Stuttgart: Schweizerbarts Verlagshandlung, 1838.

Quetelet, A. *A treatise on man and the development of his faculties.* Edinburgh: William & Robert Chambers, 1842.

Rebelsky, F. (Ed.). *Life: The continuous process.* New York: Knopf, 1975.

Reese, H. W. The development of memory: Life-span perspectives. In H. W. Reese (Ed.), *Advances in child development and behavior* (Vol. 11). New York: Academic Press, 1976.

Reinert, G. Grundzüge einer Geschichte der Human-Entwicklungspsychologie. In H. Balmer (Ed.), *Die Psychologie des 20. Jahrhunderts* (Vol. 1), *Die europäische Tradition: Tendenzen, Schulen, Entwicklungslinien.* Zürich: Kindler, 1976.

Reinert, G. Prolegomena to a history of life-span developmental psychology. In P. B. Baltes & O. G. Brim, Jr. (Eds.), *Life-span development and behavior* (Vol. 2). New York: Academic Press, 1979.

Riegel, K. F. Developmental psychology and society: Some historical and ethical considerations. In J. R. Nesselroade & H. W. Reese (Eds.), *Life-span developmental psychology: Methodological issues.* New York: Academic Press, 1973. (a)

Riegel, K. F. Dialectic operations: The final period of cognitive development. *Human Development*, 1973, *16*, 346–370. (b)

Riegel, K. F. The dialectics of human development. *American Psychologist*, 1976, *31*, 689–700. (a)

Riegel, K. F. *Psychology of development and history.* New York: Plenum, 1976. (b)

Riegel, K. F. History of psychological gerontology. In J. E. Birren & K. W. Schaie (Eds.), *Handbook of the psychology of aging.* New York: Van Nostrand–Reinhold, 1977.

Riley, M. W. Age strata in social systems. In R. Binstock & E. Shanas (Eds.), *Handbook of aging and the social sciences*. New York: Van Nostrand–Reinhold, 1976.

Riley, M. W. (Ed.). *Aging from birth to death*. Washington, D.C.: American Association for the Advancement of Science, 1979.

Riley, M. W., Johnson, M., & Foner, A. (Eds.). *Aging and society* (Vol. 3), *A sociology of age stratification*. New York: Russell Sage, 1972.

Rogosa, D. Causal models in longitudinal research. In J. R. Nesselroade & P. B. Baltes (Eds.), *Longitudinal research in the study of behavior and development*. New York: Academic Press, 1979.

Rosenmayr, L. (Ed.). *Die menschlichen Lebensalter*. Munich: Piper, 1978.

Rudinger, G. (Ed.). *Methoden der Entwicklungspsychologie*. Stuttgart: Kohlhammer, 1982, in press.

Sanford, E. C. Mental growth and decay. *American Journal of Psychology*, 1902, *13*, 426–449.

Schaie, K. W. A general model for the study of developmental problems. *Psychological Bulletin*, 1965, *64*, 92–107.

Schaie, K. W. External validity in the assessment of intellectual performance in adulthood. *Journal of Gerontology*, 1978, *33*, 695–701.

Schaie, K. W. The primary mental abilities in adulthood: An exploration in the development of psychometric intelligence. In P. B. Baltes & O. G. Brim, Jr. (Eds.), *Life-span development and behavior* (Vol. 2). New York: Academic Press, 1979.

Schaie, K. W., & Baltes, P. B. Some faith helps to see the forest: A final comment on the Horn and Donaldson myth of the Baltes–Schaie position on adult intelligence. *American Psychologist*, 1977, *32*, 1118–1120.

Schaie, K. W., & Willis, S. L. Life-span development: Implications for education. In L. S. Shulman (Ed.), *Review of research in education* (Vol. 6). Itasca, Ill.: Peacock, 1978.

Sears, P. S., & Barbee, A. H. Career and life satisfactions among Terman's gifted women. In J. Stanley, W. George, & C. Solano (Eds.), *The gifted and the creative: A fifty-year perspective*. Baltimore: Johns Hopkins University Press, 1977.

Sears, R. R. Sources of life satisfactions of the Terman gifted men. *American Psychologist*, 1977, *32*, 119–128.

Solzhenitsyn, A. I. *The gulag archipelago*. New York: Harper, 1973.

Süssmilch, J. P. *Die göttliche Ordnung in den Veränderungen des menschlichen Geschlechtes, aus der Geburt, dem Tod und der Fortpflanzung desselben erwiesen*. Berlin: Realschulbuchhandlung, 1741.

Tetens, J. N. *Philosophische Versuche über die menschliche Natur und ihre Entwicklung*. Leipzig: Weidmanns Erben & Reich, 1777.

Thomae, H. (Ed.). *Entwicklungspsychologie*. Göttingen: Hogrefe, 1959.

Thomae, H. The concept of development and life-span developmental psychology. In P. B. Baltes & O. G. Brim (Eds.), *Life-span development and behavior* (Vol. 2). New York: Academic Press, 1979.

Toulmin, S. Epistemology and developmental psychology. In E. S. Gollin (Ed.), *Developmental plasticity: Behavioral and biological aspects of variations in development*. New York: Academic Press, 1981.

Turner, J. S., & Helms, D. B. *Life span development*. Philadelphia: Saunders, 1979.

Turner, R., & Reese, H. W. (Eds.). *Life-span developmental psychology: Intervention*. New York: Academic Press, 1980.

Van den Daele, L. D. Infrastructure and transition in developmental analysis. *Human Development*, 1974, *17*, 1–23.

Van Dusen, R. A., & Sheldon, E. B. The changing status of American women: A life-cycle perspective. *American Psychologist*, 1976, *31*, 106–116.

Wohlwill, J. F. *The study of behavioral development*. New York: Academic Press, 1973.

5 Pluralism and Correlational Analysis in Developmental Psychology: Historical Commonalities

Roger A. Dixon
*Max Planck Institute for Human Development and Education,
Berlin, West Germany*

John R. Nesselroade
The Pennsylvania State University

INTRODUCTION

The term pluralism has appeared in a number of recent reviews of the state of research and theory in developmental psychology (Baltes, Reese, & Lipsitt, 1980; Baltes & Willis, 1977; Lerner, Hultsch, & Dixon, in press; White, 1977). In these appearances pluralism is cloaked with a temperate, somewhat non-specific endorsement. Accordingly, the concept it represents, as well as its presumed theoretical and methodological usefulness, remains somewhat indistinct. It would appear, however, that pluralism is intended to represent a rather generalized guideline for developmental inquiry. In particular, reviewers have juxtaposed the term with references to the desirability of fostering multiple explanatory schema, interpretive frameworks, empirical methodologies, and analytical techniques; all of these are offered in the service of furthering our understanding of the emergence and development of psychological phenomena; that is, a favored result of the dispersal of developmental psychologists into distinct scientific traditions—which, as we see below, has been in progress for at least a century—is that a variety of human behaviors have been examined from a variety of perspectives (White, 1977).

The fundamental quality of the pluralistic guidelines appears to be the following: Psychological phenomena are sufficiently dynamic, interwoven, complex and multidimensional as to require multiple theoretical renderings and multiple modes of inquiry. In this way these guidelines bear an unmistakable resemblance to Feyerabend's (1975, 1978) "first principle of intellectual morality," or *Wissenschaftstheoretische Anarchismus*. From this perspective all theories and world views, however incommensurable with prevailing systems, must have a fair opportunity to demonstrate their merits in the arena of intellectual inquiry. In every aspect and at every stage of scientific or philosophical investigation, intellectual diversity is to be not merely tolerated but actively encouraged. Indeed, without dissensus, conflict, or "sharply contending alternative views," intellectual development is in danger of stultifying or embarking upon the inherently circular path of a single-theory science.

Because the concept of psychology—indeed, the very idea of human nature—is, as Gallie (1964; see also Booth, 1977) put it, an "essentially contested concept," there may be little hope that a final resolution of the rival modes of interpretation will ever be attained. To the contrary, essentially contested concepts are not merely meaningful, not merely rational, but a way of life in the enterprises of science (Feyerabend, 1975), history (Gallie, 1964), literary criticism (Booth, 1976, 1977; see also Abrams, 1977; Crane, 1953; Peckham, 1977; Rabinowitz, 1979), and (we argue) psychology. It is fitting, then, that in psychology the call for pluralism has both a moral flavor and an intellectual component; that is, it is both a matter of intellectual freedom and intellectual responsibility that a multiplicity of perspectives and approaches be applied to the task of understanding the unremittingly complex phenomena of human psychology.

Pluralism in Contemporary Philosophy of Science

To further introduce the concept of pluralism it may be profitable to adopt a brief two-pronged line of inquiry. In the first we review the use of the concept in contemporary philosophy of science. Second, we distinguish between the concept and activities of scientific pluralism and those of scientific eclecticism. Two of the most prominent exponents of a pluralistic approach to science are Feyerabend (1975) and Popper (1972). Although differing in certain important respects, both begin their analyses by setting off pluralism from all varieties of monism in selected realms. For Popper (1972) one such realm is the perennial issue of the mind–body relationship. In his attempt to devise a pluralistic (tripartite, three-world) rendering of the mind–body problem, Popper (1972) seeks to surpass the descriptive adequacy of both monistic and dualistic portrayals: "In this pluralistic philosophy the world consists of at least three ontologically distinct subworlds . . . the first is the physical world or the world of physical states; the second is the mental world or the world of mental states; and the third is the world of intelligibles, or of *ideas in the objective sense* [p. 154]." It is the delineation of this third world—the world of theories, arguments, problem situations, and logical relations—that constitutes the critical advance for a pluralistic philosophy. For Popper the attempt to reduce the pluralistic universe to any variety of monism (e.g., idealism or positivism) is less an exercise in informed science than a pursuit of dubious philosophical merit.

Feyerabend (1975) adopts a somewhat more radical posture. Both Popper (1965) and Feyerabend believe that scientific theories are falsifiable but not confirmable, and thus that scientific knowledge grows through the proliferation of alternatives. However, whereas Popper argues for the retention of a theory until it is has been refuted by new facts, and thus for the development of self-consistent sets of theories, Feyerabend (1965, 1975) urges the simultaneous consideration of mutually inconsistent, incompatible sets of theories. Feyerabend terms this condition of scientific development *theoretical pluralism* and argues that the most comprehensive test of a scientific theory will occur only when the theory is confronted with factually adequate, but incommensurable, alternatives (see also Lakatos, 1970, who urges confrontation between interpretive and explanatory theories). In addition, Feyerabend (1970, 1975) suggests that historically the only methodological rule that can be defended under all circumstances is the rather anarchistic principle "anything goes." Thus, to achieve maximal empirical content, the scientist must adopt the pluralistic methodology of comparing theories with theories, as well as theories with data, facts, or experience (Feyerabend, 1975).

Following J. S. Mill (*On Liberty*), Feyerabend (1975, 1978, 1980) asserts that pluralism is an important principle not only for scientific methodology, but also for a more general humanitarian perspective. According to Feyerabend both personal and intellectual (scientific) development is most enhanced in the context of a free and pluralistic society. Nevertheless, although pluralism implies that all traditions or modes of thought have an equal right to demonstrate their merit in the intellectual arena (political relativism), it does not imply that all traditions are equally true or equally false (philosophical relativism).

It is on this frontier that the outward growth (and geometric extension) of pluralism—the potential philosophical malignancy—is limited. As is seen later, pluralism is intellectually and historically related to skepticism and philosophical relativism. In the present rendering, however, the most profitable connection is constructed between a limited pluralism and a moderate or critical relativism. As Booth (1977) suggested, the limits of pluralism are plural, but if pushed to construct the tenets of a pluralistic commonwealth, the following may be offered: "Pursue some chosen monism as well as you can, [but] give your neighbor's monism a fair shake [p. 423]."

Let us turn briefly to the second aspect of our two-pronged introduction to the contemporary use of the concept of pluralism. On the theoretical level pluralism may be contrasted to eclecticism. Whereas the former involves the proliferation and subsequent confrontation of autonomous theoretical structures, the latter involves the selection of strands of various autonomous sources, often in the service of constructing a more general or comprehensive theoretical system. Whereas pluralism encourages incommensurability, eclecticism, aiming for generality (or scope) through commensuration, is often designed to circumvent or overcome it. Hence, on a metatheoretical level, pluralism encourages the retention of the structural integrity of contrasting accounts of reality, whereas eclecticism attempts to blend these accounts by selecting what are considered to be the best or more useful elements of each. That is why, in the realm of scientific theory development, eclecticism is often considered confusing (Pepper, 1970). Although on many levels of psychological inquiry and practice a critical eclecticism may prove beneficial, on the theoretical level at least it may be usefully contrasted with the pluralistic guideline.

Plan of the Paper

It is perhaps no coincidence that the same writers (Baltes et al., 1980; Baltes & Willis, 1977; Lerner et al., in press) who suggest a pluralistic approach to theory and method in developmental psychology often associate this approach with a contextual or pragmatic metatheory; that is, it appears that pluralism is implied by a view of the world that embraces constant, multilevel, multirate change, and a view of psychological phenomena as context laden. It is perhaps also no coincidence that these same writers testify to the virtues of a multivariate—often multivariate correlational—approach to the validation of measures, design of experiments, and the collection and analysis of developmental data.

These three concomitant proposals—encouragement of pluralism, employment of a contextual-developmental approach to psychology, and use of multivariate correlational techniques—are often associated with the life-span orientation to developmental psychology. Further, as reviewers have noted recently, such suggestions appear in an increasingly wide range of the developmental psychology literature (Hultsch & Pentz, 1980; Lerner et al., in press, Tyler, 1981). The guiding purpose of the present chapter is one of forging some conceptual links among the three concomitant proposals. Whereas one primary objective is to explore the meaning, use, and merit of the concept of pluralism, its connection with multivariate correlational analysis techniques is also investigated.

The method of the present inquiry is primarily historical; to understand what may be called the tacit triumvirate of life-span developmental psychology, the intellectual origins of the elements, as well as their possible conceptual and historical connections, are discussed. Where applicable common or associated strands of intellectual heritage are noted. More specifically, the remainder of the chapter is organized into three sections, the first two of which are inquiries into the origins of pluralism and correlational analysis, respectively, in psychology. The concluding section offers a set of historically informed propositions in the direction of pluralistic, multivariate developmental psychology.

ORIGINS OF PLURALISM

Among William James' most salient contributions to the intellectual community is his psychological analysis of philosophical temperaments. Noting that the will to philosophize requires a peculiar combination of mental characteristics, James attempted to categorize the most commonly associated characteristics into two prevailing (somewhat trait-like) tendencies. In his Lowell Lectures James described the so-called "tender-minded" philosopher as, among other properties, rationalistic, idealistic, religious, and dogmatic. In contrast, the so-called "tough-minded" philosopher is described as empiricistic, fatalistic, irreligious, and skeptical. One other point of contrast serves the purpose of this chapter particularly well: Whereas the tender-minded philosopher is monistic, the tough-minded philosopher is pluralistic.

Whereas the monistic–pluralistic alternative is often presented as but one point of contrast contributing to the tender-minded versus tough-minded dichotomy of philosophical temperaments, it is apparent that James addressed this point of contrast with considerable gravity. Indeed, on occasion (e.g., in the essay "Pragmatism and Religion") James asserted that the monistic–pluralistic alternative was the "final question" of philosophy. This alternative was, in James' (1907) words: "the deepest and most pregnant question that our minds can frame [p. 189]." In other essays (e.g., "The one and the many" and "Pragmatism and humanism") this "final question" of philosophy is seemingly rendered as an alternative between pragmatism and rationalism, bearing upon not just the theory of knowledge but the very structure of the universe (James, 1907, p. 168). On the pragmatist (and pluralist) side, the universe is seen as an unfinished, growing *pluriverse* (James, 1977). In contrast, the rationalists (and monists) view the universe as eternally complete, but not yet accessible in its consummation to the inquiring human mind.

It appears that James himself coined the term pluralism (at least in its present application; see Allen, 1967). Nevertheless, the concept the term represents—the doctrine that there is more than one fundamental reality (Barnes, 1965)—has a rather longer history. Two interrelated strands of the prepragmatic life of this concept may be located in the 16th and 17th centuries, as the advance of science (particularly astronomy) was gathering momentum, and the age of uncertainty (in philosophy) was dawning.

Plurality of Worlds

That the universe *may* be infinite, and that it *may* contain a plurality of inhabited worlds, was an idea that arose only in part through the efforts of the great astronomers of the 16th and 17th centuries—men such as Tycho Brahe, Kepler, and Galileo. Other lesser-known astronomers and cosmographers contributed more directly to its development than did these giants of the history of astronomy. Still, the idea did not begin even here, for in the early 15th century the Jewish philosopher Crescas (in *Or Adonai*, 1410) argued that Aristotle and all others who attempted to negate the possibility of the simultaneous existence of many worlds were exhibiting neither logical cogency nor empirical evidence; they were merely caught in the sway of human vanity (Lovejoy, 1964; Wolfson, 1929). In addition, the Christian philosopher of the Middle Ages, The Cardinal Nicolaus Cusanus, asserted that it was preposterous to think that there were not other inhabited globes filling the many spaces of the heavens (Lovejoy, 1964).

Whereas in the 16th century such sentiments were occasionally entertained hypothetically, they were quite dangerous to endorse in the public arena. Already it had become clear to theologians and metaphysicians alike that the theory of the plurality of inhabited worlds was not a simple one to assimilate to rationalistic or theological monism. Nevertheless, the discovery of new stars in the late 16th century appeared to stretch—perhaps infinitely—the boundaries of the universe. Such writers of the period as the Englishman Thomas Digges (1741–1821) and the Italian Giordano Bruno (1548–1600) depicted the cosmos as infinite in reach and (especially for Bruno) as containing a plurality of worlds. In the case of Bruno—who one contemporary observer (Butterfield, 1957) has described as more a poet than a scientist and who has been called the *enfant terrible* of 16th-century cosmographers—the speculation as to the infinity of inhabited worlds was enthusiastic (see *De Immenso* and *De l'infinito universo,* both of which appeared in the late 16th century). Even though, in the final analysis, Bruno's pluralistic metaphysics was moderate—suggesting that an organic unity, in which the multiple units of reality were meaningful only in the context of their relations to one another, lay beneath the plurality of parts (Horowitz, 1952)—his enthusiasm for a theory of questionable Biblical veridicality was unpropitious in the midst of the Inquisition. The imaginative Bruno, champion of the plural worlds hypothesis, was burned at the stake as a heretic on 16 February 1600 (Butterfield, 1957; Singer, 1950; Toulmin & Goodfield, 1961).

Ideas, however, are not as easily dispatched as quixotic heretics. Widely respected astronomers—e.g., Edmund Halley (1656–1742) and Christian Huygens (1629–1695)—were influenced by the ideas of Bruno (Singer, 1950). Indeed, by the end of the 17th century the following three interrelated theses were seriously and openly regarded among educated Europeans: (1) The physical universe was, if not infinite, then far more extensive than medieval writers portrayed it; (2) the fixed stars, now viewed as suns similar to our own, might also be surrounded by planetary systems; and (3) each of these solar systems, like our own, may have at least one inhabited planet (Lovejoy, 1964).[1] Such writers

---

[1]Although most post-Copernican scientists have tacitly accepted the plural worlds hypothesis, it has continued to the present day to be a matter of some debate (see Heffernan, 1978, 1981; Hetherington, 1981 for discussions of the recent developments in this dialogue). To briefly trace this history, it appears that general opposition to the hypothesis was marshalled by William Whewell and

as Bernard de Fontanelle (1657–1757), who in 1686 wrote the *Entretiens sur la pluralité des mondes,* served to diffuse and popularize the theory of the plurality of worlds in both France and England (Lovejoy, 1964). In his aesthetic—almost poetic—style, Fontanelle (1686; in Lovejoy, 1964) entreats: "When the heavens were a little blue arch, stuck with stars, methought the universe was too strait and close; I was almost stifled for want of air; but now it is enlarged in height and breadth and a thousand vortexes taken in. I begin to breathe with more freedom and I think the universe to be incomparably more magnificent than it was before [pp. 132–133]."

As Lovejoy (1964) notes, however, such an enlargement of the possibilities of the universe, together with its ineluctable diminishment of the singularity and importance of human existence, presented unwonted difficulties to the philosophers, ethicists, and theologians of the time. One such group of thinkers—Montaigne and the skeptics—derived a measure of philosophical or theoretical pluralism. It is to a brief discussion of this group that we now turn.

Montaigne and the Skeptics

At the same time that scientists of the period were compiling ever more precise knowledge of the material universe, their understanding of the human drama was seemingly diminishing in precision and thoroughness. Taking a perverse delight in the comedy of these inversely related progressions, Michel Eyquem de Montaigne (1533–1592) adopted an "amiable skepticism" (Barnes, 1965, p. 622) regarding the common dogmas through which the human drama was interpreted. His tolerance of mutually exclusive interpretive frameworks was exceeded perhaps only by his disdain for the pretentious advocacy of one over another.[2] Indeed, his method of inquiry is steeped in intellectual humility, tolerance, moderation, and severe self-scrutiny (Barnes, 1965). As Montaigne (1948) put it: "To the really learned men has happened what happens to ears of corn. They rise high and lofty, heads erect and proud, as long as they are empty; but when they are full and swollen with grain in their ripeness, they begin to grow humble and lower their horns. [p. 55]."

As a result of his close examinations of himself and his world, Montaigne discovered and accorded unusual importance to the temporal variations in mood

---

Alfred Russel Wallace in the middle of the 19th century. Then, following the discovery of "canali" on Mars by Schiaparelli in 1877, other scientists such as Percival Lowell became forceful proponents of the plural worlds hypothesis, and in some cases, active promulgators of speculations regarding the nature of the *inhabitants* of other worlds (again, see Heffernan, 1978, 1981; Hetherington, 1981).

[2]Barnes (1965) traces Montaigne's metaphysical tolerance to his unusually diverse religious background: His father was a devout Catholic and his mother was born a Jew but later converted to Protestantism.

of the human individual and the cross-historical and cross-cultural variations in human societies. Hence, rather than emphasizing the stable or absolute characteristics of the individual or social history, Montaigne (1948) was struck by the parts that are labile or unpredictable: "And we, and our judgement, and all mortal things, go on flowing and rolling unceasingly. Thus nothing certain can be established about one thing by another, both the judging and the judge being in continual change and motion [p. 61]."

With a focus on inconstancy, diversity, and the infinity of existing things, Montaigne's pluralism was but a small step away. For Montaigne diversity was the fundamental law of nature and the grand theme of the human drama (Barnes, 1965). Apparently anticipating Bruno, Montaigne (1948, in his essay "Apologie de Raimond Sebond") hinted that it was quite possible that the diversity of life and consciousness extended beyond the earth (Lovejoy, 1964).

Blaise Pascal (1623–1662) combined Montaigne's philosophical pluralism with the Brunonian theses of the plurality of worlds. However, unlike Bruno and Fontanelle, Pascal found the prospect of existing on but one of an infinite number of inhabited worlds singularly oppressive (Lovejoy, 1964). Nevertheless, Pascal obsessively pursued the ramifications of such infinite diversity. Other French skeptics such as Pierre Bayle (1647–1706) offered similar versions of a philosophical pluralism together with a vision of the plurality of worlds and realities. Such a pluralistic version was rediscovered and confirmed by pragmatists such as Peirce, James, and Dewey in the 19th and early 20th centuries. James, of course, identified skepticism as one of the characteristics of the tough-minded (pluralistic) tendency in philosophy. Whereas the skeptics—especially Montaigne—began turning the pluralistic thresher upon the continuing human social drama, the pragmatists began to focus at a somewhat lower altitude (the individual and the individual's internal or psychological processes). Thus, for the first time pluralism was being cast explicitly in the context of individual psychology.

Toward a Pluralistic Rationality

If the discovery of new stars by the astronomers of the 16th and 17th centuries shattered the spatial boundaries of the universe, the discovery of ancient geological artifacts fractured the temporal boundaries of the earth and the cosmos. If the theory of a plurality of inhabited worlds tended to diminish the singularity of human existence on earth, the discovery of an even greater history and gradual evolution of the species seemed to further relativize the present version of the human blend. If the human species was but a temporary waystation of tens of millions of years of accidental, unpredictable evolution, and if such evolution could be duplicated (or even surpassed) on any number of other planets in a limitless universe, then what absolute value could be placed on the products of the human mind? Were they not (as Mead, 1936, suggested) simply stopping-off points in a long history of trial-and-error progression (see also Popper, 1965, 1972)? And what of rationality—the supreme accomplishment of homo sapiens—was it not unified, absolute, the final arbiter of questions mundane and profound alike?

In the late 18th and in the 19th century, the discovery of time, of a virtually limitless history to the earth and the universe, entailed a vase reorientation in the intellectual community (Toulmin & Goodfield, 1965). The work of uniformitarian geologists such as James Hutton (1726–1797) and Sir Charles Lyell (1797–1875) demonstrated that the earth had been a continuously changing stage for the evolution of life for much longer than previously believed. Significantly influenced by the uniformitarian geologists, Charles Darwin (1809–1882) provided the mechanism by which the evolution of life could have occurred in gradually shifting ecological contexts. In many ways the 19th century was, as Eiseley (1958) put it, "Darwin's Century." But the exemplar idea of this century—that of time, or, more than time, history—was the result of a particular propitious match of man and intellectual climate. Darwinism—and the advances on other fronts such as astronomy and geology that made it possible—opened the history (both past and future) of the universe to observation and speculation. As before, as knowledge of material or natural history increased, the thoroughness of understanding of man's place in nature seemed to diminish. The dogmas of the past buttressed their defenses—often by launching insidious offensive maneuvers—and closed ranks. The perfection of human knowledge, development, and destiny was brought into question. Darwinistic developmentalists and evolutionists seemed to assert that the organization of the universe, the earth, and humankind was imperfect and subject to novel and unpredictable change. Similarly, human knowledge and rationality were now being portrayed as reliable (but not *totally* reliable), as useful but fallible.

Impressed by the multiple facets of such a climate, early pragmatists set about the task of preserving human rationality while simultaneously allowing (if not embracing) its inherent imperfection. Again, as before, pragmatism came to be set off from (albeit not dichotomously) absolute rationalism. For William James the world view provided by monism was excessively rational; it provided a unity inappropriate to the disunity of human experience (Dooley, 1974). It was adequate to the task of providing unity for the inquiring mind, but it did not yield the balance of rationality required to best understand the brimming, buzzing universe (James, 1977). According to James (1977) pluralism, on balance, gave a better account of the four dimensions of rationality (intellectual, aesthetic, moral, and practical) than did monism, which focused most attention on the intellectual and aesthetic. In addition, pluralism gave credence: (1) to the human experience of an only partially unified world; and (2) thereby focused an appropriate measure of attention upon the practical, concrete, survival-oriented problems of existence. Hence, James (1977) argued, if the monism–pluralism alternative is adjudicated according to the criteria of "true" rationality, then pluralism, which appears to meet a larger variety of intellectual demands, provides a more rational view of the universe.

James' pluralistic empiricism could thus allow novelty into the world drama without sacrificing rationality. Although the introduction of novelty did disaffirm total unity, James (1977) argued, such a sacrifice was for the better and was not taken at the risk of controverting all rationality.[3] Similarly, Darwin's introduction of novelty in the form of spontaneous variations in biological evolution served to account for change in a broader, perhaps more practical, but certainly less unified, way. The pluralistic account of rationality leads to a more empirical posture regarding the growth of knowledge. Truth is relative, temporal, and fallible. It is to be found not so much in a priori eternal laws of development as in the piecemeal examination of successive problem situations. Numerous contemporary philosophers have argued for a similar account of rationality under the rubrics of evolutionary epistemology and critical realism, and the attention of the interested reader is directed to these sources (Campbell, 1974; Popper, 1965, 1972; Richards, 1977, 1981; Toulmin, 1972).

Pluralism and the Pragmatists

In the autumn of 1907, Oxford University invited William James to give the Hibbert Lectures in Manchester College the following spring. With some reservations James (whose health was deteriorating) accepted and began to work on a series of lectures that were later published as *A Pluralistic Universe*. Writing these essays diverted precious time from James' attempt to compose a philosophical magnum opus. Further, the ultimate contribution of *A Pluralistic Universe* is less as a source of novel ideas than as a refined compendium of James' maturing radical, pluralistic empiricism.

Earlier, in a 1903 letter to Flournoy, James set out the agenda he was to fulfill in the Hibbert Lectures (quoted in Allen, 1967): to develop a " 'system' of tychistic and pluralistic 'philosophy of pure experience' [p. 498]." Allen (1967) notes that James occasionally used such neologisms as tychism (from the Greek meaning chance) and pluralism. Such terms were employed by pragmatists to describe their account of the human experience of the world. Fundamental to James' mature pluralism were the following propositions: (1) the universe is unfinished, incomplete, and continually changing; (2) as such, it is "excess"

---

[3]This is an issue that continues to be addressed by both proponents and critics of a contextual lifespan developmental psychology. It is much neater and (critics suggest) more rational (read: scientific) to delimit the extent of novelty allowed in the characterization of a change process. Although agreeing that the task of science would be easier if novelty were minimized, contextual developmentalists argue that novelty is not only an unavoidable phenomenon of psychological observation but also an indispensible element of the system of rationality with which they interpret that observation.

and indeterminant; (3) thus, the universe is not a singular unidimensional fact, but a series of multidimensional, ever-changing facts; (4) hence, the universe is accepted as it appears or is experienced by the human observer (i.e., as a *pluri*verse); (5) truth is not singular or immutable, but rather multiple and contingent; (6) truth is to be evaluated largely in terms of its practical consequences; (7) knowledge of the world is incomplete and subject to addition and aggrandizement; and (8) the method of choice for the inquiring mind is pragmatic empiricism.

The fundamental hypothesis of what James (1907, "Pragmatism and Common Sense") called noetic pluralism is: "the widest field of knowledge that ever was or will be still contains some ignorance . . . Some bits of information always may escape [p. 111]." Thus, James (1907, "The one and the many") proposed to "unstiffen" both theory and method and approach the task of knowledge gathering from as nondogmatic a perspective as possible. This pragmatic, pluralistic perspective attempted to match method with problem and adapt theory in light of the tentative outcome. With continually changing problem situations, a wide armament of methods should be accessible, and a flexible, adaptive view of theory building should be adopted. Whereas James often approached intellectual problems from a Darwinian perspective, he did so primarily because it appeared to work. Further, pluralist that he was, James adopted Darwinism nonexclusively and seldom approached any problem or subject from any single point of view (Wiener, 1949).

Although James was a leading pragmatist, and perhaps the premier pragmatic pluralist, other pragmatists contributed to the pluralistic alternative. Charles Sanders Pierce (1839–1914), of course, was an early doubter of the absolute nature of rationality, as well as the unbridled application of logical analysis. He, like James, preferred the pragmatic experimental method for the practical testing of scientific hypotheses. John Dewey (1859–1952) was both a pragmatist and a Darwinist and greatly influenced by James' pluralism (Barnes, 1965). Dewey's pluralism, however, reflected his more social and political interests (see Dewey, 1948), whereas James' pluralism was primarily rationalistic or psychological. In addition, Dewey's pluralism reflected his theoretical and methodological emphasis on the historic, dynamic nature of experience. As was the case with another early pragmatist, George Herbert Mead (1863–1931), reality was not a fixed, enduring category. Rather, reality was viewed as mutable—shifting with shifting contexts—a situation that dangerously imperiled traditional rationalism (Mead, 1934, 1938; Rucker, 1969). One observer (Thayer, 1968) has suggested that a fundamental part of pragmatic contextualism is its defense of the legitimacy of the plurality of human experiences with and descriptions of the world.

Bernard Bosanquet (1848–1923), who was not a pragmatist, appears to have modified his absolutistic, conservative political theory between the 1899 first edition and the 1910 second edition of his *The Philosophical Theory of the State,* in the face of criticism emanating from the camp of political pluralists (Randall,

1977). George Holmes Howison (1834–1916) developed a personalistic pluralism in which coexisting minds were correlated and joined in a decidedly theistic manner (Randall, 1977). G. F. Stout (1860–1940), long the editor of *Mind,* set forth a pluralistic idealism clearly influenced by James. Nicholas St. John Green offered an early empiricistic pluralism based on a statistical rendering of the fallible nature of practical reason (Wiener, 1949). Chauncey Wright (1830–1875) provided perhaps the most colorful expression for empirical diversity and pluralism: his term *cosmic weather* was intended to reflect the complexity of nature, the multidimensionality of human experience and interests, and the radical pluralism required to successfully address their interpenetration (Wiener, 1949).

Appropriately, the story of the pragmatists' development of pluralism is a complex one indeed. Certainly, not all the preceding figures would concur with all the propositions of their colleagues. Still, the story told by the pen of James is perhaps the paradigm case of pragmatic pluralism. For James pluralism was a fundamental tenet of this metaphysics, and few writers with such conviction spoke so eloquently and maintained such visibility for so long. Hence, the focus of the present discussion of pragmatic pluralism has been on the version offered by James. Indeed, it is fitting that the story of the origins of pluralism both begins (recall the discussion of philosophical temperaments) and ends with James.[4]

ORIGINS OF THE METHOD OF CORRELATION IN PSYCHOLOGY

Numerous studies of the historical development of the use of mathematics and statistical theory in psychology have been undertaken (Brooks & Aalto, 1981; Cattell, 1966a; Cronbach, 1957, 1975; Leary, 1978, 1980; Richards, 1978). It is generally known that serious successful attempts to mathematize or quantify psychological phenomena may be traced to at least the 17th century. Both Gottfried Wilhelm Leibniz (1646–1716) and his early interpreter Christian Wolff (1679–1754) were instrumental in the early development of a mathematical psychology. The purpose of this section is not to recount, reinterpret, or particularly vivify the history of mathematical psychology. Rather, the purpose is to focus on one aspect of that long, complicated history (the development of relational empirical thinking and correlational analysis). As is described below, correlational thinking and analysis bears in an interesting and unmistakable way

---

[4]The proliferation of alternative logics continued in the 20th century. For example, both Rescher (1977) and Waismann (1946) contend that multiple alternative logical systems are genuinely adequate in at least selected intellectual contexts. The plurality of viable logical systems entails, as might be expected, a certain relativism in the larger realm of logical thinking (Rescher, 1977).

upon the fundamental theses of pluralism. Hence, it is no surprise that some early Darwinist psychologists, as well as pragmatists, contributed substantively to the conceptual foundation of pluralism and at least indirectly to the intellectual propagation and institutional support of correlational analysis.

Early Contributions

Although preceded by Francis Hutcheson's (1694–1746) moral algebra (Brooks & Aalto, 1981), Johann Friedrich Herbart (1776–1841) is widely credited with establishing the first systematic mathematical psychology. A recent review of Herbart's contribution in this regard (Leary, 1980) suggests that these efforts occurred in nothing less than a fecund intellectual context. Not only had Leibniz and Wolff completed their important contributions to the mathematization of psychology, but quantification-oriented empiricists such as David Hume (1711–1776), the Bernoulli family, and Pierre Simon de Laplace (1749–1827) had long been actively engaged in applying probabilistic mathematics to the natural sciences (Leary, 1980; Struik, 1967).

Wolff appears to have been particularly influential in this regard. Not only was he the first to distinguish and demarcate empirical psychology and rational psychology (in *Psychologia empirica*, 1732, and *Psychologia rationalis*, 1734), but he offered the then novel proposition that mathematical analysis was as appropriate to empirical psychological phenomena as it was to the phenomena of physics (Richards, 1978). This approach he called "psycheometriae" or "psychimetriae" (Richards, 1978). Other 17th- and early 18th-century figures (such as A. A. Cournot, Adolphe Quetelet, J. P. Süssmilch, and J. N. Tetens) were engaged in applying statistics to social and demographic matters. In the two decades, 1830–1849, which Westergaard (1932) called the "Era of Enthusiasm" in the development of statistics, the contributions of the Belgian Quetelet are particularly prominent. Although lacking in certain matters of empirical rigor (see Westergaard, 1932), Quetelet successfully demonstrated that statistical investigations possessed a wide range of applications to social and behavioral problems. Quetelet's well-known *physique sociale* (in the 1835 work, *Sur l'homme et la développement de ses facultés ou essai de physique sociale*), founded on naturalistic philosophy rather than the providential perspective of such writers as Süssmilch, offered as its protagonist *l'homme moyen* (the average man). Quetelet's focus on the average man concept distracted him from attending to deviations from the average and discovering the regularities attendant in the law of errors (Hilts, 1973; Westergaard, 1932). Hence, his contribution to correlational techniques per se was limited (Hilts, 1973). Nevertheless, Quetelet's contribution to statistical thinking in the social sciences are manifold, and, as Baltes (1979) notes, many of his techniques, suggestions, and conclusions are vivid intellectual ancestors of contemporary developmental psychology.

Toward a Correlational Psychology

Immanuel Kant (1724–1804), although ultimately denying the possibility of applying mathematics to a rational psychology (in his *Metaphysical Foundations of Natural Science,* written in 1786; see also *Prolegomena to any Future Metaphysics,* written in 1783), nevertheless provided the conceptual foundation for perhaps the earliest correlational psychologist, J. F. Herbart (Leary, 1978; Mischel, 1967). A recent observer (Leary, 1980) has carefully dissected the corpus of Herbart's early 19th-century publications on the mathematization of psychology and identified four fundamental interrelated concepts. Inspired by Wolff's early psychometry (Richards, 1978) and owing in great measure to Kant (especially his *Critique of Pure Reason,* 1781, the *Prolegomena,* and the *Metaphysical Foundations*) and Leibniz (particularly *Monadology,* 1741), these fundamental concepts are: (1) *intensity,* which indicates the strength of mental phenomena; (2) *continuity,* which provides for the relation of degrees of intensity of mental phenomena; (3) *variation,* which provides for temporal variability in the degree of intensity of a mental phenomenon; and (4) *covariation,* which describes the consistently inverse relationship of the intensity of competing mental phenomena in one individual (Leary, 1980).

As Leary (1980) notes, Herbart was particularly influenced by the relational thinking of Leibniz. Rather unlike Newtonian absolutists of the same period, Leibniz and Herbart viewed nature (and the cosmos) as an organic whole composed of parts that are necessarily in a relational (or relative) posture to one another. Further, they both attempted to develop a relative mathematical analysis appropriate to the fundamentally relational character of nature and, especially in the case of Herbart, psychological phenomena (Leary, 1980). It was Herbart's achievement to demonstrate (at least conceptually) that a mathematical representation of the covariation of the intensities of mental phenomena is possible.

The theorems of the Calculus of Probabilities—already well-developed by Jacob Bernoulli (*Ars Conjectandi,* 1713), Abraham de Moivre (*The Doctrine of Chances,* 1718), Laplace, Cournot, and others—provided the foundation for the theory of correlation (Westergaard, 1932). Not only was probabilistic statistics being developed in the context of the 19th-century progress of physics—(e.g., the kinetic theory of physical chemistry, where behaviors of individual particles were accounted for probabilistically, see Leicester, 1956)—but similar applications were developed for the particular problems of biology. The application of the statistical method to physics and evolutionary biology benefited during this period from the Darwinistic notion that chance begets order (Weiner, 1949). If it is chance variations of individual organisms in the context of a particular ecological press that produces ordered differences on the species level, then such differences on the individual level might also be described or analyzed in similar terms.

Sir Francis Galton (1822–1911) was perhaps the first representative of what might be termed an amalgamation of Darwinistic psychology and the statistical method. Viewing individual humans as complex, integral units of a developing ecological system and fascinated with the wide variations of individual mental abilities, Galton developed instruments to measure individual differences and devised statistical techniques to describe his subsequent massive collection of quantitative data (Heidbreder, 1933). The founder of systematic psychometrics, Galton was also the first to apply the statistical method of correlation to the description of individual differences in mental abilities (Hearnshaw, 1964).

In 1885 Galton published a paper ("Co-relations and their measurement") in which he produced the first coefficient of correlation (Pearson, 1920). In his burgeoning work on inheritance, Galton sought to devise a statistical representation of the *partial* relationship between the abilities and characteristics of parents and their offspring; this he found in his correlation "index," which was (earlier in 1877) and continues to be signified by the lower case r. In an 1888 paper ("Correlations and their measurement chiefly from anthropometric data") Galton writes (quoted in Pearson, 1920):

> It is easy to see that co-relation must be the consequence of the variations of the two organs being partly due to common causes. If they were wholly due to common causes, the co-relation would be perfect, as is approximately the case with the symmetrically disposed parts of the body. If they were in no respect due to common causes, the co-relation would be *nil*. Between these two extremes are an endless number of intermediate cases, and it will be shown how the closeness of co-relation in any particular case admits of being expressed by a single number [p. 39].

Karl Pearson (1857–1936), who produced perhaps the definitive Galton biography (Pearson, 1930), and who was greatly inspired by Galton's statistical (read: correlational) work (especially the latter's *Natural Inheritance*, which was published in 1889), corroborated and extended Galton's statistical methods. Although Pearson did not coin the phrase "coefficient of correlation,"[5] he did, in 1896, demonstrate the superiority of an earlier formula (devised by the French astronomer Bravais in 1846) and coined the expression "product-moment," by which it is still known today (Hearnshaw, 1964; Pearson, 1920).

As Hearnshaw (1964) notes, Pearson believed that: "correlation was not merely a technique but an idea which illuminated the whole field of scientific method [p. 68]." That is, in the continuous, novel, unrepeatable development of the universe, the pure category of simple cause-and-effect relationships is of somewhat restricted usefulness. As Pearson (1911, p. 170, quoted in Hearnshaw, 1964) himself writes:

---

[5]The economist, F. Y. Edgeworth, is credited with first using the phrase "coefficient of correlation." The zoologist, W. F. R. Weldon, used the expression "Galton's functions" (Hearnshaw, 1964). Both men were founders, with Pearson and Galton, of *Biometrika* in October, 1901.

we cannot classify by sameness, but only by likeness. Resemblance connotes variation, and variation marks limited not absolute contingency. How often when a new phenomenon has been observed do we hear the question asked: what is the cause of it? A question which it may be absolutely impossible to answer, whereas the question: to what degree are other phenomena associated with it? may admit to easy solution and result in invaluable knowledge [p. 68].

Darwinism, with its multicausal view of variation, its allowance for multiple specific mechanisms of change, and its call for examining unmanipulable causes or circumstances *in relation to* observed effects or variations (Kleiner, 1979), directly contributed to the relational thinking of Galton and Pearson. As was described previously, putative relational thinking was also developing among the early pragmatists. At the same general time that Charles Sanders Peirce was linking the intellectual strands of Darwinism, molecular physics, and the statistical method (e.g., with the concept ''change begets order,'' see Wiener, 1949), Chauncey Wright was publicly defending Darwinism on the basis of the statistical nature of biological laws (Wiener, 1949). William James accepted Peirce's probabilistic, statistically based principles as support for his pluralistic empiricism (Wiener, 1949). This apparent intellectual link between pluralistic pragmatism and statistical methods (and especially correlational techniques) is as yet tantalizingly incomplete. Although such a connection has been broached at least once before,[6] it has not as yet been thoroughly explored. The following sections address this issue in considerably more detail and in a more contemporary context.

Multivariate Correlational Analysis

In recent times a number of writers have recognized multiple streams of empirical activity in the social and behavioral sciences. Cronbach (1957, 1975) identified and discussed the approaches of correlational (differential) versus experimental psychology. The distinction between the study of *existing* variation represented in individual differences and variability *produced* by manipulative experimental designs to examine relationships among variables is a very helpful one in clarifying some of the essential differences between general approaches to understanding behavior. The distinction seems to capture in broad terms much of the history of psychology. Each approach has a long tradition, staunch adherents, and has produced both methodological innovations and a substantial body of information. Rapprochement has been called for a number of times, and useful attempts can be seen in particular domains (Cattell, 1979, 1980; Cronbach,

---

[6]See Mancuso (1977), who notes the similarity between the descriptive approaches of pragmatic contextual psychology and the correlational psychology described by Cronbach (1957, 1975).

1957, 1975; Tucker, 1966), techniques, and studies (Hultsch, Nesselroade, & Plemons, 1976), but it does not generally obtain.

The development of multivariate correlational analysis methods has occurred largely since the turn of the century, and it boasts an illustrious cast of behavioral and social scientists, statisticians, and mathematicians. Although some psychologists have been good mathematicians and even respectable statisticians, the disciplines have not necessarily collaborated heavily in the development of analytic tools. In fact, traces of multiple, distinct lineages of some analytical tools still remain. One example is the engrained distinction between factor analysis as a "psychometric" versus a "statistical" method (Gorsuch, 1974).

One psychologist who has both written about the history of multivariate correlational methods and contributed to it broadly for nearly 50 years is Raymond B. Cattell (Cattell, 1934, 1980). Because of his leadership in promoting the growth and application of multivariate correlational methods and his broad yet programmatic set of contributions to both method and substance, we have chosen to highlight the work of Cattell more than that of others who would be properly included in a review of multivariate contributions in psychology were it not for editorial constraints.

R. B. Cattell was the prime mover in the formation of the Society of Multivariate Experimental Psychology and the editor of the *Handbook of Multivariate Experimental Psychology* published in 1966. That same year he helped to launch the journal, *Multivariate Behavioral Research,* with a guest editorial (Cattell, 1966a) revealing some of the history and ideas leading to the founding of the society and journal. In that editorial Cattell furthered the discussion of differential versus manipulative experimental approaches by distinguishing between what he identified as the Wundt–Helmholtz–Pavlov tradition and the Galton–Thurstone movement. Both were seen as experimental approaches, but with the former portrayed as bivariate and manipulative in design and the latter as multivariate and "freely observing." Cattell (1966a) pointed out that the Galton–Thurstone movement involved the "extraction of connections, causal or structural by intricate statistical analysis applied to observations on naturally occurring events." In 1966, that promultivariate-corelational argument was made chiefly on behalf of factor analysis, but today it aptly describes what many aspire to do by means of causal modeling. Indeed, the elaboration of causal modeling procedures into two explicit parts—the measurement model and the structural model—has provided the basis for a clear linkage between traditional factor analysis and causal modeling.

Among the advantages Cattell described as accruing to the multivariate approach are a more adequate representation of concepts, conceptual precision and perspective, consistency of statistical inference, and economy of design and data collection. These gains are realized because of the ability of multivariate procedures to utilize information about the interrelation of numerous measures, on both the dependent and independent variable side, as well as to identify relationships between dependent and independent variables. In fact, as Cattell (1966a) pointed out, the multivariate approach is noncommittal and open-minded about the dependent–independent variable relationship. Establishing which is which is often the product of empirical investigation rather than experimental design.

Cattell's research on personality and ability fits into the long history of the Galton–Thurstone tradition and extends it into the 1980s. It would be instructive to detail his intellectual history here, but Cattell has recently done it himself in an exciting account of a "journey through hyper-space" (Cattell, 1974). For purposes of brevity, we here identify only three outstanding figures who proximally influenced Cattell's development. These three influential figures were selected to illustrate the nature of Cattell's early intellectual context because they also are closely identified with multivariate correlation work, especially factor analysis, and with shaping the field of human abilities—a substantive domain that neither day to day experience and practice could then, nor historical analyses can now, separate from the development of multivariate correlational methods. The three are Charles Edward Spearman (1863–1945), Cyril Burt (1883–1971), and L. L. Thurstone (1887–1958). Obviously, a thorough study of the history of human abilities research would turn up many more scientists who have made outstanding contributions to multivariate methods, such as Godfrey H. Thomson, Edward Lee Thorndike, Truman L. Kelley, Karl J. Holzinger, and more recently, J. P. Guilford, Louis Guttman, Lloyd G. Humphreys, John L. Horn, L. R Tucker, P. E. Vernon, and others.

Spearman published a paper on the determination and measurement of general intelligence in 1904. His influential book. *The Abilities of Man* appeared in 1927. Thurstone, who elucidated the concept of simple structure as a criterion for the resolution of factorial solutions, published *The Primary Mental Abilities* in 1938. His book, *The Vectors of Mind,* appeared in 1935. Burt, whose contributions to the multivariate correlational literature will stand for years to come, published *The Factors of the Mind* in 1941.

Psychologists such as Burt, Spearman, Thurstone, and Cattell promoted the development of multivariate correlational research both through their contributions to methodology and their substantive work in areas such as human abilities. Indeed, as noted earlier, an examination of the field of human abilities illustrates well the development and utilization of multivariate correlational methods. But growth in other substantive domains has depended on these methods, too. In the personality/temperament domain reliance on multivariate correlational methods for determining structure and developing measuring instruments by programmatic researchers like Cattell, Eysenck, and Guilford, for example, has also been well-documented. Cattell and his colleagues have utilized a variety of factor analytic methods in attempting to structure the domain of motivation (Cattell, Horn, Sweney, & Radcliffe, 1964). From a more methodological perspective, advances in the study of psychological change (Cattell, 1966b; Harris, 1963; Nesselroade & Baltes, 1979), causal modeling (Bentler, 1980), scaling (Torgerson, 1958) and psychometric theory (Nunnally, 1967), to name but a few areas, have rested to a considerable extent on developments in multivariate correlational work. These brief allusions to the role that multivariate correlational methods have played in the broad-based study of behavior convey only slightly their applicability and use.

Clearly, much discussion, presentation, and application of multivariate, correlational methods have emphasized the study of relationships among multiple dependent variables. No doubt this has been extremely valuable. For example, from a measurement point of view, multiple indicators can be argued to give a more appropriate and useful representation of broad concepts than will a single indicator, no matter how rationally it is selected. But questions related to determinants, influences, causes, etc., and their relationships have not been ignored by researchers identified with multivariate correlational research. Many of the early factor analysts regarded their "discoveries" to be functional unities that explained observable events. The concept of simple structure, which was set out by Thurstone in 1931, became one of the critical features of Cattell's scheme for using factor analysis to identify patterns of causal influences; an idea that Cattell has advanced many times. For example, in a chapter that appeared in a "festschrift" honoring Burt, Cattell (1965) identified a number of models that he argued were pertinent in developing causal networks from multivariate correlational data. One such model, the reticular network, was incorporated by McArdle (1979) as a prominent component of a recent, systematic attempt to elaborate causal modeling procedures more in line with current thinking in structural equation analysis.

The advent of high speed, large-capacity automatic computation equipment has helped to unleash the potential of multivariate correlational methods not only for exploratory analyses but for confirmatory analyses. Recent developments include the confirmatory analysis procedures that, in principle, are designed to help with the systematic appraisal of the validity of hypothesized causal chains. Approaches such as are embodied in the LISREL (Linear structural relations) programs of Jöreskog and Sörbom (1978) provide for multiple causes, multiple outcomes, and a variety of linkage patterns between them in the context of model-fitting approaches. With these modeling techniques (Bentler, 1980; Horn & McArdle, 1980) multivariate, correlational approaches to the study of behavior have made their latest and, perhaps, strongest attempt yet to lay legitimate claim to a portion of the domain of establishing causal relationships. How successful the exploitation of correlational data for the purpose of causal modeling will be is uncertain at this point. Certainly the level of statistic-mathematical work is impressive—perhaps much more so than the level of persuasiveness of the logico-philosophical underpinnings of the approach at this point.

It does seem clear from current emphases on structural equations (Bentler, 1980) that the opening pages of a new chapter on the use of multivariate correlational methods in psychology—the extension of the Galton–Thurstone movement—is being written and that it maintains threads of continuity with the earlier parts of this portion of history's manuscript. Whether the latest chapter will be a long one or a short one, we cannot say. We are convinced, however, that it will not be the final one.[7]

A century or more of correlational and multivariate correlational labor has brought us many products—both substantive and methodological ones. As these events have come about, we have been made to think multidimensionally, and to confront the representation of interesting psychological phenomena as patterns defined across many variables rather than to insist on making concepts operational as a single variable. Of the various capabilities that multivariate correlational methods have brought to the study of behavior, let us identify three that, in particular, seem to be compatible with the "pluralistic pragmatism" discussed previously. First, multivariate correlational methods provide for the utilization of samples of variables rather than single variables, both for empirically delimiting the structure and boundaries of content domains and for studying relationships among different domains, at a given point in time. Second, multivariate correlational methods allow one to identify and study patterns of relationships among variables. Third, the latest developments in studying correlational patterns such as the analysis of covariance structures provide a way to incorporate the notions of the aforementioned points one and two into the testing of putative causal relationships.

Given the Jamesian pluralistic interpretation of the nature of the universe as described earlier, the psychologist is advised to explore the use of methods that: (1) allow for multiple observable representations of underlying concepts; (2) permit the search for invariant relationships at levels more abstract than between two observables; (3) provide a way to detect changes in patterns of relationships; and (4) offer procedures for fitting alternative causal systems to a given set of data. The history and current status of multivariate correlational methods indicates a clear sensitivity to these objectives and points to at least one way of realizing them. The extent to which the early proponents of multivariate correlational techniques were *directly* influenced by their coevals, the pragmatic con-

---

[7]From the other side of the experimental versus correlational dichotomy it should be pointed out that it is possible to design univariate studies that allow for the investigation of the effects of multiple independent variables. These multiple influences may even be conceptualized as acting simultaneously. However, there are two important aspects in which univariate designs differ from the corresponding multivariate ones. First, the number of possible antecedents (independent variables) that can be incorporated in a given experiment (and whose effect pattern can be interpreted), though more than one, is quite limited. Second, the application of such multiple treatments is not designed to mimic the putative causal patterns of some real life situation. Rather, the experiment is usually (ideally?) designed so that the various treatments being applied to the experimental units are uncorrelated with each other. This enables the investigator to sort out the various contributions of the independent variables. However, because treatments in the real world are likely to be correlated in some way, this very goal flies in the face of the "multivariate ethic."

textual psychologists, is uncertain. It is apparent, however, that both burgeoning traditions partook of certain shared antecedent developments (e.g., Darwinism, especially in the case of Thorndike and, through Galton, Spearman, as well as the advent of simple correlational techniques). It is the convergence of theory and method, rather than a direct causal linkage, that is the prominent point of this section.

Multivariate Models and the Study of Development

The application of correlational methods to the study of various kinds of change has a relatively long history. In addition to the standard psychometrically oriented assessment of change discussed by Bereiter (1963), Lord (1963), and Woodrow (1932), to name but a few, there were early attempts to use multivariate correlational methods to study oscillatory behavior (Flugel, 1928), function fluctuation (Thouless, 1936), and other forms of intraindividual variability (Fiske & Rice, 1955). Cattell's (1952) initial statement of the covariation chart or "data box," which involved the identification of the six fundamental patterns of covariation, included equal emphasis on the study of structure in stable and labile psychological phenomena.

The multivariate correlational orientation is strongly linked to the study of development. Coan (1966) and Emmerich (1968), for example, clearly explicated linkages between multivariate correlational concepts and the structure concept of development. McCall (1970) reviewed the uses of multivariate procedures in developmental psychology for readers of Carmichael's *Manual of Child Psychology*. Nesselroade (1970) identified several areas of convergence between multivariate techniques and such developmental concepts as qualitative versus quantitative changes, differentiation versus integration, continuity versus discontinuity, and stability versus instability. In a comprehensive treatment of behavioral development, Wohlwill (1973) argued that a good case could be made for correlational analysis to be the method par excellence for developmental study. Further, he argued compellingly for the multivariate approach as the appropriate level of analytic complexity to match the patterning of relationships that need to be focused on if we are to understand human development. Clearly, it has been a mainstay in, for example, the development of a life-span orientation as represented in the work of Baltes, Schaie, and others (Baltes, Reese, & Lipsitt, 1980; Baltes, Reese, & Nesselroade, 1977).

In a discussion of the role of multivariate techniques in the study of life-span development, Baltes and Nesselroade (1973) specified three assumptions underlying a multivariate approach to the study of behavioral phenomena. First, any consequent is likely to be a function of multiple determinants. Second, any determinant is likely to have multiple consequents. Third, the examination of multiple systems of antecedent-consequent relationships is a useful way to study complex systems. These assumptions stand in marked contrast to those implicit in univariate experimental research paradigms (i.e., establishing relationships between a single dependent variable and one or more independent variables or determinants). Baltes and Nesselroade's observations are not limited to multivariate correlational paradigms but apply to the use of multiple variables in manipulative, experimental situations, too. Thus, although here we are mainly emphasizing aspects of correlational work, many aspects of multivariate models and approaches cut across the traditional correlational versus manipulative experimental dichotomy.

For the developmentalist, the capacity to deal with multiple dependent variables is only part of the picture. Understanding the mechanisms of development requires one to be able to deal with the multiple determinants aspect mentioned earlier. As with the dependent variable side of the equation, one needs to be able to work simultaneously with various aspects of putative determinants. In the context of measurement problems in the study of aging, for example, Labouvie (1980) pointed out that researchers need to attend as much to the measurement characteristics of the independent variables as to those of the dependent variables. One such characteristic is the patterning of covariation among causal influences. Another is the establishment of some form of measurement equivalence for "treatments" as well as for "outcomes." Thus, pinning down the nature of processes in antecedent-process-consequent approaches to studying development should benefit from the employment of multivariate correlational methods in relation to the structure they permit one to inject into the configurations of both antecedent and consequent sets of variables.

Patterns of interrelationships among variables are the raw material for much of the speculating and theorizing that characterize differential psychology. For the developmentalist even more intriguing possibilities open up. The measurement variables of interest may correlate differently at different ages, in different epochs, in different subpopulations, etc., creating not only the opportunity but the necessity to observe and understand differences and changes in such patterns. By means of multivariate correlational techniques, the study of development as the study of intraindividual change and interindividual differences in intraindividual change can be conducted at either the level of observable variables or at more abstract levels composed of patterns of interrelationships as the state of theoretical development indicates to be appropriate.[8]

Pluralism and the Concept of Development

One conceptual area not yet examined explicitly in our discussion is the intersection between the notion of pluralism and the study of psychological develop-

---

[8]It may be noted that efforts to link evolutionary processes and biological ontogenesis from a multivariate perspective have been receiving increasing attention (Real, 1980). These analyses focus on the diversity of behaviors, forms, functions, and modes of fitness, and the consequent necessity to adopt a multivariate structural perspective on variation (Real, 1980; see also Haldane, 1955; Lewontin, 1966; Van Valen, 1974, 1978 for further discussions).

ment. Obviously, there are multiple definitions and paradigms involved in the conceptualization of development, and the adherents of each view are actively engaged in their tasks of description and explanation. Each group has relatively autonomous questions, methodologies, and criteria. Thus, a metatheoretical and methodological pluralism exists with respect to the activities of developmentalists that even commonsense seems to dictate is felicitous, given the rather embryonic state of our scientific understanding of development. Moreover, within a given world view or paradigm, logical arguments can be made for the merits of a multiplicity of techniques, choices of variables for study, populations to be sampled from, etc. But these are not the only examples of pluralism to which we are trying to establish a link. A responsible call for pluralism in the study of development must mean more than simply arguing for many investigators to try many approaches, much as the novice at pool may decide that the best strategy is to get as many balls moving as possible and surely something will drop into a pocket.

Is the study of development to be confined to those robust, biologically orchestrated irreversible functions that can be observed and identified, or should it include patterns of behavioral change that appear to be susceptible to culture- and history-graded influences?; that is, does there exist a single, immutable trajectory of change (developmental monism) or are there multiple possible trajectories (developmental pluralism)? From a slightly different perspective, may development be portrayed in terms of a single mode of experience or are multiple modes required (Lyons, 1981)? From the standpoint of pluralism as we have developed the concept in earlier sections of this chapter, our interest lies mainly in empirical inquiry regarding developmental phenomena that are subject to continual change and influenced by various historically identifiable sources. The life-span conception of development, with its attendant focus on matters of data collection, design, and analysis strategies (Baltes, Cornelius, & Nesselroade, 1978, 1979) has led to findings that seem to be compatible with the pluralistic conceptions presented earlier. In the first place, an overt emphasis on the study of interindividual differences in intraindividual changes allows for alternate patterns and underlying mechanisms of development. Second, a variety of research reviewed by Baltes et al. (1977, 1979) indicates that there are several major kinds of influence on behavioral development (ontogenetic age-graded influences, evolutionary history-graded influences, and non-normative influences).

The recognition of the influence of historical, evolutionary forces on the development of behavior has clear implications if one accepts the contextual, pluralistic tenets of an ever-changing, unfinished universe. If developmental phenomena are subject to influences that are themselves undergoing evolutionary change, then the prospect of achieving a final codification of those phenomena by any one generation of researchers is dimmed. Although a semblance of finality may be approached within a single theoretical or methodological tradition, a vibrant developmental psychology will continue to produce alternative perspectives. Many of these perspectives will arrive on the scene with competing assumptions. In turn, many of these competing assumptions will beget mutually piercing criticisms, sets of preferred questions with restricted ranges of answers, as well as a poignant sense of disbelief that anyone could have ever believed what came before.

CONCLUDING PROPOSITIONS

Summary

Numerous recent reviews of the state of developmental psychology—and, in particular, life-span developmental psychology—have suggested that a pluralistic approach to both methodology and theory may be profitable (Baltes et al., 1980; Baltes & Willis, 1977; Lerner et al., in press). It is not uncommon on such occasions for this pluralism to be implicitly associated with a contextual metatheory. Setting aside for the moment the question of the intellectual persuasiveness of the contemporary recommendations—as well as their somewhat casual neglect of definition and detail—in this chapter we sought to explore the riddle of this connection; that is, this chapter originates in an interest in what is seen as a tacit triumvirate: pluralism, contextual-developmental psychology, and (often) multivariate-correlational analytical techniques.

In an attempt to explore the nature of these connections, we inquired into the origins of the three elements of the tacit triumvirate. In these inquiries we found that the intellectual ancestry of pluralism is resonant and distinguished. Although the term pluralism (especially as applied to psychology) was apparently introduced by William James, the concept it represents had already been a familiar furnishing of the intellectual scenery for more than a century. Two interwoven strands of the development of this concept were identified. First, in the 16th and 17th centuries astronomical evidence was accumulating that the universe may extend indefinitely in all directions. If this were the case (some cosmographers such as Giordano Bruno reasoned), then the stars being discovered may (as our sun) sport a system of orbiting planets. Further, if this were the case in a presumably infinite number of circumstances, then the probability that many of these planets would possess life-sustaining conditions would be relatively high. Thus is born the plurality of worlds hypothesis.

The second strand of the development of the pluralistic concept is in some ways the "dark" side of the first. As the realm of possibilities of the universe is enlarged, the singularity of human existence on this particular planet is diminished. This, at least, is a pervasive thesis of such 16th- and 17th-century skeptics as Montaigne and Pascal. For Montaigne, change, diversity, and the indefinite extension of life are fundamental propositions of his pluralism. The early philosophical pluralism of the skeptics suggests that a plurality of worlds begets a plurality of realities. Hence, Montaigne advocates a philosophical tolerance that bears a structural kinship with such contemporary pluralists as Paul Feyerabend, and such contemporary contextual psychologists as James Jenkins (1974).

The shattering of the temporal boundaries of the universe that occurred in the late 18th and early 19th centuries by geologists and naturalists amplified the sense of philosophical relativism. Human knowledge and rationality were now being portrayed as mutable, fallible, and (not to despair) as adaptive or useful. The evolutionary model of knowledge is, as some contemporary writers have shown (Popper, 1972; Toulmin, 1972), consonant with Darwinistic evolutionism and pragmatism. Thus, it was seen that James seemingly gathered the historical strands of the pluralistic concept and wove them together in his pragmatic psychology. In James one may see the concept of a pluralistic universe, a fallible view of rationality, and an evolutionary or temporal perspective on human behavioral and social functioning.

In the second part of our inquiries, we explored the origins of relational empirical thinking and correlational analysis in psychology. Although halting short of making explicit causal historical inferences, we suggested that the intellectual climate that yielded the concept of pluralism may have also engendered correlational thinking in psychology. Except to note common strands of intellectual heritage, only a weak causal chain is advanced. It is noted that Wolff and Herbart put some distance between an empirical (or quantifiable) psychology and a purely rational psychology. It is also noted that Quetelet founded a social science on naturalistic principles rather than providential ones. It is observed that Herbart proposed a relational cosmology and was among the first to seriously attend to the concept of covariation in psychology. It is further observed that Galton, influenced by naturalism and evolutionism, developed the first application of the correlation index to psychological problems. The emergence of the Pearson product-moment correlation coefficient is seen to be the capstone of many strands of these developments. Finally, the multivariate correlational approach, one element of the tacit triumvirate of developmental psychology, is traced to these 19th-century developments. The "factor school" of psychology is portrayed simply as a recent moment in the development of relational, multidimensional, empirical thinking in psychology.

Certainly our attempt to describe historical and intellectual antecedents common to both pluralism and multivariate correlational analysis originates in an interest in explanation. Nevertheless, it is at this point that discretion prevails. Our acknowledged interest in *interpreting* the preceding rather descriptive inquiries has been until now cautiously suppressed. In what follows we loosen ever so slightly the shackles that have bound our "intellectual libido." First, we attempt to describe the conceptual tenets shared by the elements of the so-called tacit triumvirate. Finally, we describe our view of a historically informed foundation for a pluralistic multivariate-correlational developmental psychology.

The argument we wish to advance at this point (hopefully with a certain measure of historical support) is that pluralism (à la James) and multivariate correlational approaches to the study of behavior share some common tenets, if not deliberately, then at least through temporal accident. We have described a historical context in which ample opportunity existed for the mutual influence of pluralism and multivariate correlational psychology, although, admittedly, we lack the testimony of participants and eye witnesses who could make the case absolutely convincing. To make this connection more concrete we summarize, at some risk of oversimplification, the principles of Jamesian pluralism detailed earlier as representing two general lines of thought.

First, many of the principles reflect a notion of incompleteness or "changingness" about the universe and about our understanding of it. The devices that we manufacture to represent the universe ultimately will fall short of the ideal. Putative causal mechanisms will not be fully dependable and relationships among variables will not be demonstrably invariant.

In an unfinished, everchanging world, the question "To what degree are other phenomena associated with phenomenon x?" is one that must be asked over and over. The answers may differ with time. Asked in the context of a pluralistic orientation, the question is more one of exploring or "discovering" relationships than one of testing hypothesized, bivariate causal mechanisms (although both approaches are valuable). The situation leads to a need to explore relationship or covariance systems both within antecedent and consequent classes of variables and between them as well. A set of experimentally verified, well-ordered causal connections does not seem to be a reasonable expectation from the pluralistic viewpoint.

The extensions of spatial and temporal boundaries noted earlier further dramatized the empirical diversity that scientific disciplines had to confront. Limitations in existing systems of lawful relationships had to be recognized and then the systems either replaced or altered to increase their range of applicability. That, it is clear, is the concern of *external validity* or generalizability, and it is a need that is not met by the highly controlled, precise, and in other respects desirable laboratory work as well as it is by the activities associated with the "freely observing" multivariate Galton–Thurstone movement identified by Cattell.

Second, there is a marked thread of multidimensionality woven through the fabric of pluralism. Observed events depend on many influences. Interesting behavioral phenomena arise from the concerted effects of a multitude of causes. Both antecedent and consequent concepts that are likely to be of interest may require multiple indicators to be pinned down as unambiguously as possible.

Both the incompleteness and multidimensionality notions are compatible with, even inherent in, the multivariate correlational approach. Whether doing exploratory analyses to identify possible causal relationships or causal modeling to test hypothesized causal sequences, the multivariate correlational approach supports the examination of possible explanatory schemes.

Toward a Pluralistic Developmental Psychology

A pluralistic multivariate developmental psychology may or may not arise primarily in a "tough-minded" assumptive context; that is, although such a psychology may often embody a certain skepticism and a certain empiricism, it may also incorporate a certain measure of idealism and rationalism. In the very least, the pluralist will recognize the inherent value of: (1) the independent simultaneous existence of multiple representations or schemes of reality; and (2) multiple competing interpretive frameworks *within* each of those schemes. Further, the pluralist will deny an inherent or necessary a priori superiority to one scheme or another. All such schemes must be allowed an opportunity to demonstrate their worth in the arena of intellectual inquiry. For the pluralist such a credo is both intellectually sound—providing a context for the rigorous testing and advancement of empirical knowledge—and ethically cogent—insuring that the psychological enterprise operates in a free society (Feyerabend, 1978).

It is interesting (but not surprising) to note that most pluralistic developmental psychologists have evidenced the empirical tendency. Nevertheless, most openly recognize the valuable contributions of more rationalistic (read: less-empiricistic) approaches to developmental problems (e.g., the biographical method of Charlotte Bühler, 1935 and, more recently, Daniel Levinson [see Levinson, Darrow, Klein, Levinson & McKee, 1978]). All this is to say that a pluralistic psychologist may (and perhaps should) adopt a preferred scheme of reality, even preferred methods (e.g., multivariate correlational), whereas at the same time appreciating the contributions of other methods, or even other interpretive frameworks. To accomplish this coincident appreciation it may be incumbent upon the psychologist to adopt the "inside" view of the interpretive framework. Much as ethnomethodologists immerse themselves in the framework of the target culture, and Collingwoodian historians view historical events from within the historical context, pluralistic psychologists may evaluate alternative models from within their own (the models) system of rationality. Thus the pluralist is in some sense at least a moderate relativist. Of course, the flag of alarm that is often raised when the term relativism is broached does not go unheeded by the pluralist. Extreme or pure relativism is considered to be as dangerous or dogmatic as extreme absolutism. The pluralist may simply endorse what some writers have called a moderate relativism or a healthy skepticism (Kagan, 1967; McHoul, 1981; Radnitzky, 1970). Relativism, even as explicit as that of Wittgenstein (1972), has informed numerous flourishing empirical programs (Collins, 1981). It is neither appropriate nor possible in this setting to further develop these ideas. Let us simply close with a set of propositions that, together, may contribute to an historically informed pluralistic multivariate-correlational developmental psychology.

To facilitate the presentation these propositions are presented in the following manner. Each proposition is viewed as a higher-order convergence of two lower-order themes. The lower-order themes derive from, first, the fundamental propositions of pluralism and, second, the fundamental propositions of multivariate correlational analysis. In this way, the first theme is the obverse of the second; the first being the theoretical side of the proposition and the second the empirical side. Our intention in juxtaposing the themes of the propositions is to both summarize principal ideas of the two domains as well as make explicit a basis for their integration.

Proposition 1
    First Theme: The universe—the to-be-known—is accepted as it appears to the observer.
    Second Theme: Free, nonmanipulative, naturalistic, observations of relationships is encouraged *in addition to* highly controlled, laboratory observation.

Proposition 2
    First Theme: The universe is a series of multidimensional, ever-changing facts.
    Second Theme: Concepts are defined as (temporal) patterns of relationships among variables, each of which may be multidimensional, thus making the concept a multidimensional one.

Proposition 3
    First Theme: Because the universe is excess and indeterminant, it, and knowledge of it, appears to be unfinished, incomplete, continuously changing.
    Second Theme: There is a contingency of patterns of relationships among variables and this contingency has two aspects: (1) the patterns are temporally mutable; and (2) they are contextually dependent.

More specifically, in terms of the mission of a pluralistic developmental psychology these three propositions may be rendered as follows:

Proposition 1. The human individual is accepted as it "naturally" appears to the observer and studied in terms of both nonmanipulative observations of relationships and highly controlled laboratory observation.

Proposition 2. The human individual comprises an ever-changing multidimensional system, and the concepts by which the facts of that system are interpreted are defined temporally and multidimensionally.

Proposition 3. Knowledge of the course(s) of psychological development is(are), like the development per se, unfinished and incomplete. Because the patterns of relationships used to represent that change are temporally mutable, each observed pattern is in some way contingent upon the context of observation.

ACKNOWLEDGMENT

The first author's work on this chapter was supported in part by National Institute of Aging predoctoral grant No. T32 AG00048. The chapter was initially written while the first author was at The Pennsylvania State University.

REFERENCES

Abrams, M. H. The deconstructive angel. *Critical Inquiry*, 1977, *3*, 425–438.

Allen, G. W. *William James*. New York: Viking, 1967.

Baltes, P. B. Life-span developmental psychology: Some converging observations on history and theory. In P. B. Baltes & O. G. Brim, Jr. (Eds.), *Life-span development and behavior* (Vol. 2). New York: Academic Press, 1979.

Baltes, P. B., Cornelius, S. W., & Nesselroade, J. R. Cohort effects in behavioral development: Theoretical and methodological perspectives. *Minnesota Symposium on Child Psychology*, 1978, *11*, 1–63.

Baltes, P. B., Cornelius, S. W., & Nesselroade, J. R. Cohort effects in developmental psychology. In J. R. Nesselroade & P. B. Baltes (Eds.), *Longitudinal research in the study of behavior and development*. New York: Academic Press, 1979.

Baltes, P. B., & Nesselroade, J. R. The developmental analysis of individual differences on multiple measures. In J. R. Nesselroade & H. W. Reese (Eds.), *Life-span developmental psychology: Methodological issues*. New York: Academic Press, 1973.

Baltes, P. B., Reese, H. W., & Lipsitt, L. P. Life-span developmental psychology. In M. R. Rosenzweig & L. W. Porter (Eds.), *Annual Review of Psychology* (Vol. 31). Palo Alto, Calif.: Annual Reviews, 1980.

Baltes, P. B., Reese, H. W., & Nesselroade, J. R. *Life-span developmental psychology: Introduction to research methods*. Monterey, Calif.: Brooks/Cole, 1977.

Baltes, P. B., & Willis, S. L. Toward psychological theories of aging and development. In J. E. Birren & K. W. Schaie (Eds.), *Handbook of the psychology of aging*. New York: Van Nostrand Reinhold, 1977.

Barnes, H. E. *An intellectual and cultural history of the western world* (Vol. 3). *From the nineteenth century to the present day*. New York: Dover, 1965.

Bentler, P. M. Multivariate analysis with latent variables: Causal modeling. In M. R. Rosenzweig & L. W. Porter (Eds.), *Annual Review of Psychology* (Vol. 31). Palo Alto, Calif.: Annual Reviews, 1980.

Bereiter, C. Some persisting dilemmas in the measurement of change. In C. W. Harris (Ed.), *Problems in measuring change*. Madison: University of Wisconsin Press, 1963.

Booth, W. C. M. H. Abrams: Historian as critic, critic as pluralist. *Critical Inquiry*, 1976, *2*, 411–445.

Booth, W. C. "Preserving the exemplar": or, How not to dig our own graves. *Critical Inquiry*, 1977, *3*, 407–423.

Brooks, G. P., & Aalto, S. K. The rise and fall of moral algebra: Francis Hutcheson and the mathematization of psychology. *Journal of the History of the Behavioral Sciences*, 1981, *17*, 343–356.

Buhler, C. *From birth to maturity*. London: Kegan Paul, 1935.

Burt, C. *The factors of the mind*. New York: MacMillan, 1941.

Butterfield, H. *The origins of modern science 1300–1800* (Rev. ed.), New York: Free Press, 1957.

Campbell, D. T. Evolutionary epistemology. In P. Schilpp (Ed.), *The philosophy of Karl Popper* (Vol. 1). Lasalle, Ill.: Open Court, 1974.

Cattell, R. B. Friends and enemies: A psychological study of character and temperament. *Character and Personality*, 1934, *3*, 54–63.

Cattell, R. B. The three basic factor-analytic research designs—their interrelations and deviations. *Psychological Bulletin*, 1952, *49*, 499–520.

Cattell, R. B. Higher-order factor structures and reticular-versus-hierarchical formulae for their interpretation. In C. Banks & C. L. Broadhurst (Eds.), *Studies in psychology in honor of Sir Cyril Burt*. London: University of London Press, 1965.

Cattell, R. B. Guest editorial: Multivariate behavioral research and the integrative challenge. *Multivariate Behavioral Research*, 1966, *1*, 4–23. (a)

Cattell, R. B. Patterns of change: Measurement in relation to state-dimension, trait change, lability, and process concepts. In R. B. Cattell (Ed.), *Handbook of multivariate experimental psychology*. Chicago: Rand McNally, 1966. (b)

Cattell, R. B. Travels in psychological hyperspace. In T. S. Krawiec (Ed.), *The psychologist* (Vol. 2). New York: Oxford University Press, 1974.

Cattell, R. B. *Personality and learning theory* (Vol. 1). *The structure of personality in its environment*. New York: Springer, 1979.

Cattell, R. B. *Personality and learning theory* (Vol. 2). *A systems theory of maturation and structural learning*. New York: Springer, 1980.

Cattell, R. B., Horn, J. L., Sweney, A. B., & Radcliffe, J. *The motivation analysis test, MAT*. Champaigne, Ill.: Institute for Personality and Ability Testing, 1964.

Coan, R. W. Child personality and developmental psychology. In R. B. Cattell (Ed.), *Handbook of multivariate experimental psychology*. Chicago: Rand McNally, 1966.

Collins, H. M. Stages in the empirical programme of relativism. *Social Studies of Science*, 1981, *11*, 3–10.

Crane, R. S. *The languages of criticism and the structure of poetry*. Toronto: University of Toronto Press, 1953.

Cronbach, L. J. The two disciplines of scientific psychology. *American Psychologist*, 1957, *12*, 671–684.

Cronbach, L. J. Beyond the two disciplines of scientific psychology. *American Psychologist*, 1975, *30*, 116–127.

Dewey, J. *Reconstruction in philosophy*. Boston: Beacon Press, 1948.

Dooley, P. K. *Pragmatism as humanism: The philosophy of William James*. Totowa, N.J.: Littlefield, Adams, 1974.

Eiseley, L. *Darwin's century*. Garden City, N.Y.: Doubleday, 1958.

Emmerich, W. Personality development and concepts of structure. *Child Development*, 1968, *39*, 671–690.

Feyerabend, P. Problems of empiricism. In R. Colodny (Ed.), *Beyond the edge of certainty*. Englewood Cliffs, N.J.: Prentice–Hall, 1965.

Feyerabend, P. Against method: Outline of an anarchistic theory of knowledge. In M. Radner & S. Winokur (Eds.), *Minnesota Studies in the Philosophy of Science* (Vol. 4). Minneapolis: University of Minnesota Press, 1970.

Feyerabend, P. *Against method*. London: NLB, 1975.

Feyerabend, P. *Science in a free society*. London: NLB, 1978.

Feyerabend, P. Democracy, elitism, and scientific method. *Inquiry*, 1980, *23*, 3–18.

Fiske, D. W., & Rice, L. Intraindividual response variability. *Psychological Bulletin*, 1955, *52*, 217–250.

Flugal, J. C. Practice, fatigue, and oscillation. *British Journal of Psychology*, Monograph Supplement, 1928, 4 (No. 13), 1–92.

Gallie, W. B. *Philosophy and historical understanding*. New York: Schocken, 1964.

Gorsuch, R. L. *Factor analysis*. Philadelphia: W. B. Sanders, 1974.

Haldane, J. B. S. The measurement of variation. *Evolution*, 1955, *9*, 484.

Harris, C. W. *Problems in measuring change*. Madison: University of Wisconsin Press, 1963.

Hearnshaw, L. S. *A short history of British psychology 1840–1940*. New York: Barnes & Noble, 1964.

Heffernan, W. C. The singularity of our inhabited world: William Whewell and A. R. Wallace in dissent. *Journal of the History of Ideas*, 1978, *39*, 81–100.

Heffernan, W. C. Percival Lowell and the debate over extraterrestrial life. *Journal of the History of Ideas*, 1981, *42*, 527–530.

Heidbreder, E. *Seven psychologies*. Englewood Cliffs, N.J.: Prentice–Hall, 1933.

Hetherington, N. S. Percival Lowell: Professional scientist or interloper? *Journal of the History of Ideas*, 1981, *42*, 159–161.

Hilts, V. L. Statistics and social science. In R. N. Giere & R. S. Westfall (Eds.), *Foundations of scientific method: The nineteenth century*. Bloomington: Indiana University Press, 1973.

Horn, J. L., & McArdle, J. Perspectives on mathematical/statistical model building (MASMOB) in research on aging. In L. W. Poon (Ed.), *Aging in the 1980s: Selected contemporary issues in the psychology of aging*. Washington, D.C.: American Psychological Association, 1980.

Horowitz, I. L. *The Renaissance philosophy of Giordano Bruno*. New York: Coleman–Ross, 1952.

Hultsch, D. F., Nesselroade, J. R., & Plemons, J. K. Learning-ability relations in adulthood. *Human Development*, 1976, *19*, 234–247.

Hultsch, D. F., & Pentz, C. A. Encoding, storage, and retrieval in adult memory: The role of model assumptions. In L. W. Poon, J. L. Fozard, L. S. Cermak, D. Arenberg, & L. W. Thompson (Eds.), *New directions in memory and aging: Proceedings of the George A. Talland memorial conference*. Hillsdale, N.J.: Lawrence Erlbaum Associates, 1980.

James, W. *Pragmatism*. New York: New American Library, 1907.

James, W. *A pluralistic universe*. Cambridge: Harvard University Press, 1977.

Jenkins, J. J. Remember that old theory of memory? Well forget it. *American Psychologist*, 1974, *29*, 785–795.

Jöreskog, K. G., & Sörbom, D. *LISREL IV—A general computer program for estimation of linear structural equation systems by maximum likelihood methods*. Chicago: International Education Services, 1978.

Kagan, J. On the need for relativism. *American Psychologist*, 1967, *22*, 131–142.

Kleiner, S. A. Feyerabend, Galileo and Darwin: How to make the best out of what you have—or think you can get. *Studies in History and Philosophy of Science*, 1979, *10*, 285–309.

Labouvie, E. W. Identity versus equivalence of psychological measurement and constructs. In L. Poon (Ed.), *Aging in the 1980s: Selected contemporary issues in the psychology of aging*. Washington, D.C.: American Psychological Association, 1980.

Lakatos, I. Falsification and the methodology of scientific research programs. In I. Lakatos & A. Musgrave (Eds.), *Criticism and the growth of knowledge*. London: Cambridge University Press, 1970.

Leary, D. E. The philosophical development of the conception of psychology in Germany, 1780–1850. *Journal of the History of the Behavioral Sciences*, 1978, *14*, 113–121.

Leary, D. E. The historical foundation of Herbart's mathematization of psychology. *Journal of the History of the Behavioral Sciences*, 1980, *16*, 150–163.

Leicester, H. M. *The historical background of chemistry*. New York: Dover, 1956.

Lerner, R. M., Hultsch, D. F., & Dixon, R. A. Contextualism and the character of developmental psychology in the 1970s. *Annals of the New York Academy of Sciences*. New York: New York Academy of Sciences, in press.

Levinson, D. J., Darrow, C. N., Klein, E. B., Levinson, M. H., & McKee, B. *Seasons of a man's life*. New York: Knopf, 1978.

Lewontin, L. C. On the measurement of relative variability. *Systematic Zoology*, 1966, *15*, 141–142.

Lord, F. M. Elementary models for measuring change. In C. W. Harris (Ed.), *Problems in measuring change*. Madison: University of Wisconsin Press, 1963.

Lovejoy, A. O. *The great chain of being*. Cambridge: Harvard University Press, 1964.

Lyons, J. Why human development requires more than one mode of experience. *Journal for the Theory of Social Behaviour*, 1981, *11*, 167–187.

McArdle, J. J. The development of general multivariate software. In *Proceedings of the Association for the Development of Computer-Based Instructional Systems*. Akron, Ohio: University of Akron Press, 1979.

McCall, R. B. Addendum. The use of multivariate procedures in developmental psychology. In P. H. Mussen (Ed.), *Carmichael's Manual of Child Psychology* (3rd ed.). New York: Wiley, 1970.

McHoul, A. W. Ethnomethodology and the position of relativist discourse. *Journal for the Theory of Social Behaviour*, 1981, *11*, 107–124.

Mancuso, J. C. Current motivational models in the elaboration of personal construct theory. In J. K. Cole & A. W. Landfield (Eds.), *Nebraska Symposium on Motivation* (Vol. 24). Lincoln: University of Nebraska Press, 1977.

Mead, G. H. *Mind, self, and society*. Chicago: University of Chicago Press, 1934.

Mead, G. H. *Movements of thought in the nineteenth century*. Chicago: University of Chicago Press, 1936.

Mead, G. H. *The philosophy of the act*. Chicago: University of Chicago Press, 1938.

Mischel, T. Kant and the possibility of a science of psychology. *The Monist*, 1967, *51*, 599–622.

de Montaigne, M. E. *Selections from the essays of Montaigne*. New York: Appleton–Century–Crofts, 1948 (Trans. and Ed. by D. M. Frame).

Nesselroade, J. R. Application of multivariate strategies to problems of measuring and structuring long-term change. In L. R. Goulet & P. B. Baltes (Eds.), *Life-span developmental psychology: Research and theory*. New York: Academic Press, 1970.

Nesselroade, J. R., & Baltes, P. B. (Eds.). *Longitudinal research in the study of behavior and development*. New York: Academic Press, 1979.

Nunnally, J. C. *Psychometric theory*. New York: McGraw–Hill, 1967.

Pearson, K. Notes on the history of correlation. *Biometrika*, 1920, *13*, 25–45.

Pearson, K. *The life, letters and labors of Francis Galton* (Vol. 3A). *Correlation, personal identification and eugenics*. Cambridge: Cambridge University Press, 1930.

Peckham, M. The infinitude of pluralism. *Critical Inquiry*, 1977, *3*, 803–816.

Pepper, S. C. *World hypotheses*. Berkeley: University of California Press, 1970.

Popper, K. R. *Conjectures and refutations: The growth of scientific knowledge*. New York: Harper & Row, 1965.

Popper, K. R. *Objective knowledge: An evolutionary approach*. London: Oxford University Press, 1972.

Rabinowitz, P. J. Who was that lady? Pluralism and critical method. *Critical Inquiry*, 1979, *5*, 585–589.

Radnitzky, G. *Contemporary schools of metascience* (Vol. 2). *Continental schools of metascience*. Göteborg: Scandinavian University Books, 1970.

Randall, J. H., Jr. *The career of philosophy* (Vol. 3). *Philosophy after Darwin*. New York: Columbia University Press, 1977.

Real, L. A. On uncertainty and the law of diminishing returns in evolution and behavior. In J. E. R. Staddon (Ed.), *Limits to action: The allocation of individual behavior*. New York: Academic Press, 1980.

Rescher, N. *Methodological pragmatism*. Oxford, Basil Blackwell, 1977.

Richards, R. J. Discussion: The natural selection model of conceptual evolution. *Philosophy of Science*, 1977, *44*, 494–501.

Richards, R. J. *Christian Wolff's prolegomena to empirical and rational psychology: Translation and commentary*. Unpublished manuscript, 1978. (University of Chicago).

Richards, R. J. The natural selection model and other models in the history of science. In M. B. Brewer & B. E. Collins (Eds.), *Scientific inquiry and the social sciences: A volume in honor of Donald T. Campbell*. San Francisco: Jossey-Bass, 1981.

Rucker, D. *The Chicago pragmatists*. Minneapolis: University of Minnesota Press, 1969.

Singer, D. W. *Giordano Bruno: His life and thought*. New York: Schuman, 1950.

Spearman, C. *The abilities of man*. New York: MacMillan, 1927.

Struik, D. J. *A concise history of mathematics* (3rd ed.). New York: Dover, 1967.

Thayer, H. S. *Meaning and action: A critical history of pragmatism*. Indianapolis: Bobbs–Merrill, 1968.

Thouless, R. H. Test unreliability and function fluctuation. *British Journal of Psychology*, 1936, *26*, 325–343.

Thurstone, L. L. *The vectors of mind*. Chicago: University of Chicago Press, 1935.

Thurstone, L. L. The primary mental abilities. *Psychometric Monographs*, 1938. (No. 1)

Torgerson, W. S. *Theory and methods of scaling*. New York: Wiley, 1958.

Toulmin, S. *Human understanding*. Princeton: Princeton University Press, 1972.

Toulmin, S., & Goodfield, J. *The fabric of the heavens: The development of astronomy and dynamics*. New York: Harper & Row, 1961.

Toulmin, S., & Goodfield, J. *The discovery of time*. Chicago: The University of Chicago Press, 1965.

Tucker, L. R. Learning theory and multivariate experiment: Illustration by determination of generalized learning curves. In R. B. Cattell (Ed.), *Handbook of multivariate experimental psychology*. Chicago: Rand McNally, 1966.

Tyler, L. E. More stately mansions—Psychology extends its boundaries. *Annual Review of Psychology*, 1981, *32*, 1–20.

Van Valen, L. Multivariate structural statistics in natural history. *Journal of Theoretical Biology*, 1974, *45*, 235–247.

Van Valen, L. The statistics of variation. *Evolutionary Theory*, 1978, *4*, 33–43.

Waismann, F. Are there alternative logics? *Proceedings of the Aristotelian Society*, 1946, *46*, 77–104.

Westergaard, H. *Contributions to the history of statistics*. London: P. S. King & Son, 1932.

White, S. H. Social proof structures: The dialectic of method and theory in the work of psychology. In N. Datan & H. W. Reese (Eds.), *Life-span developmental psychology: Dialectical perspectives on experimental research*. New York: Academic Press, 1977.

Wiener, P. P. *Evolution and the founders of pragmatism*. Cambridge: Harvard University Press, 1949.

Wittgenstein, L. *Philosophical investigations*. Oxford: Blackwell, 1972.

Wohlwill, J. F. *The study of behavioral development*. New York: Academic Press, 1973.

Wolfson, H. A. *Crescas' critique of Aristotle: Problems of Aristotle's physics in Jewish and Arabic philosophy*. Cambridge: Harvard University Press, 1929.

Woodrow, H. Quotidian variability. *Psychological Review*, 1932, *39*, 245–256.

6 The Context of Development and The Development of Context

Urie Bronfenbrenner
Cornell University

PURPOSE AND PROCEDURE

This chapter began as an inquiry into the scientific past and has ended with an uncertain but optimistic vision of the scientific future. The first of these undertakings turned out to be a long, arduous, and initially frustrating process. For many hours I struggled and stumbled through deep woods, in truth could not see the forest for the trees, and finally came out in my own backyard—or so it seemed when I first got back home. The woods were thousands of pages in histories, handbooks, and texts in developmental psychology. To my surprise and disappointment, the histories did not offer much for my purpose. The handbooks and manuals served me much better. I worked through them all: the two volumes of Murchinson (1931, 1933), two of Carmichael (1946, 1954), one of Goslin (1969), and two of Mussen (1960, 1970), the last consisting of two volumes (it would be harder work in the future—the next edition is planned in four mighty tomes). Then there was a series of volumes reviewing *Child Development Research*. The first, edited by Hoffman and Hoffman, appeared in 1964; the last one I looked at was Number 5 (1975), but they will probably go on forever. For dessert, I turned to lighter fare and sampled successive editions of two widely used textbooks in developmental psychology. One by Mussen and Conger—later joined by Kagan—ran to five editions between 1956 and 1979. The second text covered an even longer time span. Hurlock's *Child Development* first appeared in 1942. The most recent lineal descendent of the same volume was published in 1980 under the title *Developmental Psychology: A Lifespan Approach*. Hurlock has produced a revised text about every 4 years during almost half a century, probably, a record for the field.

Note: This chapter documents the results of the first phase of an analysis to be published in full in the forthcoming revision of the Mussen *Handbook of Child Psychology*.

What was the purpose of this scholar's journey through time? My aim was to trace the evolution of the concept of environment in systematic research on human development. The focus was not on theory directly, but on the constructs that were actually being employed, explicitly or implicitly, in empirical investigation. I was interested in how, over the years, the concept of the environment has evolved, how it has been operationalized and legitimized as scientifically acceptable, and how successive operationalizations have functioned to delimit or expand the scope of the knowledge acquired.

In pursuing this inquiry, I discovered a curious fact. Insofar as I have been able to determine, no comprehensive history has been written of research on human development. To be sure there are histories of theories and theorists of childhood (e.g., Grinder's study, 1967, of the basic tenets of genetic psychology as developed by G. Stanley Hall and his disciples). There are also comprehensive histories of childhood itself (Bremner 1974). But, in contrast to other branches of psychology—notably experimental—there has been no systematic historical account of the progressive growth of empirically based knowledge about human development.[1] It would be a fascinating story.

I am not giving away much of that story here, because my concern was the evolution of underlying concepts rather than the growth of substantive knowledge. But, because I was interested in the constructs implicit in operational definitions, I had to look at empirical work. To make manageable the task of selection from mountains of material, (and to minimize the awesome responsibility for choice), I relied mainly on compedia compiled by others. For the early period, the only summary source I could find was Dennis's *Historical Readings in Developmental Psychology* (1972). The studies reprinted in that volume conveniently extend into the 1930s and 40s, when *the great handbooks,* to use Sear's term, take over. Finally, for work published in the last few years, I had no recourse but to rely on my own judgment.

For the earlier decades, much of what I learned is already well-known. It had been recorded in the histories of theorists and theories that I had set aside as not directly relevant to my interests. It turns out that, until recently, the main sources of significant change in the operational definitions of the environment as a context of human development have been overarching theoretical ideas, what Kuhn (1962) has called "paradigmatic shifts." The creators of the new paradigms are all familiar names to students of human development. They begin with Francis Galton and formulation of the nature/nurture problem (1876). Next in line is probably G. Stanley Hall, whose inquisitive mind ranged beyond problems of ontogeny to undertake the first American study of environmental influences in development (1883). (As we see, it was a replication and significant expansion of a German prototype conducted more than a decade earlier.) He also brought to America the man who produced what is probably the greatest paradig-

---

[1]The closest approximations are found in two remarkably concise and comprehensive historical surveys of child development as a total field, one by Sears (1975) and the other by Hartup (1978).

matic shift in research on the context of development—Sigmund Freud. As the result of Frued's clinically derived theoretical ideas, the microenvironment of the child came alive as a complex of affectively charged and evolving interpersonal relationships. It would take a quarter century, however, before this differentiated conception was to serve as the basis for systematic investigations by developmental psychologists. What had to be accomplished first was some act of legitimatization by establishment scientific psychology. To judge from subsequent events, that seal of approval finally came through the inclusion in the Murchison *Handbook* (1931) of a short chapter by Anna Freud summarizing the basic elements of her father's theory, with emphasis on its implications for child development. The same Handbook contained chapters by two other Europeans who revolutionized scientific conceptions of the child's environment: Piaget and Lewin. But I am getting ahead of my story.

EARLY PARADIGMS

The story begins about 100 years ago. For the purposes of this chapter, I defined systematic research as a procedure requiring the collection of data that could contradict the expectations of the investigator in so salient a fashion that it would be difficult to disregard contrary evidence. As a result of this requirement, investigations that consisted solely of anecdotal reports or individual case studies did not qualify. The earliest researches I have been able to find that meet the stipulated criterion do not appear until the 1870s. Interestingly enough, they encompass two of the major conceptions of the environment that still prevail today. The first appears in a work referred to by Dennis (1972) as: "the first published study in educational psychology [p. 68]"; it is the report of a survey, conducted by the Pedagogical Society of Berlin (Schwabe & Bartholomai, 1870), on "The Contents of Children's Minds on Entering School at the Age of Six Years."[2] A passage describing the purpose of the inquiry has a curiously modern ring:

> It is an undeniable fact that the average knowledge of the child in the metropolis, hense also in Berlin, is a different one, in consequence of the influence of his surroundings, from that of a child living in a rural district or in a small town. It is also a fact that the conditions of the various parts of the city exercise different influences upon the knowledge of children, in consequence of which the mental receptivity of children of different wards shows a noticable inequality (U.S. Commissioner of Education, 1902, p. 710).

Although the survey sample was gratifyingly large, over 1000 children, the method of administration, the content of the questions, and especially the scope

---

[2]An English translation was published under this title 30 years later in the Annual Report of the U.S. Commissioner of Education 1900/1901 (U.S. Commissioner of Education, 1902).

of the findings leave much to be desired from a contemporary scientific perspective. The children were asked to answer questions orally in groups of 10. The questions themselves dealt primarily with facts of nature and geography and were phrased in very abstract terms; for example, the children were asked, "How many have an idea of a birch, oak, or pine tree standing in the woods?" Other concepts inquired about included supposedly familiar locations in the city, numbers, fairy tale characters, as well as God, Christ, and biblical stories. At the end of the survey, the youngsters were asked how many had attended a concert, could sing a song, or recite a memorized poem.

Curiously enough, the reported results have nothing to do with the opening statement of the purpose of the study. The assertion that "conditions of the various parts of the city exercise different influences upon the knowledge of children" had not been based on empirical findings but had appeared in a circular letter sent to the teachers of Berlin to induce their cooperation in the research. No analyses bearing on this issue are reported in the 13 tables summarizing survey results, perhaps because the members of the Society were overwhelmed by their two major findings. The first had to do with marked sex differences, and the second with even more pronounced variations between children who had entered school directly from home versus those who had had prior experience in a kindergarten or day care center. To quote the authors of the report:

> From the foregoing table, we see that by far the greater number of ideas . . . were found more frequently in boys than in girls. Greater even than that is the difference between children coming directly from home and those coming from the kindergarten. The latter have a much greater wealth of ideas than the former. The difference is less marked between children coming direclty from home than those having been kept in créches (Bewahranstalten). It is plain, therefore, that the school must assume an attitude with reference to boys different from that assumed thoward girls; likewise different attitudes as regards home children, kindergarten children, and children from créches [op. cit., p. 718].

The members of the Society were especially impressed by the greater number of responses produced by children with prior preschool experience. This contrast prompted a strong policy recommendation, uttered with some conviction in 1870, that speaks provocatively to issues of preschool intervention arising a century later:

> The greater wealth of ideas among children coming from the créches (Bewahranstalten), and the still greater wealth among children coming from the kindergarten as compared with those who have attended neither of these institutions, is so striking that the decision as to whether kindergarten for the prescholastic age is desirable or not cannot remain doubtful for a single moment [p. 720].

With the two major findings of the study before us, we are in a position to pose the central question to which this chapter is addressed: What is the model of the environment, and its relations to the development of the child, that is explicit or implied in this pioneering work? The stated purpose of the investigation, although never fulfilled, provides one direct answer to this query: The geographic location in which a child lives (country versus city, and different neighborhoods in the latter) was presumed to produce varying degrees and types of knowledge about the natural environment. In the actual analysis of the data, two other environmental parameters were employed. Considerable importance was attributed to the exposure of children to supervised preschool settings. And, perhaps most surprising in an era dominated by the biological determinism of Darwin, sex differences were explained as a function of the differential treatment of boys and girls within the school setting. It is noteworthy that no reference was made to an analogous possibility in the sphere of parental upbringing. As we see, it would take half a century before the family came to be seen as the primary environmental influence on children's development. And even within the formal educational context, the Berlin research design made no provision for obtaining information about the actual experience of children in preschool or school settings.

We are now in a position to formulate the first and simplest paradigm employed for investigating development in context; it can be described as *the comparison of children living at different social addresses*. As we see, although the social addresses become more sophisticated, this century-old model continues to characterize the majority of investigations being conducted today on the role of environmental factors in human development. For this reason, it is useful to take note of three distinctive and delimiting properties of the paradigm. First, the model may be characterized as child centered in the sense that no one else's behavior is being examined except the child's. Second, the model is unidirectional, with the child being a passive recipient and product of environmental influences. Third, no explicit consideration is given in research operations to intervening structures or processes through which the environment might affect the course of development. One looks only at the *social address*—that is, the environmental label—with no attention to what the environment is like, what people are living there, what they are doing, or how the activities taking place could affect the child. In Lewin's terms (1935), the model is class-theoretical rather than field-theoretical; observed differences in children from one or another setting are "explained" simply as attributes of the children in the given context.

The comparison of children living at different social addresses was not the only model of the environment in developmental research to emerge in the 1870s. A contrasting conception of context was implied in Galton's classic study, published during the same period, on "The History of Twins as a Criterion of the Relative Power of Nature and Nurture" (1876). In this monograph, Galton proposed and applied what he called "a new method" for unraveling the effects of heredity and environment. It involved the comparison of two groups of twins: those who were perceived by family and close acquaintances as having been much alike in childhood, versus those who were described as rather dissimilar during the same early period. The relative impact of nature versus nurture could then be assessed, Galton argued, by inquiring as to whether over the years the twins in each of the two groups became more similar or less similar.[3]

Galton's examination of data on 55 cases that he studied intensively brought him to what he describes as an unexpected answer. He found that the degree of reported similarity between twins showed very little variation throughout life despite exposure to different conditions. In the few instances in which marked departures occurred, they could be ascribed almost entirely to some form of illness. Galton speculated: "whether nature could do anything at all, beyond giving instruction and professional training [Ibid., p. 404]." Nevertheless, his final statement of the case contained an important qualification seldom heeded by his successors: "There is no escape from the conclusion that nature prevails enormously over nurture *when the differences of nurture do not exceed what is commonly to be found among persons of the same rank of society and in the same country* [loc. cit. p. 404, italics supplied]."

The preceding limitation is critical, for, in effect, it confines any generalization to the restricted range of environments existing for persons living in similar social strata of the same society. As a result, Galton's statement regarding the primacy of nature over nurture risks criticism as a foregone conclusion. Moreover, the criticism does not rest with Galton's ingenious pioneering study, for the conception of the environment implicit in his research design has survived and flourished in the work of later investigators—most notably Spearman (1914), Burt (1972), and Jensen (1980). Galton's implied conception, and that of his successors, may be described as a definition by exclusion; that is, the environment becomes that portion of the variance that cannot be explained by genetic factors under conditions in which major potential sources of environmental influence are not taken into account, either through oversight or conscious exclusion.

Ironically, it was Galton himself who identified a number of environmental factors that have proved to be significant mediators of developmental processes and outcomes up to the present time. Two years prior to the study of twins, he had published his classic monograph entitled "English Men of Science: Their Nature and Nurture" (1874). Therein he documented a statistically significant relation between scientific eminence and primogeniture; a heavily disproportionate number of his highly selected sample were firstborns. Galton was the first to introduce family structure as a key environmental context affecting the course of human development.

Galton also went beyond structure to investigate family functioning by calling attention to the role of parents in the early lives of his subjects: "Nearly a third of the scientific men have expressed themselves indebted to encouragement at home

---

[3]Although Galton was aware that some twins were born from the same ovum and others from two different ova (op. cit., p. 392), no technique existed at that time for differentiating monozygotic and dizygotic twins in vivo. Hence his strategy represents an ingenious approximation of this distinction made on the basis of the twins' external appearance and behavior.

[op. cit., p. 205]." The influence of parents, however, was qualified in two respects. The first concerns genetic factors; the second relates to the comparative influence of fathers versus mothers:

> I ascribe many of the cases of encouragement to the existence of a hereditary link; that is to say, the son had inherited scientific tastes, and was encouraged by the parent from whom he had inherited them, and who naturally sympathized with him.
>
> Attention should be given to the relatively small encouragement received from the mother . . . In many respects the character of scientific men is strongly anti-feminine . . . In many respects they have little sympathy with female ways of thought. It a curious proof of this, that in the very numerous answers which have reference to parental influence, that of the father is quoted three times as often as that of the mother [op. cit., pp. 206–207].

Although Galton's conclusions in this domain reflect more than a dash of subjectivity, the fact remains that he appears to be the first researcher to have identified and investigated the effect of parents on the development of their offspring through the medium of personal interaction. It would take more than a half a century, however, before this interpersonal context would become a primary focus of scientific study.

Yet another aspect of the environment studied by Galton was to find quicker adoption as an essential consideration in developmental research. Galton was concerned not only with the position of the child within the family, but also with the position of the family in the external world. To assess what he called the parents' "position in life," he classified the families of his outstanding scientists into five categories, ranging from "farmers" to "noblemen and private gentlemen [op. cit., pp. 21–22]." The resulting frequency distribution led him to the following conclusion: "There can be no doubt but that the upper classes of a nation like our own, which are largely and continually recruited from selections from below, are by far the most productive of natural ability. The lower classes are, in truth, the "residuum [Ibid. p. 23]."

Here we see the origin of the scales of occupational and socioeconomic status that today constitute the backbone of environmental assessment in studies of human development.[4]

Another core dimension was introduced in a replication of the Berlin survey in Boston, Massachusetts by the American psychologist G. Stanley Hall in 1883. The new parameter is adumbrated in his introductory comments about the original Berlin study; Hall saw the survey in cross-cultural perspective: "In Germany

---

[4]Galton was actually not the first to examine systematically the social background of eminent scientists. A year earlier de Candolle (1873) had published a study of French "savants" in which he divided his sample into three social classes.

it is more common than in our country to connect songs, poetry, reading, and object lessons, instruction in history, geography, botany, geology, and other elementary branches with the immediate locality . . . holiday walks conducted by teachers for educational purposes and for making collections for the school rooms are more common [op. cit., p. 144].''

In the light of these considerations, Hall eliminated some of the original German questions that he thought were inappropriate to the American scene and added others he regarded as more suitable. The two major findings of the original Berlin study reappeared in Boston two decades later and 4000 miles away. As in the German sample, boys surpassed girls except in the area of home and family life (as well as in knowledge of parts of the body). Similarly, a comparison of children entering first grade with and without previous kindergarten experience revealed: ''in a striking way the advantage of the kindergarten children, without regard to nationality, over all others [p. 152].'' Moreover, Hall was not unaware of the possible selective bias: ''Many were from charity kindergartens, so that superior intelligence of home surroundings can hardly be assumed [loc. cit].'' Hall also carried out a comparison anticipated but never implemented in the original German survey. Of the total sample of over 200 children, there were 36 from rural backgrounds, and these tested higher than their urban counterparts. In explanation, Hall pointed out that the content of primers being used in the schools at that time dealt in substantial measure with country life, and that experiences of nature had a powerful impact on the young: ''Many children locate all that is good and imperfectly known in the country, and nearly a dozen volunteered the statement that good people when they die go to the country— even here from Boston [Ibid., p. 156].'' Consistent with his cross-cultural perspective, Hall then proceeded to examine two additional contrasts. The first was between the Boston and the Berlin children on the 11 questions that were common to the two groups: There were no appreciable differences. The next assessment was in terms of ethnic background; a comparison of responses given by: ''children of Irish and American parentage [op. cit., p. 152].'' The former achieved significantly lower scores. The differences were especially marked for Irish boys, a finding that prompted Hall to speculate whether: ''the five and six year old Irish boys are not after all so constituted as to surpass their precocious American playmates later in school or adult life,'' as slow children ''are proported to do [loc. cit.].''

Although Hall's findings are not without substantive interest, what is significant about them from the perspective of this analysis is their extension of the concept of social address along a new dimension. To my knowledge, his was the first systematic cross-cultural study. Moreover, it was carried out not only across but also within national boundaries. In the latter instance, the criterion of classification was no longer where the children lived, but the country of origin of their parents and grandparents.

It is clear from the foregoing accounts that, by the late 1880s, the characteristics of the environment selected for study had become more complex, primarily through involving aspects of social structure both within the family and in the society at large. The addresses employed for classifying and comparing the characteristics of the children were becoming increasingly more social and far less linked merely to a geographic location. It is instructive to examine the environmental taxonomies that exist as research on development in context enters the 20th Century. In general, the environment is being analyzed at two different levels, which may be differentiated in the following way. Each is still defined by a social address, but in one instance the address describes the social location of the child, whereas in the second it is determined by the location of the family within the larger society. Examples of the former include the child's ordinal position, or his exposure to different settings (e.g., home versus kindergarten). The latter is represented by differences in parental occupation and the family's ethnic background. At each level, there is the presumption that somehow the child's experience in these different contexts influences the course of development, but, as of the turn of the century, the processes through which environmental factors might influence the child's behavior and development had not yet become an explicit focus of investigation, primarily because no theory of transmission had been proposed capable of being translated into operational terms. Such a theory was actually in the making in Europe during the first three decades of the present century, but it was not until the 1930s that an American was able to transform the elusive conceptions into replicable research designs.

THE TRANSITION FROM STRUCTURAL TO DYNAMIC MODELS

The change started on a small scale, with crude concepts and measures, but these were soon refined and applied on a broader front. The new developments took the form of three successive research trajectories.

1. The Parent–Child Paradigm.   The new model emerged in studies on parent-child relationships and their effect on the child's behavior and development. The initiator and principal protagonist of this early work was the pediatrician and psychiatrist, David Levy. Unfortunately, his first effort was burdened with an awesome and awkward title: "A Method of Integrating Physical and Psychiatric Examination with Special Studies of Body Interest, Over-protection, Response to Growth, and Sex Differences" (1929). In collaboration with colleagues at the Smith College School of Social Work, Levy proceeded to gather and analyze systematic clinical data on cases representing contrasting patterns of parent–child relationship along the continuum from what he called "rejection" to "over-protection." The results were published in a series of papers by himself and his students (Figge, 1931, 1932; Foley, 1932; Hough, 1932; Levy, 1930,

1932, 1933; Lewenberg, 1932; Lewis, 1930). The sphere of inquiry also included the role of the father (Barlow, 1924), and the developmental significance of sibling rivalry (Ross, 1931; Sewell, 1930). Although Levy's statistics were primitive, they revealed consistent relationships between modes of parental care and the corresponding behavior and personality characteristics of children. Levy continued to accumulate and follow up cases so that by 1943 he was able to publish data on 100 children, 20 of whom had been studied longitudinally for 10 to 15 years (Levy, 1943).

In the interim, Percival Symonds, a psychologist at Columbia, conducted a study based on Levy's work but employed a more rigorous design by supplementing clinical interviews with checklists and behavior-rating scales filled out by teachers and other professional personnel who had worked with the child. The results were published in a volume entitled "The Psychology of Parent–Child Relationships" (1939). A new era in developmental research had been born. Levy's and Symond's investigations constitute the prototype for a sequence of more sophisticated studies of child rearing in succeeding decades, notably the work of Baldwin (1946, 1948, 1949; Baldwin, Kalhorn & Breese, 1945), Sears, Maccoby, & Levin (1957), and Baumrind (1967, 1971, 1980; Baumrind & Black, 1967).

2. *Socialization and Social Structure.*   A second major wave of studies followed upon the first. The underlying model can be viewed as a grafting of a new paradigm onto the old: The comparison of persons living at different social addresses is expanded to include not just children but also parents. The initial contrasts to be investigated were those by socioeconomic status. In a series of surveys conducted in 1932 for the White House Conference on Child Health and Protection (Anderson, 1936), data were reported on social class differences in parent practices, including onset and duration of breast feeding, scheduled versus self-demand feeding, toilet training, permissiveness, modes of punishment, and training for independence. This was the first in what was to become a series of investigations of socialization and social class over a period spanning a quarter of a century. The accumulated results were analyzed midway by Bronfenbrenner (1958), who identified a secular trend, over a 25-year period, toward greater permissiveness, especially on the part of middle-class parents, who reversed their relative position vis-a-vis the working class in this respect.

Although ethnographic studies of cultural differences in child rearing had become a major focus of anthropological research by the late 1920s, primarily through the work of Margaret Mead (1928), the first study in this domain meeting our methodological criteria seems to have been Davis and Havighurst's investigation (1948) of "Color Differences in Child Rearing" within American society. Within a decade, however, systematic information about differences in child rearing at social addresses scattered all over the world were made available through the publication of Whiting and Child's volume *Child Training and Personality* (1953).

Variations in parent–child relationships associated with internal family structure were first reported in relation to the sex of the child (Cavan, 1932; Wang, 1932). The findings were soon further qualified by sex of parent (Simpson, 1935; Mott, 1937; Terman, 1938). For example, Mott, in interviews with 500 elementary-age children, found boys were more often spanked by father, girls by mothers. Curiously enough, variations in parental treatment associated with other aspects of family structure were relatively late in attracting the attention of investigators. Thus reports on differences in patterns of child rearing associated with family size and birth order do not begin to appear until the middle 1950s (Bossard & Boll, 1956; Koch, 1954; Lasko, 1954; Sears, Maccoby, & Levin, 1957). More striking is the paucity of research, even up to the present day, on patterns of child rearing in families consisting of only one adult. Despite the now extensive literature on the effects of the father's absence, such studies were not initiated until after World War II (Bach, 1946; Sears, Pintler, & Sears, 1946). The first investigation to focus direct attention on the child-rearing behavior of the single-parent mother was apparently Hetherington's work published in 1978 (Hetherington, Cox, & Cox, 1978).

3. Models of Group Context. The third major development in concepts underlying field research designs was provision for analyzing structure and process in children's groups as contexts for human development. Two types of research models can be distinguished in the early investigations conducted in this sphere. The first focused primarily on relations between children and adults, the second on relationships among the children themselves. In the former category, the earliest studies were conducted in children's institutions. Although the best known of these is the investigation by Spitz (1946a,b), the pioneering study in this domain appears to have been conducted in Austria more than a decade earlier by Durfee and Wolf (1933).[5] These investigators compared developmental quotients of 118 infants in various institutions and correlated the scores with the amount of maternal care that the infants had been given. No differences in performance were discerned before the age of 3 months, but thereafter the developmental levels dropped in inverse relationship to the amount of maternal care received. Children who had been institutionalized for more than 8 months during the first year manifested such severe psychological disturbances that they could not be tested. The study marks the beginning of a series of investigations of institutional deprivation by Spitz, Goldfarb (1943a,b, 1955), Bowlby (1951), Dennis and Najarian (1957), Pringle and Bossio (1958), through the contempo-

---

[5]The Kaethe Wolf, who was the coauthor of this pioneering study, is later acknowledged in a footnote as having served as a collaborator in Spitz's work (1946a, p. 56).

rary work of Tizard (Tizard, Cooperman, Joseph, & Tizard, 1972; Tizard & Hodges, 1978; Tizard & Rees, 1974, 1976).

The second and complementary line of research, using a rather different model, also had its origins in the late 1930s in the work of Skeels, Updegraff, Wellman, and Williams, (1938). This investigation preceded Skeel's better-known longitudinal study of orphanage children placed for care on a ward of an institution for mentally retarded adults (Skeels, 1942, 1966; Skeels & Dye, 1939). This earlier research also involved an experimental intervention. The sample consisted of 21 pairs of children matched on chronological age, sex, intelligence, nutritional status, and length of residence in the orphanage. The experimental group was randomly assigned to a preschool established on the premises and remained there for 3 years; the control group continued under the established orphanage regime. In contrast to their controls, the experimental children showed impressive gains in IQ, vocabulary, and social adjustment but were still below the norms for their age. The most dramatic findings of the study were related to the effects of upbringing in the institutional environment. At the outset of the experiment, both groups were described as: "lacking in information about the commonest of objects and experiences . . . either lethargic or destructive . . . lacking in flexibility, and tied to nothing in past experience [p. 184]." All these characteristics were aggravated for the children in the control group who remained under the institutional regime:

> Certainly no one could have otherwise predicted, much less proved, the steady tendency to deteriorate on the part of children maintained under what had previously been regarded as standard orphanage conditions. With respect to intelligence, vocabulary, general information, social competence, personal adjustment, and motor achievement the whole picture is one of retardation. The effect from one to three years attendence in nursery school . . . was to reverse the tide of regression which, for some, led to feeblemindedness [p. 2].

Again, my purpose in citing this study is not to focus on its substantive findings, but to illustrate a new departure in research design. To my knowledge, this investigation by Skeels and his colleagues represents the first example of experimental early intervention as a strategy for studying the impact of the environment on human development. Thus is marks the beginning of a long trajectory reflected in the work of such investigators as Gordon (1971), Gray and Klaus (1965), Heber, Garber, Harrington, & Hoffman (1972), Karnes, Studley, Wright, and Hodgins (1968), Kirk (1958), Levenstein (1970), and Weikart (1967).

Complementing studies of the developmental effects on children of deprived social environments were investigations focusing on the power of the group to shape and sustain the behavior of its members. Perhaps the first study in this regard was Shaw's analysis (1933) of juvenile delinquency as a gang phenonemon. Shortly thereafter, Murphy (1937) documented the role of the group in shaping and sustaining the behavior of nursery school children. This line of investigation entered on experimental phase with the classic study by Lewin, Lippitt, and White on group atmospheres (1939). This work set the stage for an evolving program of research on group influences and child behavior and development (for a summary see Hartup, 1970).

THE IMPLEMENTATION OF THEORETICAL PARADIGMS

How can one account for the remarkable innovation and enrichment that suddenly emerged during the 1930s in the conceptions underlying research models for the study of human development in context? Although a number of factors contributed to this rapid evolution, the main sources of significant change were new theoretical ideas that postulated linkages between particular features of the environment and the developing organism. Before the 1930s, the only theory employed in empirical work that approximated this requirement was classical conditioning (Holt, 1931; Pavlov, 1928), but it was not equal to the task, despite Watson's grandiose promise (1918).[6] But there were three candidates waiting in the wings and their formal admission into the scientific establishment of psychological science was signified by their inclusion in the first edition of Murchinson's *Handbook* in 1931. The three were Freud, Piaget, and Lewin. Freud's name is of course much more closely associated with theories of intrapsychic structure than with the analysis of external contexts. Nevertheless, it was on Freud's clinically derived theoretical ideas about family dynamics that Levy explicitly relied in designing his studies of parent–child relationships and their developmental effects. Similarly, it was Freud's emphasis on the importance of the mother–infant bond that provided the framework for the early investigations of the effects of institutionalization by Durfee, Wolf, Spitz, and their successors.

A rather different view of the organism–environment interface was presented by both Paiget and Lewin. Whereas for Freud the primary context was one of intense emotional relationships, Piaget saw the environment through the eyes of the child as a congitive structure incorporating physical as well as social dimensions. Moreover, the child was no longer a passive victim of external forces as conceived in Freud's formulation, but an active creator and transformer of the world about him. In support of this view, Piaget adduced experimental evidence

---

[6]"Give me a dozen healthy infants, well-formed, and my own specified world to bring them up in, and I'll guarantee you to take any one at random and train him to become any type of specialist I might select—doctor, lawyer, artist, merchant-chief, and, yes, even beggerman and thief, regardless of his talents, tensions, tendencies, abilities, vorations, and race of his ancestors (Watson, 1930, p. 82)."

showing how the child used objects, shapes, and activities available in the environment to achieve his own "construction of reality" (Piaget, 1926, 1954).

Whereas sharing Paiget's phenomelogical orientation, Lewin assigned to the environment an even more explicit and powerful role. He conceptualized it as having "demand characteristics" that attract or repel and cited experiments showing how the child's behavior could be changed by altering the psychological situation (Lewin, 1935). Lewin's abstractly defined field theory was to generate his classic experiments on group atmospheres (Lewin, Lippitt, & White, 1939), and culminating ultimately in the conception and execution of what he called "action research" (Lewin, 1948).

Credit for the next paradigmatic shift in research on environmental factors in human development belongs to a psychologist whose star seems to be falling. Whereas references to Freud, Paiget, and Lewin in scientific journals and texts have remained frequent throughout recent decades, Clark Hull would appear to have reached his peak of prominence in the middle 1950s. Yet, the long-range impact of his learning theory on investigations of environmental influences has been profound. There is a direct line from his experiments on contingent reinforcement to the behavior strategies so widely used in contemporary studies and applied programs on experimental intervention in clinics, schools, and social institutions. But even more significant from an environmental perspective is the indirect contribution of Hull's work to the explosion of research on *socialization* that occurred in the middle 50s as the result of the systematic integration, in a series of seminars planned and directed by Hull at Yale, of concepts from learning theory, psychoanalysis, sociology, and cultural anthropology. As documented by Sears (1980), the participants in the seminar included, among others, psychologists Leonard Doob, Carl Hovland, Neal Miller, and O. H. Mowrer; anthropologists George Murdock, Clellend Ford, and John Whiting; and psychoanalysts John Dollard and Earl Zinn. The theoretical integration set a pattern for empirical studies linking processes at the individual and cultural level (Dollard, 1939; LeVine, 1970; Miller & Dollard, 1941; Whiting & Child, 1953).

A dramatically different paradigm of the role of culture in human development, emerging from a contrasting cultural and intellectual context, is found in the work of the Soviet psychologists Vygotsky and Luria. The hallmarks of this orientation are telegraphed in the titles that Michael Cole, their American editor, has given to the two books that present these ideas in English translation: the volume by Vygotsky is called *Mind in Society* (1978); the one by Luria, *Cognitive Development: Its Cultural and Social Foundations* (1976). The general thesis of both volumes is that the evolution of cognitive processes in the individual is shaped by the definitions of reality provided by the broader cultural context, with particular emphasis on the impact of large-scale social changes, both planned and unplanned. The origins of theory, and its first application, date back to the late 1920s and early 1930s, when Vygotsky and Luria undertook to test their hypotheses by investigating the effects on cognitive functioning of the transformation of Soviet society that followed the October Revolution. The field work, which involved intensive psychological interviews and tests, was carried out by Luria himself in the remoter regions of Soviet Asia (Vygotsky was too ill from tuberculosis to be able to leave Moscow). The investigation focused on a comparison of cognitive functioning in members of communities that had been exposed in varying degrees to the planned social changes being introduced across the entire country.

The results of the study are best conveyed in Luria's (1976) own words: "The facts show convincingly that the structure of cognitive activity does not remain static during the different stages of historical development and that the most important forms of cognitive processes . . . vary as the conditions of life change and the rudiments of knowledge can be mastered [p. 161]." Because Luria's reliance on psychological tests was incompatible with the Communist ideology of the 1930s and succeeding decades, he was not permitted to publish the results of his research until 40 years later, just before his death in 1976. In the middle 1960s, however, Michael Cole, then an exchange graduate student at Moscow University, had the opportunity to work with Luria. He subsequently applied sophisticated elaborations of the Soviet cultural cognitive model in an influential series of studies conducted both in Africa and the United States (Cole, Gay, Glick, & Sharp, 1971; Cole & Scribner, 1974).

The last paradigmatic shifts that can be identified with any confidence both have their roots in biological research, one line being naturalistic, the other experimental. The former is reflected in the impact on developmental psychology of the etological conceptions of the American Nobel laureate, Konrad Lorenz (1935, 1965), and their subsequent refinement by Tinbergen (1951) and Hinde (1966). In studies of the evolution of social behavior in human beings, the framework has been particularly influential in research on mother–infant relations (Ainsworth, 1963; Ambrose, 1961, Blurton–Jones, 1974; Schaffer, 1963). A second biological model stems from the experiments of a Canadian psychologist, Donald Hebb, on the effects of environmental restriction and enrichment on development in rats (1937a,b, 1938, 1949). Hebb's work served as a major theoretical and empirical base for Hunt's (1961) influential volume on the effects of infant stimulation, which, in turn, contributed to the rationale for establishing early intervention programs in the middle and late 1960s (Bronfenbrenner, 1974; Horowitz & Paden, 1973).

Finally, although the evidence is as yet meager and most of it indirect, it would appear that another theoretical paradigm of long standing is at last beginning to be implemented in investigations of human development. I refer to the role of theory of the "Chicago School" of sociologists, chief among them being Cooley (1902), G. H. Mead (1934), and W. I. and D. S. Thomas (Thomas, 1927; Thomas & Thomas, 1928; Thomas & Znaniecki, 1927). Their theory of socialization focused on the evolution of a concept of self through the person's interaction, throughout the life-span, with "significant others," both within and outside the family. It is a reflection of the long history of isolation between disciplines that only in recent years has this conception begun to influence research in child development, an area of inquiry heavily dominated by psychologists. The scholar who finally broke the disciplinary barrier was a sociologist, Glen Elder. Using longitudinal data gathered by psychologists, Elder assessed the impact of the Great Depression (Elder, 1979) on the development of children at successive stages of transition in their lives. Elder explicitly credits the Chicago School, particularly Thomas and Znaniecki's study of *The Polish Peasant in Europe and America (1918–1920),* as the source for the research model on which his investigation was based. His work, in turn, has stimulated other researchers (Furstenberg, 1976) to use similar designs in pursuing what Elder has called "the life course" approach in studies of human development. The approach focuses attention on stability and shift in developmental trajectories as a function of role statuses and transitions experienced by a particular age cohort during a given period in history.

Although my analysis yielded few surprises in identifying the originators of paradigmatic shifts in conceptions of the role of the environment in human development, it illuminated aspects of the evolution of operational concepts that I had not previously recognized. First, I had not appreciated the extent to which the most influential theroetical ideas had been produced by scholars from other countries and other disciplines. Second, I had not realized how long the typical "refractory period" was between the publication of a theory and its application in scientific work. Indeed, it is this "sleeper effect" that makes it difficult, as we approach our own times, to identify which contemporary theoretical ideas, if any, will eventually lead to new and fruitful directions in scientific work.

Confronted with this phenomenon, I pondered on the forces that might account for its existence. Fortunately, my labors had yielded some evidence bearing on the issue. In the course of analysis, I found myself identifying not only persons whom I called "creating theorists," but also "translating theorists," those who were able to transform new, highly general, and often strange theoretical ideas into delimited researchable problems and corresponding operational definitions. Inventive translators were not always at hand at the time the theory was conceived. It often took a decade or two before the translation was finally accomplished. Thus, as we have seen, the first implementation of Freud's theories in systematic research on parent–child relationships did not take place until the early 1930s; moreover, the translation was made from outside developmental psychology by David Levy, who was a psychoanalytically oriented psychiatrist. It was only thereafter that a psychologist (Symonds) entered the picture, primarily to provide a more rigorous research design and more objective methods of data gathering and analysis.

Another productive Freudian research trajectory was also set in motion by a psychiatrist, with a psychologist taking over to provide a more objective methodology. Bowlby (1958, 1969) gave sufficient theoretical concreteness to

Freud's concept of maternal attachment so that Ainsworth and her colleagues (1969) were able to develop the widely used "strange situation" experiment as a method for assessing the quality and consequence of stability versus disruption in the mother–infant bond.

The implementation of Freud's theory of identification ran a more convoluted course via a detour through learning theory. It finally emerged in somewhat altered but readily operationalized form in the concept of modeling and observational learning as developed and applied by Bandura and his colleagues (Bandura, 1969; Bandura & Huston, 1961).

Analogous roles in relation to Piaget's theories of social influences in development were played by Berenda (1950), Kohlberg (1963, 1964), and Flavell (1963, 1970). Similarly, it was Lewin's students—and later colleagues—Lewin, Lippitt, and White (1939), who applied his field theory to the study of children's groups. Some years later, Barker translated Lewin's elusive concept of "life space" into concrete naturalistic "behavior settings," thereby establishing a new research domain of ecological psychology (Barker, 1965, 1968; Barker & Wright, 1951, 1955).[7]

I have already commented on the critical role of Hull's interdisciplinary seminar in integrating his learning theories with psychoanalytic and anthropological approaches, thus setting the stage for field studies of socialization processes and outcomes. The fact that the gap between conception and application was far longer in the case of role theory at the University of Chicago suggests that borders between disciplines can be as powerful barriers as those of language and geographic distance.

It is instructive to ask whether an examination of empirical work reveals any other sources of new operational definitions of the environment besides those generated by overarching theoretical systems. One such creative influence may be described by the term *domain theory*—that is, a conception that identifies a hitherto unexplored area of investigation and offers descriptive concepts and methods appropriate for exploring the uncharted terrain. A good example in Moreno's invention of sociometry (1934) as a technique for analyzing the social structure of a group and the individual's position within it. Moreno's constructs and procedures provided the impetus for a large number of studies of social development, in which the child's sociometric status was used either as the independent or the dependent variable.

A more significant and sophisticated contribution is represented by Baltes and Schaie's development of a conceptual-methodological framework for the systematic study of what they called "life span developmental psychology" (Baltes &

---

[7]Although Barker (1968) equates his conception of the psychological environment with "the life space in Kurt Lewin's terms [p. 1], "he also credits another psychological theorist of European origin, Brunswik (1956), as influencing the definition of environment as employed in ecological psychology (Barker, 1965, p. 1).

Schaie, 1973). Their formulations have had two important implications for research on development-in-context. First, they have called attention to the importance of the cohort as a group of persons experiencing a distinctive environmental history through the life-span. Second, and more important, the orientation focuses attention on the developmental impact of contexts that human being enter in the years following adolescence, thus reinforcing the scientific power of the "life course" approach developed by Elder (1974).

HISTORICAL CHANGE AS A SOURCE OF SCIENTIFIC INNOVATION

The analysis of empirical studies over the years reveals yet another influence on operational concepts of the environment—an influence that emanates from an entirely nonscientific source. I refer to the impact of historical and cultural changes in focusing the attention of investigators on new features of the environment that effect developmental processes. For example, the scientific revolution occurring in the second half of the 19th century clearly set the stage for Galton's studies of the genesis of scientific genius. Freud's neurotics were the products of a special brand of Viennese Victorianism. As clearly revealed in his first published paper (Lewin, 1917), Lewin's theoretical ideas of "psychological life-space" were stimulated by his experience as a foot soldier in World War I. In his analysis of the *Kriegslandschaft* (War landscape), he described how, as a soldier nears the front line, the perceived reality of the landscape changes from one of pastoral peace to threatening terrain. History can also speak to the researcher without the intervening translation of a theorist. For instance, the first studies of the impact of the father on the functioning of the family as a child-rearing system were prompted by the massive unemployment of fathers during the Great Depression (Angell, 1936; Caven & Ranck, 1938; Komarovsky, 1940; Morgan, 1939). A second flurry of investigation in this sphere occurred a few years later, when World War II gave rise to a spate of studies on the effect of father absence on children's development (Bach, 1946; Sears, Pintler, & Sears, 1946; Stolz, 1954). Research on the impact of maternal employment first appeared in the 1930s as women began to enter the labor force in larger numbers to supplement family income in the aftermath of the Great Depression (Glueck & Glueck, 1934a,b; Hodgkiss, 1933; Mathews, 1934).

In a different domain, the experiment with orphanage children conducted by Skeels and his colleagues in the 1930s was stimulated not by a theoretical concern with the effects of maternal deprivation but as one of a series of studies being conducted at the University of Iowa on the educational effect of kindergartens, which were then becoming more common on the American scene. Despite the promising result of this and other early experimental programs (reviewed in

Bronfenbrenner, 1974), research on the effects of preschool intervention exhibited a low profile through the 1940s and 1950s but became a major social science industry in response to President Johnson's call to arms for a "War against Poverty" and a "Head Start" for poor children and their families. With the growing divorce rate and entry of mothers into the labor force, single parenthood and day care became primary research concerns of the 1970s. As we look ahead to the 1980s, should we anticipate new scientific knowledge, and possibly new theory as well, about the effects on children and families of inflation, unemployment, and the drastic reduction of health and welfare programs? Time will tell. In the interim, we had better begin to heed the methodological requirements of what may be called the "new demography." The well-designed study of the future must not only control for the familiar confounding variables of class and race; to these we must add maternal employment status, new forms of family structure, the type and extent of substitute care, and the numbers of hours spent by fathers in housework and child rearing. Such are the forces determining the future of our science.

THE EVOLUTION OF LATENT STRUCTURES

The scientific developments of the past few decades have involved more than a proliferation of the contexts presumed to affect psychological growth. The underlying research models have undergone changes not only in scope but also in structure. Their organization has become more differentiated. To pursue our original metaphor, the doors at social addresses have been opened to disclose dwellings in which human beings relate to one another and engage separately and jointly in a variety of activities. The variation in these relations and activities results, over time, in differences in the development of persons living at each address. Moreover, the various locales are no longer isolated from each other but are linked together in complex ways that, in turn, influence the operation and outcome of processes taking place within each setting.

This brings me to what emerges as the most intriguing outcome of the analysis. The evolution, during recent years, of more complex research models for investigating development-in-context has, for the most part, not been the result of conscious, coordinated effort. It emerges as an unplanned achievement, the product of seemingly ad hoc innovations by different investigators working independently, but nevertheless proceeding in complementary and covergent directions. The resultant integrated structure has not been made explicit, but it can be inferred from the operational designs employed by different investigators in the field. The implicit evolution has proceeded by stages. Each stage builds upon the preceding and involves greater complexity. The evolving models, however, do not spring de novo from contemporary research; they have their roots in the earlier paradigms, both explicit and implicit, traced in the preceding pages. To convey the total picture, I have incorporated the old and the new in a single series.

From this perspective, the successive stages have a twofold significance. On the one hand, making latent paradigms explicit illuminates the path of progress in the past. On the other hand, because all the operational models are currently in productive use, and most are only beginning to be employed, their explication can adumbrate a trajectory of possible scientific advance for the future.

1. The Ecology of Developmental Outcomes.   The first trend has its origins in the earliest systematic studies of development-in-context, conducted 100 years ago. It is defined by the application of the prototype social address model to an increasing variety of environmental contexts. From the crude geographic and national contrasts of the late 19th century, they proceed to indices of social structure, and, in recent decades, to the analysis of concrete naturalistic settings (e.g., home, school, peer group, day care, work place) and to the assessment of experimental programs of environmental intervention. Each new environmental contrast involves a comparison of the behavior and characteristics of children exposed to the contexts in question.

Although this traditional trajectory sheds little light on the processes through which the environment influences behavior and development, it still has important scientific utility in at least two areas. First, it remains a strategy of choice for exploring the developmental potential of newly emerging domains. For example, increasing numbers of offspring are growing up in so-called ''merged families,'' in which children of different biological parents are living in the same household. The effects of remarriage on children is as yet an uncharted terrain for which the social address model is well-suited as a tool for scientific discovery. A second area, defined more by practical than scientific needs, is that of program evaluation where child outcomes define the major goals to be achieved.[8]

2. The Ecology of Environmental Influences.   The second trend was made possible by the emergence of theories of organism–environment interaction in human development and their translation into operational definitions. With these at hand, researchers were able to apply the environmental contrasts generated in the preceding stage to a new set of dependent variables—indices of the specific environmental forces presumed to affect psychological growth. For example, the measures of child-rearing attitudes and practices that were derived first from psychoanalysis and then from learning theory became the focus of a still-continu-

---

[8]The exclusive use of a social address model for either of the previous purposes does not imply that more scientific knowledge would not be gained through application of the more sophisticated paradigms described later. But with limited resources, this model represents the minimal strategy adequate to the problem at hand.

ing series of comparative studies of socialization across settings, classes, and cultures.

Although considerable knowledge has been acquired about contrasting contexts of development, much terrain still remains to be explored. First, not all the creative ideas of the paradigmatic theorists have been exploited. For example, research on parent–child interaction has drawn heavily on the concepts and hypotheses of Freud, Hull, and thier theoretical successors, but the constructs of Piaget, Lewin, and Vygotsky have yet to be translated into dyadic terms. These cognitive theorists share in common an emphasis on the importance of goal-oriented activities both as the producers and the products of developmental advance. In consequence, the research that such perspectives have generated has involved extensive observation of the ways in which children act upon, transform, and even create their environments. But the fact that all three theories are essentially child centered in their approach to development has inhibited recognition of their implications for adult-child interaction. Specifically, neither the originators of these cognitive paradigms, nor their scientific descendents, have spent much time observing the activities of parents with their children. Yet, given the assumption of organism–environment reciprocity common to all three cognitive theories, it is not unreasonable to expect that the content and complexity of parent–child activities—analyzed in terms of the concepts of Piaget, Vygotsky, or Lewin—would have a great deal to do with the content and complexity of the activities spontaneously engaged in by the children in their parents' absence. There is also the unexplored question of how parental activities, again viewed in cognitive terms, are differentially distributed across the well-established socioenvironmental contexts of social class, ethnicity, and family structure. The same issue can be raised with respect to the much-researched socialization mechanisms of reinforcement and modeling. Are these equally prevalent in families of varying structure and cultural background? Finally, there is the question of the socialization correlates of the new demography. Since 1960 an increasing number of investigations have assessed differences in the behavior and characteristics of children of working versus nonworking mothers, or of youngsters reared entirely at home versus in day care settings. But very few studies have been directed at the parents of these children. Does a mother begin to treat her child differently once she goes to work, or the child enters day care? Such unanswered questions highlight the fact that there are still many missing cells at critical junctures in the matrix that constitutes the ecology of environmental influences.

3. The Ecology of Developmental Processes. The third developmental trend represents a convergence of the two preceeding, but it differs from either of its origins. Whereas both predecessors are derivatives of explicit theoretical formulations, the third trajectory has evolved primarily as a latent structure. Beginning in the 1960s, researchers on environmental influences began to report that the relationship between independent and dependent variables varied from one structural context to another. Specifically, there were differences by social address not only in the characteristics of parents and of children, but in the relation between the two. For example, parental treatment in early childhood was found to predict subsequent behavior in adolescence much better for boys than for girls (Kagan & Moss, 1962; Schaefer & Baley, 1963). Even earlier in life, the same prenatal and perinatal traumas (e.g., birth injuries) correlated with later IQ for children from lower-class families but not for those from middle-class homes (Drillien, 1964; Werner, Simonian, Bierman, & French, 1967; Willerman, 1972; Willerman, Naylor, & Myrianthopoulos, 1970). Convesely, the association between adolescents' reports of parent–child relationships and ratings of their behavior at school by teachers and peers was stronger for middle-class than for lower-class groups (Bronfenbrenner, 1961). It appears that both biological and interpersonal influences can have different effects depending on the context in which they operate. To put it more colloquially, good things get better for those who are well-off to start with, and bad things get worse for those who aren't.

The dynamics of the processes involved in such contextual contrasts were illuminated in a series of studies by Tulkin and his colleagues (Tulkin, 1973a,b; Tulkin & Cohler, 1973; Tulkin & Covitz, 1975; Tulkin & Kagan, 1972). These investigators focused on differences in development during infancy and early childhood as a function of the family's socioeconomic status. To control for the child's sex and ordinal position, the sample was limited to firstborn girls, first studied when they were 10-months old. The initial publication (Tulkin & Kagan, 1972), based on home observations, reported that middle-class mothers engaged in more reciprocal interactions with their infants, especially in verbal behavior, and provided them with a greater variety of stimulation. The second study (Tulkin & Cohler, 1973) documented parallel differences in maternal attitudes; middle-class mothers were more likely to subscribe to statements stressing importance of perceiving and meeting the infant's needs, the value of mother–child interaction, and the moderate control of aggressive impulses. Furthermore, the correlations between maternal behavior and attitudes were substantially greater in middle-class than lower-class families. Next, in two experiments Tulkin (1973a,b) found that middle-class infants cried more when separated from their mothers but were better able to discriminate the mother's voice from that of an unfamiliar female from the same social class. Finally, several years later, Tulkin and Covitz (1975) reassessed the same youngsters after they had entered school. The children's performance on tests of mental ability and language skill showed significant relationships to the prior measures of reciprocal mother–infant interaction and strength of maternal attachment and voice recognition when the children had been 10-months old. Once again, the observed correlations were higher for middle-class families. Even more important from a developmental perspective, the relationships of maternal behavior at 10 months to the child's

behavior at age 6 were considerably greater than the contemporaneous relationships between both types of variables in the first year of life. The investigators,
however, were quick to reject the hypothesis of a delayed "slepper effect."
Rather, they argued that mothers who engage in adaptive reciprocal activity with
their infants at early ages are likely to continue to do so as the child gets older,
thus producing a cumulative trend.

This new area of investigation is truly a *terra incognita*. For example, we
know very little about whether or how socialization techniques differ in their
effectiveness from one ecological context to another. Under what environmental
circumstances are biological potentials most likely to be realized or biological
limitations most readily transcended? Does social reinforcement operate more
successfully in certain types of family structure? Does modeling produce behavior change more quickly in conforming societies? Do socialization processes
become less effective for families under severe economic or psychological
stress? At a more general level, what are the ecological conditions that affect the
capacity of a family, day care setting, school classroom, or other socialization
context to function effectively? This is the central issue to which this developmental trajectory is leading us.

4. The Ecology of Second-order Effects.   The next developmental trend involves a latent structure that has somewhat longer history. Researches on the
effects of father absence during World War II (Bach, 1946; Sears, Pintler, &
Sears, 1946), in keeping with the then-prevailing research model, collected
systematic data only on the perceptions and behavior of the child. But, in interpreting their findings, the investigators suggested that the child may have been
affected not only directly by the absence of the role model, but also indirectly
through the impact of her husband's absence on the parental behavior of the
mother. It took a decade before this possibility was investigated systematically
and confirmed in Tiller's study of children in Norwegian sailor families (Gronset
& Tiller, 1957; Tiller, 1958, 1961). The operational model of the parent–child
relationship was thereby expanded from a dyad to a three-person system. It was
not until the 1970s, however, that the model was formally explicated (Bronfenbrenner, 1974, 1979; Lewis & Feiring, 1979) and applied in a still growing
number of investigations. The basic mechanism revealed in such studies has been
referred to by Bronfenbrenner (1974) as a "second-order effect"—the mediation
of a dyadic process through the influence of a third party. Second-order effects
were first demonstrated in studies documenting the impact of the father on the
mother's treatment of the child (Parke, 1978; Pedersen, 1976). More recently, in
a symposium on second-order effects, Pederson and his colleagues (1981) reported that 5-month olds timed their bids for parental attention to periodic lapses
during conversations between husband and wife. The authors (Pederson, Cain, &
Anderson, 1981) comment: "In spite of the complexity of selective engagement
and disengagement of the different dyadic units, the five-month old infant ap-

pears sufficiently sensitive and adaptive to maintain synchrony with these changes [p. 3]."

In the investigations carried out to date, the triadic model has been applied only to the nuclear family, but it has much wider implications. For example, the third party role can be played, with as yet unknown effects, by grandparents (including the much maligned but as yet unresearched role of the mother-in-law); aunts and uncles; other members of the extended family; friends and neighbors; as well as teachers, counselors, or others providing services to children and families.[9]

5. The Analysis of Ecological Transitions.   An ecological transition occurs whenever, during the life course, a person enters a new role or setting. Such transitions occur at all ages and often serve as the impetus for developmental change. In infancy and early childhood they are typically triggered by external events, but, especially from adolescence onward, can be self-initiated as well. Examples of such events include arrival of a younger sibling, entry into day care or school, graduation, finding a job, going on vacation, becoming ill—and well again, marrying, moving, becoming divorced, changing jobs, remarrying, retiring, and that final transition to which there are no exceptions—dying. From the viewpoint of research design, every ecological transition constitutes, in effect, a ready-made experiment with a built-in, before–after design in which each subject can serve as his or her own control. Thus the transition provides an excellent opportunity for investigating development as a function of environmental change.

Yet, few scientific investigators have exploited naturally occurring events of this kind. Early on, Baldwin (1947) observed the mother's behavior toward the first child before, during, and after the mother's pregnancy with a second child. More recently, Hetherington, Cox, and Cox (1978) have traced the progressive influence of divorce on the mother–child relationship and the child's behavior in school. The disruptive effects of separation reached their peak 1 year afterwards and declined through the second year, although the divorced mothers never gained as much control as their married counterparts in the control group. Evidence for a second-order effect appeared in the finding that the mother's effectiveness in dealing with the child was directly related to the amount of support she received from her ex-husband. But, with the notable exception of Elder's study of *Children of the Great Depression* (1974), the common transition of life during adolescence, youth, and adulthood have remained uninvestigated.

And even at younger age levels, an important aspect of the transition has often been overlooked. I refer to what might be called "ecological feedback." The typical investigation of a child's entry into day care, school, or informal peer

---

[9]Of particular interest in this regard is the person, who after the parents, is the most pervasive but forgotton figure in the lives of American children—the babysitter.

group focuses on changes of behavior only in the new setting. The ecological feedback model emphasizes the importance of observing changes in other settings as well. Does the arrival of a younger sibling alter a child's orientation toward the peer group? Do children treat their parents differently once they have entered school? The demonstration of such feedback phenomena permits distinguishing generalized developmental effects from mere situational adaptation to a new setting.

6. The Ecology of Multiple Settings.   The fact that ecological transitions can involve movement across settings illustrates another closely related form of latent structure increasingly frequent in research designs of the past two decades. Beginning with the earliest studies of socialization, there has been a recurring, but apparently unremarked, discrepancy in the types of experimental designs being employed. For example, in investigations of the effects of child-rearing practices, some workers measured the developmental outcomes in the home, others in some external setting like nursery, preschool, or school classroom. Once it is pointed out, the theoretical significance of this difference in research design becomes readily apparent. In the first case, both independent and dependent variables are occurring in the same setting; the second design permits assessing the impact of events in one setting on behavior in another. A conception of the environment as involving more than one setting has evolved only gradually in developmental research. Insofar as I have been able to discover, it first received recognition in Hartshorne and May's classical experiments on deceit (1928), in which the authors reported on the relative impact of parents versus peers on the child's attitudes about right and wrong. It was not until the 1950s that there appeared a significant number of studies incorporating a multisetting conception of the environment. There are three sequential aspects to this development: (1) studies of the impact of events in one setting on the child's behavior and development in another; (2) investigations of the joint effect of the child's experience in two or more settings; and (3) research on the role of linkages between settings in affecting developmental processes taking place within them. Elsewhere (Bronfenbrenner, 1979), I have reviewed this body of research and sought to give a formal statement of the underlying research model. I describe it as the system of settings containing the developing person and suggest the term *mesosystem* to identify it.

Perhaps the greatest potential contribution of mesosystem models for research on human development lies in the importance they place on the nature of the connections existing between settings and the impact of these connections on intrasetting processes. How do the relations between family and school affect the child's capacity to learn in the classroom or the child's behavior within the home? Very few systematic studies have dealt with linkages of this kind. An outstanding example in Smith's research on "School and Home" (1968). Smith saw as a basic problem of American public education the growing alienation between parents and schools prevailing many segments of our society. With this issue as the focus, she designed a program to improve school performance of low-income minority pupils in the elementary grades. The project involved approximately 1000 children from low-income families, most of them Black, attending public elementary schools. The principal strategy employed for enhancing children's school performance was that of involving parents and teachers "as partners, not competitors, in the child's learning process." A core group of low-income parents mobilized others to become involved in the program. Parents were urged to provide supports for their children. Youngsters were given tags to wear at home that said, "Please read to me." Older children were given tags imprinted: "May I read to you?" Business students from the high school typed and duplicated teaching materials thus freeing teachers to work directly with the children. Teachers' in-service sessions focused on the influence of environmental factors in the children's classroom behavior and performance. In short, reciprocal support systems were established for all participants in the program. Regrettably, the innovativeness of Smith's intervention strategy was not matched by equal originality in the selection of outcome measures. Measured effects were limited to significant gains on tests of reading achievement, and overwhelmingly favorable attitudes expressed toward the program in a questionnaire that brought a gratifying response rate of 90%.

Since Smith's work was published, there has been only one substantial foray into the borderland between family and school, an ethnographic study by Lightfoot (1978), appropriately entitled "Worlds Apart." The area clearly merits further systematic investigation.

7. The Ecology of Exosystems.   The next emerging trend represents an extension of, but one step farther out on, the environmental continuum. Whereas the mesosystem deals with relations between settings containing the developing person, it does not take into account yet another possibility: the potential impact of events in settings in which the developing person is not present. An example is found in research carried out over the past 50 years on the influence of the conditions of parental work on family functioning and the development of the child (for a recent review, see Bronfenbrenner & Crouter, 1982). An analogous situation still be be explored is the influence of the parent's social life on the functioning of the family as a child-rearing system. Such influential settings external to the behavioral world of the developing person are referred to as *exosystems* (Bronfenbrenner, 1979). Among the most powerful exosystems are those agencies and institutions, both in the private and public sector, that design and administer policies affecting the well-being and functioning of families, schools, social service programs, and other socialization settings.

To consider a contemporary example, as these words are being written, family policies of long standing are being disowned, and the programs they sustain are being reduced or dismantled with little more than cursory examination of the consequences of such decisions for the well-being of the nation's families and children. Only 2 years ago we saw the first research evidence that some of the strategies employed in these programs were having lasting effects (Darlington, Royce, Snipper, Murray, & Lazar, 1980). Children enrolled in preschool intervention programs more than two decades ago later showed significantly higher rates of meeting school requirements than did controls, as measured by lower frequency of placement in special education classes and being retained in grade. Today, preliminary reports of the most recent findings indicate that the same children, as they grew older, were better school achievers and were more likely to graduate from high school. These experiences, in turn, predicted indices of subsequent success as measured by such criteria as continuing one's education, being gainfully employed, or having income other than public assistance (Lazar, 1981). In short, children who were the beneficiaries of such programs as preschoolers are today more likely to be productive citizens. In the meantime programs continue to be reduced. Social scientists are subject to an ethical code that prohibits them from exposing children to situations that are injurious to their welfare. Unfortunately, there is no such restriction on the nation as a whole, or on its duly empowered leaders and policy makers. The latter are free to run their economic and social experiments without such niceties as prior parental consent or review by qualified professionals. It remains the responsibility of researchers, however, to monitor these experiments and give an early warning of any unintended effects. What will be the consequences of cutting back funds for prenatal care, child nutrition and health, day care, and recreational and vocational programs for school-age children? In assessing these effects, we must use the best scientific methods at our command. There may be some difficulties in finding matched control groups, but there should be no problem with sample size. It is the irony and limitation of our science that the greater the harm done to children, the more we stand to learn about the environmental conditions that are essential for the human condition. It, therefore, becomes our professional obligation to employ the most advanced research designs at our disposal in order to forestall the tragic opportunity of significantly expanding our knowledge about the limits of the human condition on developing human beings.

8. *The Ecology of Developmental Trajectories.*   A number of the designs illustrated in this analysis have dealt with the impact of events and conditions in early childhood on development in later years. Such a demonstration is a recent phenomenon made possible by a reconceptualization in research design. Until the late 1960s, the results of longitudinal studies in human development had been interpreted as revealing psychological growth as a function of age. Then the sophisticated analyses of Baltes, Schaie, and their colleagues (Baltes, 1968; Nesselroade & Baltes, 1979; Schaie, 1970) demonstrated the confounding effects of age and cohort. Not only did persons in the same age group share a life history of common experience, but those of a given age in different generations

could have quite diverse experiences depending on the period in which they lived. Baltes and his associates sought to clarify these complexities through the use of ingenious statistical models designed to separate out the influences of age and cohort. It remained for a group of sociologists (Elder, 1974; Furstenberg, 1976; Riley, 1973) to turn a methodological problem into a substantive solution by transforming the individually oriented study of life-span development into a context-oriented analysis of the progression of particular groups along contrasting social trajectories throughout the life course. For example, Furstenberg (1976) has shown that, in contemporary America, when a teenager becomes pregnant before marriage, much of the rest of her life is foreordained and, indeed, foreclosed in terms of future education, work opportunities, income, marriage, and family life. In other domains, Entwisle and Doering (1981) have traced the effect of changing patterns of prenatal education over time on the mother's birth experience and on her subsequent treatment of the infant; and Hogan (1981) analyzed how the transition from adolescence to adulthood has changed in successive cohorts since 1900.

On an even broader scale, the long-term influence of historical events on individual development is traced in Elder's study of "Children of the Great Depression" (1974, 1979; Elder & Rockwell, 1979). Using archival material from two logitudinal studies begun in the 1930s, Elder divided each sample into otherwise comparable groups, differentiated on the basis of whether the loss of income as a result of the Depression exceeded or fell short of 35%. The fact that the youngsters in one sample were 8 years older than those in the other permitted a comparison of the effects of the Depression on children who were adolescents when their families became economically deprived, versus those who were still young children.

The results for the two groups presented a dramatic contrast. Paradoxically, for youngsters who were teenagers during the Depression years, the family's economic deprivation appeared to have a salutary effect on their subsequent development. They did better in school, were more likely to go to college, had happier marriages, exhibited more successful work careers, and, in general, achieved greater satisfaction in life, both by their own and societal standards, than nondeprived children of the same social class. These favorable outcomes were more pronounced for adolescents from middle-class background but were also evident among their lower-class counterparts. Elder hypothesized that the loss of economic security forced the family to mobilize its own human resources, including those of its teenagers. The youths had to take on new responsibilities to work toward the goal of getting and keeping the family on its feet. This experience provided them with effective training in initiative, responsibility, and cooperation. In the words of the banished Duke, "Sweet are the uses of adversity."

Alas, adversity was not so sweet for children who were still preadolescents when their families suffered economic loss. Compared to controls from nondeprived families, these youngsters subsequently did less well in school, showed less stable and successful work histories, and exhibited more emotional and social difficulties, some still apparent in middle adulthood. These disruptive effects were found only for males. Elder and his colleagues carefully traced the source of this downward trajectory to the "role-loss" experienced by the father as a result of the Depression.

The researches of Furstenberg and Elder take on long-range social significance in the light of changes currently taking place in the structure and status of families in contemporary American society. But their work, along with that of other protagonists of the life-course approach, has equally long-range implications for basic developmental science. Studies in this domain focus attention on the nature and sequence of the environments and events a person experiences from early childhood onward, and the effect of these experiences on subsequent development. Once set in motion, such developmental trajectories (Bronfenbrenner, 1979) have a momentum of their own. To employ an outmoded metaphor, development takes place on a moving train. One can walk forward or backward through the cars, but what really matters is where the train is going, for in most countries there are few places where one can change tracks. America probably presents more possibilities in this regard than many other societies, but, even here, many transfers are forced rather than free, especially those leading to unwelcome destinations. Within a particular culture, opportunities to change trains vary with one's age, social position, and the period of history in which one lives. The life-course approach involves the systematic study of such variations and its effects on development. By transforming elapsed time into historical time, Elder, Furstenburg, and other workers in this domain have added a new third dimension to developmental research that endows substantive content to what had previously been mere temporal duration.

RETROSPECT AND PROSPECT

The delineation of a third dimension completes this analysis of the evolution of scientific models of the environment in studies of human development. The analysis has identifed three major sets of forces contributing to the scientific advance. The first, and the most explicit, were new theoretical paradigms developed by scientists themselves. The fact that the creators of these paradigms were frequently theorists from other disciplines and other cultural backgrounds may account for the frequently long refractory period between the exposition of a theory and its ultimate application in empirical research. A critical role in this regard was played by researchers whom I called "translating theorists," those who were able to operationalize unorthodox concepts in more orthodox ways. A constructive contribution was also made by so-called "domain theorists," investigators who called attention to previously uncharted domains and provided tools for their systematic mapping.

Having established that theorists have made creative contributions to scientific progress, what use can we make of this hardly surprising discovery in order to advance scientific work in the future? Our progress in understanding the conditions conducive to human development relegates to science fiction any possibility of raising the quantity and quality of creative scientists in years to come. But if we cannot create paradigm-makers for the future, we can still learn from paradigm-makers in the past. As I indicated, I believe we have yet to reap the full harvest of their revolutionary conceptions.

The second stimulus to scientific progress identified in this analysis emanates from a source outside the pale of science itslef. It would appear that, over the decades, developmental researchers have been carrying on a clandestine affair with Clio—the muse of history. To put the issue more discretely, the course of social change has itself provoked investigators to a broader and more complex conception of the environment as it affects processes of human development. Initially, this broader conception involved recognition of newly emerging social structures in the society, but more recently history has provided the framework for tracing what Elder has called "the life course" of human beings living in the same cultural epoch and, thereby, progressing together through a distinctive succession of common experiences, critical events, and ecological transitions. To be sure, social scientists cannot shape the course of history; but they can learn to pay attention to its vicissitudes. I suggest that, after so many years, the developmental researcher's illicit liaison with Clio is no longer a tenable arrangement; it is time we embraced her as a legitimate partner in our creative scientific efforts.

Finally, I have tried to show that, over the last three decades, the most significant changes that have occurred in the evolution of scientific models in the study of human development have been a closet phenomenon—the gradual elaboration of latent structures underlying the research designs employed by investigators in the field. I suggest that herein lies the greatest promise for moving forward in our scientific endeavors. The evolution of these latent structures has proceeded at an uneven pace, with greater advances in some sectors than in others; as a result, some regions have been by-passed leaving gaps in the terrain. These gaps not only reveal the scope of our ignorance; they also delineate the ground for useful exploration. More importantly, the latent structures are not static forms, but dynamic trajectories with a momentum of their own. In Lewin's terminology, they represent uncompleted tasks that call for scientific closure. Our opportunity lies in recognizing and responding to that challenge by selecting those trajectories that have penetrated farthest into new scientific terrain and accelerating their momentum.

ACKNOWLEDGMENTS

Appreciation is expressed to Ann Pitkin and, especially, Gerri Jones for dedication beyond the call of duty in carrying out bibliographic work and totaling hundreds of index entries.

REFERENCES

Ainsworth, M. D. S. The development of infant–mother interaction among the Ganda. In B. M. Foss (Ed.), *Determinants of infant behavior* (Vol. 2). London: Methuen, 1963.

Ainsworth, M. D. S., & Wittig, B. A. Attachment and exploratory behavior of one-year-olds in a strange situation. In B. M. Foss (Ed.), *Determinants of infant behavior* (Vol. 4). London: Methuen, 1969.

Ambrose, J. A. The development of the smiling response in early infancy. In B. M. Foxx (Ed.), *Determinants of infant behavior* (Vol. 1). New York: Wiley, 1961.

Anderson, H. E. *The young child in the home*. New York: Appleton Century, 1936.

Angell, R. C. *The family encounters the Depression*. New York: Scribner, 1936.

Bach, G. R. Father-fantasies and father-typing in father-separated children. *Child Development*, 1946, *17*, 63–80.

Baldwin, A. L. Differences in parent behavior toward three- and nine-year old children. *Journal of Personality*, 1946, *15*, 143–165.

Baldwin, A. L. Changes in parent behavior during pregnancy: An experiment in longitudinal analysis. *Child Development*, 1947, *18*, 29–39.

Baldwin, A. L. Socialization and the parent–child relationship. *Child Devel.*, 1948, *19*, 127–136.

Baldwin, A. L. The effect of home environment on nursery school behavior. *Child Development*, 1949, *20*, 49–62.

Baldwin, A. L., Kalhorn, J., & Breese, F. H. Patterns of parent behavior. *Psychology Monographs*, 1945, *58*, #5.

Baltes, P. B. Longitudinal and cross sectional sequences in the study of age and generation effects. *Human Development*, 1968, *11*, 145–171.

Baltes, P. B., Reese, H. W., & Lipsitt, L. P. Life-span developmental psychology. *Annual Review of Psychology*, 1980, *31*, 65–110.

Baltes, P. B., & Schaie, K. W. *Life-span developmental psychology: Personality and socialization*. New York: Academic Press, 1973.

Bandura, A. *Principles of behavior modification*. New York: Holt, Rinehart, & Winston, 1969.

Bandura, A., & Huston, A. C. Identification as a process of incidental learning. *Journal of Abnormal and Social Psychology*, 1961, *LXIII*, 311–318.

Barker, R. G. Explorations in ecological psychology. *American Psychologist*, 1965, *20*, 1–14.

Barker, R. G. *Ecological psychology: Concepts and methods for studying the environment of human beings*. Stanford, Calif.: Stanford University Press, 1968.

Barker, R. G., & Wright, H. F. *One boy's day*. New York: Harper, 1951.

Barker, R. G., & Wright, H. F. *Midwest and its children: The psychological ecology of an American town*. New York: Row, Peterson, 1955.

Barlow, D. *The passive father as a factor in the adjustment of the child*. Smith College Studies in Social Work dissertation, 1924.

Baumrind, D. Child care practices anteceding three patterns of preschool behavior. *Genetic Psychology Monographs*, 1967, *75*, 43–88.

Baumrind, D. Current patterns of parental authority. *Developmental Psychology Monographs*, 1971, *4*(1), 1–102.

Baumrind, D. New directions in socialization research. *American Psychologist*, 1980, *35*, 63–661.

Baumrind, D., & Black, A. Socialization practices associated with dimensions of competence in preschool boys and girls. *Child Development*, 1967, *38*, 291–329.

Berenda, R. W. *The influence of the group on the judgements of children*. New York: King's Cross Press, 1950.

Blurton–Jones, N. G. *Biological perspectives on parenthood. The family in society: Dimensions of parenthood*. London: DHSS, HMSO, 1974.

Bossard, J. H. S., & Boll, E. S. *The large family system*. University of Pennsylvania Press, 1956.

Bowlby, J. *Maternal care and mental health*. Geneva: World Health Organization, 1951.

Bowlby, J. The nature of the child's tie to his mother. *International Journal of Psychoanalysis,* 1958, *39,* 350–373.

Bowlby, J. *Attachment and loss* (Vol. 1). *Attachment.* London: Hogarth, 1969.

Bremner, R. H. (Ed.). *Children and youth in America.* Cambridge, Mass.: Harvard University Press, 1974.

Bronfenbrenner, U. Socialization and social class through time and space. In E. E. Maccoby, T. M. Newcomb, & E. L. Hartley (Eds.), *Readings in social psychology.* New York: Henry Holt, 1958.

Bronfenbrenner, U. Toward a theoretical model for the analysis of parent–child relationships in a social context. In J. C. Glidewell (Ed.), *Parental attitudes and child behavior.* Springfield, Ill.: Charles C. Thomas, 1961.

Bronfenbrenner, U. *Is early intervention effective?* Washington, D. C.: DHEW Publications no (OHD) 76–30025, 1974.

Bronfenbrenner, U. *The ecology of human development: Experiments by nature and design.* Cambridge, Mass: Harvard University Press, 1979.

Bronfenbrenner, U., & Crouter, A. C. Work and family through time and space. In S. B. Kamerman & C. D. Hayes (Eds.), Families that Work: Children in a Changing World. Washington, D.C.: National Academy Press, 1982.

Brunswik, E. *Perception and the representative design of psychological experiments.* Berkeley: University of California Press, 1956.

Burt, C. The inheritance of general intelligence. *American Psychologist,* 1972, *27,* 175–190.

Carmichael, L. (Ed.). *Manual of child psychology* (1st ed.). New York: Wiley, 1946.

Carmichael, L. (Ed.). *Manual of child psychology* (2nd ed.). New York: Wiley, 1954.

Cavan, R. S. The wish never to have been born. *American Journal of Sociology.* 1932, *37,* 547–559.

Cavan, R. S., & Ranck, K. H. *The family and the depression: A study of 100 Chicago families.* Chicago: University of Chicago Press, 1938.

Cole, M., Gay, J., Glick, J. A., & Sharp, D. W. *The cultural context of of learning and thinking.* New York: Basic Books, 1971.

Cole, M., & Scribner, S. *Culture and thought: A psychological interpretation.* New York: Wiley, 1974.

Cooley, C. H. *Human nature and the social order.* New York: Scribner, 1902.

Darlington, R., Royce, J. M., Snipper, A. S., Murray, H. W., & Lazar, I. Preschool programs and later school comparisons of children from low-income families. *Science,* 1980, *208,* 202–204.

Davis, A., & Havighurst, R. J. Color differences in child rearing. *American Psychological Review,* 1948, *11,* 698–710.

de Candolle, A. L. P. *Historie des sciences et des savants depusi deux siècles, suivie d'autres études sur des sujets scientifiques, en particulier sur la sélection dans l'espèce humaine.* Genève: H. Georg, 1873.

Dennis, W. (Ed.). *Historical readings in developmental psychology.* New York: Meredith Corporation, 1972.

Dennis, W., & Najarian, P. Infant development under environmental handicaps. *Psychological Monographs,* 1957, *71* (#7).

Dollard, J. Culture, society, impulse, and socialization. *American Journal of Sociology,* 1939, *45,* 50–63.

Drillien, C. *The growth and development of the prematurely born infant.* Baltimore: Williams & Wilkins, 1964.

Durfee, H., & Wolf, K. Anstaltspflege und Entwicklung im ersten Lebensjahr. *Zeitschrift für Kinderforschung,* 1933, *42,* 273–320.

Elder, G. H., Jr. *Children of the great Depression.* Chicago: University of Chicago Press, 1974.

Elder, G. H., Jr. Historical change in life patterns and personality. In P. H. Baltes & O. Brim (Eds.), *Life-span development and behavior* (Vol. II). New York: Academic Press, 1979.

Elder, G. H., Jr., & Rockwell, R. C. The life-course approach and human development: An ecological perspective. *International Journal of Behavioral Development*, 1979, *2*, 1–21.

Entwisle, D. R., & Doering, S. G. *The first birth: A family turning point*. Baltimore: Johns Hopkins Press, 1981.

Figge, M. *The etiology of maternal rejection: A study of certain aspects of the mother's life*. Thesis at the Smith College School for Social Work carried on in the Institute for Child Guidance, New York, 1930; abstracted in *Smith College studies in social work, I: 407*, June 1931.

Figge, M. Studies of maternal overprotection and rejection: V, Some factors in the etiology of maternal rejection. *Smith College studies in social work, 2: 209–223*, March 1932.

Flavell, J. H. *The developmental psychology of Jean Piaget*. Princeton: Van Nostrand, 1963.

Flavell, J. H. Concept development. In P. H. Mussen (Ed.), *Carmichael's manual of child psychology* (Vol. 2). New York: Wiley, 1970.

Foley, P. Studies in maternal overprotection and rejection: V, Some factor in the etiology of maternal rejection. *Smith College studies in social work, 2: 209–223*, March 1932.

Furstenberg, F. *Unplanned parenthood: The social consequences of teenage child bearing*. New York: Free Press, 1976.

Galton, F. *English men of science: Their nature and nurture*. London: Macmillan, 1874.

Galton, F. The history of twins as a criterion of the relative power of nature. *Anthropological Institute Journal*, 1876, *5*, 391–406.

Glueck, S., & Glueck, E. *One thousand juvenile delinquents*. Cambridge, Mass. Harvard University Press, 1934(a).

Glueck, S., & Glueck, E. *Five hundred delinquent women*. New York: Knopf, 1934(b).

Goldfarb, W. The effects of early institutional care on adolescent personality. *Journal of Experimental Education*, 1943, *12*, 106–129. (a)

Goldfarb, W. Infant rearing and problem behavior. *American Journal of Orthopsychiatry*, 1943, *13*, 249–265. (b)

Goldfarb, W. Emotion and intellectual consequences of psychological deprivation in infancy: A re-evaluation. In P. H. Hock & J. Zubin (Eds.), *Psychopathology of childhood*. New York: Grune & Stratton, 1955.

Gordon, I. J. *A home learning center approach to early stimulation*. Gainsville, Fla.: Institute for Development of Human Resources, 1971.

Goslin, D. A. *Handbook of socialization theory and research*. Chicago: Rand McNally, 1969.

Gray, S. W., & Klaus, R. A. Experimental preschool programs for culturally deprived children. *Child Development*, 1965, *36*, 887–898.

Grinder, R. E. (Ed.). *A history of genetic psychology, the first science of human development*. New York: Wiley, 1967.

Gronset, E., & Tiller, P. O. Father absence in sailor families. In *Studies of the family*, (Vol. II). UNESCO Institute for Social Research and International Seminar on Family Research. Gottingen: Vandenhoeck et Ruprecht, 1957.

Hall, G. S. The contents of children's minds on entering school. *Princeton Review*, Jan./June 1883.

Hartshorne, H., & May, M. *Studies in deceit*. New York: MacMillian, 1928.

Hartup, W. W. Peer interaction and social organization. In P. H. Mussen (Ed.), *Carmichael's manual of child psychology* (Vol. 2). New York: Wiley, 1970.

Hartup, W. W. Perspectives on child and family interaction: Past, present and future. In R. M. Lerner & G. B. Spanier (Eds.), *Child influences on marital and family interaction: A life-span perspective*. New York: Academic Press, 1978, 23–42.

Hebb, D. O. The innate organization of visual activity: I. Perception of figures by rats reared in total darkness. *Journal of Genetic Psychology*, 1937, *51*, 101–126. (a)

Hebb, D. O. The innate organization of visual activity: II. Transfer of a response in the discrimination of brightness and size by rats reared in total darkness. *Journal of Comparative Psychology*, 1937, *24*, 277–299. (b)

Hebb, D. O. Studies of the organization of behavior: I. Behavior of the rat in a field orientation. *Journal of Comparative Psychology,* 1938, *25,* 333–352.

Hebb, D. O. *The organization of behavior.* New York: Wiley, 1949.

Heber, R., Garber, H., Harrington, S., & Hoffman, C. *Rehabilitation of families at risk for mental retardation.* Madison: Rehabilitation Research and Training Center in Mental Retardation, University of Wisconsin, 1972.

Hetherington, E. M., Cox, M., & Cox, R. The aftermath of divorce. In J. H. Stevens, Jr., & M. Mathews (Eds.), *Mother–child, father–child relations.* Washington, D. C.: National Association for the Education of Young Children, 1978.

Hinde, R. A. *Animal behavior: A synthesis of ethology and comparative psychology.* New York: McGraw-Hill, 1966.

Hodgkiss, M. The delinquent girl in Chicago: II. The influence of broken homes and working mothers. *Smith College Studies of Social Work,* 1933, *3,* 259–274.

Hoffman, M. L., & Hoffman, L. W. *Review of child development research* (Vol. 1). New York: Russell Sage Foundation, 1964.

Hogan, D. *Transition in social change: The early lives of American men.* New York: Academic Press, 1981.

Holt, E. B. *Animal drive and the learning process* (Vol. 1). New York: Holt, 1931.

Horowitz, F. D., & Paden, L. Y. The effectiveness of environmental intervention programs. In B. M. Caldwell & H. N. Ricciuti (Eds.), *Review of child development research* (Vol. 3). Chicago: University of Chicago Press, 1973.

Hough, E. Studies in maternal overprotection and rejection: II. Some factors in the etiology of maternal overprotection. *Smith College Studies in Social Work,* March 1932, *2,* 118–208.

Hunt, J. Mc. V. *Intelligence and experience.* New York: Ronand Press, 1961.

Hurlock, E. B. *Child development.* New York: McGraw-Hill, 1942.

Hurlock, E. B. *Developmental psychology: A life-span approach.* New York: McGraw-Hill, 1980.

Jensen, A. R. *Bias in mental testing.* New York: Free Press, 1980.

Kagan, J., & Moss, H. A. *Birth to maturity.* New York: Wiley, 1962.

Karnes, M. B., Studley, W. M., Wright, W. R., & Hodgins, A. S. An approach to working with mothers of disadvantaged preschool children. *Merrill–Palmer Quarterly,* 1968, *14,* 174–184.

Kirk, S. A. *Early education of the mentally retarded.* Urbana: University of Illinois Press, 1958.

Koch, H. L. The relation of "primary mental abilities" in five- and six-year olds to sex of children and characteristics of his sibling. *Child Development,* 1954, *25,* 209–223.

Kohlberg, L. Moral development and identification. In H. W. Stevenson (Ed.), *Child psychology.* Chicago: National Society for the Study of Education, 1963.

Kohlberg, L. The development of moral character. In M. L. Hoffman & L. W. Hoffman (Eds.), *Review of child development research* (Vol. 1). New York: Russell Sage Foundation, 1964.

Komarovsky, M. *The unemployed man and his family.* New York: Dryden Press, 1940.

Kuhn, T. S. *The structure of scientific revolutions.* Chicago: University of Chicago Press, 1962.

Lasko, J. K. Parent behavior toward first and second children. *Genetics Psychological Monographs,* 1954, 49–50, 97–138.

Lazar, I. Personal communication, 1981.

Levenstein, P. Cognitive growth in preschoolers through verbal interaction with mothers. *American Journal of Orthopsychiatry,* 1970, *40,* 426–432.

LeVine, R. A. Cross-cultural study in child psychology. In P. H. Mussen (Ed.), *Carmichael's manual of child psychology* (3rd ed.). New York: Wiley, 1970.

Levy, D. M. A method of integrating physical and psychiatric examination with special studies of body interest, over-protection, response to growth, and sex differences. *American Jounral of Psychiatry,* 1929, *9,* 121–198.

Levy, D. M. On the problem of delinquency. *American Journal of Orthopsychiatry,* 1932, *2,* 197–211.

Levy, D. M. Relation of maternal overprotection to school grades and intelligence tests. *American Journal of Orthopsychiatry,* 1933, *3,* 26–34.

Levy, D. M. *Maternal overprotection.* New York: Columbia University Press, 1943.

Lewenberg, M. Studies in maternal overprotection and rejection: IV: Marital disharmony as a factor in the etiology of maternal overprotection. *Smith College Studies in Social Work, 2:* 224–236, March 1932.

Lewin, K. Kriegslandschaft. *Zeitschrift fur Angewandte Psychologie,* 1917, *12,* 440–447.

Lewin, K. *A dynamic theory of personality.* New York: McGraw–Hill, 1935.

Lewin, K. *Resolving social conflicts, selected papers on group dynamics.* New York: Harper, 1948.

Lewin, K., Lippitt, R., & White, R. K. Patterns of aggressive behavior in experimentally created "social climates." *Journal of Social Psychology,* 1939, *10,* 271–299.

Lewis, M. How parental attitudes affect the problem of lying in children. *Smith College Studies in Social Work, 1, 403,* 1930.

Lewis, M., & Feiring, C. The child's social network: Social objects, social functions, and their relationship. In M. Lewis & L. A. Rosenblum, *The child and its family.* New York: Plenum, 1979.

Lightfoot, S. L. *Worlds apart.* New York: Basic Books, 1978.

Lorenz, K. Z. Der Kumpan in der Umwelt des Vogels. *Journal für Ornithologie,* 1935, *2,* 137–413.

Lorenz, K. Z. *Evolution and modification of behavior.* Chicago: University of Chicago Press, 1965.

Luria, A. R. *Cognitive development: Its cultural and social foundations.* Cambridge, Mass. Harvard University Press, 1976.

Mathews, S. M. The effects of mothers' out-of-home employment upon children's ideas and attitudes. *Journal of Applied Psychology,* 1934, *18,* 116–136.

Mead, G. H. *Mind, self, and society.* Chicago: University of Chicago Press, 1934.

Mead, M. *Coming of age in Samoa.* New York: Morrow, 1928.

Miller, N. E., & Dollard, J. *Social learning and imitation.* New Haven, Conn.: Yale University Press, 1941.

Moreno, J. L. *Who shall survive?* Washington, D. C.: Nervous and Mental Diseases Publishing Co., 1934.

Morgan, W. L. *The family meets the Depression.* Minneapolis: The University of Minnesota Press, 1939.

Mott, S. M. Mother–father preferences. *Character and Personality,* 1937, *5,* 302–304.

Murchison, C. (Ed.). *A handbook of child psychology.* Worcester, Mass.: Clark University Press, 1931.

Murchison, C. (Eds.). *A handbook of child psychology* (second rev.) Worcester, Mass.: Clark University Press, 1933.

Murphy, L. B. *Social behavior and child personality.* New York: Columbia University Press, 1937.

Mussen, P. H. (Ed.). *Handbook of research methods and child development.* New York: Wiley, 1960.

Mussen, P. H. (Ed.). *Carmichael's manual of child psychology.* New York: Wiley, 1970.

Mussen, P. H., & Conger, J. J. *Child development and personality.* New York: Harper, 1956.

Mussen, P. H., Conger, J. J., & Kagan, J. *Child development and personality* (2nd ed.). New York: Harper, 1963.

Mussen, P. H., Conger, J. J., & Kagan, J. *Child development and personality* (3rd ed.). New York: Harper, 1969.

Mussen, P. H., Conger, J. J., & Kagan, J. *Child development and personality* (4th ed.). New York: Harper, 1974.

Mussen, P. H., Conger, J. J., & Kagan, J. *Child development and personality* (5th ed.). New York: Harper, 1976.

Mussen, P. H., Conger, J. J., & Kagan, J. *Child development and personality* (6th ed.). New York: Harper, 1979.

Nesselroade, J. R., & Baltes, P. B. *Longitudinal research in the study of behavior and development.* New York: Academic Press, 1979.

Parke, R. D. Children's home environments: Social and cognitive effects. In I. Altman & J. F. Wohlwill (Eds.), *Children and the environment.* New York: Plenum Press, 1978.

Pavlov, I. P. *Lectures on conditioned reflexes* (trans. by G. V. Antrep). London: Oxford University Press, 1928.

Pederson, F. A. *Mother, father, and infant as an interaction system.* Paper presented at the annual meeting of the American Psychological Association, Washington, D. C., 1976.

Pederson, F., Cain, R., & Anderson, B. *Second-order effects involving interactions among mother, father, and infant.* Paper presented at the biennial meeting of the Society for Research in Child Development, Boston, 1981.

Piaget, J. *The language and thought of the child.* New York: Harcourt, Brace, 1926.

Piaget, J. *The construction of reality in the child.* New York: Basic Books, 1954.

Pringle, M. L., & Bossio, B. A study of deprived children. *Vita Humana 1, 1958,* 65–92, 142–170.

Riley, M. W. Aging and cohort succession: Interpretations and misinterpretations. *Public Opinion Quarterly,* 1973, *37,* 35–49.

Ross, B. M. Some traits associated with sibling jealousy in problem children. *Smith College Studies in Social Work, 1: 364–376,* 1931.

Schaefer, E. S., & Baley, N. Maternal behavior, child behavior, and their correlations from infancy through adolescence. *Monographs of the Society for Research on Child Development,* 1963, *28,* 3 (serial #87).

Schaffer, H. R. Some issues for research in the study of attachment behavior. In B. M. Foss (Ed.). *Determinents of infant behavior* (Vol. 2), New York: Wiley, 1963.

Schaie, K. W. A reinterpretation of age-related changes in cognitive structure and functioning. In L. R. Goulet and P. H. Baltes (Eds.), *Life span developmental psychology: Research and theory.* New York: Academic Press, 1970.

Schwabe, H., & Bartholomai, F. Der Vorstellungskreis der Berliner Kinder beim Eitritt in die Schule. *Stadtisches Jahrbuch der Stadt Berlin, Vierter Jahrbuch.* Berlin: Guttentag, 1870, 59–76.

Sears, R. R. Your ancients revisited: A history of child development. In E. M. Hetherington (Ed.), *Review of child development research* (Vol. 5). Chicago: University of Chicago Press, 1975, 1–74.

Sears, R. R. In G. Lindzey (Ed.), *A history of psychology in autobiography* (Vol. 7). San Francisco: Freeman, 1980.

Sears, R. R., Maccoby, E. E., & Levin, H. *Patterns of child rearing.* Evanston, Ill.: Row, Peterson, 1957.

Sears, R. R., Pintler, M. H., & Sears, P. S. Effect of father separation on preschool children's doll play agression. *Child Development,* 1946, *17,* 219–243.

Sewell, M. Some causes of jealousy in young children. *Smith College Studies in Social Work, 1: 6–22,* 1930.

Shaw, C. R. Juvenile delinquency—a group tradition. *Child welfare pamphlets* (No. 23). Bulletin of the State, University of Iowa News Services, No. 700, 1933.

Simpson, M. *Parent preferences of young children.* Teachers College Center of Education, No. 652, 1935.

Skeels, H. M. A study of the effects of differential stimulation on mentally retarded children: A follow-up report. *American Journal of Mental Deficiency,* 1942, *46,* 340–350.

Skeels, H. M. Adult status of children with contrasting early life experience. *Monographs of the Society for Research in Child Development,* 1966, *13,* (#3, serial No. 105).

Skeels, H. M., & Dye, H. B. The study of the effects of differential stimulation on mentally retarded children. *Proceedings and Addresses of the American Association of Mental Deficiency,* 1939, *44,* 114–136.

Skeels, H. M., Updegraff, R., Wellman, B. L., & Williams, H. M. *A study of environmental stimulation: An orphanage preschool project.* Iowa City: The University of Iowa, 1938.

Smith, M. B. School and home: Focus on achievement. In A. H. Pasow (Ed.), *Developing programs for the educationally disadvantaged.* New York: Teachers College Press, 1968.

Spearman, C. The heredity of abilities. *Eugenics Review,* 1914, *6,* 219–237.

Spitz, R. A. Anaclitic depression: An inquiry into the genesis of psychiatric conditions in early childhood, II. *Psychoanalytic Study of the Child,* 1946, *2,* 313–342. (a)

Spitz, R. A. The smiling response: A contribution to the onotogenesis of social relations. *Genetic Psychology Monographs,* 1946, *34,* 57–125. (b)

Stolz, L. M. *Father relations of war-born children.* Stanford: Stanford University Press, 1954.

Symonds, P. M. *The psychology of parent–child relationships.* New York: Appleton–Century, 1939.

Terman, L. M. *Psychological factors in marital happiness.* New York: McGraw–Hill, 1938.

Thomas, W. I. *The unadjusted girl.* Boston: Little, Brown, 1927.

Thomas, W. I., & Thomas, D. S. *The child in America.* New York: Knopf, 1928.

Thomas, W. I., & Znaniecki, F. *The Polish peasant in Europe and America.* Chicago: University of Chicago Press, 1927.

Tiller, P. O. Father absence and personality development of children in sailor families. Copenhagen: *Munksgaard Nordisk Psykologi's Monograph Series,* 1958, *9.*

Tiller, P. O. *Father separation in adolescence.* Oslo: Institute for Social Research, 1961.

Tinbergen, N. *In the study of instinct.* London: Oxford University Press, 1951.

Tizard, B., Cooperman, O., Joseph, A., & Tizard, J. Environmental effects on language development: A study of young children in long-stay residential nurseries. *Child Development,* 1972, *43,* 337–358.

Tizard, B., & Hodges, J. The effect of early institutional rearing on the development of eight year old children. *Journal of Child Psychology and Psychiatry,* 1978, *19,* 99–118.

Tizard, B., & Rees, J. A comparison of the effects of adoption, restoration to the natural mother, and continued institutionalization on the cognitive development of four-year-old children. *Child Development,* 1974, *45,* 92–99.

Tizard, B., & Rees, J. A comparison of the effects of adoption, restoration to the natural mother, and continued institutionalization on the cognitive development of four-year-old children: further note: December 1975. In A. M. Clarke & A. D. B. Clarke (Ed.), *Early experience: Myth and evidence.* London: Open Books, 1976.

Tulkin, S. R. Social class differences in infant's reactions to mother's and stranger's voices. *Developmental Psychology,* 1973, January, *8*(1), 137. (a)

Tulkin, S. R. Social class differences in attachment behaviors of ten-month-old infants. *Child Development,* 1973, March, *44*(1), 171–174. (b)

Tulkin, S. R., & Cohler, B. J. Child-rearing attitudes and mother–child interaction in the first year of life. *Merrill–Palmer Quarterly,* 1973, *19,* 95–106.

Tulkin, S. R., & Covitz, F. E. *Mother–infant interaction and intellectual functioning at age six.* Paper presented at the meeting of the Society for Research in Child Development, Denver, April 1975.

Tulkin, S. R., & Kagan, J. Mother–child interaction in the first year of life. *Child Development,* 1972, *43,* 31–41.

U.S. Commission of Education. Annual Report for 1900/1901 (Vol. 1). Washington, D.C., 1902.

Vygotsky, L. S. *Mind in society: The development of higher psychological processes.* Cambridge, Mass.: Harvard University Press, 1978.

Wang, C. K. A. The significance of early personal history for certain personality traits. *American Journal of Psychology,* 1932, *44,* 768–774.

Watson, J. B. *Psychology from the standpoint of a behaviorist.* Philadelphia: Lippincott, 1918.

Watson, J. B. *Behaviorism* (2nd ed.). New York: Norton, 1930.

Weikart, D. P. *Preschool intervention: A preliminary report of the Perry Preschool Project.* Ann Arbor: Campus Publishers, 1967.

Werner, E., Simonian, K., Berman, J. M., & French, F. E. Cumulative effect of perinatal complicating and deprived environment on physical, intellectual, and social development of preschool children. *Pediatrics,* 1967, *39,* 480–505.

Whiting, J. W., & Child, I. L. *Child training and personality: A corss-cultural study.* New Haven, Conn.: Yale University Press, 1953.

Willerman, L. Bisocial influences on human development. *American Journal of Orthopsychiatry,* 1972, *42,* 452–462.

Willerman, L., Naylor, A., & Myrianthopoulos, N. Intellectual development of children from interracial matings. *Science,* 1970, *170,* 1329–1331.

7 A Trio of Trials*

Bernard Kaplan
Clark University and *Heinz Werner Institute for Developmental Psychology*

I. THE PAST AS PROLOGUE, PRELUDE, AND PRETEXT

Benedetto Croce is notorious for having formulated the profound banality that all true history is contemporary history. Although Croce was too much of a philosopher and statesman to urge the full force of that dictum, it has been taken by many to suggest that we posit and construct the past of any entity—cosmos, humanity, nation, individual—in terms of our current values and concerns, in

---

*The three papers comprising this chapter were written at different times and for different occasions. The first was prepared for a Symposium on Developmental Psychology: History of Philosophy and Philosophy of History, held in Montreal in 1980. The second was prepared for a Symposium on Life-Span Developmental Psychology, held in Santo Domingo, June, 1981. It is included here because it seemed more appropriate to the changed title of this volume, which was originally to correspond with the title of the Montreal Symposium. A change of scene changes the character of the act, and so I sought an act that would fit the altered scene, characterized by the present title of this volume. The third paper mushroomed as I began to reflect on the papers I had heard and read by other symposiasts at the Montreal Conference or by those who had been invited to contribute chapters to this volume under its altered title. I considered, in my "call to controversy," only those papers to which I had access and have therefore omitted any critique of several of the chapters here included. If my comments on those chapters I considered have prompted the authors to change or qualify their earlier drafts, so that some of my comments may seem to have no point of reference in their chapters, I hope the reader takes my seemingly irrelevant remarks as applying to anyone who takes the positions I have here attributed to specific authors. The issue here as elsewhere is not who says it but what is said, and whether what is said is warranted or not. *Non quo, sed quomodo!* I especially thank those I criticized for providing solid meat to chew on. I hope they take the occasion, here or elsewhere, to expose my papers to the same kind of critique I have addressed to theirs.

terms of our current interests. Where goals differ or concerns vary, the histories that are presented are likely to diverge: sometimes to such an extent that two historians, putatively referring to the "same" set of events, will present characterizations of what took place that scarcely overlap—the well-known *Rashomon* phenomenon. In some instances, it will not be merely a disagreement as to the interpretation of the "data," or the weightings attributed to different "facts," but as to the existence of the very facts themselves. The implication seems to be that the world is a gigantic Rorschach blot, and any structurization—including one into past, present, and future—is at bottom (or is it at top?) a personal confession and a personal expression.

The possibility that descriptions of what happened in history are governed by the values and concerns of individual historians—professional or amateur—threatens, of course, to dissolve historiography into mythology, to blur the sacred boundaries between Fact and Fancy. To forestall such an unbridled descent into Hell—which would certainly carry along with it all claims to dispassionate knowledge and truth in any discipline whatsoever—we, as responsible scientists, critical philosophers of history, hypercritical philosophers of science, and just plain serious persons, have erected a number of sacred canons: responsible methods of inquiry, responsible ways of ascertaining the facts, responsible ways of using language, responsible ways of drawing inferences and conclusions. It has long been asserted that inflexible adherence to these canons would enable us to keep strong and intact the walls between the subjective and the objective, fact and fiction, the true and the false, and so on. Alas—or is it happily?—we now live in an era in which a number of pagans outside the fold and a number of heretics within the walls of the academy have cast aspersions on our sacred canons: They have had the temerity to assert that our procedures to insure accountability and preserve natural class distinctions are merely shibboleths to maintain stability and insure law and order. They have questioned the Autonomy of Fact, rejected the Sanctity of Method, sneered at the Sovereignty of the Syllogism, and even depreciated the value of Value—Free Inquiry. In their "rage for chaos," they seem to have let mere anarchy loose upon the world.

I must admit that I am not unsympathetic to this new movement or cluster of movements, although I resist marching under the banner of the extreme hermeneuticists, the dissolute deconstructionists, the high priests of misprision. Whether this resistance derives from the severity of my superego, my "blessed rage for order," or my fear of eliminating all constraints over the vagaries of mind, I prefer to accept some distinctions between the True and the False, Fact and Opinion, Appearance and Reality, as difficult as it may be firmly to establish the grounds for such distinctions.

My prologue was intended to alert you to the fact that I deal with the general theme of this book—DEVELOPMENTAL PSYCHOLOGY: PHILOSOPHY OF HISTORY AND HISTORY OF PHILOSOPHY—in a way different from that which I think psychologists are likely to expect, given their *déformation profes-sionelle*. I believe that individuals construe the Philosophy of History and the History of Philosophy in quite different ways depending on their interests and concerns. As a special case, I believe that individuals who take themselves to be developmental psychologists will reconstruct the domains, Philosophy of History and History of Philosophy, in quite different ways depending on their values and interests. Thus, it is likely that what we take to be Philosophy of History and History of Philosophy will depend not only on what we take current versions of developmental psychology to be, but also—and more importantly—what we think developmental psychology ought to be about, and what developmental psychologists ought to be doing.

With these considerations in mind, I try to make explicit what my values and concerns are with regard to developmental psychology and then pick and choose among philosophers of history and philosophers in history to demonstrate, with incontestable bias and irrefrageable illogic, that the thesis I advance about the true mission of developmental psychology has been foreshadowed, indeed even explicitly promoted, by many of the leading philosophers of history and many of the great philosophic minds of our culturally consitututed past. Because I suffer from an incurable predilection for polemics, I parenthetically smote hip and thigh much of contemporary developmental psychology. This may serve to promote a future symposium, in which individuals confront each other in dialogue and not as an aggregate of monads.

Developmental Psychology

What is developmental psychology? Lurking beneath this seemingly simple and innocuous question is a serpentine ambiguity. Developmental psychology can be defined in terms of what self-proclaimed or officially canonized developmental psychologists do, or in terms of what one thinks they ought to be doing. The issue here is analogous to questions such as "What is justice?," "What is art?," "What is science?." Although such questions, on the surface, seem to ask for straightforward descriptions, it inevitably turns out that the answers are "persuasive definitions" (Charles Stevenson). And those who define in terms of the "mainstream"—the operationalists who hold, for example, that "developmental psychology" is what developmental psychologists do, are as much engaged in persuasive definition (maintaining the status quo) as those who suggest a radically different definition of the enterprise.

It should be obvious that persuasive definitions are not regulated simply or mainly by "what is the case." They are advanced in terms of certain interests and therefore reflect ethical and axiological considerations as well as logical and methodological ones. Inevitably, they are political and ideological, even though they may be presented as neutral and dispassionate (see Black, 1954). I want to make this explicit because all of us, considering the relations of developmental psychology to history of philosophy and philosophy of history, bring to the discussion persuasive definitions of these three domains.

Now, my definition of "developmental psychology". *Developmental psychology is a practico-theoretical discipline, a policy discipline, concerned with the perfection (including liberation or freedom) of the individual.* Its aim is to facilitate—and here I use many of the terms sneered at by academic developmentalists—the self-actualization, self-realization, freedom from bondage, individuation, etc.—of human beings. To do so, it undertakes inquiries into the variety of factors, operative at particular times and places, that facilitate or impede progress toward the goal and suggests policies and practices to institute the facilitative factors and eliminate those factors that interfere with optimal development. It should be obvious, in terms of this definition of the field that *human development* itself is not defined by observations, systematic or otherwise, of what actually occurs in childhood, over the life-span, etc. To use Northrop's formulation, "development" is a *concept by postulation,* not a *concept by intuition.* It pertains to a rarely, if ever, attained ideal, not to the actual. We do not discover the nature of human development through longitudinal studies, cross-sectional studies, cross-cultural studies, experimental studies, etc., although all these kinds of studies—*carried out with the telos of "development" in mind*—may help us to recognize our own egocentricities, ethnocentricities, *préjuges du monde;* and may provide us with information about factors, at any and all levels of analysis, that facilitate or impede human development. *I emphasize the necessity for having the telos of "development" in mind:* It entails, in my view, that developmentalists specify how their inquiries and the results of their inquiries bear on issues of human freedom and liberation.

Far be it from me to assume or suggest that the proposed telos of development is transparent or easy to articulate. The nature of human perfection and human freedom have been problematic throughout history. Mortimer Adler (1958, 1961) has devoted two thick volumes to summarizing the diverse and conflicting views of philosophers on the nature and conditions for human freedom and has surely omitted many important contributions to the debate. This suggests that one of the tasks of developmental psychologists is to work to clarify the ideal of human development. And such a work inevitably involves us with the writings of those who have concerned themselves with that issue: among them, philosophers of history and philosophers in history.

Before I discuss some of the relationships between developmental psychology as I conceive it, and the philosophies in and of history, I do want to note that few, if any, official developmental psychologists have explicitly advanced the definition I propose, even though some—typically those concerned with the cure of bodies, minds, and souls—have tacitly accepted the notion that development pertains to a movement toward increasing liberation from bondage and the perfecting of human beings. Thus, Freud and Jung both assumed an immanent telos of development—a movement toward genitality or toward individuation—and both worked or claimed to work to remove certain factors inhibiting the relative attainment of such relatively more advanced modes of being-in-the-world. Unfortunately, these two great minds were inclined to take their teloi as immanent in the biographico-historical process: ineluctable, if only the inhibiting forces could be overcome. Freud was, of course, far more pessimistic than Jung concerning the possibility of eliminating the inhibiting forces, and thus his teleological assumption is less obvious.

I see no good reason to assume such an immanent finalism in ontogenesis, any more that I see a good reason to assume such a teleological factor operative in world history. It seems that the eschatological vision of one of the earliest of our philosophers of history in the West—St. Augustine—led a number of 18th- and 19th-century thinkers to conflate historical change, development, evolution, and progress, and to discern—if through a glass darkly—an immanent progressive movement in the actual processes of history (see K. Löwith, 1949). This conflation seems to have penetrated the minds of some developmental psychologists—even some other than Freud and Jung—who see actual ontogenesis as moving through a series of stages in a fixed and quasi-necessary sequence toward some ideal end state of affairs or mode of operation.

Although I bear no animus towards those who wish to attribute to the human organism an inclination to move stepwise, stagewise, or otherwise toward Ultima Thule in the course of ontogenesis, I sense some dangers in positing such an indwelling telos; one may espy necessity in the process of actual change where there is only contingency; and one may equate the telos with an actual state in the history of the organism, such as Hegel is reputed to have done with regard to the world-historical process. I, therefore, bracket the issue of whether or not such finalism is inherent in historical processes on the individual level, and radically distinguish development, as an ideal process, from ontogenesis as an actual one (Kaplan, 1966a,b, 1967, 1981a,b).

History of Philosophy/Philosophy of History

I turn now to the other domains referred to in the title of the symposium from which this volume derived: History of Philosophy and Philosophy of History. Given the context of this colloquy, I have construed my task as showing the relevance or irrelevance of these domains to developmental psychology, as I have formulated the goals of that discipline.

Unfortunately, there is no single History of Philosophy or Philosophy of History. With regard to the first realm, a cursory survey of presumptive histories of philosophy and a close scrutiny of one critical examination of histories of philosophy (Smart, 1962) indicate that historians of philosophy have often disagreed as to the aim of such a history, the subject matter to be included in such a history, the significance of such a history for the philosophical enterprise itself, and a number of other issues as well.

With regard to the second domain, there is even a more radical dispersion: There are philosophers of history—speculative—concerned to delineate the pattern, purpose, direction, meaning, and/or value of historical processes in the history of mankind as a whole or/and in the "biography" of nations or civilizations comprising that larger history; there are other philosophers of history—critical, analytical—who focus on the categories of historical analysis, the criteria of historical explanation, or the nature and warrant of claims to historical knowledge, and so on. In both of these more or less segregated subdomains, civil and incivil wars are rampant.

Among the speculators, despite some alliances, it is obvious that Augustine, Vico, Herder, Kant, Hegel, Marx, Croce, Spengler, and Toynbee, to mention only some, advance different theses concerning the goal of history, the patterns to be discerned in history, the factors leading to the rise and fall of states, the roles of different groups within societies, and so on. Among the critical philosophers of history, one will recall the *Methodenstreit* of the late 19th century, when Dilthey, Windelband, Rickert, Max Weber, and others, however much they squabbled among themselves, took up arms against the positivists and scientific historians of the period (see Cassirer, 1961, 1950); and more recently the sometimes rabid controversies between Popper–Hempel–Nagel and Collingwood–Dray as well as between the Popperians and Adorno, Habermas, and others. It would be an overwhelming task to know what to do with this embarrassment of riches even if I had world enough and time. In the limited space available, I discuss the values of philosophy in, and philosophy of, history in both global and personal terms.

Over the past 25 years, I have offered seminars in developmental theory to graduate students at Clark University. In these seminars, we often discussed Plato, Aristotle, Spinoza, Herder, Kant, Schelling, Fichte, Hegel, Marx, Cassirer, Croce, Dewey, Horkheimer, Marcuse, and others and scrutinized their works for relevance to the formulation of an adequate concept of development; to the establishment and clarification of the telos of human development; to an appreciation of the characteristics that mark a highly developed human being; to a grasp of the cultural factors that might promote or militate against optimal human development, etc. In sum, we looked at those philosophers in history who concerned themselves with issues relevant to the condition of being fully human. Admittedly, we did not look at the writings of these thinkers from the perspective of a putatively dispassionate historian of philosophy. Nor did we look at them from the point of view of one who wants to grasp one or another philosophical system for its own sake. We took these philosophers as voices in an ongoing symposium concerned with human self-realization and human self-perfection. We took them as individuals, who, limited as they might be due to their particular sociohistorical circumstances, did not immure themselves inside the ghettos of a segregated discipline, did not blind themselves to the interrelations of what we, today, call psychology, with what we, today, call politics, sociology, education, economics, ethics, axiology, etc.

They helped at least some of us to see the folly of collapsing human development into so-called "cognitive development," whether of the ordinary or meta-variety; the insipidity of taking the ultimate telos of human development to be formal operations; the inanity of collapsing the ideal of human development into the actualities of ontogenesis, parochial or cross-cultural; the sterility of trying to deal with human development solely through so-called value-neutral inquiry; etc.

I may add that, more recently, we have added other voices to the symposium, thinkers who are not usually included in our standard works on History of Philosophy, but who are surely concerned with the nature of human beings, optimal human development, the human being's place in nature, the kinds of factors that impede human development, and so on. I refer to religious and philosophical thinkers from the Far East and Near East and others influenced by such thinkers, for example, the Gurdjieff–Ouspensky–Bennett "school" (see J. Bennett, 1977, 4 vols.; P. Ouspensky, 1973, 1974;). These thinkers have often been considered by workers in the area of "transpersonal psychology," but so rigid is the *apartheid* within academic psychology, that they are rarely explored by so-called developmental psychologists.

Now, *philosophy of history,* first critical, then speculative. Because it is clear to me that the principal subject matter of developmental psychology demands methods of analysis and modes of interpretation at least as much akin to those of the historian as to those of the physicist of biologist, I also devoted and continue to devote seminars to the problems of historical knowledge, trying to acquaint myself and my students with the issues and controversies concerning historical reconstruction, historical understanding, historical explanation. We have spent considerable time going over the writings of Vico, Marx, Dilthey, the Marburg neo-Kantians, Collingwood, M. R. Cohen, Mandelbaum, Walsh, Dray, Danto, and others who have dealt with the categories, concepts, and methods of historical inquiry. And we have done so because I believe that developmental psychology and developmental psychologists must liberate themselves from the methodological straitjackets imposed on them by philosophers and philosophies of science so long dominant on the academic scene.

Now, to speculative philosophy of history. Of little relevance to me, in the present context, and perhaps in any context, are the claims, dubious at best, of many speculative philosophers of history to have discerned necessary patterns or directions either in the universal history of mankind, or the separate histories of states or civilizations, each taken as an exemplar of the same universal archetype. With the proper prisms, one can descry circles, lines, or spirals everywhere. To be sure, one may learn from such extravagant exercises the dangers of leaping from empirically ascertained sequences in a few cases to generalizations taken to be applicable to all cases; or the hazards of transforming an empirically observed sequence of stages or steps into a fixed and *necessary* sequence of stages, *destined* to succeed each other in every case. But such lessons can be learned elsewhere.

The speculative philosophies of history most relevant to us here are those that have taken freedom or liberation from bondage as the telos of the historical process (for example, Hegel, Marx), and those that have taken the telos of human striving (viz., salvation) as lying outside the domain of actual history (for example, Augustine, Niehbuhr, and perhaps Toynbee). Both of these species of philosophers of history have been led in their interpretations to treat factors that block the achievement of the telos, and to try to delineate the factors "outside" or "inside" the individual that may promote the attainment of the telos. Whatever one may think of their formulations of these factors, it should be clear how and why I take their writings to have some relevance to developmental psychology as I conceive it. Indeed, there is an interesting paradox—one may be led to reject their conclusions and prophecies and yet find their categories and their modes of interpreting historical phenomena extremely fruitful for developmental analysis.

Now, my concluding remarks. Had we retained the vision of some of the leading philosophers in history and some of the speculative philosophers of history and considered both the history of humankind and the history of the individual as scenes of the struggle for human liberation and human perfection, we would not have separated the "is" from the "ought" in developmental psychology. We would have recognized that development, as distinct from mere chronological change, is an ideal movement toward freedom, autonomy, individuation, liberation from the various forms of bondage, external and internal.

The mistake is to think that such a movement occurs "naturally" in history and therefore unfolds unconsciously, under "normal conditions," without the persistent and deliberate involvement and intervention of individuals in their own self-making. One may acknowledge in Stephen Toulmin's fine phrase, that there is operative an "ideal of natural order," but this ideal, like others, requires strenuous efforts to be approximated or attained.

If we had followed this path as developmental psychologists—orienting ourselves toward the achievement of self-perfection in ourselves and others—there would not now be such a radical diremption between so-called developmental psychologists and personality psychologists, transpersonal psychologists, clinical psychologists, anthropologists, sociologists, philosophers, etc. All would be concerned with the processes of attaining human "perfection," freedom, and liberation, and all would realize that their principal raison d'être is to examine and eliminate the factors that obstruct that attainment; determine and facilitate the factors that promote that attainment. There would, in sum, be far more connection and integration in psychology than now obtains. There would also be far more linkage to other disciplines. All psychology would be recognized as developmental psychology, and developmental psychology, itself, would be the guiding star for all the other disciplines in the academy. For should not the achievement of human freedom and perfection for others and ourselves be the aim of all of us?

II. SOME PROBLEMS AND ISSUES FOR A THEORETICALLY ORIENTED LIFE-SPAN DEVELOPMENTAL PSYCHOLOGY

In recent years, a new movement has sprung up in the United States among those who refer to themselves as ''developmental psychologists.'' This movement, a quasi-political one, marches under the banner of ''Life-Span Developmental Psychology.'' Although its main centers still seem to be in the United States, like the ''pox'' it threatens to spread to all corners of the world. Its principal contribution to the world of scholarship and inquiry, up to now, has been to assert that ''developmental psychology,'' so often limited to the study of infants, young children, and adolescents, should appropriately extent its territory to include the middle-aged, the senescent, and even the dying. This outstanding proposal, this revolutionary manifesto, has brought together in one party the most divergent elements. Behaviorists, phenomenologists, information processors, naturalistic observers, cross-cultural enthusiasts, experimentalists, and even psychoanalysts may now all join hands and jointly subscribe to a political platform consisting of a single plank: ''Yesterday the infant and child; today, the adolescent too; tomorrow, the entire life-span.''[1] A jaundiced sociologist of knowledge might wonder whether this new party has come into being as a consequence, at least in part, of the shift in the median age of North Americans. But we know that such callous and opportunistic considerations play no role in the world of intellectuals.

One remarkable quality of this movement is that it is concurrently motley and monolithic. Invoking some obscure principle of pure tolerance, its choirmasters call for a multitheoretical, multiperspectival, multimethodological, and multivariate approach to developmental psychology. Everyone is invited to contribute his/her voice to the songfest without any restrictions on melody, lyrics, or arrangement. All must, however, pledge fealty to the one and only Life-Span. Enjoining neither a theory nor a concept of development and hence enjoying the obvious advantage of not knowing what it is that they are studying in examining individuals over the life-span, the leaders of this movement apparently expect that some Master Builder will eventually take all the ''data'' generated by the

---

[1] Were it not for the double entendre, and the danger of provoking the cessation of grant funds and a Senate Investigation, one might expect that the name of the Society for Research in Child Development (SRCD) would momentarily be changed to Society for Research in Life-Span Development (SRLSD).

diverse members of the movement and demonstrate with irrefrageable logic the decisive and determining influence of the 18th century on the 19th or the 20th century on the 21st.

It is obvious that neither the study of phenomena over the life-span nor the *developmental analysis* of phenomena over the life-span are novel enterprises. G. Stanley Hall, the first President of Clark University, clearly concerned himself with the investigation of human life from birth to senescense. And my teacher and colleague, Heniz Wener, clearly sought to apply developmental conceptualization not only to all phases of the life-span, but to cultural phenomena, neurological phenomena, pathological phenomena, transient episodes of human beings at all ages, and so on. I do not deal here with the conception of development held either tacitly or explicitly by Hall. Nor do I consider whether Hall expected to arrive at the nature of "development" through empirical methods rather than through postulation or stipulation. I do, however, deal with Werner.

In his classic work, *Comparative Psychology of Mental Development,* Werner (1948) operated with a hybrid notion of development. On one hand, he treated it as a *concept by postulation;* on the other, as a *concept by intuition* (Northrop, 1947, pp. 82ff); that is, he took development as having a specific *meaning,* and this meaning governed his selection and ordering of empirical and experimental facts; at the same time, he seemed to believe that the facts of ontogenesis, evolutionary change, change in the central nervous system, cultural variation and cultural change, and so on, naturally fell into a developmental sequence, and that he was merely reading off the facts. Thus, he (Werner, 1948) wrote:

> It is no mere coincidence that Goethe, a man of powerful intuition who saw deep into the nature of all things, should be the first to express in clear language the idea of organic development. For him, the very essence of the development of biological forms is symbolized by the differentiation of the organic parts and their subordination to the whole of the organism [p. 40].

Werner (1948) goes on to cite Goethe's introduction to his *Morphologie.* There Goethe remarked:

> The more perfect the creature becomes, the less similar become the /morphological/ parts to one another. On the one genetic pole, the whole is more or less similar to the parts, and on the other the whole is dissimilar to the parts. The more nearly equal the parts, the less they are subordinated one to another. Subordination of the parts indicates a perfect creature [pp. 40–41].

Now it should be clear that Goethe leaves open (or ambiguous) the issue of whether "development"—movement toward perfection—is to be *defined* in terms of increasing differentiation and hierarchic integration or is found to obtain through empirical examination of phenomena over time (ontogenesis, evolution, etc.). In his seminal book, Werner maintained that ambiguity.

Whether for good or ill, it was through his association with me (Werner & Kaplan, 1956) that Werner came to recognize the necessity for distinguishing the meaning of development from the actualities of life. Together, we formulated the "orthogenetic principle," which served to *define* the nature of development irrespective of what actually took place over the life-span or as a function of age. It was only through such a separation of the normative and the factual that one could justifiably use the concept of development in the various domains to which Werner had applied the notion (see Kaplan, 1966a, 1967). "Development" was unabashedly recognized as an heuristic concept, serving to order phenomena from the most diverse domains, including that of cultural differences (see Kaplan, 1966a).

This distinction freed us from the specious supposition that changes with age were necessarily or intrinsically developmental and indeed warranted the use of such notions as "arrested development," "regression," and so on as applied to individuals during the course of ontogenesis or in pathological conditions.[2] It freed us, in general, from the unwarranted doctrine that Time was the mother of Perfection or that Progress either in history or biography was inevitable. It allowed us to make explicit our view that any investigator who claimed to discover a necessary sequence of stages in ontogenesis, with regard to personality development, intellectual development, moral development, or any other partitive development, was doubtless constructing an artificial child (*"the* child") or an artificial human being (*"the* human being over the life-span"), assimilated to an unacknowledged a priori system of interpretation.

Normally, I would not think it necessary to state that this differentiation of the *meaning of development* from the *facts of ontogenesis* demands a full and complete focus on ontogenetic phenomena. But the character of the "orthogenetic principle" and the implications of its use have been so widely misunderstood or misrepresented that I want to take some time to render clear what should never have been obscure. Precisely because the facts of individual ontogenesis do not necessarily, or even as a rule, conform to the orthogenetic principle, precisely because change over time is not necessarily progress or a movement toward perfection, one examines actual individuals as they engage in various performances or actions; as they operate in different situations or settings; as they are motivated by different goals or ends. But one does not examine them helter-skelter, without some firm conception of what development means. *One examines them from a developmental point of view* (see Kaplan, 1981a).

And it is because one examines them from a developmental perspective that one looks—in terms of the ever-present operation of forces of differentiation

---

[2]The notion of "pathology" itself presupposes such a normative conception of development.

(many) and integration (one)—for the factors that promote or inhibit *develop-mental advance;*[3] that, as a practitioner in any domain, one works to introduce those factors that will promote development (''movement toward perfection'') and seeks to eliminate or mitigate those factors that seem to bar the way. Such noxious or beneficial factors, it is recognized, may operate at every level, from the physical to the cosmic, from the material to the spiritual. The first issue, then, for a theoretically oriented life-span developmental psychologist to face is that of the locus of development: *Development does not lurk directly in the population(s) studied but resides fundamentally in the perspective used.* A developmental perspective, as Werner has shown, can be used to study individuals and groups; ontogenesis and phylogenesis; intellectual history and cultural variations; short-duration and long-duration phenomena; normal functioning and ''pathological'' functioning; the ups and downs of everyday life; the formation of persons as well as the formation of percepts.[4] And, again, as Werner has shown, a truly developmental perspective can help us to avoid that temptation to take any delimited domain of development (e.g., ''cognitive development'') as if it were the whole of the development of human beings or even the linch pin.[5] Such a perspective may therefore keep us on guard against ''vicious abstractions'' or ''fallacies of misplaced concreteness.''

---

[3]See Kaplan (1966, 1967). A developmentalist in the Wernerian tradition does not (or should not) ritually invoke the orthogenetic principle as an afterthought. The principle is intended to guide problem setting, methodology, and analysis-synthesis. Like Plato, Werner was concerned with the big issues of the One and the Many, Being and Becoming, etc. In all domains of human life, collective and individual, Werner presupposed forces that tended to break up unities and forces that tended to unite distinguished elements; such forces, materially different on different levels—biological, social, interpersonal, intrapsychic—were, in Werner's terms, *functionally analogous* or *formally parallel*. For an imaginative application of Werner's conception of ''formal parallels,'' see Brent (1981).

[4]It should be obvious why a developmental perspective is intrinsically comparative.

[5]It is remarkable how often scholars of reputation write about ''cognitive development'' or edit books on ''cognitive development,'' without specifying or being able to specify what they intend by either ''cognition'' or ''development.'' Ostensibly, this would suggest that they have no principle for recognizing instances of either; for distinguishing cognition from any other human or infrahuman activity; for distinguishing ''developmental change'' from any other form of change. Consequently, they often use a tautologous makeshift, ''Cognition is what (self-styled) cognitive psychologists study''; and/or make ''regular'' or ''systematic'' changes with age the criterion of development. Some who do the latter—equating changes over age with development—attempt to obscure the vacuity of this move: They say that they are merely assuming or hypothesizing that changes with age will reflect development. In fact, *unless they have a notion of development independent of age changes,* they are *positing* or *presupposing* that whatever happens in the course of time is development. This would not be unduly serious for those who collapse the distinction between development and change. For those who seek to maintain the distinction (i.e., to talk about ''higher'' and ''lower,'' ''more advanced'' and ''less advanced''), it is disastrous: It suggests that the later is the more advanced simply by virtue of occurring in older individuals.

The word, "theory" in psychology and kindred disciplines is much abused. One would almost think that psychologists and other "social scientists" have had a collective affair with Madison Avenue. Every guess is an hypothesis, and every hypothesis is denominated a "theory." One may hope that Art Buchwald or George Carlin will one day devote an article or a monologue to satirize this inclination to hyperbole.

Of course, theory has taken on a specialized meaning in the natural sciences and in some branches of psychology, suggesting a hypothetico-deductive system, rigorously derived predictions, etc. And just as barbers hope to accrue some rewards by adopting an honorific title for their enterprise ("tonsorial science"), so investigators of individual and social phenomena in the human sciences seem to have used "theory" to surround their approaches and perspectives with an aura of rigor, precision, and exactitutde.[6]

In its original and unpretentious meaning, a theory was a way of looking at or contemplating phenomena. In other words, a *perspective*. As a consequence of the sophistication inculcated in us by Kant, it may be taken today, as Toulmin (1953) has taken it, as a way of representing phenomena; or, as a way of transforming "data" into "facts." Ostensibly, most of us, by this time, have renounced the "myth of the given," rejected the "dogma of immaculate perception," realized that there is no "innocent eye." These abjurations, especially among those who style themselves "constructivists," should have led to the recognition that there is no "data base" that theories must take into account or explain, and that the prime function of theory is to "transform" ineffable data into facts ("things given into things made"); or, better, to transform "first-order" facts into second- and third-order facts.[7]

If this is so, then different theories will yield "different facts." Indeed, what are taken as facts by those adopting one perspective may well be invisible to those who are wearing other spectacles. It is preposterous to expect any perspective, except that of G–D, to account for, or explain, these different species of facts, generated by different theories, as if these "facts" were theory neutral. To constitute a life-span developmental psychology in terms of a catalogue, or telephone book, of facts garnered from every perspective, utilizing every method, and examining the functional relations between every variable and every other variable is not only a vain endeavor; it is an inane one.[8] The second issue,

---

[6]Some, dismayed by the limited rewards accruing to mere "theoreticians," have added a pretentious prefix—which has now spread like Gypsy moths—and have become metatheoreticians (see Cirillo & Kaplan, 1981).

[7]See Goethe, "All facts are already theory" (cf. Peirce's "firstness," "secondness," and "thirdness").

[8]J. H. Woodger suggested the inanity of this kind of approach in his influential monograph on *Theory-Construction*, International Encyclopedia of Unified Science (Woodger, 1939).

then, for a theoretically oriented life-span developmental psychologist to face is *the choice of theory or perspective for examining the phenomena of human life*.[9].

Some decades ago, Robert Lynd wrote a book called *Knowledge for What?* Against a prevailing trend that involved the seeking for knowledge for its own sake ("knowledge for knowledge's sake" analogous to "art for art's sake"), Lynd's title and work suggested that knowledge—and especially the kind of knowledge sought by social scientists—was not an intrinsic value but rather an instrumental one. Lynd's view stems from an ancient heritage. The value of knowledge was to make us free. The goal of knowledge was to liberate us from bondage (see Kaplan, 1982).[10] "Know ye the truth and the truth shall make ye free." Even those who construed *theoria* as contemplation took the contemplative life as the Way (*met-hodos*) to freedom. And as Socrates emphasized, the most fundamental knowledge on which all other knowledge depends is self-knowledge (*gnothi sauton*).

This view of the instrumental character of knowledge, or knowledge as a means for "living, living well and living better" (Whitehead), gave way in academic circles during the late 19th and 20th centuries to a doctrine of "value-free inquiry." The purposes or goals for which knowledge was sought were now taken to be subjective or irrational, and insusceptible to rational justification (see Strauss, 1953). Each individual could pose his/her own problem, without seeking to justify it, and then accumulate the facts relevant to the solution of his/her problem. Given the diversity of "idiotic" motives,[11] there was a proliferation of studies, many characteristically without any relation to anything else.[12] Concurrently, there was a division of labor between the fact accumulators and the policymakers. "Scientists" merely gathered the data and accumulated the facts. The policymakers determined what ought to be done with the facts. Some pious scientists, repelled with what was done with their facts, were inclined to believe that the remedy for the life-destroying and spirit-destroying use of facts by policymakers was the provision of more and better facts. Due to a "trained

---

[9]One of the more boorish phenomena of current practice is for a psychologist to say "developmental theory predicts or maintains" when he/she intends his/her own point of view. Such identification of self with cosmos—"inflation" in Jung's sense—is unfortunately common among some developmental psychologists. It is especially presumptuous when the individual using that expression has no theory at all.

[10]This was the theme of my second lecture in my Heinz Werner Lectures. Now, after the proverbial 7 years in limbo suggested by Cato, I plan to publish them in final form in the near future. The title of the lectures is *Rationality and Irrationality in Development*.

[11]I use "idiotic" here in its original sense of "private."

[12]A group, constituting a school (e.g., Psychoanalytic, Piagetian), might produce studies linked to others carried out by members of the school, but the distance between schools is often as great or greater than the distance between nonaffiliated individuals.

incapacity'' (Veblen) to appreciate anectodal evidence of millions when un-verified by laboratory experimentation, or by studies run on 400 subjects ranging in age from 5 to 15 or 1 to 80, these pious men and women were blind to the fact that values (a central ingredient in perspectives) determine the nature of the facts, the significance of the facts, and the use of the facts. Not only for policy makers, but for themselves.

These considerations suggest a third issue for a theoretically oriented life-span psychology, or, better, psychologist: *whether one should adopt a perspective that unites theory and praxis or opt for a point of view—positivistic, in fact—that seeks merely to describe and explain "the facts."* It should be clear that either choice implicates a value. The issue is whether we as human beings, first, and psychologists, a distant second, pursue our "knowledge" in the interests of self-perfection and other-perfection (one may argue that they are interdependent and correlative) or continue to indulge in the exercise of accumulating facts for facts' sake, leaving the issue of values to a Hobbesian war of all against all. In the latter case, all our psychological stories will be tales told by idiots, full of sound and fury, signifying nothing.

From a good newspaper reporter, if not from Aristotle and Kenneth Burke (1945), we learn to ask at least six questions in any attempt to comprehend what has taken place or what is going on: Who? What? Why? Where? When? and How? I have written this brief chapter—in constitutes a symbolic action—for at least two kinds of audiences: those who may have already joined the "life-span" movement, and those who are attracted to it for a variety of reasons, not least of which is that it is a current fad. One of my goals has been to persuade those who read the chapter that the kind of developmental psychology proposed by *some* exponents of life-span developmental psychology is both vain and inane. An-other has been to suggest that a *developmental approach* to all the phenomena of life, from conception to biological death, and even beyond on either side, is a desideratum. A third goal has been to get others to see that such a developmental approach, doubtless amenable to modification and improvement (development), has been with us long before the present proponents of a life-span psychology appeared on the scene. A fourth goal—a hidden agenda—has been to convince you that the modification and extension of the Wernerian perspective that I have called Genetic-Dramatism (G–D), which directly confronts all the issues I men-tion in my chapter, provides the kind of perspective I hope you see fit to adopt. I say this in all modesty, because the perspective I have articulated is, I submit, the perennial perspective, and the perspective that you recognize as the one you take in everyday life.[13] The time and place of this symbolic action is here/now. Whether it is also everywhere and everywhen, in one incarnation or another, is to be determined. The "how" I leave to you to decide.

---

[13]See B. Kaplan (1981a,b) and L. Cirillo and B. Kaplan (1981).

III. SWEENEY AMONG THE NIGHTINGALES—A CALL TO CONTROVERSY

In a spirit that may tarnish the cherished traditions of collections such as this one, I offer this chapter as the first step in a colloquy with some of those who have submitted chapters for this volume. I have always found it frustrating to participate in a collective enterprise in which the various participants in that undertaking either do not talk to one another or do so in such an oblique way that it is difficult to know who is being addressed. It is, in part, to challenge this custom of monadism, that I have written this chapter. I hope that this step prompts the other authors in this work to offer their critiques of the claims and contentions in my articles and in those of their other fellow authors.

Because I find myself least likely to cavil with White's treatment of "The idea of development in developmental psychology," I begin with his chapter. If one senses an undue amount of nit picking in my discussion of this informative article, I hope it is taken as a manifestation of that well-known principle in academic circles, "the maximization of minimal differences"—a "sharpening" needed to counterbalance tendencies to homogenize and to level important distinctions.

As should be clear from my other sections in this chapter, and elsewhere (Kaplan, 1966a,b; 1967; 1981a), I challenge the interpretation of "developmental psychology," which I believe is characteristic in the field. Like "history," "developmental psychology" may be taken as a subject matter of concern or as a way of representing or even constituting a subject matter. As pertaining to a subject matter, developmental psychology is typically used to refer to what children up to any arbitrary cut-off point do or what individuals do over the life-span. The subject matter is, so to speak, taken to *be there,* and exponents of different theories or approaches are presumed to offer different accounts and explanations of that subject matter. From this point of view, the theories or approaches are not *developmental;* the subject matter is! The object is taken as already constituted—much as one might say that the past is whatever it was—and the various theories are putative attempts to describe the object adequately and to explain its variations and vicissitudes. It is recognized that the different theories or approaches, like different species of insects or animals, may chew on different parts of the corpus of ontogenesis, or some arbitrarily selected segment of it; but if someone finally puts together, in some way, all the pieces chewed over by the variegated theorists, we will somehow get a full and recognizable picture of what it was they were all nibbling at.

With regard to such a view of developmental psychology—as subject matter—surely every social group, from time immemorial, has entertained one or another idea of development. Is it not apparent that every social group entertains beliefs as to how human beings come into existence, how and why they change, how adverse changes might be forestalled or remedied, and so on? If one were to treat the "ideas of development" in developmental psychology so conceived, without any préjuge du monde, without ethnocentrism or "nunccentrism," then surely one would have to go far beyond Europe and the 19th century in the search for such ideas.

On the other hand, if developmental psychology is taken not as a subject matter within psychology, but as a set of presuppositions or categories—ontological, methodological, epistemological, etc.—for viewing and even constituting the subject matter of psychology, then one might still have to go far beyond Europe and the 19th century, but one would be looking for different origins, forerunners, precursors, and histories. Developmental psychology would then be like "behaviorism," "psychoanalysis," etc.—a mode of constructing the object of psychology, and would not be limited to ontogenesis or any other domain. Now, of course, there have been at least several such "developmental" approaches to psychological phenomena in the course of history. And during the 19th century, some of these approaches seemed to have a kinship that distinguished them from "mechanical materialist" approaches, associationistic approaches, etc. But, despite this kinship, they were also distinguishable from each other. As elsewhere, depending on the criteria that one uses, one may emphasize similarities or differences. White has grouped together a number of theorists who shared certain doctrines, however they might have disagreed on others. These theorists seemed to assume that "time was the mother of perfection"; that the course of history was one of progressive change; that later modes of thought and action, though built on earlier ones, were an advance over earlier ones; that later, and hence more advanced, forms of thought and action, were, and had to be, in some unspecified way, more adequate to reality than the earlier and more primitive ones. Once some version of the Meckel–Haeckel "law of recapitulation" was accepted, it was inevitable that those who adopted the formula that time was the mother of perfection would see this formula as applying not only to history and evolution but also to ontogenesis. Thus, if history and evolution were ineluctably progressive, so too, would be biography; and if not the biographies of human beings *in vivo,* then at least the biographies of laundered and skeletonized human beings as processed by the methods of science (see Kaplan, 1966b, 1967/74/82; 1981a). Of course, there was the recognition—how could it be ignored?—that in actuality there might be setbacks or prolonged stasis in the historical process, large-scale or small. And, surely, presupposition was not so powerful as to blind observers to the fact that individuals in the course of their existence might be arrested or might "regress." But these very terms suggested that the natural course was onward and upward. If this were the case, then the impartial examination of ontogenesis, necessary excisions and exclusions being made, would reveal, to the innocent eye, the "development" of human beings.

Now, White may be quite correct in taking such a belief to be "truistic" among most of those who call themselves developmental psychologists. It is, however, questionable, that a "developmental psychology" demands the belief that a child's mind must necessarily develop as the child gets older. As I have urged elsewhere, developmental psychology may well be articulated in such a way, as applied to ontogenesis, to avoid any claim that human beings necessarily develop, just as applied to "objectified mind"—political instituitions, economic arrangements, legal ideas, etc.—it can avoid any claim that such institutions necessarily develop. It may take "development" (i.e., movement toward perfection) as an "ideal of natural order" (Toulmin, 1953) and concern itself with the factors in ontogenesis or in society that promote and militate against development. This formulation radically distinguishes between development and the actualities, ontogenetic or sociohistorical; and therefore rejects precisely those assumptions that White presupposes in his rhetorical question.

Linked with my rejection of the identification of ontogenesis with development, I would also reject White's contention that such an identification is alive in Werner's 20th-century perspective, whatever may be said about Piaget. Although there is surely such conflation in Werner's formulation of the concept of development in his classic *Comparative Psychology of Mental Development,* Werner (1948) expressly rejected the identification of developmental psychology with evolutionistic psychology. "We ask," he writes, "not whether a pattern of functions is relatively early or late in the historical scale, but whether it represents a low or high level of mentality [p. 17]." Just as we may and do rank our performances and the performances of others as relatively high or low, relatively primitive or advanced, irrespective of the time of occurrence, so we may assess, from a developmental point of view, performances and personalities, sociopolitical organizations or legal institutions, without regard to dates. As A. O. Lovejoy once put it: "Rationality knows no dates."

I stress this point because Werner and Piaget have often been lumped together. Piaget may well have believed that the human being in the course of ontogenesis goes through a fixed and necessary sequence of stages. Werner did not. Whether or not, in the course of ontogenesis, specific human beings or human beings in general, manifest progressively higher levels of functioning was, for Werner, an empirical question. If they *developed,* they would: That is what "development" means. But there was no immanent law either in history or biography that insured that they would develop.

I do not contest here White's choice of early exemplars of "stage theorists." Nor do I contest the claim that their conceptions of what took place in ontogenesis were not based on data in the way in which the views of some stage theorists today are said to be "based on data." And I demur only slightly at the suggestion that 20th-century idealization of the philosophy of science holds that "theories" ought to be based on data. Only some philosophers of science in the 20th century maintained that view; and there are not a few philosophers of science (Hanson) who would insist, with Goethe, that all facts are already theory, and that there are no theory-neutral data for individuals to build theories on.

I would further agree with him that none of the stage theorists to whom he refers proceeded inductively. Indeed, I think a spendid case can be made to show that none of the contemporary stage theorists have proceeded inductively. It is another matter whether these 19th-century ancestors thought they were doing so. Given the prevalent view of scientific inquiry at that time, I would hazard a guess that they did think they were so proceeding. It would have been against the grain for them to take themselves as drawing their conclusions deductively from premises, and it would be anachronistic to attribute to them that kind of sophistication with regard to "hermeneutic circles" that one finds in some disciplines today. In any case, whether they thought they were proceeding inductively or not, it is likely that others thought they were presenting generalizations from the facts. One need only reflect on the number of developmental psychologists who believe(d) that Piaget arrived at his stage theory via induction. Or Freud.

White suggests that the early "stage theorists" proceeded "abductively" in C. S. Peirce's sense. Now Peirce seems to me to intend by "abduction" one phase of a two-phase process-the other being "retroduction"—both of which together constitute what today we might call the hypothetico-deductive method.[14] It does not seem to me that either the entire process (called "qualitative induction" by Peirce) or either phase of the process constituted or constitutes the procedure of "stage theorists." Rather, I believe they had (and their descendents now have) a system of categories that they applied (or apply) to diverse materials, interpreting the various phenomena in terms of these categories and presuppositions. In other words, Peirce allowed for general ideas from any source to enter into attempts to explain phenomena; stage theorists, with more or less "fixed ideas" interpret various phenomena in terms of these ideas; characteristically, I suppose, without cognizance of the fact that they do so. In the context of current controversies over whether so-called natural sciences are also hermeneutic disciplines (see Dreyfus, 1980; Rorty, 1980; Taylor, 1980), it may be that the prototypical stage theorists were all doing, without awareness, what we all do now. Presumably, we have less excuse for being unconscious about it.

With regard to White's conclusion, after his examination of the views of Romanes, Sechenov, Spencer, and Baldwin, I am in almost complete agreement. The various "theories," including those of the moderns, "do not sit directly on the data of child development and they do not jeopardize in the easy and com-

---

[14]N. Rescher (1978) puts it thus (*Peirce's philosophy of science*):

Phenomena are observed. A series of explanatory hypotheses . . . is imaginatively projected to account for these [by the process of conjectural hypothesis-proliferation that Peirce called *abduction*]. These hypothesis are then tested by the familiar process of exploiting them as a basis for predictions, which are then checked against the actual course of developments. The hypothesis that fares best under such trial is tentatively adopted over the alternatives until it is itself overthrown by a further sequence of projection and testing of hypotheses. Peirce gave the name *retroduction* to this process of eliminating hypotheses by experiential/experimental testing [p. 3].

plete way that falsificationist tradition says scientific theories ought to." Again, as he observes, "the developmental theories are cross-disciplinary and eclectic (sic!), sitting on facts and conclusions coming out of many fields of inquiry." And, finally, "the older theories of development were not designed to be regulated solely by facts. They were designed to bring facts into patterns having simplicity, coherence, orderliness and harmony."

My reservations are as follows: As mentioned before, I do not see these approaches or perspectives—I eschew the term *theories*—as abductive in the Peircian sense; I do not see them as "eclectic" in the usual meaning of the word, but rather diversified in their application; I do not see that what he says about developmental approaches applies any less to contemporary developmental approaches than to the "older ones." And finally, I do not see the kinds of stages outlined by the different developmental "theorists" as of 19th-century provenance or 18th or 17th. Long before the "temporalizing of the great chain of being" (Lovejoy, 1936), and reflected in Arabic commentaries on Alexander of Aphrodisias' commentaries on Aristotle, we find the same kinds of distinctions among different grades or levels of intellect as we find in the stage theorists of history or biography, who have fallen into time.

One section of White's chapter demands special attention from me. Despite Heinz Werner's antipathy to Spencer and despite his explicit alignment of his view of development with that of Goethe (as opposed to Darwin) (Werner, 1948), the statement is made that: "the simplification of Spencer's principle that developmental psychologists are most familiar with is Heinz Werner's orthogentic principle [p. 46]. Now, because I formulated the "orthogentic principle" with Werner (Werner & Kaplan, 1956) and therefore have some of the responsibility and blame for it, I want to insist that it *defines* development in terms of increasing differentiation and hierarchic integration *but in no way maintains that the processes of ontogenesis are inherently developmental.* Nor does the principle refer to "a general efficient force." With regard to this issue, I maintain that White is correct only in his view that ontogenesis (as distinct from development) was and is an excellent field in which to observe differentiation and integration as well as dedifferentiation and disintegration. But there were (and are) many other excellent domains for developmental analysis.

A final comment on White's extremely stimulating and enlightening chapter: a comment directed toward his last section, "Development as the Idea of the Good." As I have argued elsewhere (Kaplan, 1981a,b; and the second paper contained herein), development, as distinct from change, has been and ought to be an axiological and normative notion. It has been, and ought to be, comprehended as "movement toward perfection," "movement toward liberation," "movement toward the Good or God." As Karl Löwith (1949) has shown, at least to my satisfaction, most of our contemporaries' views of development, especially those that conflate development with history, evolution, or biography, are secularizations of eschatological doctrine. I believe that White is correct in his thesis that the secular developmentalists hope(d) to read off from the facts of history and biography a developmental progression in time ("movement toward perfection," "toward freedom," "toward the good") and thereby dispense, with transcendent values and norms, nonderivable from data or facts. I would, of course, deny that this has been done or can be done. Where individuals have claimed to find or discover values and norms in facts of history or biography, it is only because they have unwittingly sneaked them into their analyses. One reason why I have urged the radical distinction between development and ontogenesis is to eliminate such conscious or unconscious conflation.

Whether or not it was intended as such, I take Kagan's essay "The premise of connectivity" to be primarily one in epistemology. He seems to be concerned with the assumptions we make, wittingly or otherwise, in constituting the objects and object-properties, not only of our "refined" knowledge, but also of our everyday world. Of course, he may not put his problem in quite this way, but that may stem from the fact that he accepts certain ontological and epistemological presuppositions that I either question or reject.

For example, he seems to accept without question some form of ontological realism: There is a (noumenal) reality "out there" that we (or at least Someone) can know and that we seek to know. Alas, in our knowing operations, and especially in our perceptions, that "reality" is distorted" or is susceptible to distortion. It is understood that I attribute the presupposition of (some form of) Realism to him, because unless he assumes such a "reality," somehow ascertainable through an unmediated and hence nondistorting vision, it would make no sense to talk about "distortion." Distortion, to utilize a distinction he seems to draw elsewhere, has as its correlative nondistortion, and if instruments of knowing are taken to enter into the constitution of what is known and hence "change them" from what they "really are," there is no way through the mediation of cognition to get at the undistorted "Reality." Hence the need for an unmediated vision (Cassirer, 1910/23/, Chapter 6; 1953, 1955, 1957).

His suggestion that contemporary physicists and chemists, recognizing the "arbitrariness" of the division between the knower and the known, still "manage to contain the distortion" is, of course, questionable. If one *stipulates* a norm, standard, or criterion, then deviations from such a norm, standard, or criterion may be called distortions, but they are not distortions from an independently known "Reality." What is taken as the standard of the real is determined by human stipulation and conventions. One recalls, during the beginnings of modern physical science, that Descartes set out a methodological prescription for the "real," and, because experience of human beings diverged from that methodologically stipulated "reality," psychology was initially a discipline devoted to the study of "error" or "distortion."

Now, if I read Kagan correctly, he sees the physical sciences as able to contain distortion, although the disciplines devoted to the study of human nature seem to be unable to do so. Human beings studying other human beings commit errors, and, it would seem, developmental psychologists studying the ontogenesis of human beings are especially likely to do so; that is, they are more likely to distort reality than many other students of human behavior. All this, of course, presupposes that there is Someone there who knows what the reality of ontogenesis is "really like" so that they can attribute errors or distortion to the ordinary frail folk. Such an omniscient observer would also have to be around to determine whether an investigator has exaggerated what happened, ignored most of what happened, or invented phenomena that never happened.

As I see it, the main thrust of Kagan's chapter is to show that the ontological presuppositions of investigators, their pretheoretical or perhaps tacit conceptions of the nature of human beings, their preconceptions as to what is important and what is matter of fact (Whitehead, 1937), their involvements with their models and hypotheses, etc. determine how they select events, how they classify events, how they classify "motives," etc. Furthermore, he suggests—or do I take him beyond where he wishes to go?—that not only the statements describing observations are affected by the method of observing, but the very observations themselves. To be sure, all this is merely to iterate Nietzsche's opposition to the "dogma of immaculate perception" and to specify in a particular domain a thesis advanced by Stephen Pepper (1942) in his *World Hypotheses*. One problem here, of course, is that Kagan, in making *his* classifications about the activities of other human beings, must be subject to the same kinds of "idols" as the rest of us. And just as he enjoins others to make presuppositions explicit, he would be expected to make the same demand on himself.

I cannot refrain here from mentioning one of those presuppositions, not acknowledged but more or less obvious from his discussion. He seems to assume some kind of ontological priority for "matter in motion" ("facial muscles") and allows only a derivative status to the perception of emotion in another. Thus, he seems to take the displacements in space of bodily parts as hard data, whereas the attribution of fear involves inference or construction. This bias, rooted in physicalist ontology and epistemology, surely needs justification as well as open avowal. (For a radical critique of this view, see Cassirer, 1960.) It is a holdover from the doctrine of primary and secondary qualities (Descartes, Galileo, Locke), and the assumption, undermined by Berkeley, that the former are mind independent, whereas the latter are intruded into the object by the knower.

To those in the vineyards of "developmental psychology" who may not have been aware of it before, Kagan has done a considerable service in pointing out that temporal continuity between the earlier and the later is not a datum but a constructum. Moreover, because change, as opposed to difference, presupposes something invariant, "substance"—Aristotle's *ousia*—is also a constructum. And so, also, the apparatus of transformations, precursors, Anlage, etc., which are taken by historians, developmentalists, religious enthusiasts, and the rest of us as somehow being there, in reality, independent of our cognitive operations. One may, of course, regard all these as "fictions" in Bentham's or Vaihinger's sense, fictions that alone enable us, as human beings, to make sense out of "data," fictions necessary to transform (fictional or "mythic") data into facts. (Perhaps the etymological relationship between fact and fiction is not so strange after all; see Kaplan, 1960.)

But what is the upshot of all this?; that human beings studying anything cannot have an unmediated vision of reality but can only mediate whatever there is through a variety of "symbolic forms" as Cassirer has suggested (Cassirer, 1944, 1953, 1955, 1957, 1960); that psychologists in general, and developmental psychologists in particular, ought to be more aware of their ontological and epistemological assumptions in their putatively "empirical" or "scientific" attempts to understand human beings and their ontogenesis?; that in talking about the child and the child's construction of reality, it would behoove us to consider how we *construct* the child and *construct* the child's construction of reality?; that the Eastern thinkers and the Delphic oracle were right—that before we can hope to know anything else we must first know ourselves?

It is doubtless my own predilection for Platonism, paranoia and the a priori, as well as my own theoretical persuasion, but whenever I read someone suggesting that he/she undertook some kind of empirical inquiry to find out, for example, about "the evolution of the concept of environment in systematic research on human development," I wonder about the interpretation he/she has given to the principal terms; interpretations that I assume guided and determined the enterprise. I wonder about the motivation for such interpretations when others were possible. I wonder whether the interpretations conform to the usual meanings of the terms used or whether they are idiosyncratic. In the latter case, I wonder whether the terms were chosen rhetorically to suggest something far more rigorous and praiseworthy than is justified by what was done. And so on. Given that many, if not all, terms in psychology are "systematically ambiguous," by which I mean that they take on different values and meanings in different theoretical systems, I also wonder about the tacit ontological and epistemological commitments the enquirer makes, wittingly or not, in undertaking the particular piece of research.

Now, Bronfenbrenner tells us that he undertook such an inquiry into "the evolution of the concept of environment in systematic research on human development." So I wondered what he meant by "evolution," "environment," "concept of environment," "systematic," and "human development." He doesn't quite tell us what he intends by "evolution." Does he distinguish it from potted history? Does he distinguish it from chronicle? Does he distinguish it from "development"? Does he distinguish it from "evolution" as that term is usually taken? Perhaps all he means, operationally wise, is that evolution refers to his reconstruction of what took place on the basis of a limited number of texts taken as somehow canonical. Because he had some plan in mind in selecting these texts, his inquiry, in one sense of the term, may be said to have been "systematic."

What about "environment" and "concept of environment"? Let us just consider the latter. That seems to be the key phrase in his chapter. It seems clear that if one is going to trace "the evolution of the concept of environment," one must have some tacit conception of what one is going to consider a "concept of environment." Otherwise, one would not know how to distinguish a concept of environment from a concept of anything else. One would not know what to include and what to exclude. Does he take as an individual's concept of environment what the individual says it is? Or does he infer the individual's concept of environment from what the individual does? Or does he scientifically operationalize "concept of environment" to mean whatever an individual takes to have some effect on the form, behavior, and experience of an individual over the life-span? Or does he intend whatever a "systematic scientific researcher" takes in particular research activities to have some effect, excluding those effects that might be attributed to the "organism" or to the organism's heredity? All of the above? None of the above? Some of the above?

Now, it may be seen that it depends on the researcher's concept of what a concept of environment is whether he takes two inquirers to have similar concepts of the environment or different ones. For example, if we take as "concept of environment" what an individual takes to be independent of mind, and "out there," then those who take the world as they see it as thus mind independent might be said to have a similar "concept of environment" as contrasted, for example, with those who take the environment to consist of physical energies that elicit or evoke the "construction" of objects by a subject. On the other hand, if we take as "concept of the environment" what one takes to be causally efficacious in affecting, influencing, or occasioning changes in an individual, then those who were taken to have similar concepts of environment under the first reading might have radically different notions under the second. It should be clear that an experimenter who takes the environment of a "subject" to be what he or she, the experimenter, takes the environment to be has a quite different concept of environment than one who takes the environment of a "subject" to be "the definition of the situation" by that subject. In this sense, the early Freud seems to have had quite a different conception of the environment than the later Freud.

Let us turn to "systematic research." Bronfenbrenner alludes only in a general way to what he means by that phrase. It is research involving more than anecdotal reports or individual case studies. Though that isn't too much, it suggests that at least a necessary condition for something to be systematic research for him is that the research involves, if not large numbers of subjects, at least an N larger than 1. It may also mean, if we follow a dictionary definition, that those who carried out the research did so with respect to a theoretical system; or that they proceeded according to some method or plan (J. Buchler, 1961); or that they proceeded in an orderly fashion. But such considerations would surely have led to the examination of a larger number of individuals than he considers in this survey, *if he had been systematic*. Finally, perhaps eccentrically, it may mean that kind of research that is accepted by those authorities that he accepts. Thus Freud's case studies may become "systematic research" when Freud's views are accorded recognition in some received text or handbook.

And finally "human development." Does Bronfenbrenner equate human development with ontogenesis from birth to childhood?, from birth to maturity?, from birth to death? Is the idea of human development that he holds behavioral change, whatever it is, over the life-span or some portion of it? Or does he take development to mean something more than behavioral change? Obviously, what one looks for, and what one looks at, will depend upon what one means.

So much now for what one might call "philosophical perspectives." I turn to a closer consideration of Bronfenbrenner's "historical perspective." He initiates his historical survey of "concepts of environment" held by systematic researchers by discussing an inquiry into the contents of children's minds carried out by the Pedagogical Society of Berlin. As Bronfenbrenner presents it, the study seems to deal with what *children* took their environment to be or knew about the objects of the social reality of the investigators. True, the investigators seemed to consider *their environment* as "exercising an influence" on the minds of the children, and in this sense, they may have (naively) viewed their adult constructions as having some vague kind of causal efficacy. The environment is somehow construed as "entering the mind" of children. Such a view would, of course, not be markedly different from that held by many today, even in august psychological circles. In the main, however, it seems that the study was directed toward determining whether and to what extent the children had concepts that the Deutsche Gelehrter had, or whether they could denote the referents or give the definitions of certain terms. It is not at all obvious to me that the study cited indicates any early "concept of environment" by systematic researchers.

Nor is it clear to me that Sir Francis Galton, the next researcher to be dealt with, had a markedly different conception of environment than the German pedagogues. He seems to have asked different kinds of questions about the environment and may have held different views as to its relative efficacy in affecting behavior or fundamental characteristics of individuals. But it is doubtful that Sir Francis, despite his passion for nature over nurture, would deny that identical twins reared in different environments would have different mental contents "in their minds." Is it not possible that individuals with similar concepts of environment may ask quite different questions of subjects?

And then there is Hall. It is suggested that Hall somehow provides a crude operational definition of the environment in his work, and that he differs fundamentally from the Germans with regard to what the environment is. I must confess that the basis for these claims eludes me. If Bronfenbrenner means by *his* concept of "concept of environment" whatever a researcher takes to have some bearing on human behavior of experience that is not due to hereditary factors, then perhaps G. Stanley considered a wider range of such factors than his

German colleagues. I doubt, however, that in ordinary parlance we mean by someone's concept of environment any and all nongenetic factors that are taken to be actually or potentially efficacious in occasioning behavior or behavioral variation. For example, I doubt that many would take "social class" as predicated by an investigator of an individual to be environmental, although one might take variations in social class as influencing the environments in which an individual lives, the way in which an individual acts, the way in which an individual interprets his/her environment, etc.

Moreover, it seems quite clear to me that Bronfenbrenner does not consider such agent attributes or ascribed statuses as "environmental." Thus, he remarks, in criticizing what he refers to as "composite operational definitions of the environment" that they do not take into consideration the "intervening structures or processes through which the environment might affect the course of development." He continues: "One looks only at the social address—that is, environmental label—with no attention to *what the environment is like, what people are living there, what they are doing, or how the activities taking place could affect the child*" (my italics). This suggests that for him the environment is places, people, and activities external to the subject. Social status or ethnic status are no more "environmental" that ordinal position in the family or age, although ostensibly they all may affect "what the environment is like."

And yet, from Bronfenbrenner's discussions of various people and movements, it appears that although the term, environment, has a commonplace referent for him, it is also used to refer to something quite different. As Lovejoy (1936) points out in his chapter on "The study of the history of ideas," even the greatest minds are likely to hold distinct and conflicting ideas together under a single term; the unity of name deceiving them into believing that they hold a unity of notion. Although I may well misread Bronfenbrenner, it seems to me that he also means by "environment" whatever factors, visible or invisible, intersubjectively denotable or theoretically posited, that might be demonstrated, through respectable methods, as having some effect on organismic (read here, human) behavior.

Once the abstract possibility that a human being might be *causa sui* is rejected, then the "causation" that results in human beings coming-into-being, undergoing transformations (changes), and ceasing-to-be must come from "outside" or the environs. A variable degree of "self-determination" may still be allotted to the organism—usually under some rubric referring to some "intrinsic nature"—but even this intrinsic nature is likely to be dissolved into a network of "environmental" conditions that occasion its coming into being. Although, initially, Environment is hypostatized in opposition to Organism or Heredity, the slow march of scientific inquiry will dissolve the substantiality of human beings, including ourselves, into complexes of processes, themselves determined by complexes of processes, themselves determined by complexes of processes, ad infinitum. Some may still persist in giving aery nothings a local habitation and a name, but scientists—nay Science, for scientists after all are merely hypostatizations of the Heracleitian flux—will know that a subsistent organism undergoing transformations is merely an artifact of imperfect human thought and metaphysical pathos. One will no longer speak of Environment in opposition to Organism or Heredity. The only Substance will be God or Nature, a la Spinoza, or Space considered as God (M. Jammer, 1953).

As Science (or Thought), in its ephemeral embodiments in transitory "human beings," takes cognizance of the ecological truth that everything is, in one way or another, dependent on everything else—the well-known doctrine of internal relations—then it will breed researchers who will seek to make manifest—to whom? to what?—how every phenomenon is, in varying ways and to varying degrees, affected by every other phenomenon. This, of course, is a never-ending enterprise, because Time, one of the others names for God (or Nature) keeps generating (at least to our finite minds) new processes that interact with all the old ones that like Old Man River, "jes keep rollin' along."

But I have lapsed into "philosophical considerations" again. Although Bronfenbrenner's program might have its principle of perfection in such an unqualified doctrine of "internal relations," he seems content with pointing out how, in the limited course of a limited history (or evolution) among a limited group of individuals, using a limited number of methods in a limited profession, there seems to be an increasing awareness of the range and kind of processes that may have some influence on the variable "motions" (e.g., cognitive, affective, interpersonal) of an abstracted and reified entity called *the human being over the life-span,* or alternatively *the developing human being.* Although Science may question such partiality (Polanyi, 1962, p. 16, 33ff), the anthropocentrism and acrasia that seem to afflict those processes-in-context we euphemistically call human beings seem to "cause" those human beings to think of themselves as having some substantial unity, some "physis," and to be concerned mainly with the kinds of "entities" or "processes" in the totality of what there is and what there will be that affect their specific comings-into-being, transformations, and passings-away.

Now, for those who wash out any distinction between "development" and change, and who dissolve the distinction between "form" and "causality" (see E. Cassirer, 1960, Ch. 10), eliminating hierarchies of value and perfection as testimony of their fidelity to the modern world view (Cassirer, 1927/53, Koyre, 1957; Lovejoy, 1936; Randall, 1962; Tillyard, 1942; Willey, 1953), the enlargement or restriction, differentiation or fusion, "monistic" integration or "pluralistic" aggregation, of the factors or processes individuals take to influence the vicissitudes of human life are merely phenomena themselves to be explained or dissolved into processes-in-context. It would reflect an unscientific or prescientific intrusion of anthropocentric human values to assess or evaluate the varied conceptions of the efficacious environment in *developmental terms* (in my sense): In the world of science, there is no higher or lower, no less advanced and more advanced, only neutral phenomena to be explained "as a function of." This would hold for what the "operationalizing scientists" do as well as for the subjects studied by such operationalizing scientists. A futurologist might prophesy that in the course of time, those processes-in-context called human beings will, through various trajectories, come to entertain a greater number and variety of "causal factors" in human affairs. A scientist might predict that, under certain conditions (processes-in-context), human beings will vary, irrespective of their time in history, as to the number and kind of factors they take as relevant to explaining the vicissitudes of human action. But it would be extrascientific for anyone to evaluate what they do as being more advanced, less advanced, etc. The futurologists or scientists will simply record that through the momentum of history or the conjunction of processes various human beings called scientists held this or that conception of the environment; and carried out these or those studies with these or those operationalized conceptions of environment.

It is, of course, likely that Bronfenbrenner is not only a scientific psychologist of "development" (ontogenesis) but also a developmental psychologist, who delights in the fact that human beings called "scientific psychologists" consider an ever-increasing, differentiated and hierarchically integrated number of factors as possibly entering into the determination of human action over the life-span. He is likely, I would surmise, to regard this posture as a *developmental advance* whenever and wherever it took place; and he would doubtless consider it a *regression* if at some future time—for who can predict history?—psychologists of ontogenesis limited and conflated the factors or processes-in-context taken to occasion change.

Having again lapsed back into philosophical considerations, I should get back on course with regard to Bronfenbrenner's historiography and historical reconstruction, on which he seeks to base his view of "the development of context" or "the evolution of concepts of environment." I will, however, forego such an excursion. It is clear from my previous remarks why I think he deals with neither, although he can claim to do both by "operationally specifying" what he means by both.

I should not close this commentary, however, without affirming how important I take it to be, irrespective of historical interpolation and extrapolation, that Bronfenbrenner has been among the very few to stress the need for psychologists of ontogenesis and developmental psychologists to differentiate, articulate, and hierarchically integrate the range of factors—concrete and abstract—that may influence the variegated aspects of human behavior and facilitate or militate against human development. May I only offer the pious, and probably vain, hope that psychologists of all persuasions consider the possibility that those processes-in-context we call human beings may, at least sometimes, respond to their environments, not in terms of the processes or factors operationally specified by a certain group of "scientists," but in terms of their definitions of the situation (their "scenes"), which may have little or nothing to do with the contexts antiseptic scientists take to be operative or influential. At least on some occasions, the environment may turn out to be what a subject takes it to *mean* rather than what a "tough-minded" scientist takes it to *be*.

I come, finally, to the last chapter I consider in this call to controversy: that by Dixon and Nesselroade, representing, at least in sympathy and sentiment, the life-span movement I attacked in my second paper (1981a; see also 1981b). In their chapter, which is offered both as an argument for, and a genealogy of, three fundamental tenets of the life-span movement, or at least of its "movers and shakers," they offer us brief "histories" of *pluralism* and a *multivariate approach*, argue for their affinities, and set forth an outline for a pluralistic, multivariate correlational approach to "developmental" psychology. It is, perhaps, an unintended irony that they do not discuss the "history" of views of the *context-dependency of phenomena*—the third component of their triumvirate, although their identification of it with "pragmatic metatheory" may constitute at least an historical allusion for them; ironic, because their "historical exposition" is characterized, among other things, by a remarkable disregard of context.

Now, a term may be introduced in the context of an ostensibly dispassionate description of some state of affairs to call attention to the fact that something rather than something else is taking place. Thus, one may say, with a mien of mature impartiality, that among those who call themselves developmental psychologists today one finds a multiplicity as opposed to a unity of perspectives, a multiplicity as contrasted with a unity of method, a multiplicity as counterposed to a unity of objects studied, and so on. Without sanction or disdain, one may then say that "pluralism" characterizes the current scene. In the same way, perhaps, as a computer may record that crime is on the increase in various cities and states.

On the other hand, one may use a term not to record but to advocate; to provide guidelines and not characterizations; to endorse, not to describe. Dixon and Nesselroade, although here and there adopting the guise of dispassionate describers of the historical scene, are, in their chapter, clearly advocates, and their seemingly neutral descriptions of what happened in history are surely in the service of persuasion. I have elsewhere (see p. 185ff) indicated my "tough-minded" scepticism of even third-party chroniclers, not intoxicated by *parti pris*. When instant historians reconstruct an ancient and honorable ancestry to exalt their current cause, one's scepticism may easily verge on suspicion. This is not to suggest that the advocate will have any intent to deceive. It is just that *credula res amor est*. I need not remark that because I am an antagonist of the life-span movement, one should be wary of my commentary on the Dixon and Nesselroade chapter.

Our authors, as noted, are enthusiasts of "pluralism." Now, pluralism, like most other big words, and perhaps little ones too, may mean different things to different people. A detached student of the uses of the word might uncover, as A. O. Lovejoy (1908/1963) once did with regard to "pragmatism" (another of

Dixon and Nesselroade's words of power), 13 meanings or more. Surely, it is incumbent on an advocate not to pretend to uncover what x or y or z might mean by the term, but to specify what he/she means by it; not what pluralism appears to mean in the writings of x, y or z, but what I or we intend by the term. Of course, if one tries to swing back and forth between a detached and involved posture, this course might be difficult. It is also convenient, for it allows one to say, "They said it, I didn't." Unless otherwise stated, I assume that their tacit endorsements of the views of others they cite in approving tones reflect their own views.

One who advocates a pluralism akin to that of Dixon and Nesselroade thus advocates, among other things, multiple explanatory schemes, multiple interpretative frameworks, multiple empirical methodologies, and multiple analytical techniques. Given the acknowledged complexity of psychological phenomena—and, in indeed, one might add, our difficulties and disagreements even in locating all the places where psychological phenomena are—we should be tolerant. Nay, more than tolerant. We should encourage different theoretical perspectives and different modes of inquiry. To put their proposal in more familiar terms: There should be a free market for ideas as well as methodologies, techniques, etc. All theories and world views should have an equal opportunity—they suggest a "fair" one, but let us be more generous—to demonstrate their "merits" in the "arena of intellectual inquiry." Such competition and conflict is essential to avoid stultification. Such a posture, urging that anyone and everyone be allowed to put on the "intellectual"—or should one say, "ideological"—market place whatever one wishes is a moral imperative. It is a clarion call for intellectual freedom. They also urge that it conduces to "intellectual responsibility," but it is not quite clear what that means. If one is to consider the analogy of the "market place," in which all regulatory agencies are dissolved, and in which *caveat emptor* prevails, it is not at all clear that the right of everyone to sell what he/she wishes leads to any special kind of responsibility for the product that one purveys.

Irrespective of the merits of their plea—and one might be taken to challenge God, country, mother, and apple pie if one voiced objections to it—it is gratuitous in a democratic society where everyone ostensibly has the right to advocate what he or she wishes to advocate; it is also empty unless one can insure that everyone has an *equal* opportunity—access to journals, access to media, access to grants—to demonstrate their merits. One might, of course, challenge this advocacy of what seems to be a doctrine of "pure tolerance" (O'Brien, 1967; Wolff, Moore & Marcuse, 1956). I do not do so. If the Nazis wish to advance their world views and marshal their evidence, they should be encouraged to do so. If the "creationists" wish to have an equal opportunity to present their doctrines, they should be encouraged to do so. If some wish to teach astrology, chiromancy, and numerology in the universities, they should be both allowed and encouraged to do so. Of course, there is a codicil to their ecumenicism: The various world views and perspectives have to demonstrate their "merits" in the "arena of intellectual inquiry." Alas, there is, however, a slight problem here. Who is to decide on the "merits" or the nature of "intellectual inquiry?" If different world views entail different conceptions of merit and intellectual inquiry, who is to be the ultimate arbiter, the Supreme Court? One might appeal to "truth" or "rationality." But given their seeming adherence to a pragmatist (or better, Jamesian, not that of either Perice of Dewey) conception of "truth" and a "pluralistic rationality," this would be an appeal to the void. Does it finally come down, for them, to *Vox populi, vox Dei* (Boas, 1969)?; world history as the world court? Or will the Wissenschaftliche anarchists surreptitiously make themselves or those of like mind the judges of merit and the nature of intellectual inquiry, dogmatically (and hence, monistically) introducing their criteria or standards to assess the one and the other. Well, let us see.

One who advocates pluralism of world views surely will not decide *ex cathedra* that a pluralist ontology is preferable to a monistic one; or suggest that a philosopher of science *qua* ontologist, who insists on a pluralist ontology has any a priori merit over one who argues for a monistic one. That would be dogmatically to advocate one of several world views over others. That one obliquely applauds such a metaphysician's attack on ontological monism as "less an exercise in informed science than a pursuit of dubious philosophical merit" only shows that the pluralist for all seasons has chosen sides. Again—and I trust that this is not too paradoxical—for an advocate of pluralism, open to multiple positions on the philosophy of science, would it not be inconsistent to advocate "theoretical pluralism" as opposed, let us say, to "theoretical dualism" or "theoretical monism"? Would not that be advocating one philosophy of science as opposed to other alternatives? Perhaps not, if one has some *authority* to warrant the preference for the theoretical pluralist. What might that be, especially if the only methodological rule is that "anything goes"? Aha. One way to decide among all the competing claims concerning Being and Truth is to compare theories with theories as well as theories with data, facts or experience! But who is to compare, and on what grounds? On some world views, there are no data, facts, or experiences that are theory independent, no Protokol statements to check the theories against. This they have surely learned from their reading of Pepper (1942). Are we arbitrarily to adopt those points of view that hold that theories are to be compared with (sic!) data, facts, or experience? Are we, who extol the dictum that "anything goes," to raise the red herring of "nonscientific" to exclude the views of those we do not like?

In advancing these questions, I should not be taken to oppose ontological pluralism—indeed I am sympathetic to doctrines that advocate even more than three kinds of "stuff" (body, mind, and objectified mind). Nor should I be taken to oppose cognitive pluralism or multiple ways of "knowing" the world; indeed, I am open to the acceptance of "modes of knowing" that many who claim to be scientists would automatically disallow. But that is not because I am a pluralist in the Dixon and Nesselroade sense. It is precisely because I *reject* those alternative views that take other positions, ontologically or epistemologically. If I took the view that "anything goes" and rejected any trans-systemic standard for comparing and evaluating different world views, then it would be difficult for me to see how I can favor "relativism" (political, cultural, or otherwise) and still claim that I am not committed to the thesis that all these different views are equally true or equally false (Kaplan, 1967, 1974/82, 1981a,b). In sum, it is not that I oppose a perspective (one), positing ontological pluralism, methodological pluralism, etc. I oppose a *pluralistic perspective,* which would, in principle, allow for everything and its opposite. That may be fine, *sub-specie-eternitatas,* or for the *Ein-Sof,* or at that point in infinity where there is a *coincidentia oppositorum.* But for any mortals to claim that position is *hubris.* And its "cash-value," as we pragmatists say, would on the mundane level be relativism, pure and simple. From the vantage point of the Empyrean, one may say of a plurality of conflicting and contradictory contentions, "That's right! And that's right! And that's right, too!". For most of us, however, the judgment that any claim and its contradictory were both right or both wrong would usually be taken as an indication of *intellectual irresponsibility.* Or the first step on the road to monism (of the organismic variety), mysticism, or gnomic silence.

Dixon and Nesselroade are obviously sensitive to the possibility that the pluralism they advocate might lead one to think that they are eclectics or perhaps syncretists—picking and choosing here and there from the goodies offered by different perspectives with different methodologies and even different criteria of evidence and truth. No. Pluralism, as they advocate it, urges the proliferation of "autonomous theoretical structures" and does not suggest that one should select bits and pieces from different sections of the market place. To concretize, a pluralist would urge that the behaviorist, the psychoanalyst, the humanistic psychologist, the Jungian—let us assume for the moment that each possesses or advances an "autonomous (law unto itself) theoretical structure"—each retain their "structural integrity" and their "autonomy" and, incommensurable though they be, somehow confront each other. A remarkable feat! An eclectic, on the other hand, would urge, for example, that one constitute one's views of what takes place in the complex, multidimensional psychological domain by buying a little psychoanalytic stuff, a little behaviorist stuff, a little Marxist stuff, a little Piagetian stuff, a little Maslovian stuff, and so on. Of course, if a "Pluralist" engages in this kind of potluck purchasing in psychological inquiry and practice, then it gains status and becomes "critical eclecticism." Would it not be more intellectually responsible to drop all the talk about "pluralism" and urge a good pragmatic eclecticism. Whatever happens to work in this context or that, or whatever satisfies me is "true" and becomes part of my comprehensive psychological "theory" whatever its provenance?

Now, Dixon and Nesselroade perspicaciously observe that they and some of their neighbors in the life-span movement happen to share a number of doctrines and beliefs. They are *pluralists,* as we have seen, in some vaguely defined and amorphous manner; perhaps ontological pluralists; perhaps perspectival pluralists; with attendant strabismus and nystagmus; perhaps methodological pluralists. They are *contextualists* in some vaguely defined and amorphous manner; perhaps holding that every seemingly isolated phenomenon is affected by context, and every context is affected by a wider context; but surely not maintaining the extreme doctrine of "internal relations," which might lead them to lapse into some form of organicism and monism. Although their pluralism does not entail a notion of levels, one may say that they are *strataphiles,* believing in many levels; of course they happen to share that view with many others who are not contextualists and not even ontological pluralists. They also believe that phenomena change at different rates; so they may be called *multiratists.* And finally, they also advocate a multivariate—often multivariate correlational—approach to the validation of measures, to the design of experiments, to collection of data over the life-span, and to the analysis of data over the life-span. *Multivariatists.*

Now, as dedicated pluralists and contextualists, they might just take this agglomeration of beliefs and attitudes as an *aggregate:* different strands of their shared outlook. But perhaps a passion for "monism" prompts them to seek some unity or coherence among this aggregate, this plurality. Going beyond the brute facts that these beliefs just happen to be among the ones shared by members of a particular "community," they search for reasons or rationales. Are they closet monists and rationalists in this respect?; tender-minded underneath despite their tough-minded exterior? No tychistic or merely happenstance relationships among these various doctrines! There must be some conceptual links. Nor are they satisfied with conceptual links. They present us with putative historical links. Let us therefore examine Dixon and Nesselroade's search for, and reconstruction of, their genealogy and ostensibly the genealogy of the life-span movement.

First, however, I want to set the stage for my examination of their historical quest with a quotation from that eminent historian of ideas, A. O. Lovejoy, the source of much of the "information" cited by Dixon and Nesselroade. In the introductory chapter of his magisterial work, *The Great Chain of Being* (1936), Lovejoy observes:

> that the doctrines or tendencies that are designated by familiar names ending in −ism or −ity, though they occasionally may be, usually are not, units of the sort which the historian of ideas seeks to discriminate. They commonly constitute, rather, compounds to which his method of analysis needs to be applied. Idealism, romanticism, transcendentalism, pragmatism, [may one add, pluralism?], all these trouble-breeding and usually thought-obscuring terms, which one sometimes wishes to see expunged from the vocabulary of the philosopher and historian altogether, are names of complexes, not of simples—and of complexes in two senses. They stand as a rule, not for one doctrine but for several distinct and often conflicting doctrines to whose way of thinking these appellations have been applied, either by themselves or in the traditional terminology of historians; and each of these doctrines, in turn, is likely to be resolvable into simpler elements, often very strangely

combined and derivative from a variety of dissimilar motives and historical influences [pp. 5f, my insert].

Clearly, Lovejoy here invites the amateur historian of ideas to expose the felony, not to compound it. As we see, Dixon and Nesselroade not only compound the felony; they plurally and multiply compound it. Had they said openly, "These are the doctors and doctrines we have decided to take as our intellectual ancestors, and here is how we have decided to interpret what they say," they could have selected anyone they wished and interpreted them in any way they desired. Oriented thusly, one can freely make a silk purse out of a sow's ear.

But our advocates of "pluralism," and life-span "developmental psychology" do not indicate that this is what they are doing. Rather, they intimate that the masters and the movements to which they refer have something to do with the doctrine they now advocate. Thus, they claim, or at least suggest, that the beliefs in a plurality of inhabited worlds and in an infinite universe—these are, of course, two distinct beliefs—foreshadowed the kind of pluralism they propose. And thus they at least appear to invoke Crescas, Cusanus, Brahe, Kepler, Galileo, Digges, and Giordano Bruno, among others, as forerunners and ancestors. Again they take, or appear to take, the 16th-century scepticism, as embodied in the writings of Michel de Montaigne, to be both an expression of a pluralistic outlook and a propellant toward modern pluralism. And we find classified among the sceptics of the 17th century Rene Descartes—did he also advocate methodological pluralism and opt for empiricism?—who is taken to advocate "a philosophical pluralism," the kind of pluralism and pluralistic vision "rediscovered and confirmed by pragmatists such as Peirce, James, and Dewey in the 19th and early 20th centuries."

Now, as a "pluralist" myself, in one of the "interminate"[15] meanings that one has assigned to that word, I could construe this kind of genealogical reconstruction in an "interminate" number of ways. From one perspective, it can be taken to confirm the thesis that every historian makes up his/her own history (see Kaplan, this volume); from another, it may be taken to exemplify the well-known maxim of utter credulity, "If you believe that, you'll believe anything"; from a third, it may be taken to illustrate the disadvantages of "misprision," whose advantages for the creative imagination have been amply documented elsewhere (Bloom, 1972, 1976); from a fourth, it may be taken to confirm the cynical observation to the effect that histories are tricks that the living play upon the dead; and so on. But, I must admit, despite a latitudinarian attitude toward "validity in interpretation," the readings Dixon and Nesselroade give to many of the doctrines and views they cite seem to me to be idiosyncratic in the extreme. Did space permit, I could give the grounds for this judgment by directly citing

---

[15]Following Cusanus and Descartes, I say "interminate" rather than "infinite," because "infinity" is reserved for God alone (see A. Koyre, 1958, pp. 7f).

Dixon and Nesselroade. In some cases I do just this. In the main, however, I rely on some respected historians of ideas, including two, Lovejoy and Randall, who are apparently taken as quite credible by Dixon and Nesselroade.

It is quite clear that Dixon and Nesselroade are much taken with William James and would like to have him and the pluralistic pragmatism he advocated as a grandfather for their kind of contextualistic pluralism. Thus, they begin their section on "origins of pluralism" by referring to James' typology of "philosophical temperaments." It is, perhaps, representative of their historical method that they do not indicate the context (or scene) in which James proposed his dichotomous typology or the purposes for which James introduced his polar opposites. Nor do they mention all the "traits" James introduces to constitute his "ideal types." And, perhaps through a venial sin of omission, they appear to suggest that James aligned himself with one of these types in opposition to the other. Let us supply the omissions and restore the context.

In his initial Lowell Lecture, "The present dilemma in philosophy," James, addressing a popular audience, was deeply concerned to show that philosophies, rather than being impersonal constructions of autonomous thought, were determined, in large measure, by temperament. Just as Jung, subsequently, was to take any psychological theory as a "personal confession," James considered philosophical viewpoints as motivated by extrarational factors. Using a later terminology, James could easily be taken to say that articulated world views were simply or mainly rationalizations of subjective, temperamental tendencies. This posture is, of course, one reason why Popper finds at least Jamesian pragmatism so reprehensible (Popper, 1975, pp. 125, 145).

To illuminate and illustrate his thesis, James considered extreme types: the Platos, Leibnizes, Hegels, and Royces, on one side; the naturalists, exmpiricists, and positivists, on the other. Rationalists and emprircists, architects and bricklayers. To show what he had in mind, James constructed his dichotomous typology from eight pairs of contrasting predicates and dubbed the two constellations of predicates "tough-minded" and "tender-minded." Thus, the *ideal type* "tough-minded" philosopher constructed by James was empiricistic (going by "facts"), sensationalistic, materialistic, pessimistic, irreligious, fatalistic, pluralistic, and sceptical. In contrast, the hypothetical "tender-minded" philosopher was rationalistic (going by "principles"), intellectualistic, idealistic, optimistic, religious, free-willist, monistic, and dogmatical.

Now, it should be clear—it is more so in James than in Dixon and Nesselroade—that James did not happen to find a group of "tough-minded" individuals and "tender-minded" individuals and determine, as a matter of observation and fact, that the one possessed this constellation of traits and the other possessed the opposing constellation of traits. James *defined* what he meant by "tough-minded" and "tender-minded" in terms of these opposing lists of predicates. As he (1907/1943), himself, noted: "every sort of permutation and combination is possible in human nature [p. 21]." He drew the typological opposition, which he acknowledged as "to a certain extent arbitrary [p. 21] as a foil to help him is his "ulterior purpose of characterizing pragmatism [p. 21]."

Any examination of James' thought would show that, despite his vaunted pluralism, he did not align himself with the tough-minded. Indeed, his "pragmatism" was intended to overcome the seemingly intransigent opposition between the two types. As he (James 1907/1943) noted, to his popular audience: "few of us are tender-footed Bostonians pure and simple, and few are typical Rocky mountain toughs in philosophy. Most of us have a hankering for the good things on both sides of the line [p. 23]." The "ordinary philosophic layman," never being a radical or extremist, never overly concerned about system, oscillates between being tender-minded and tough-minded "to suit the temptations of successive hours [p. 23]." For most of us, "consistency is the hobgoblin of small minds," as one of James' Transcendentalist forbears put it. But not for the professional philosopher, who is "vexed by too much inconsistency and vacillation [p. 23]." Ostensibly, according to Dixon and Nesselroade (this volume), it is professional philosophers, seeking to be unvexed, who would fall into one or the other of James' types extolled as one of his "most salient contributions to the intellectual community [p. 117]."

I digress for a moment from my examination of Dixon and Nesselroade's treatment of James to consider whether philosophers who are "pluralists"—in the sense that they assert the doctrine that there is more than one fundamental "stuff" constituting reality—tend to possess those other "traits" that make up the tough-minded type. Instead of promoting my own exemplars of "pluralism," I follow John Dewey (1902) in his article on Pluralism in James Mark Baldwin's *Dictionary of Philosophy and Psychology*. Dewey defines "pluralism"—note carefully how this deviates from Dixon and Nesselroade's presentation (p. 123)—as: "the theory that reality consists in a plurality or multiplicity of distinct beings [p. 306]." Are those who are pluralists tough-minded "materialists"? Dewey (1902) observes that pluralism: "may be materialistic, as with the Atomists; hylozoistic as with Empedocles; or spiritualistic, as with Leibniz." That is the *pluralistic* Leibniz, by the way, who is the arch representative for James of the rationalistic, intellectualistic, optimistic, "tender-minded" type.

As Dewey observes, the opposition between ontological monism and pluralism does not emerge with James, with the move from "the closed world to the infinite universe" (Koyre, 1957), with Cusanus, or even with Crescas. Dewey (1902) states that the opposition is: "one which was among the earliest to attract attention, and about which the conflict is most stubborn [p. 306]." Those who advocated a pluralistic ontology against the monists were motivated, Dewey (1902) suggests, by a desire to ground:

> the possibility of real change, or an objectively valid dynamic view, since monism seems to make change a mere incident in the totality of being, or even a partly illusory phenomenon [Heraclitus and Hegel, however, seem to be dynamic monists

in asserting the one reality to be essentially process]; the possibility of real variety, particularly in the differences of persons, as monism appears to lend itself to a pantheistic view, regarding all distinctions as simply limitations of the one being; the possibility of freedom, as a self-initiating and moving power inherent in every real *qua* real [p. 306].

As we see, Giordano Bruno, whom Dixon and Nesselroade wish to claim for their pluralistic ancestry, was precisely one of those *pantheistic monists* (see Lovejoy, 1936, pp. 189ff, Randall, 1962, pp. 326–338, especially p. 336), who foreshadowed and influenced the "tender-minded" Leibniz, whose monadology was, paradoxically, both monistic and pluralistic.

Let us now return to the exposition of James by Dixon and Nesselroade. If James did not advocate, or align himself with, one or the other of his caricatures of philosophic temperaments, why do Dixon and Nesselroade make so much of it? A plausible reason it seems to me, is that by presenting the typology as they do, and hinting at some intimate and intrinsic connection of the traits on any one list, they can claim as progenitors not only those who are admittedly "ontological pluralists," but even those who are not but are marked by some other term on the list containing pluralism. Conversely, they can blot out from their genealogy some of those pluralists who happen to be otherwise "tender-minded." In other words, they can thus practice some version of "guilt by association" or "kinship by contiguity." Whether or not this is their conscious intent, I try to show that this is, in fact, what they do.

To be sure, there is another form of "linkage by association," which may override the types I have just mentioned: the linkage of "pluralism" with "plurality." This near-homophonic connection leads them to suggest that those who argue for a "plurality of worlds" are pluralists in some significant sense. Thus Crescas, Cusanus, and Bruno, among others, are taken as belonging to the ancestral tree of contemporary "pluralism" by virtue of their advocacy of a "plurality of inhabited worlds." Now it should be obvious that a belief in the plurality of inhabited worlds no more entails a belief in ontological pluralism or methodological pluralism than a belief in the plurality or multiplicity or organs in a body, rooms in a house, or people on earth. And, indeed, none of the three putative progenitors would be considered "pluralists" in any significant sense.

Hasdai Crescas was a late 14th-century religious Jew who opposed, within the Jewish community, the Aristotelianism advanced by Maimonides and Gersonides. Informed, in part, by the passion that affected Halevi and Al Gazali in Jewish and Islamic thought of the 11th century, Crescas, *on behalf of revelation and faith,* used dialectical weapons to challenge the intellectualistic rationalism of the Aristotelian school. Without resorting to empirical observation or multivariate correlational analysis, Crescas (in Husik, 1916/1940), arguing from Holy Writ and the Almighty's infinite power, maintained: "that an infinite magnitude *is* possible and exists actually; that there is an infinite fullness or void outside of this world, and hence there may be many worlds [p. 390]." This thesis did not lead him to reject rationalism exclusively or urge more empirical observation. This thesis was not coupled with any scepticism, except with regard to either *rational or empirical* claims to knowledge, not sustained by the Bible. This thesis did not lead him to reject a single (monistic) ultimate cause (viz., God). Of course, if "pluralism," in some idiosyncratic way, is taken to mean the belief that natural knowledge, whether rational or empirical, is always fallible, then Crescas could be considered a "pluralist." But that is surely not the meaning "pluralism" usually carries, although some who are "pluralists" may also be "fallibilists."

What about Nicholas of Cusa, the 15th-century Cardinal, also claimed as a forerunner because of his advocacy of a plurality of inhabited globes? This is the Cusanus who, in Cassirer's words (1927/1963), is the only thinker of his period: "to look at all the fundamental problems of his time from the point of view of *one* principle through which he masters them all [p. 7]." This is the Cusanus who, according to Randall (1962) devoted all his writings to: "the medieval problem of the relation of God to the world"; who formulated "the very modern ideas of the relativity of human knowledge and the essential *homogeneity of the universe [p. 178, my italics]." This is the Cusanus who took over the "great Platonic tradition" and transformed it into "what the world has since known as German transcendentalism." This is the Cusanus whose: "metaphysical system stands . . . as the culmination of the mystic Platonism of medieval thought, and found in Bruno a wholehearted disciple [p. 179]." This is the Cusanus whose thought is: "an unmistakable link in the German tradition from Eckhart to Leibniz and transcendental idealists like Schelling," and hence one who is linked to those rationalistic, religious figures James ridicules in his Lowell lecture. This is the Cusanus: "firmly impressed by the older Platonic conviction of the unity of all things in Supreme Being"* who "emphasizes the interconnectedness and relations of things, their nexus, as their intelligible aspect and hence the proper object of knowledge [p. 180]." This is the Cusanus (De conjecturis, I, 3, in Randall, 1962) who insists that: "Truth is not susceptible of more or less, but is of an indivisible nature, and whatever is not itself the True is unable to measure it with precision [p. 181f]."

As Randall (1962) remarks:

In such fashion Cusnaus expresses the old Platonic distinction between the vision of the intellect, beholding the world as One, as a Unity of diversity, and the plodding work of reason lost amidst the Many—that distinction made by the Augustinians between *sapientia* and *scientia* . . . this vision man can see, but he can give it rational expression only in the form of relative and comparative knowledge, of 'conjectures' [p. 182].!

Is this ontological pluralism? It may be epistemological dualism, with one way of knowing superior to the other. Does Cusanus advocate a plurality of methods? As stated in Randall (1962): "It is mathematics which alone can give even a limited and conjectural knowledge of the Infinite of God [p. 182]." What is there, then that prompts Dixon and Nesselroade, to claim Cusanus as one of their ancestors?

And what about Giordano Bruno? A *pantheistic monist*, driven by principle (plenitude, later sufficient reason, and hence *rationalistic*) to assert *dogmatically*, and without any empirical evidence, the existence of a plurality of inhabited worlds and an infinite universe (see Cassirer, 1927/1963, passim; Koyre, 1957, pp. 39ff; Lovejoy, 1936, pp. 116–121, especially p. 120; Randall, 1962, pp. 328–329). In what way is this Bruno, who believed that there is throughout the infinite universe the life of the great divine ordering force, a pluralist? Indeed, it is Bruno (De immenso et innumerabilibus, Book VIII, Ch. 10, in Randall, 1963) who says: "Beneath the fluctuating surface of things it is closer to all things than they are to themselves, the living principle of being, the source of all forms, mind, God, being, one, true, fate, word, order [p. 333]."

It seems to me that if one looks closely at these figures, taken as progenitors of pluralism by Dixon and Nesselroade, they are, in fact, just the opposite. It is they who set the stage for the homogenization of reality and the exclusive methodology of mathematical rationalism that one finds at the rise of modern physical science.

I close this discussion of the chapter by Dixon and Nesselroade with an examination of their treatment of Montaigne, whom they also take as one of their precursors. Now, it is clear that Montaigne was aware of a multiplicity of views concerning nature; a multiplicity of views regarding theological doctrine; a multiplicity of different customs. And he is sceptical with regard to all of them. For Montaigne, our ignorance is universal, and multiplying our claims to knowledge on the basis of rational deductions or observations would not reduce our ignorance in the slightest. The upshot of Montaigne's scepticism, as Randall (1962) notes (p. 100) is relativism pure and simple. This relativism is, for Montaigne, rooted in human nature and in "universal reason" implanted in every man. This nature is *not to be described by science* but can only be grasped by self-critical introspective examination. Thus, Montaigne advocated not a plurality of methods, but a single method—that of portraying oneself candidly. As Randall notes (1962), in portraying himself, Montaigne took himself to be portraying Everyman, for: "every man has in himself the whole form of human nature [p. 99]."

In sum, one might say not that Montaigne's scepticism led to an advocacy of pluralism, but rather his awareness of the plurality of beliefs, the plurality of creeds, the plurality of customs, etc. led to his scepticism. It is thus that he advocated turning away from all the presumptuous claims to knowledge about the outside world and a hearkening to that natural wisdom, that universal wisdom, imprinted in each and all of us; a wisdom identical with the divine wisdom, save that ours is transient, whereas the latter is eternal. As Popkin observes (1964, p. 45), the overriding aim of Montaigne's *Apologie de Raimond Sebond* was not to provoke multiple world views, multiple empirical methodologies, multiple analytic techniques, etc.; it was to establish a new form of *fideism*—Catholic Pyrrhomism. Do Dixon and Nesselroade find him an eminent forerunner of theirs because of his anti-intellectualism?; because of his advocacy of cultivating ignorance in order to rely on faith alone?; because of his advocacy of complete doubt and a life lived in accordance with custom and nature?; because of his apparent support of the thesis that all views are equally true and equally false?

One can surely demonstrate a number of other instances of the loose and superficial treatment of the history of ideas in this genealogy of Dixon and Nesselroade. Although Descartes might be regarded as a sceptic by some thinkers who followed him, he scarcely viewed himself as one and indeed regarded himself as having resolved the *crise pyrrhonien* (Popkin, 1964, 175ff). Surely, neither Peirce, James, nor Dewey took themselves to be continuators or rediscoverers of French scepticism! Certainly, Dixon and Nesselroade needed little access to the literature of pragmatism to known, despite their source, that it was Peirce and not James who introduced and developed the doctrine of "tychism." Nor would it have taken much to discover how much both Peirce and Dewey objected to James' pragmatic definition of truth. Such errors of commission and omission do not prompt me to give much credence ("tough-minded" sceptic that I am) to this philosophical and historical perspective in "life-span developmental psychology"; but, then, as I have indicated elsewhere, I don't place much value on the movement itself.

I have been admittedly critical of the chapters of my colleagues in this collection, stressing issues on which I believe that distinctions have been fudged, questionable theses advanced, mistakes of commission and omission made. I have doubtless been too caustic on occasion; sometimes, perhaps, captious. Inevitably, those I have challenged may feel wronged in some respects. And there is clearly the possibility that I may have read them wrongly, imputing to them, or to their words, meanings beyond or other than those intended. If so, I apologize, suggesting Gurdjieff's sage advice: If one is criticized fairly, one should thank the critic for the illumination; if wrongly, out of ignorance, one should ignore what has been said as reflecting that ignorance and as not applying to one's self.

I trust that my disagreements with my colleagues will not hide major points of concurrence. Although White, in his historical survey, does not directly advocate a *developmental approach* to the phenomena of human existence, he does indicate that the application of such an approach was the intent of some of the major figures in "developmental psychology." I, of course, advocate such a "strong developmental approach," a developmental framework, not to be confused with ontogenesis as a subject matter or population. Such an approach would not look for the place of "developmental psychology" *within* "psychology" *but would look at all of psychology in developmental terms*.

I am in accord with Kagan's continuing emphasis on the necessity for developmental psychologists to turn inward and examine the operations by and through which we constitute our objects of knowledge, including the child and the child's activities. The focus in the field has for so long been "extroverted," with little regard for the ontological, axiological, and epistemological assumptions we insinuate into the phenomena we claim dispassionately to describe and explain.

Although I have questioned Bronfenbrenner's reconstruction of the changing "concepts of environment" in developmental psychology, I surely agree with him as to the importance of understanding such concepts. I would only suggest that we ought to concern ourselves with the whole range of concepts of environment (and correlative concepts of the "organism") in the history of thought, without regard for whether those who advanced such notions were "operationalizing scientists" or not. It may well be that other notions of organism–environment, some long buried as antiquated or demolished, are more alive than we imagine, and more relevant to us than those advanced by the perpetuators of the Cartesian "bifurcation of nature" (see Barfield, 1965; Cassirer, 1923/53, 1925/55, 1929/57; Feyerabend, 1975).

Finally, despite the fact that my most acerb remarks have been directed against the chapter by Dixon and Nesselroade, as representative of the "life-span movement," I am, in many respects, in agreement with the general aims of that movement: that developmental psychology concern itself with human beings throughout their lives as imbedded in, and, *in part,* constituted by sociohistorical circumstances; that developmental psychologists break away from their bondage to "methodolatry" (A. Kaplan, 1964, pp. 24–27); that developmental psychologists struggle to bracket their own *préjuges du monde* in order to appreciate the multiple and different worlds in which human beings (including ourselves) dwell and have dwelled; that developmental psychologists, as mortals, recognize their inevitable "fallibility" (presupposing, I would argue, some regulative principle of "truth") and hearken to Cromwell's injunction (cited in Whitehead, 1925)— "By the bowels of Christ, I beseech you, bethink you you may be wrong"—; and so on.

My objection to their historical reconstruction, and to the movement for which it seeks to provide an ancestry, is that it fails to deal with the distinction between "development" and change, behavioral or otherwise; that it does not take into account that development is a culture concept (Cassirer, 1960, p. 117 ff), and, moreover, a normative and axiological notion; that, as Dewey points out, a pluralism without a corresponding monism inclines toward total chaos; that it is not seemly for those who argue against the hegemony of any single methodology, and who insist on "anything goes," to plead for their own preferred methodology, and their own ways of going about inquiry, etc.

In sum, it is gratuitous for human beings to advocate multiple world views and perspectives, because groups and individuals will have such diverse Weltanschauungen and points of view willy–nilly. In my view, a *developmental psychology* pertaining to the life-span must take a stand as to what "development" means and cannot collapse it into behavioral change, leaving it to a limited group to observe and record the antecedents and consequents of changes in the passing parade. Nor can one rely on the "evolutionary process" to generate developmental progress in any meaningful sense (see Kaplan, 1967/74/82, Kaplan, 1981a,b). Without a stand on what "development" is to mean, without that posited center, which is admittedly taken from an anthropocentric perspective, "things fall apart"—and we are left with a telephone book of intercorrelations, tales told by idiots signifying nothing.

ACKNOWLEDGMENT

This chapter is dedicated to the memory of my analyst and friend, Silvano Arieti, who died August 7, 1981. Dr. Arieti was not only a fine man and a great man. He was an extraordinarily wise one.

REFERENCES

Adler, M. *The idea of freedom*, Vol. 1. Garden City: Doubleday, 1958.

Adler, M. *The idea of freedom*, Vol. 2. Garden City: Doubleday, 1961.

Barfield, O. *Saving the appearances: A study in idolatry.* New York: Harcourt Brace & World, 1965.

Bennett, J. *The dramatic universe,* 4 vols. Sherbourne: The Coombe Springs Press, 1977.

Black, M. The definition of scientific method. In *Problems of analysis.* Ithaca, N. Y.: Cornell University Press, 1954.

Bloom, H. *Anxiety of influence.* New York: Oxford, 1972.

Bloom, H. *Poetry and repression.* New York: Oxford, 1976.

Boas, G. *Vox Populi.* Baltimore: Johns Hopkins Press, 1969.

Brent, S. *Changes in size and changes in form in the development of psychological structures.* Presented at conference on developmental psychology for the 1980's: Werner's influence on theory and praxis. Clark University, Worcester, Mass., 1981.

Buchler, J. *The concept of method.* New York: Columbia University Press, 1961.

Burke, K. *Grammar of motives.* Englewood Cliffs, N. J.: Prentice-Hall, 1945.

Cassirer, E. *Substance and function.* (1910) Lasalle, Ill.: Open Court, 1923.

Cassirer, E. *An essay on man.* New Haven, Conn.: Yale University Press, 1944.

Cassirer, E. *The problem of knowledge.* New Haven, Conn.: Yale University Press, 1950.

Cassirer, E. *Philosophy of symbolic forms,* I. (1923) New Haven, Conn.: Yale University Press, 1953.

Cassirer, E. *Philosophy of symbolic forms,* II. (1925) New Haven, Conn.: Yale University Press, 1955.

Cassirer, E. *Philosophy of symbolic forms,* III. (1929) New Haven, Conn.: Yale University Press, 1957.

Cassirer, E. *Logic of the humanities.* New Haven, Conn.: Yale University Press, 1960.

Cassirer, E. *The individual and cosmos in renaissance philosophy.* (1927) New York: Harper, 1963.

Cirillo, L., & Kaplan, B. *Figurative action from the perspective of Genetic-Dramatism.* Presented at conference on developmental psychology for the 1980's. Werner's influence on theory and praxis. Clark University, Worcester, Mass., 1981.

Dewey, J. Pluralism. In J. M. Baldwin (Ed.), *Dictionary of philosophy and psychology.* New York: Macmillan, 1902.

Dreyfus, H. Holism and hermeneutics. *Review of Metaphysics,* 1980, *34,* 3–23.

Feyerabend, P. *Against method.* New York: Schocken, 1975.

Husik, I. *A history of medieval Jewish philosophy,* (1916). New York: Atheneum, 1940.

James, W. *Pragmatism.* (1907). New York: Meridian, 1943.

Jammer, M. *Concepts of space.* Cambridge, Mass.: Harvard University Press, 1953.

Kaplan, A. *The conduct of inquiry.* San Francisco: Chandler, 1964.

Kaplan, B. *Lectures on developmental psychology.* Worcester State Hospital & Clark University, 1960.

Kaplan, B. The comparative-developmental approach and its application to symbolization and language in psychopathology. In S. Arieti (Ed.), *American handbook of psychiatry,* (Vol. 3). New York: Basic Books, 1966. (a)

Kaplan, B. The 'latent content' of Heinz Werner's comparative-developmental approach. In S. Wapner & B. Kaplan (Eds.), *Heinz Werner: Papers in memoriam.* Worcester, Mass.: Clark University Press, 1966. (b)

Kaplan, B. Meditations on genesis. *Human Development,* 1967, *10,* 65–87.

Kaplan, B. *Genetic-dramatism: Old wine in new bottles.* Presented at conference on developmental psychology for the 1980's: Werner's influence on theory and praxis. Clark University, Worcester, Mass, 1981. (a)

Kaplan, B. *Reflections on culture and personality from the perspective of genetic-dramatism.* Presented at conference on Developmental psychology for the 1980's: Werner's influence on theory and praxis. Clark University, Worcester, Mass., 1981. (b)

Kaplan, B. *Rationality and irrationality in development.* Heinz Werner Lectures presented in 1974. Worcester, Mass.: Clark University Press, 1982.

Koyre, A. *From the closed world to the infinite universe.* New York: Harper, 1957.

Lovejoy, A. O. *The great chain of being.* Cambridge, Mass.: Harvard University Press, 1936.

Lovejoy, A. O. *The thirteen pragmatisms and other essays* (1908). Baltimore: Johns Hopkins Press, 1963.

Löwith, K. *Meaning in history.* Chicago: University of Chicago Press, 1949.

Northrop, F. S. C. *Logic of the sciences and humanities.* New York: MacMillan, 1947.

O'Brien, C. C. Politics and the morality of scholarship. In M. Black, (Ed.), *The morality of scholarship.* Ithaca, N. Y.: Cornell University Press, 1967.

Ouspensky, P. *The fourth way.* New York: Vintage, 1973.

Ouspensky, P. *The psychology of man's possible evolution.* New York: Vintage, 1974.

Pepper, S. *World hypotheses.* Berkeley: University of California Press, 1942.

Polanyi, M. *Personal knowledge.* New York: Harper, 1962.

Popkin, R. H. *The history of scepticism: From Erasmus to Descartes.* New York: Harper, 1964.

Popper, K. *Unended quest.* Lasalle, Ill.: Open Court, 1975.

Randall, J. H. *The career of philosophy,* I. New York: Columbia University Press, 1962.

Rescher, N. *Peirce's philosophy of science.* Notre Dame: Notre Dame University Press, 1978.

Rorty, R. A reply to Dreyfus and Taylor. *Review of Metaphysics,* 1980, *34,* 39–48.

Smart, H. R. *Philosophy and its history.* Lasalle, Ill.: Open Court, 1962.

Strauss, L. *Natural right and history.* Chicago: University of Chicago Press, 1953.

Taylor, C. Understanding in human science. *Review of Metaphysics,* 1980, *34,* 25–38.

Tillyard, E. M. W. *Elizabethan world picture.* New York: Modern Library, 1942.

Toulmin, S. *The philosophy of science.* London: Hutchinson, 1953.

Werner, H. *Comparative psychology of mental development,* (1948). New York: International Universities Press, 1960.

Werner, H., & Kaplan, B. The developmental approach to cognition: Its relevance to the psychological interpretation of anthropological and ethnolinguistic data. *American anthropologist,* 1956, *58,* 866–880.

Whitehead, A. N. *Science and the modern world*. New York: Macmillan, 1925.

Whitehead, A. N. *Modes of thought*. New York: Macmillan, 1937.

Willey, B. *The seventeenth century background*, (1935). New York: Anchor, 1953.

Woodger, J. H. *The technique of theory construction*. International Encyclopedia of Unified Science. Chicago: University of Chicago Press, 1939.

Woolf, R. P., Moore, B., & Marcuse, H. *Critique of pure tolerance*. Boston: Beacon, 1956.

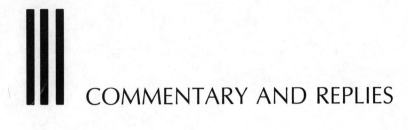

COMMENTARY AND REPLIES

8 A Reply to Kaplan

Jerome Kagan
Harvard University

Kaplan's tart and telling essay parses easily into a prologue containing a clear statement of his presuppositions and critiques of four chapters in this volume. Because my three colleagues are capable of defending themselves, I take as my assignment Kaplan's comments on my contribution and the theme of his initial statement.

In his critique of my chapter Kaplan claims that I assume a reality that humans attempt to know. I am guilty of that assumption. With Russell, I believe there is for each organism a world of events that humans try to capture, always incompletely, with symbols. Obviously the world as experienced by humans has a special quality, different from that of the clam. As Quine (1969) notes, the wavelength of light is a salient quality for our species but not for the majority of living forms. Although all symbolic descriptions of events are necessarily fallible, I suggested that some were more influenced by private presuppositions than others and implied that psychological descriptions of behavior were more guilty than the botanist's statements on mitosis, even though the biologist's words are also the product of beliefs having little to do with the phenomenon being studied. Specifically, I argued that many descriptions of infants are influenced in a profound way by the presupposition of connectivity.

The only misreading in Kaplan's comments is his attributing to me the belief that matter in motion has a special priority. I take quite the opposite position. Emotions and the perception of emotion in others are as real as smiles and frowns, and I have disagreed with those who want to classify affective states on the basis of external responses alone, changes in facial expression being only one example.

The essential theme in the first part of his commentary is a distinction between the facts of psychological growth, which Kaplan chooses to call ontogenesis, and the sequence that describes how children approach the metaphysical ideal each theorist believes children should grow toward, which he calls development. This is a reasonable and useful distinction. Kaplan does not waffle on the ideal states he regards as primary: movement toward freedom, autonomy, and individuation, which he acknowledges are constructions and asserts by sheer force, without the advantage of reasoned argument or analogy. Although one cannot charge him with being wrong—a declaration of values cannot be judged as true or false—it is fair to ask why Kaplan selected freedom and liberty as the teloi of preference. Imposition of this ideal for nonhuman organisms is confusing, for a frog seems to me to be less free than a tadpole and the pair-bonded adult gibbon appears to have a more restricted life than the prepubertal animal.

Even though Kaplan does not supply a target or context for the predicate of freedom, I assume he means freedom to think and act as one chooses, states of mind Thomas Jefferson would certainly celebrate. It is reasonable to ask why those states are more desirable than feeling obligated to nurture others, even when one does not wish to do so. Kant's categorical imperative restricts a great deal of individual freedom to deceive another or to rid oneself of anger through acts of aggression to those who are regarded as the source of the unpleasant feelings. As Kaplan knows, the Chinese and Japanese regard a love of humanity as the primary goal of development, and I am persuaded that *jen* is as reasonable a telos as freedom, although not synonymous with it. Thus, I applaud the clarity with which Kaplan announces his values, but my sense of gratitude does not require agreement.

I would like to believe that over the past 25 years I have been studying ontogenesis, not development. For I have tried, although not always sufficient to the task, to keep what I would like to believe is the meaning of development from influencing what I hope are real changes in the coherences among events that accompany growth from birth forward. With Kaplan, I also hold private wishes regarding what the child should become, but they emphasize compassion, nurture, and love. Such a trio of final purposes places obligations on children and adults that restrict seriously the freedom Kaplan cherishes.

REFERENCE

W. V. Quine. *Ontological Relativity and Other Essays.* New York: Columbia University Press, 1969.

9 Developmental Psychology, Bewildered and Paranoid: A Reply to Kaplan

Sheldon H. White
Harvard University

Kaplan's discussion is, as is characteristic of him, directed toward the pretheoretical and definitional commitments that form a floor upon which my chapter's historical discussion is built. I use the term *development* as a concept by postulation as he does. There is really no other way to get a concept on the table, posed for discussion. But my persuasive definition of development is one that he considers and rejects on the way to his own. He accepts this definition: "*Developmental psychology is a practico-theoretical discipline, a policy discipline, concerned with the perfection (including liberation or freedom) of the individual.*" My persuasive definition of developmental psychology is, in Kaplan's words: "*Developmental psychology can be defined in terms of what self-proclaimed or officially canonized developmental psychologists do.*"

Both definitions are argumentative and both reflect values. I point to something in the world more clearly than does Kaplan, but he indicates more clearly why one would want to take the trouble to point in the first place. My definition looks "behavioral" and so less ambiguous and complicated than Kaplan's. But physical events are not psychological events, and it takes some rather complicated maneuvers to make one kind of event an index of the other. Psychology's operationalistic phase of the 1940s fostered the belief that behaviors are simple physical things like rocks and trees. But behaviorism, far from standing on "naive realism," represents a very sophisticated kind of realism. The world does not cut itself up into smiles, lever presses, acts of aggression, or eye blinks for you without your skilled and energetic cooperation. And "smiles," etc., are not things that endure and that can be repeatedly visited and measured. They are dynamic patternings of things in motion, no two ever the same, classed with one another so as to be regarded as recurrences of the "same thing." So any decision

233

to look at something and count it embodies a theory, and the something is always what Kaplan terms a concept by postulation.

Still, my more behavioral way of getting ''developmental psychology'' on the table may have some advantages. In what direction? Alfred North Whitehead says somewhere, ''The object of symbolization is the enhancement of the importance of that which is symbolized.'' Kaplan symbolizes, and therefore draws attention to, one way in which developmental psychology intentionally inexists in the world, I another. He centers our gaze on the value positions that developmental psychologists move toward in their work—self-realization, self-perfection, self-actualization, freedom.

Developmental psychologists share some fundamental value commitments, but they are not our only ones, nor are our many other common purposes and agreements logically entailed in our deepest agreements. A fisherman's life is grounded upon humankind's need for self-maintenance through a food supply, but this principle alone doesn't explain much about a fisherman. What a fisherman is and does is ruled by the tides of the ocean, the kind of boat he has, the weather, the feeding habits of his target fish, the market, financing, crew, etc. I want to understand developmental psychology as a human enterprise and so I examine the status quo. Developmental psychology is a dynamic patterning of people in motion. I do not think I ''defend'' the status quo in any serious sense by taking the-way-things-are as an entry point and anchor for the examination of developmental psychology. There is Don Quixote's view of the world and there is Sancho Panza's view, both with some merit. And then there is Sancho Panza nervously going along with Don Quixote and Don Quixote reluctantly acquiescing to Sancho Panza's perspective. A remarkable and interesting collaboration.

I use the status quo as one point of reference for the examination of very complex questions about what we are all doing together simply in the interest of finding a clear point of re-entry. I want to be able to look again and again from a context of gradually changing perspectives, definitions, and beliefs. James Mark Baldwin's ''Thought and Things'' argued that your definition of what things are changes as your thoughts change. There is the possibility of a somewhat devastating negative loop. You begin thinking about something. Your train of thought leads you to gradually deny the existence of the something you began with in favor of other and presumably higher-order somethings. But then your thought has cancelled itself out. Here you are in full flight, bearing in mind your question and trying this way and that way to answer it, and suddenly you reach a point where the terms of your question have vanished. Now where, exactly, are you and what are you doing? This sounds all very farfetched, something only a philosophical type might dream up, but researchers will recognize that something like this regularly happens in scientific work. You start out trying to find answers but your work leads you inexorably toward different and better questions.

How do you find your way back to the things you were thinking about after your thoughts change? It helps to pick some pretty simple, classical things to think about—like the existence of a group of cooperating people. Here are these developmental psychologists. What are they all doing together? We could get into some soul-searching about exactly who is in the set "developmental psychologists" and who is not. We know that a core group is centered in SRCD and Division 7 of the APA, and we have a little trouble defining the edges of the group—but then we have a little trouble defining the edges of most concepts. Because we attribute about 100 years of historical continuity to the group, the soul-searching becomes more intense as we wonder whether or not the lineage of developmental psychologists goes directly back to the child development movement in the 1930s and the child study people of the 1890s. These groups are not exactly like one another in membership requirements, training, interests, goals, and collateral affiliations. But they form, across historical time, a community that recognizes itself as forming a heritage. One generation has been taught and befriended by the one before. There are common ideas and some common goals that all members of the heritage distributed across time recognizably hold in common.

So now, ackwardly to be sure, I have arranged to treat the designation *developmental psychology* as a pointer, directing attention to a group of people and their common activities. The people are not "developmental psychologists" entirely, of course, just as neither Kaplan nor I are entirely developmental psychologists. We are only so with our official hats on, when we are acting in a certain role or mode of being. How can you tell when a nominal developmental psychologist is actually *being* a developmental psychologist? This is one of the complexities of my behavioral definition, of course. People committed to developmental psychology do not purely and cleanly define the enterprise. Some of their behaviors, some of the time, do.

Martin Rein and I have recently discussed social workers as individuals bound together by a body of common skills, purposes, myths, and power arrangements (Rein & White, 1981). Social work is a group game. Developmental psychology is a no-less-complicated social system for synergizing individual actions into composite action patterns. What are developmental psychologists trying to do together? Why does society pay them a salary to let them try to do it?

Suppose I ask people within the group what they are all doing together? A funny thing happens. The group divides. Some developmental psychologists offer what I would call a "Bewildered" view of what the group is up to. A minority offer a radically contrasting "Paranoid" theory. I have been interested in the differences between Bewildered and Paranoid developmental psychologists for some time. I am quite sure these two groups exist. Bewildered developmental psychologists look at the collective activity of the group in this way:

1. *Developmental psychology is not seriously unified. It is a political convention, not a field. Many people do research with children under the tent of developmental psychology, studying everything from evoked potentials to single-*

parent families from a great range of basic and applied viewpoints. In the journals and conventions shared by developmental psychologists, people give one another miscellaneous political and intellectual support, but it is a mistake to think of all this heterogeneous activity as in any serious way constituting a common intellectual discipline.

2. Developmental psychologists work with the trappings of scientific analysis, but in truth they are working with feeble or empty stuff. You can't really do science unless you explore the effects of some independent variables. The independent variable of the developmental psychologist, age, is empty. Developmental psychologists endlessly document age effects through their longitudinal designs and cross-sectional designs, but any high school senior can tell you that age doesn't cause anything. Age is a dimension in which things happen—biological variables, environmental variables. Those are the causes. When you say that such-and-such happened with age, you say almost nothing.

3. Developmental psychologists find with monotonous regularity that children get better at everything with age. Sometimes they seem to find cases in which children's performance worsens with age, but then they explore those cases and—aha!—what the older children do really is better after all. Developmental findings are largely nonnutritious and boring.

Postulates of the Bewildered view of developmental psychology are set forth regularly, by insiders and outsiders. Is there a kind of despair latent in these arguments? I do not think so—or, at least, I do not advance them for consideration here because I am trying to advance a simple optimist–pessimist dichotomy among developmental psychologists. The existence of the Bewildered view says that a good many developmental psychologists do not have a very structured view of what they are doing together that is meaningful. This is an excellent reason for a volume exactly like the present one. Interestingly, one can recognize members of the community of developmental psychologists who hold out a very different image of mutuality to the group. Consider the Paranoid view—Paranoid not in the sense of everyone-is-out-to-get-me but rather in the sense of I-am-the-King-of-the-world. The Paranoid position subscribes to postulates like these:

1. Developmental psychology is only superficially the study of children. Really, you are studying many things that go beyond childhood but whose nature is clarified by the patterning of age changes in children's behavior.

2. The proper and only way to approach behavior is through the study of development.

3. Time series phenomena in evolution, organizational change, history, geology, cultural practices, the history of science, etc. show interesting and useful communalities. At the same time, psychopathology, neuropathology, social dissolution, and other forms of human disorder may be usefully interpreted as reversions in universal human organicist patterns of growth.

4. *The study of developmental pscyhology yields values. It takes you from is to ought.*

My chapter in this volume traces a path backward in time toward some of the more important historical sources of the Paranoid view. How can developmental psychologists differ so much in their self-concepts? I have been interested in these contrasting perspectives for some time. My chapter here is one of several efforts to explore the Paranoid view (White, 1976b). An analysis of the Child Study movement done with Alexander Siegel (Siegel & White, 1982) follows several previous efforts to explore the diversity of life in a heterogeneous, Bewildered scientific community (White, 1976a, 1977, 1978).

What is my perspective as a developmental psychologist? My outlook is Bewildered, with streaks of Paranoia that have grown over the years. (I recognize a trifle ackwardly that some of my Paranoid friends would refer to what I call "streaks of Paranoia" as what they would call "growth," but I am honestly not sure about the authority or the complete coverage of issues given by Paranoia, and, like Peter Pan, I refuse to grow any faster than I absolutely have to.) The brilliance and the substantial contributions of the Paranoid lineage do compel you to examine the intellectual position, even though it seems arbitrary and counterintuitive and against the commonsense of the conventional scientific orientation of American psychologists.

Werner was Paranoid, of course, in his recognition of developmental parallelisms governing many phenomena of organizational change. I overestimated his affiliation with Spencer, as Kaplan points out. The problem of attributing intellectual influence and kinship among people living in a richly communicating community of crisscrossing writings is difficult. There are nonetheless, to my mind, strong resemblances between Spencer and Werner. Both men used formidable scholarship and considerable intellectual resourcefulness in the effort to formulate a comparative psychology of mental development. I remember how astonished I was some years ago to find that this odd figure, Spencer, who seemed to pop up on so many historical trials leading to so many diverse modern Psychologies—a culture-hero in his own day, the Svengali of Social Darwinism to many today—that this 19th-century figure, Spencer, was like Werner in his systematic belief that Development was everywhere and in everything. Piaget is slightly Paranoid, of course, with his idea that a child's cognitive development is an evolution of evolution, and his belief that there are resemblances between the growth of a child's thought and the history of science.

Kaplan's piece in this volume is a significant formulation of this very broad view of what the study of development entails. Children are a vehicle for the study of universal processes of development. One should sharply distinguish development as an ideal process from ontogenesis as an actual one. We commune with large principles when we study children, but we do not do so only in the interest of amassing more facts and theories. We invest our time and effort in the actual only to grasp the ideal. We want to recognize what is necessary in us and in the world. We have basic human sentiments and emotions, non-negotiable urges toward freedom and self-respect. In a world run by symbols and articulate thought, we want to think about where and how we can have what we need to have as human beings. In *Reconstruction in Philosophy,* John Dewey (1920) argues that it is the eternal task of the philosopher to transpose the faiths and beliefs of the old generation into the conceptual and social forms of the new. Here, as in so many other places, Psychology carries an inheritance from Philosophy. Kaplan, I think, looks beyond the clatter and the clutter of everyday developmental psychology toward essential meaning.

Developmental psychology an ethical discipline? Make no mistake about it, there are many developmental psychologists, Bewildered and Paranoid, who believe they touch ideality through their work. They do not take the bull by the horns as Lawrence Kohlberg did a few years ago when he wrote his classic essay, "From is to ought: How to commit the naturalistic fallacy and get away with it." Most developmental psychologists take comfort in the belief that they are practicing value-free science. From that authoritative standpoint, nevertheless, they believe they can made judicious recommendations about what it is good or bad for children to watch on television, about good child development, good education, what adolescents need, etc. They may refuse to prescribe for children—not on principle, because it is impossible for them as value-free scientists, but because "more research is needed." Developmental psychologists regularly and unconflictedly take on research evaluations of preschools, schools, curricula, television programs, therapies, day care centers, social service agencies, mental health facilities, etc. Some very complicated social processes have to go on to allow value-free scientists to evaluate projects and programs when nobody tells them what the values are (Rein & White, 1977).

Kaplan has caught, and expressed, a deep, hidden, and slightly uncomfortable truth about developmental psychology. The establishment of the social and behavioral sciences near the turn of the last century took some impetus from a several-centuries-old quest for a "natural religion," a body of rules and meanings to guide life based on facts and reason rather than on revelation and faith. Developmental psychologists act as though they espoused Kaplan's persuasive definition. They treat developmental psychology as though it were an ethical science. The Creationists' argument that contemporary scientific teachings have somewhat the thrust of a secular religion are not entirely without merit.

Why do I seek to maintain my gaze on actuality if I accept the validity of Kaplan's centration on ideality? The social organization of developmental psychology is complicated, entailing many kinds of operational necessity, political structure, skills, holy and unholy motives, etc. I want to keep open the possibility of exploring all facets of the interorganization of developmental psychology. I want a signpost, a phenomenon, something I can come back to time and time again, something I can get everyone to agree is there. In the essay that launched Pragmatism, "The Fixation of Belief," C. S. Peirce said: "To satisfy our doubts, therefore, it is necessary that a method should be found by which our beliefs may be determined by nothing human but by some external permanency—by something upon which our thinking has no effect."

Designating developmental psychology as the external permanency of the group of developmental psychologists, I feel I have the change to explore the numerous intentional inexistences of the group. I do not disagree with Kaplan's definition of one such intentional inexistence. It is a significant weakness of his persuasive definition that he does not designate what community of humans is embraced and obligated by his it—developmental psychologists?; psychologists?; behavioral and social scientists?; human service workers and human scientists together?; humankind?. I do not understand if a method exists to "ground" his definition, to affix it to a particular group of humans. Just looking at the definition, I am quite sure its scope of application is broader than the community of developmental psychologists. I do not think I am quibbling about a carelessness in wording, a loophole in the formulation of his persuasive definition that might be closed with a little careful editing. The transition from particulars to universals is very difficult for me in one direction and equally difficult for him in the other.

Perhaps the Bewildered and Paranoid perspectives need each other, as Don Quixote and Sancho Panza needed once upon a time to travel together. Perhaps both visions together are needed to place values in a world of facts.

REFERENCES

Dewey, J. *Reconstruction in philosophy.* New York: Henry Holt, 1920.

Rein, M., & White, S. H. Can policy research help policy? *The Public Interest,* 1977, *49,* 119–136.

Rein, M., & White, S. H. Knowledge for practice. *Social Service Review,* 1981, *55,* 1–41.

Siegel, A. W., & White, S. H. The child study movement: Early growth and development of the symbolized child. In H. Reese & L. P. Lipvitt (Eds.), *Advances in child development and behavior* (Vol. 17). New York: Academic Press, 1982.

White, S. H. The active organism in theoretical behaviorism. *Human Development* 1976, *19,* 99–107. (a)

White, S. H. Developmental psychology and Vico's concept of universal history. *Social Research,* 1976, *43,* 659–671. (b)

White, S. H. Social proof structures: The dialectic of method and theory in the work of psychology. In N. Datan & H. Reese (Eds.), *Life-span developmental psychology: Dialectical perspectives in experimental research.* New York: Academic Press, 1977.

White, S. H. Psychology in all sorts of places. In R. A. Kasschau & F. S. Kessel (Eds.), *Psychology and society: In search of symbiosis.* New York: Holt, Rinehart, & Winston, 1978.

10 Rumours of Historiography

Roger A. Dixon
John R. Nesselroade
*Max Planck Institute for Human Development and Education,
Berlin, West Germany*

> *And as if there was less animosity and bitterness in commenting
> than in inventing!*
> ——Montaigne ("Of Experience")

A PAUSE IN HISTORY

The title of our initial contribution to this volume is "Pluralism and correlational analysis in developmental psychology: historical commonalities." It is, we think, a rather modest title reflecting a broad but carefully circumscribed historical venture. It is a deliberately commodious title in that it permits exploration of moments of primitive pluralism occurring in a number of intellectual settings and similarly dispersed moments of relational mathematical thinking in early psychological literature. The theme of the chapter is restricted in that we have no intent (and make no such claim) of producing a history of pluralism, nor a history of mathematical psychology, nor even a history of life-span developmental psychology. For these worthy projects we must, for the time being, defer to others. Our present purpose is to explore historical commonalities and (occasionally) connections in these arenas of thought and, thus, contribute to the understanding of their contemporary manifestations. Insofar as we are successful, the present coincidence of pluralism, contextual developmental psychology, and correlational analyses becomes less arcane.

From this perspective, then, the portion of Kaplan's chapter to which we are "responding" seems substantially ill-begotten. The theme of our chapter—our stated purpose and our openly rather speculative conclusions—stands largely untouched and unaddressed by the putative critic. Further, as we show below, the series of animadversions that constitute his "call to intellectual controversy" is, although often insightful and eloquent, frequently provincial, irrelevant, and manipulative. There is an air of combative potency to Kaplan's writing, but one is never completely certain that he hasn't confused the sharpening of swords with the grinding of axes. Whereas, as pluralists, we generally countenance constructive intellectual exchange, we nevertheless have little interest in adopting our interlocuter's chosen intellectual weapons (i.e., secondary sources bolstered by bombast) and engaging him on his preferred turf.

Monism and its Discontents

Just as it is no simple matter to classify Kaplan's original (i.e., noncritical) contribution to this volume, it is difficult to decode the positive work of his critical contribution. He proclaims in the maiden sentence of his chapter *part* of (the "notorious") Croce's "banal" historiographical observation and thus, presumably and admirably, reveals his historical perspective at the outset. And yet there is very little that is Crocean about either his original historical contribution or his subsequent critical analyses.

In psychological respects Kaplan's *parti pris* is more clearly identified (viz., he [naturally] favors Werner and a classically strong definition of development and [anatomically] disfavors ["smiting hip and thigh"] much of the rest of contemporary developmental psychology). In particular, although his definition of developmental psychology differs only moderately from that of proponents of the life-span movement (Baltes, Reese, & Nesselroade, 1977, p. 4), it is this group (or, rather, his impression of this group, because virtually no representative work is cited) that is the object of much of his censorious remarks. He is at once a fervent partisan (perhaps a monist) and a self-proclaimed pluralist (of one sort or another). On one early page he lists a veritable historical hit parade of some 30 eminent philosophers and social historians with which he is familiar but neglects to distinguish among them nor to even identify those that influence his own thinking, or in other ways inform the arguments of his chapter.

All of this is, perhaps, *hors de propos,* so let us proceed forthwith to Kaplan's treatment of our chapter and our proposals. To begin, the very concept of pluralism is a troubling one for Kaplan, and it is troubling we think for basically the right reasons; that is, the real ("slight") problem with pluralism for Kaplan is (and we quote liberally) the nagging question: "Who is to decide on the merits or the nature of "intellectual inquiry?" If different world views entail different conceptions of "merit" and "intellectual inquiry," who is to be the ultimate arbiter, the Supreme Court?" He goes on to suggest that perhaps what *we* really want to do is "surreptitiously," "dogmatically (and, hence, monistically)" make ourselves the judges of intellectual merit and academic virtue.

Now, the question of just how and on what grounds such intellectual confrontations are made in a pluralistic science (or, for that matter, in society) is an extremely interesting one. Indeed, Kaplan has identified perhaps *the* issue that follows most naturally from our arguments. Although we did address this issue in a cursory manner (and cite references for further reading), Kaplan is correct to note that we presented no fully articulated proposals. But he was incorrect to assume that the issue has not been addressed elsewhere; indeed, such a view of incommensurability is at least partially consonant with one interpretation of the history of the natural sciences; that is, it is really not such a novel idea and it most certainly does not boil down to our "surreptitiously, dogmatically, monistically" assuming the role of ultimate intellectual arbiter. His concomitant exposition of our hopelessly nefarious, secret intentions is quite unremarkable. Yes, we leave it at that: *Satis verborum.*

Would it that we could elaborate this perspective on the history and philosophy of science further, but, alas, space is at a premium (see, however, Booth, 1977; Feyerabend, 1975, 1978). It is appropriate—and perhaps inevitable—at this juncture, with so much more to address in the Kaplan piece, and so little space in which to do it, to sign plaintively (and with no small measure of irony) along with Kenneth Patchen, who must have felt much as we do: It is as though we "have but a bullet left and there are so many things to kill."

Tilting at Historical Windmills

Let us turn now to the very premise of Kaplan's more detailed disputations. Kaplan is, again, quite convinced that our fundamental mission is one of genealogy, establishing an "ancestral tree" or intellectual lineage such that the brachiations observed in, for example, the plural worlds hypothesis, skeptical philosophy, mathematical psychology, and 19th-century pragmatism converge logically, ineluctably upon the recently vaunted trunk of life-span developmental psychology. Quite admittedly recoiling at the very enterprise of this movement, Kaplan seeks to destroy this putative historical foundation by attacking these purported intellectual linkages. Although his method of attack (viz., the simple invocation of secondary sources couched in a righteous bluster) is itself considerably suspect, the object of his animadversions is really rather hypnagogic, belonging to the ambiguous realm between flesh and eidolon.

That is, we took (and so declared) our mission to be one of careful historical information gathering and hypothesis generation, noting (and we quote from our own chapter) "where applicable common or associated strands of intellectual heritage." That we were not attempting to construct precisely a genealogy should be clear from our summary statements. Here, even when the moments of pluralism (etc.) are necessarily contiguous, we sought to eschew the explicit advocation of causal historical inferences.

For example, we suggest not that pluralism in any way caused correlational thinkng in psychology, but that the contexts of their respective emergences may have been, in part, a shared intellectual climate. This is really a rather mild claim, and one, we continue to believe, quite defensible. Repeatedly, we eschew the imputation of a causal chain by assiduously *noting* (observing, and further observing) generally intraindividual cases of the simultaneous existence of a modicum of pluralism and (e.g.) correlational psychology. At one point very late in the chapter, we acknowledge that "our attempt to describe historical intellectual antecedents common to both pluralism and multivariate correlational analysis originates in an interest in explanation." But we go on to say, "Nevertheless, it is at this point that discretion prevails." Our acknowledged interest in *interpreting* the preceeding rather descriptive inquiries was (until then) cautiously suppressed. It is here, and only here in the final section of the chapter, that we begin speculating about possible connections relevant to the *contemporary* scene in developmental psychology.

Let us turn now to some of the more specific problems with Kaplan's critique. Kaplan unabashedly marshals a handful of secondary sources to dispute a claim he attributes to us (which was also based on secondary sources) that Crescas, Cusanus, and Bruno represent instances of pluralism in embryo. Indeed he devotes several rather strident, altogether persuasive pages to his confutation of this claim. However, after reading Kaplan's brief exegeses of the writers in question, then consulting our original chapter, and then rereading his remarks, we found ourselves rather perplexed: *Cui bono?* To what end is his criticism? In this case it is not simply a matter of having arrogated our motives. True, it is that, but it is more than just that. The three writers in question are mentioned in an early subsection entitled: "Plurality of Worlds." Two of them (Crescas and Cusanus) are broached only in the first paragraph of this subsection and exit the stage as quickly as they enter, with all of one sentence devoted to each. Now, let us look at the context and the content of these pernicious sentences.

First, the context. We introduce this section by writing: The idea that "the universe *may* be infinite, and that it *may* contain a plurality of inhabited worlds" (italics in original) arose in part through the observations of great astronomers but did not necessarily originate there. Now, the content. In the sentence referring to Crescas we write (simply) that in the course of his critique of Aristotle and others he argued that to gainsay the possibility of the simultaneous existence of many worlds is more a function of human vanity than of logical ascendency or empirical testimony. In the sentence referring to Cusanus, we write (simply) that he "asserted that it was preposterous to think that there were not other inhabited globes filling the many spaces of the heavens." As is customary, after each sentence, we cite our (secondary) sources. Clearly, we do not claim that these men are pluralists nor assert that they are progenitors of life-span developmental psychology, or in any necessary way our "ancestors." Yet, these putative claims are precisely the subject of Kaplan's desultory malediction. Again, *cui bono?*

A similar befuddlement resulted from our reading of Kaplan's remarks about Bruno. We indeed write quite explicitly that Bruno was an enthusiastic proponent of the plural worlds hypothesis. Kaplan (apparently) doesn't dispute this assertion (indeed, he cites several secondary sources supporting it). Kaplan's point (apparently) is that Bruno, because of an unmistakable underlying monism, is not a pure pluralist. But this is another imaginary contradiction. We write: Whereas "Bruno's pluralistic metaphysics was moderate—suggesting that an organic unity, in which the multiple units of reality were meaningful only in the context of their relations to one another, lay beneath the plurality of parts," it was his active advocacy of the plural worlds hypothesis during the Inquisition that led to his infamy as a heretic and, ultimately, his execution in 1600. Even so, Bruno did not explicitly reject the existence of multiple monads (which was Democritus' position). Bruno simply went beyond that essentially descriptive view to assert that for him the monads were important only in their dialectical interpenetration (Horowitz, 1952).

It is in these modest ways that Crescas, Cusanus, and Bruno contributed to the development of the plural worlds hypothesis. In addition to being one of the most influential sources for Bruno, Cusanus was one of the pioneers of the experimental era in the physical sciences, more experimental indeed than Bruno, who lived at the dawning of the age of secular science (Singer, 1950). Both came to believe that an infinite universe was without restriction, limitation, weight, and absolute position. Both were fascinated by the possibility of inhabitants in these other worlds, a fascination that continues to be in the forefront of modern astronomical science (Billingham, 1981; Crick, 1981; Goldsmith, 1981). The reader interested in a more precise treatment of the place of Cusanus' thought in the development of Bruno's ideas is directed to Singer (1950). This source may also repair several gashes in Kaplan's perfunctory presentation of Cusanus. The important point for us is that insofar as the plural worlds hypothesis was a necessary part of the intellectual scenery that spawned pluralism—insofar as it helped set the stage for subsequent, related concepts—it contributed to the development of (let us say) a pluralistic psychology. But that is a claim quite apart from the one Kaplan ponders so sonorously.

Kaplan's piquant, summary gloss of Montaigne is equally inapposite as a criticism of any portion of our chapter. In these particular comments Kaplan appears to take the concept of pluralism to mean the explicit advocation of a plurality of methods. This, we agree, is one kind of pluralism. However, in contrast to Kaplan's implicit attribution, we do not link such methodological pluralism to Montaigne. Quite the contrary, indeed: at one point we refer to his method of inquiry in the singular. Nevertheless, it is not entirely implausible to wring from the writings of Montaigne himself a certain leniency with regard to the simultaneous deployment of multiple methods. The following quote from Montaigne's (1948) essay, "Of Experience," will amply illustrate this point:

"There is no desire more natural than the desire for knowledge. We try all the ways that can lead us to it . . . truth is so great a thing that we must not disdain any medium that will lead us to it [p. 94]."

Throughout his writing, as we emphasize, Montaigne argues for intellectual tolerance and moderation, and against the vanity of humans and their knowledge—especially *absolute* knowledge—claims. This is the aspect of pluralism to which the comments of Montaigne in our original chapter refer. Historically, there has been considerable controversy as to precisely why and for what purpose Montaigne drafted his famous "Apologie de Raimond Sebond." Certainly, however, irrespective of his intentions—whether they are as Kaplan asserts or not—the essay has contributed to his legacy as a skeptic, a vigorous debunker of intellectual vanity. Kaplan pushes Montaigne's supposed "anti-intellectualism" to the extreme where, of course, it is brittle (which is probably fair) and implies that because of the well-known weaknesses of extreme skepticism modern pluralists can take no lessons from Montaigne (which, if fair, is probably not accurate).

In any event, Kaplan failed to note that very late in our own chapter we explicitly dissassociate ourselves from the extreme relativism he attacks. We write: "Extreme or pure relativism is considered to be as dangerous or dogmatic as extreme absolutism. The pluralist may simply endorse what some writers have called a moderate realtivism or a healthy skepticism." Nevertheless, we note, such relativism *can* inform philosophy, philosophy of science, and empirical research programs. Incidentally, a careful reading of Montaigne will reveal several instances of a developmental perspective akin to that of both Kaplan and life-span developmental psychologists (e.g., "Of the Inconsistency of our Actions," and the aforementioned "Apologie").

CONCLUSION: IT'S NOT NICE TO FOOL MOTHER CLIO

The work of the critic is rather like that of the historian: There is an inherent, unequivocal obligation not only to anatomize the target work but also to read it, and, more than read it, to read it carefully, to understand it (as it were) from the inside-out as well as from the outside-in. It would appear that somewhere on the line between the cardinal poles of a simple reading and an anatomization dangles our putative critic. However, we are far from assuming the pose of hangmen: Our modest task in this brief response has been one of simply pointing to some of the means by which our critic may have done himself in.

Reading our chapter and reading Kaplan's caustic criticism is like driving an automobile on a sheet of ice. Sometimes one is on the road seemingly in control, and sometimes one, at unpredictable intervals, is entirely misdirected. Many of Kaplan's comments are quite interesting and elucidating. Some contribute eloquently to the refinement of our (clearly) imperfect chapter. Still, one occasionally has the distinct impression that: (1) Kaplan disallows our choice of roads; (2) he defines his own road in spite of our stated choice; or (3) the road, glazed with ice, goes on without him. Perhaps at different junctures different impressions match the case. All in all, it gives a reader pause.

REFERENCES

Baltes, P. B., Reese, H. W., & Nesselroade, J. R. *Life-span developmental psychology: Introduction to research methods*. Monterey, Calif.: Brooks/Cole, 1977.

Billingham, J. (Ed.). *Life in the universe*. Cambridge: The MIT Press, 1981.

Booth, W. C. ''Preserving the exemplar'': or, How not to dig our own graves. *Critical Inquiry*, 1977, *3*, 407–423.

Crick, F. *Life itself: It's origin and nature*. New York: Simon & Schuster, 1981.

Feyerabend, P. *Against method*. London: NLB, 1975.

Feyerabend, P. *Science in a free society*. London: NLB, 1978.

Goldsmith, D. *The quest for extraterrestrial life*. Mill Valley, Calif.: University Science Books, 1981.

Horowitz, I. L. *The Renaissance philosophy of Giordano Bruno*. New York: Coleman–Ross, 1952.

de Montaigne, M. E. *Selections from the essays of Montaigne*. New York: Appleton–Century–Crofts, 1948 (Trans. & Ed. by D. M. Frame).

Singer, D. W. *Giordano Bruno: His life and thought*. New York: Schuman, 1950.

11 Plato Out of Place and Time: A Rejoinder to Professor Kaplan

Urie Bronfenbrenner
Cornell University

Professor Kaplan takes a position from which my chapter falls short of his high expectations. I am saddened, for he is a respected and congenial colleague, whose good opinion I cherish. But, given his starting point, his disparaging conclusion follows as the night the day, and, in accord with the stipulated sequence, leaves him mainly in the dark. Small wonder, for Professor Kaplan has imposed objectives on my work rather different from those that I had sought to achieve.

In his opening comment on my analysis, Professor Kaplan proudly declares himself a Platonist. True to the teachings of his mentor, he begins by looking for ideal types. Noting that my chapter deals with "the evolution of the concept of environment in systematic research on human development," he wants, at the very outset, to know—and me to tell him—what is *truly* meant by each of these terms and is clearly prepared to dispute the answers given. These are indeed appropriate subjects for a Platonic dialogue, but that was not my aim. The task that I undertook was not the a priori formulation of concepts, but the a posteriori analysis of the operational definitions of the environment employed over successive decades by scholars engaged in the empirical investigation of psychological growth. In pursuit of my inquiry, the first models I came upon were Aristotelian, but, in accord with Lewin's admonition (1935), these soon turned Galileian and, in recent decades, have become increasingly relativistic, both across time and space, an outcome that should have kindled Professor Kaplan's Platonic ire even more than did my failure to speak to the essence of things, or as he puts it, to hypostatize.

To be sure, it can be argued that no one should presume to analyze how others have defined the basic concepts in the field who has not previously placed his own formulations on the record. If so, I suspect I am guilty of overfilling the norm. In a recent book on the "Ecology of Human Development" (1979), I presented no less that 50 a priori propositions—50 (and not a lemma among them!) undergirded by a dozen formal definitions of basic concepts, including most of those Professor Kaplan calls for: development, environment, and even "systematic" research. The only one I missed was "evolution." Here I risked the reader's acquaintance with the first definition given in my dictionary: "a process of change in a certain direction." It is this process of change, and its direction, that I sought to identify and describe in my chapter.

It is not clear to me whether Professor Kaplan would agree with the results of my analysis, for, as he himself says, he has chosen to "forego such an excursion." He does appear to take issue, however, with what he describes as my "delight in the fact that human beings called 'scientific psychologists' consider an ever-increasing, differentiatted and hierarchically integrated number of factors as possibly entering into the determination of human action over the life span." Moreover, he suspects that I "regard this posture as a developmental *advance.*" I confess to the charge (although I do not wish to parse the sentence). Professor Kaplan correctly infers, although he does not say so explicitly, that my conception of development draws heavily on the formulations of a man whom we both admire, Heinz Werner. Werner defined development as progressive differentiation and hierarchical integration of mental functioning. In acknowledging our common indebtedness to a great psychologist, I must also confess that Professor Kaplan has done better justice to the master than I, for Werner was remarkable in his capacity to bring philosophical sophistication to bear on the psychological study of human development. It is a pleasure to see that sophistication still flourishing, even on inappropriate terrain.

REFERENCES

Bronfenbrenner, U. *The ecology of human development: Experiments by nature and design.* Cambridge, Mass.: Harvard University Press, 1979.

Lewin, K. The conflict between Aristotelian and Galileian modes of thought in contemporary psychology. In K. Lewin, *A dynamic theory of personality.* New York: McGraw–Hill, 1935, 1–42.

IV CONCLUSION

12
Some Dynamic and Subjective Features of the History of Developmental Psychology

Richard M. Lerner
The Pennsylvania State University

In the Preface to the first edition of his *A History of Experimental Psychology* (1929), Edwin G. Boring wrote that: "the gift of professional maturity comes only to the psychologist who knows the history of his science [p. xii]." However, in the Preface to the second edition (1950), in response to the question "can history be revised?," Boring said: "Yes. As time goes on, there come to be second thoughts about the interpretation of it. There are also new discoveries [p. xiii]."

Given its largely descriptive and normative emphases even into the 1940s, developmental psychology has matured as a discipline at least insofar as Boring's criterion of knowledge of one's history is concerned. Indeed, as the preceding chapters illustrate, leading developmental psychologists are today both aware of their discipline's history—and particularly of the historical role of philosophical issues—and see the mutual articulation of philosophical concerns and theoretical and methodological issues as pertinent to their current endeavors. In fact, as exemplified by the philosophical disputes in the preceding pages regarding the role of the context and of contextual change in individual development, the history of philosophy in developmental psychology has today led to major disagreements about the philosophy of history. Such disagreements have been seen in the preceding chapters to have implications not only for definitions and theories of development, but also for one's research methods and, ultimately, for the "facts" of development one generates.

This situation leads us to make some observations relevant to Boring's (1950) second point. Despite the level of maturity developmental psychology may have reached by being aware of its history and by actively incorporating historical and philosophical concerns into its current scientific agenda, this history is open to an array of interpretations. As evidenced too by the preceding chapters, historical and philosophical issues are today approached in ways sufficiently different to evoke intense controversy among leading developmentalists. These scholars have in no small way shaped much of contemporary developmental psychology; their continued work along the different paths evident in their essays and their continued disputes create the future history of the discipline that later scholars will recount. Thus, our history and our currently evolving discipline are, and are likely to remain, dynamic.

Let me use the contents of the preceding chapters to project into the future what some key philosophical and historical issues may be. One of the key themes in the different perspectives evident in the preceding chapters involves what Boring (1950) labeled the personalistic versus the naturalistic theories of history. For example, Boring (1950) asked: ''Did Wundt found the new experimental psychology somewhere around 1860 or did the times compel the changes to which Wundt merely gave expression [p. 4]?'' In other words, and more generally, is it the spirit of the times—the *Zeitgeist*—that inculcates, or at least permits the influence of, ideas or discoveries, *or* is it the ''great person,'' who through his or her independent insight and/or efforts creates a new feature of science and therby changes the spirit of the times?

We see the tension between these two positions reflected, on the one hand, in the ideas of Bronfenbrenner and, to some extent, of Baltes and of Dixon and Nesselroade and, on the other hand, in the ideas of Kaplan. Bronfenbrenner describes how events in the social context of science, and social change itself, altered the nature of empirical research, provoking it to investigate broader and more complex conceptions of the environment as it affects human development. Baltes describes how the presence of specific features of data sets in the adult development and aging literatures forced developmentalists to seek ideas derived from philosophical paradigms other than organismic or mechanistic ones in order to achieve better integration of information. Similarly, Dixon and Nesselroade describe how a multivariate correlational approach to development arose in a scientific context suggesting the empirical usefulness of such a perspective. Interestingly, all three of these positions are views that incorporate the role of the historically changing context in the development of the discipline *and* link individual development to contextual change. Kaplan, however, stresses the use of an idealistic theory of development, one that highlights the difference between development and ontogenetic change; and he emphasizes the role of the scholar's perspective in advancing developmental theory.

Of course, the naturalistic and personalistic perspectives are not mutually exclusive. As Boring (1950) has explained, the role of the Zeitgeist and of the great person in determining scientific progress are, in actuality, the: ''obverse and reverse of every historical process [p. xiii],'' and that ''you get the person-alitic view when you ignore the antecedents of the great man, and you get the naturalistic view back again when you ask what made the great man great [p. 4].'' We indeed see this synthesis between a person- and a context-emphasis in several of the previously noted essays. For instance, Baltes emphasizes the 18th-century contributions of Tetens, Carus, and Quetelet as forerunners of current life-span developmental thinking, and Dixon and Nesselroade emphasize the major contribution of James' pragmatics and pluralism to current life-span and multivariate/correlational approaches.

The synthesis between the personalistic and naturalistic theories of history may presage a synthesis between idealistic and contextual approaches to developmental theory. Although it would be difficult to find a developmental psychologist who would disagree with Kaplan's point that one needs to approach empirical work with a theory-based definition of development—in order to discriminate developmental from nondevelopmental change—such a theoretical perspective need not exclude the context or the relations between organism and context. Indeed if, in agreement with White, we contend that the key feature of a developmental theory is its generic nature, then both the context and organism-context relations should show developmental progression. In fact, in two previous papers I have indicated the use of precisely the principle that Kaplan promotes—the orthogenetic principle—for integrating data pertinent to the development of organisms, their context, and the relations between organisms and contexts (Lerner, 1979; Lerner & Busch–Rossnagel, 1981). Kaplan, in his critique of the life-span perspective does not make reference to these papers or in fact to any specific publications in the life-span developmental psychology literature. Nevertheless, life-span developmental psychology is a theory-based approach to studying human lives, one particularly sensitive to the need for deriving a concept of individual development that precisely details the ways in which contextual variation within and across time influences the human life course. Indeed, chapters by Bronfenbrenner and by Dixon and Nesselroade, as well as the one by Baltes, may be seen as vitally concerned with this definitional issue. Although much work remains to be done before any such definition of development has demonstrated substantial empirical utility, the present point is that considerable theoretical and empirical work has been done and continues to be generated (Baltes, Reese, & Lipsitt, 1980; Bronfenbrenner, 1979). Indeed, this work leads me to my next point.

The synthesis between personalistic and naturalistic theories of history may also reflect the nature of the relation between individual development and historical change. In the introductory chapter to this volume I indicated that a key issue in contemporary developmental psychology is the nature of the relation between individual and contextual history, as well as between these "types" of history and historical analysis per se. This issue is involved in much of the controversy between Kaplan, on the one hand, and Bronfenbrenner, Dixon and Nesselroade, and Baltes, on the other. If, as Boring (1950) suggests, emphasis on individual or Zeitgeist distorts what is actually a synthesis between the two, then analogously, at the level of individual development, one may say that individuals—by acting to influence a context that feeds back to shape them—provide a basis not only of their historical context but also of their own development. Evidence exists that such reciprocal influences exist in regard to both evolutionary and ontogenetic processes (Johanson & Edey, 1981; Lerner & Busch–Rossnagel, 1981; Lovejoy, 1981).

Thus, an inclusive, synthesizing view of human development would be one that, analogous to the relation between personalistic and naturalistic views of historical progress, reciprocally links developing individuals to their changing contexts. Such a conception would have to specify not only the ways in which such bidirectional processes may proceed, but too the constraints on and limits of such reciprocal influence. It is just such a concept of development—one that incorporates the active, constructive role of the person (the subject) in his or her own development, one that sees the person both as influenced by and an influence on the shaping context—that is being explored for its use by life-span and ecological developmental psychologists.

The adequate formulation of such a conception of development may prove evasive; there may never be a *theory* of development that grows out of the current life-span view of human development (Baltes et al., 1980); and the empirical utility of the life-span perspective for all portions of the life course and for all substantive areas may never be entirely demonstrated. However, at this writing such pessimism is by no means warranted. As such, the attempts of life-span developmentalists to devise such a conception of development and to demonstrate its scientific use should not be dismissed by pre-empirical fiat or, more precisely, by dictates derived from our presuppositions about what is the nature of development and about what phenomena may be classified as developmental and what as nondevelopmental. As the scholarship of Kagan, in this volume and elsewhere (Kagan, 1980), has demonstrated, our presuppositions constrain and limit our theoretical and empirical activities. And because many attempts to optimize human life derive from such activities (Brim & Kagan, 1980), the constraints of presuppositions may seriously circumscribe our ability to enhance human life.

If we accept the lessons taught us by Werner (1948, 1957), by Reese and Overton (1970; Overton & Reese, 1973), and by Kagan (1980)—that our implicit and explicit philosophical orientations always influence our theoretical and methodological endeavors—then as mature scientists we cannot ignore, in our present or future work, the role of philosophy in general, or any particular philosophical view in particular.

ACKNOWLEDGMENTS

The writing of this chapter was supported in part by a grant from the John D. and Catherine T. MacArthur Foundation. I am grateful to Roger A. Dixon, David F. Hultsch, and Karen Hooker for their comments on an earlier draft of this chapter.

REFERENCES

Baltes, P. B., Reese, H. W., & Lipsitt, L. P. Life-span developmental psychology. *Annual Review of Psychology,* 1980, *31,* 65–110.

Boring, E. G. *A history of experimental psychology.* New York: Appleton– Century–Crofts, 1929.

Boring, E. G. *A history of experimental psychology* (2nd ed.). New York: Appleton–Century–Crofts, 1950.

Brim, O. G., Jr., & Kagan, J. Constancy and change: A view of the issues. In O. G. Brim, Jr. & J. Kagan (Eds.), *Constancy and change in human development.* Cambridge, Mass.: Harvard University Press, 1980.

Bronfenbrenner, U. *The ecology of human development.* Cambridge, Mass.: Harvard University Press, 1979.

Johanson, D. C., & Edey, M. A. *Lucy: The beginnings of humankind.* New York: Simon & Schuster, 1981.

Kagan, J. Perspectives on continuity. In O. G. Brim, Jr. & J. Kagan (Eds.), *Constancy and change in human development.* Cambridge Mass.: Harvard University Press, 1980.

Lerner, R. M. A dynamic interactional concept of individual and social relationship development. In R. L. Burgess & T. L. Huston (Eds.), *Social exchange in developing relationships.* New York: Academic Press, 1979.

Lerner, R. M., & Busch–Rossnagel, N. A. Individuals as producers of their development: Conceptual and empirical bases. In R. M. Lerner & N. A. Busch–Rossnagel (Eds.), *Individuals as producers of their development: A life-span perspective.* New York: Academic Press, 1981.

Lovejoy, C. O. The origin of man. *Science,* 1981, *211,* 341–350.

Overton, W. F., & Reese, H. W. Models of development: Methodological implications. In J. R. Nesselroade & H. W. Reese (Eds.), *Life-span developmental psychology: Methodological issues.* New York: Academic Press, 1973.

Reese, H. W., & Overton, W. F. Models of development and theories of development. In L. R. Goulet & P. B. Baltes (Eds.), *Life-span developmental psychology: Research and theory.* New York: Academic Press, 1970.

Werner, H. *Comparative psychology of mental development.* New York: International Universities Press, 1948.

Werner, H. The concept of development from a comparative and organismic point of view. In D. B. Harris (Ed.), *The concept of development.* Minneapolis: University of Minnesota Press, 1957.

Author Index

Italics denote pages with bibliographic information.

Subject Index